Two-Bit Culture

THE PAPERBACKING
OF AMERICA

Two-Bit
Culture

KENNETH C. DAVIS

HOUGHTON MIFFLIN COMPANY

BOSTON 1984

Library of Congress Cataloging in Publication Data

Davis, Kenneth C.
    Two-bit culture.

    Bibliography: p.
    Includes index.
        1. Paperbacks — Publishing — United States.   2. Book industries and trade — United States.   3. Books and reading — United States.   4. Popular literature — United States.   5. United States — Popular culture.   I. Title.
    Z479.D38 1984   070.5'73'0973   83-22767
    ISBN 0-395-34398-4
    ISBN 0-395-35535-4 (pbk.)

Printed in the United States of America

V 10 9 8 7 6 5 4 3 2 1

To Kurt Enoch
1895–1982

"Do you realize there are towns in America where there are no libraries at all? Not even a bookstore! The only place the people in those small towns can get a book is at the drugstore. And what do they read? Our books."

"My heavens," she said.

"We are responsible for the changing literary taste of America," he went on. "People have to learn to crawl before they can walk. First they won't read anything but the most obvious kind of lurid adventure stories. Then we sneak in a good book or two. We train them. Eventually all our books will be as good as or better than the best so-called literary hardcover books. Do you think all hardcover books are good just because they cost four dollars? Most of them stink. . . . It's *our* books, with *our* sexy covers, and *our* low cost, and *our* mass distribution that are teaching America how to read. Let people who don't know anything say Derby Books are trash. They'll see."

— from Rona Jaffe's *The Best of Everything* (1958)

Contents

Preface

DISMISSING DR. JOHNSON's assertion that "No man but a blockhead ever wrote except for money," it is safe to say that most writers aren't in it for the wages, fringe benefits, or short hours. There are much easier ways to make a buck and few better ways to stay poor. No. Lurking in the shadows behind every writer is the relentless spirit of the zealot. The act of writing is an act of faith; someone will read and perhaps be changed.

Joseph Conrad expressed this dream in his preface to *The Nigger of the Narcissus* when he wrote: "The task which I am trying to achieve is, by the power of the written word, to make you see. That — and no more, and it is everything. If I succeed, you shall find there according to your desserts: encouragement, consolation, fear, charm — all you demand — and perhaps also that glimpse of truth for which you have forgotten to ask."

New York's colorful mayor Jimmy Walker once put it more simply. "No woman was ever ruined by a book."

I begin with this simple assertion: books can change people and societies. I was surprised by several publishers and editors who downplayed this seemingly basic article of faith. I suspect that they are lying either to me or to themselves. Or they really belong in another business. But the belief that *paperback* books have been responsible for significant changes in the American consciousness is another matter, more debatable perhaps. To many people, the paperback book has always been little more than second-rate trash. Literary flotsam. Schlock turned out to appease a gluttonous mass appetite for sex and sensationalism. And that view, to a considerable extent, is accurate.

But not exclusively so. The point of this history is to paint another portrait of the paperback, one that shows its better side (although not ignoring its warts, crooked teeth, cross-eyes, and cauliflower ears).

During its first forty-odd years of existence in America, the mass market paperback has made an enormous contribution to our social, cultural, educational, and literary life. *Mass market paperback* is the term used for the rack-sized paperbound book that was introduced by Pocket Books in the United States in 1939 and sold principally through periodical distributors in drugstores, chain stores, bus stations, and airport terminals — that is, the mass market. By contrast, *trade* (or "quality") paperbacks, were introduced later and sold primarily through college stores and the general bookstore trade. Today, the distinction has blurred because both types of books are almost universally available. While this history discusses both kinds of paperbacks, it focuses on the impact of the mass market paperback.

Before these inexpensive, widely distributed books came along, only the rarest of books sold more than a hundred thousand copies; a million-seller was a real phenomenon. Bookstores were for the elite "carriage trade" of sophisticates, mostly in big cities; public libraries, few and far between, were not much better. Overnight, the paperback changed that. Suddenly, a book could reach not hundreds or thousands of readers but millions, many of whom had never owned a book before. Universally priced at twenty-five cents in its early years, the paperback democratized reading in America. The Paperback Revolution had begun. The phrase has lost much of its luster from misuse, but its essential meaning remains: more Americans read more books than ever before.

This is the story of that revolution — of the writers, publishers, booksellers, and readers who made it, and of what it meant to America. But it is essentially a story of the books themselves. In advance, I offer apologies for the many books not mentioned and editors not named. I have attempted to touch on the major currents within the business and the books that best represented the spirit of the times or were consequential in a way that exceeds simple sales statistics or company profits. Obviously, many have been overlooked. I must particularly apologize to the editors in hardcover houses who were originally responsible for many of the books discussed here. Their role was pivotal. But my purpose is to examine the various books as paperbacks, the format in which they reached the broadest audience.

Personally, the Paperback Revolution was very real. I belong to that large and nebulous group labeled the Paperback Generation. For us, there had always been paperbacks, so they were as legitimate as anything bound in hard covers — save that they were cheaper, more comfortable to read, and more convenient to carry in the blue-jeans pocket or backpack.

I grew up in Mount Vernon, New York, a city of some seventy thousand people that had more in common with its neighbor, the North Bronx, than with the more exclusive Westchester enclaves of Bronxville and Rye. Amazingly, this large city had no legitimate bookstore. (There still isn't one.) But there were always paperbacks in Bob's Luncheonette. And there was the respected Mount Vernon Public Library, where, as far back as I can recall, there were racks for paperbacks. The books I remember most from my adolescence and that had the most impact on me were those paperbacks.

There were many, but a few bear note. One of my most powerful early reading recollections is Upton Sinclair's *The Jungle.* I read it when I was thirteen years old. In 1967, I was pretty typical for an American kid. God and John Wayne were in their rightful places. Vietnam was not yet on the map of our minds. But with Sinclair's exposé of the Chicago meat-packing industry and the treatment of immigrant workers, I had my first taste of reality. It was like a slap in the face or a splash of cold water; the veneer of America posed by Bob Hope and *Bonanza* suffered its first crack. It was the first time I had read anything that suggested that this country was not what I had been led to believe it was. *The Jungle* was later followed by another library paperback, *Johnny Got His Gun.* (Did those librarians know what they were unleashing?) To a young boy raised on a steady diet of war movies, Dalton Trumbo's painful story of a physically devastated war casualty was eye-opening. I didn't know anything about Upton Sinclair or Dalton Trumbo or left-wing politics, only that these books went to the heart of the matter.

Other books soon followed. *Animal Farm* and *1984.* Dick Gregory's *From the Back of the Bus. Black Like Me.* I was being introduced to a fearfully different world. In junior high, I was also introduced to a few other books that teachers and librarians had nothing do with. None is more memorable than 1967's hot book *The Harrad Experiment.* I can clearly remember the way that dog-eared copy was passed from one boy to the next. It was a major source of encouragement for going to college. A few years before, my real baptism had come with *Candy.* Knowing nothing of satire or Voltaire's *Candide,* I got my first sexual education from Terry Southern and Mason Hoffenberg and their wild story of a young girl's sexual adventures. The first taste of forbidden fruit.

There were nobler moments. My introduction to Shakespeare came from *Five Great Tragedies,* a Pocket Book with an introduction and commentaries by British poet laureate John Masefield. I can now confess to writing a book report on *Macbeth* based purely on my reading of the plot synopsis in that book. If my English teacher was the wiser, she didn't let on. Smart lady. An unkind word might have dashed my fervor for the Bard. In later years, I encountered *Catch-22, Z, The Catcher in the Rye,* and *Lady Chatterley's Lover* — each in its paperback incarnation. Each left its mark. And I have discovered that I am not alone. These experiences are universal. Only the titles change. A number of people have shared some of their paperback memories with me:

- "For many years I was an avid buyer of paperback books, purchasing four or five a week. . . . Some of my early ones — from the late thirties — in laminated covers (Dorothy Parker's *Enough Rope,* Selden Rodman's anthology *100 American Poems*) I cherish beyond all expectations of the publisher in setting his twenty-five-cent price. Further, I might mention some of the series: *Best American Short Stories, New World Writing, Panorama, Modern Writing,* and *discovery* made it possible for me to keep up with writing trends."

- "After the war, I was chief pilot for KLM. In about 1948, we started flying from Amsterdam to New York. As I was an author of about fifteen books, I started then to spend many hours in New York bookshops and became quite impressed by your 'Paperback Revolution.' At this moment, *The Pocket Book of Popular Verse* is on my table. . . . Treasures and treasures made available in abundance for everybody to take home, almost free. The best cultural values for hardly any money! Something great had started. . . . Your Paperback Revolution had dealt the trump card to whoever was interested in the life of the spirit."

- "As a youngster, I borrowed the Ballantine edition of Tolkien's *Lord of the Rings* and was promptly transported to Middle-earth. I was enthralled and proceeded to reread the trilogy at regular intervals. . . . Such books as the trilogy cannot be properly savored during the day. No, I saved the trilogy for late-night perusal — something to curl up in bed with. This cannot be comfortably accomplished with a hardcover book. The wave of Tolkien's popularity crested during the late-sixties counterculture and was undoubtedly linked with it, since Tolkien's protagonists embraced idealistic causes and saw them through with perseverance and determination. Truly a myth for the times. A hardcover edition would never have attracted such a following, since it would seem too 'Establishment,' resembling the much-feared textbooks wielded by stodgy professors."

Some people have considerably less high-minded recollections. "Personally, the most specific advantage of reading paperbacks that I can recall relates to the fact that the cover can be removed, allowing the teenager to indulge in banned literature on the bus, in study hall, etc. In my case, it was *Lady Chatterley's Lover* and *The Story of O*. Of course, look where I wound up!" So said Kate Nolan, an associate editor at *Playboy*.

Those and others like them were the books that made the Paperback Revolution a living, pulsing force in contemporary America. They helped shape a culture and very often showed where it was heading. Looking back at the books that have appeared in paper covers since 1939 is a little like uncovering shards of pottery at an archeological dig; they provide a glimmer of insight into the way we thought and lived. I have tried to find out how these books did that and what they meant to America. I have also tried to look at the paperback business as it exists today; the report is not encouraging. In the process of completing this project, the worth of books has been reconfirmed for me, and I hope that if this book accomplishes nothing else, it will help restore the essential meaning of publishing.

I could not have learned anything about paperbacks and books without the help of a great many people who provided insights, information, and encouragement and gave generously of their time. First is the man who was there when the idea for this book was hatched on Overlook Mountain in Woodstock: Ian Ballantine. For more than forty years, Ian Ballantine and his dear wife Betty have been taking the rest of the paperback world by surprise, and they're not finished yet. To the Ballantines, I owe a great many thanks.

Another early supporter who helped shape my thinking about this book and about the art and science of paperback books is Oscar Dystel, whose contribution to making paperbacks a part of American life has been overwhelming. Among the many others I would like to thank are Vance Bourjaily, Knox Burger, Ed Butler, George and Barbara Davidson, Judy-Lynn and Lester del Rey, E. L. Doctorow, Bud Egbert, Donald Fine, Marc Jaffe, Stanley Kauffmann, Peter Mayer, Leona Nevler, Patrick O'Connor, Walter Pitkin, Jr., Arabel J. Porter, Leon Shimkin, Theodore Solotaroff, Dr. Benjamin Spock, Truman Talley, Frank Taylor, Carl Tobey, Robert Wyatt, and Walter Zacharius. These are but a few of the people who assisted my research by agreeing to be interviewed. If no note or citation follows a quote in the text, it may be assumed that the quote comes from an interview I have conducted, either in person or by telephone, with the person cited.

I acknowledge with gratitude the assistance of the librarians at Columbia's Butler Library Rare Books Division, the Special Collection at New York University's Bobst Library, and Yale University's Beinecke Library. I also am indebted to my local library, the Ottendorfer, a beleaguered, underbudgeted little jewel in the New York Public Library system. The *Publishers Weekly* files and their keeper, Miriam Phelps, as well as the R. R. Bowker librarians, Jean Peters and Peggy Spier, were inexhaustible sources of information. I am also grateful to the best little bookstore in Manhattan, The Bookstore, and its owner, Wallis Cooper, who had all the books I needed or got them if she didn't. (And she gave me my first job, too!) For their special support, encouragement, and friendship, I thank Tom Hart, the editor who adopted this project as his own, Sarah Flynn, who copy-edited the manuscript with great care and competence, and my agent, Nat Sobel.

For personal reasons, researching this book became very important to me because it introduced me to Kurt Enoch, whom I was fortunate enough to meet and get to know before his death in 1982 in his eighty-seventh year. One of the true pioneers of the paperback, Kurt Enoch provided me with a wealth of information about the publishing industry and was an enthusiastic friend to this project. More important, he taught me about standards of excellence and clarity of thought. He was a man of great courage, intellect, and integrity. I regret that he will not be able to read this book.

Above all, I want to thank my wife, Joann, for her collaboration, guidance, assistance, suggestions, support, typing, and, most of all, patience when the going got rough. And for Jenny Davis, who managed to arrive before the book did.

Two-Bit Culture

ONE

In the Beginning, There Was Spock

Trust yourself. You know more than you think you do.
— Dr. Benjamin Spock,
Baby and Child Care (1946)

IRST THEY WERE CALLED the Baby Boom Generation. Then came the Now Generation. Never slow to catch on, Madison Avenue anointed them the Pepsi Generation (Come Alive!). When they rebelled, the media proclaimed a generation gap. And a few years later, when they had grown up and traded in their Levi's for designer jeans, Tom Wolfe conveniently labeled them the Me Generation.

They were the postwar kids. They grew up more affluent, more literate, and better educated, perhaps more self-assured, and certainly more restless than any American generation that had preceded them. They were the first children to be reflected in the blue glare of television's gaze. The music rocking out from transistor radios and stereo sets molded them, as did the movies cranked out for them by a hip Hollywood. Besides the electric blizzard bending their minds, there also remained — Marshall McLuhan be damned — the influence of books. Because along with all the other neat labels pinned on them by an uncertain adult world, these were the children of the Paperback Generation.

Paperback books and the baby boomers were made for each other, a mass medium for a mass generation. Paperbacks were cheap and readily available. The "boomers" were the first generation to have paperbacks in the classroom. Unlike their parents and grandparents,

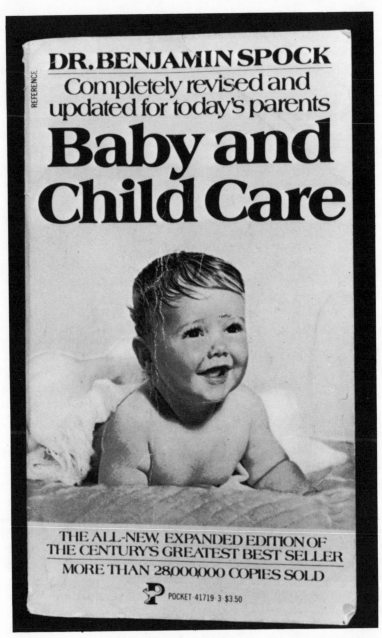

REFERENCE

DR. BENJAMIN SPOCK
Completely revised and
updated for today's parents

Baby and Child Care

THE ALL-NEW, EXPANDED EDITION OF
THE CENTURY'S GREATEST BEST SELLER
MORE THAN 28,000,000 COPIES SOLD

POCKET 41719-3 $3.50

Published in 1946, Dr. Spock's book is second in sales only to the
Bible. (Photo by Jerome Frank; by permission of Pocket Books, a division of Simon & Schuster, Inc.)

they read their classics in soft covers, having been assigned reading lists filled with inexpensive paperbacks that they could *own*, not borrow. And they had their own favorite authors, such as J. D. Salinger and Kurt Vonnegut, whose resistance to orthodoxy seemed to travel best in paperback. But if there was a single book that bonded together this bundle of contradictions called the baby boom, one paperback did the trick. The book and its author were controversial, widely read, and perhaps just as widely misunderstood. The book was *Baby and Child Care.* For these were the children of the Spock Generation.

Since its appearance in June 1946 as *The Pocket Book of Baby and Child Care,* Dr. Spock's book has become the second-best-selling book in American history, trailing only the Bible. In fact, for two generations of American parents, it has been the bible for coping with their newborns. In its first ten years, the paperback edition went through fifty-nine printings and sold about one million copies every year. Besides the Bible, no other book — hardcover or paperback — comes close in either sales or influence. A comparison of new mothers to the number of books sold during the baby boom's peak years — from 1946 to 1964, when nearly seventy-five million babies were born in the United States — put the estimate of "Spock babies" at one in five, and that failed to account for the number of women who shared or borrowed the book or used it to raise more than one child.[1]

(Was it simply coincidence that one of the generation's principal cult figures was a pointy-eared, nonviolent half-human named Spock? No doubt Dr. Spock would approve of his namesake's behavior: Mr. Spock's strictly logical side tempered by the emotions of his human maternal side.)

To the young mothers of America, Dr. Spock was a savior. To the children he had helped to raise, he became a sort of spiritual godfather when they took up the crusade for peace in the late sixties. But to Lyndon Johnson, Spiro Agnew, and Richard Nixon, he was a criminal, a bum, and the cause of a good many of their problems.

Benjamin McLane Spock seemed an unlikely candidate for either cultural hero or villain. Born on May 2, 1903, in New Haven, Connecticut, he was — in 1980s parlance — the ultimate preppy. The son of Benjamin Ives Spock, the general counsel to the New Haven Railroad, the younger Spock attended Phillips Academy and then went on to Yale. If he had never written the book, his moment of glory might have come while crewing on the eight-oared shell that won the gold medal in the 1924 Olympics.

After working summers in a camp for handicapped children in Hartford, Spock knew what he was meant to do. He graduated from Yale in 1925, spent two years at Yale Medical School, and then transferred to the College of Physicians and Surgeons at Columbia University. After graduating in 1929, he completed internships in medicine, pediatrics, and, significantly, it would later turn out, psychiatry. He supplemented his medical studies with six years of psychoanalytic training.

But starting a new pediatrics practice in New York City was no simple matter in 1933, the depths of the Depression. As Spock later recalled, "Established pediatricians were sitting on their hands at the time. It took me three years before I earned enough to pay my office rent and for the gas for a secondhand car that I'd inherited from my mother-in-law."[2]

By 1938, he had acquired enough of a reputation to warrant the first call from a publisher eager to have Spock write a book about child rearing for parents. Spock's standing came not because he tended to famous patients but because of his training. At the time, he was perhaps the only pediatrician in the United States, and maybe the world, who had psychiatric and psychoanalytic experience. According to Spock, anyone who made inquiries at university pediatrics departments would have learned that if they wanted a pediatrician with this training, Spock was the one.

When approached by an editor from Doubleday, Spock rejected the proposal that he write a book, claiming that he was too inexperienced to offer advice with authority. He was still trying to reconcile what he had learned from mothers about child behavior with the psychological concepts he had studied in the classroom. Five years later, however, when he received his second offer from an editor, he felt ready. This time it came from Donald Porter Geddes of Pocket Books, the four-year-old paperback publishing house. Spock later recalled Geddes as a droll fellow who had a somewhat unorthodox book proposal. He told Spock, "It doesn't have to be a very good book because at twenty-five cents a copy, we'll be able to sell a hundred thousand a year."

This strange appeal worked with Spock, who as a self-professed "do-gooder" liked the idea of reaching so many people. The editor's assurance that the book didn't have to be a very good one was also comforting; if the young pediatrician had been asked to write the best book ever on the subject, he might have been intimidated and turned down the offer.

It was 1943 and Spock was convinced that he could knock the book out in six months' time. But as the war heated up, his practice was expanding because more physicians were called up for active duty, and Spock himself served two years in the navy. Spock dictated the book to his first wife, Jane Cheney, and work on it often didn't begin until one o'clock in the morning. While he was away, the two of them sometimes worked long into the night by telephone. The six-month project had soon stretched into two years and then three.

In order to win the requisite review attention for the book once it had been completed, Pocket Books suggested arranging for a hardcover edition, and Spock mentioned the earlier overture from Doubleday. The notion of a co-publishing venture with a paperback house was sniffed at and quickly passed over by the traditionalists at Doubleday. Instead Spock suggested the name of an old classmate from Yale, Charles Duell of Duell, Sloan & Pearce, a relative newcomer to the publishing scene who had shown he was unafraid of the risks of testing the conventions of publishing. In 1946, Duell, Sloan & Pearce published the hardcover edition as *The Common Sense Book of Baby and Child Care*. In June, 248,000 copies of Pocket Book 377, *The Pocket Book of Baby and Child Care*, hit the newsstands, Rexalls, and Woolworths of America. That first printing sold out in five months. Two additional printings of 50,000 copies were ordered. Then *Parents' Magazine* gave Spock its 1946 award for the outstanding book for parents. A new printing of 400,000 copies was ordered, followed by a fifth printing of another quarter of a million copies in January 1948. Clearly Pocket Books and the unheralded baby doctor had tapped into an extraordinarily rich vein.

One reason for its immediate and surprising success was the book's acceptance by Spock's colleagues in the medical world. The American Medical Association called it a generally sensible book and cited only one fault — too often the book advised parents to consult their own physicians. That was criticism Spock could live with easily. He had been apprehensive about the book's reception, fearing that his colleagues would accuse him of usurping their role as chief consultant to new mothers. And indeed there were complaints. Occasionally other physicians told Spock that some parents were contradicting their advice with the refrain, "But Dr. Spock says . . ." But he also found that the book was winning the recommendation of many pediatricians. In fact, Spock was soon being thanked by fellow doctors who told him that the book had spared them many a midnight call from worried parents who were instead turning confidently to Dr. Spock.

Despite the book's amazing acceptance and its phenomenal sales record, Dr. Spock found that the role of America's Pediatrician was not making him rich. He may have been brilliant when it came to babies, but he had a lot to learn about the book business. "I didn't have an agent in those days and they gave me a miserable royalty rate," said Spock.

> I got no advance and I started with a half-a-cent-per-copy royalty and after so many hundreds of thousands of copies, it went to three-quarters of a cent. After I proved to be sought after, I tried to raise my royalty rate, because Pocket Books didn't have to pay Duell, Sloan & Pearce anything. [The standard practice with Pocket Books and other paperback houses was to pay a royalty that was split between the author and the original hardcover publisher; since Pocket Books was the book's originator, this situation did not apply.] They had a very popular book and they were getting it cheap, so I began to nag them about the royalty. In the first several years, although it was selling close to a million copies a year, I was only getting five thousand dollars. And that didn't seem like enough. So I kept nagging the publisher, Bob de Graff, who was the hardhearted one. Freeman Lewis [editor in chief] was sort of in my corner. But de Graff said no.

Spock later won out when he refused to write any new books — Pocket Books had proposals for two more — until they agreed to double his royalty rate. Ironically, neither of the other two books, *Feeding Your Baby and Child* and *A Teen-Ager's Guide to Life and Love*, ever approached the incredible stature of *Baby and Child Care*.

Undoubtedly, the success of the book depended largely upon its low price and wide availability. Although it was initially sold for twenty-five cents, as was every Pocket Book at the time, the price was later raised to thirty-five cents. For the extra dime it was still a bargain for uncertain mothers who could buy it at more than a hundred thousand retail outlets. The timing of the book was also perfect. Returning from the war, former GIs and their wives were soon busy on the burst of baby making that reshaped American society in the latter half of the twentieth century.

But there was something more fundamental behind the book's popularity and longevity: Dr. Spock's message. *Baby and Child Care* presented the most current medical information available, both in its description of the physical development of children and in its introduction of newly emerging theories of psychological development. Yet the major difference between Spock's book and other pediatrics books that preceded it lay in Spock's tone. He wrote a friendly book, speaking to new mothers with a voice of gentle reassurance rather than the condescendingly stern tones of medical authority. It was in the book's first line, the admonition to "trust yourself," and in the notion that parents should enjoy their babies. As Spock commented, "The previous attitude was, 'Look out, stupid, if you don't do as I say, you'll kill the baby.' I leaned over backwards not to be alarming and to be friendly with the parents."

This was simply revolutionary in comparison to the widely read baby doctors of the previous generations, whose thinking belonged more to Victorian convention and puritanical notions of man being born in sin than to twentieth-century medical practices. One popular doctor, Emmet Holt, cautioned against coddling. Others told parents to remedy thumb-sucking by tying the infant's arms to the crib, painting its thumb, or forcing the child to wear mitts. And just a few years before Spock's book appeared, the most influential thinker had been behaviorist John B. Watson. In *The Psychological Care of Infant and Child*, Watson advised mothers against kissing, holding, or rocking the child; feeding and toilet training were matters of clockwork precision.

Against this background, it is simple to see the roots of the charge most often leveled against Spock: permissiveness with a capital *P*. When compared with his predecessors, Spock was far more liberal and flexible in his advice to new parents, favoring, for instance, the "demand concept" of feeding the baby when it is hungry rather than on a strict but artificial schedule. The notion that he was promoting a kind of wild-eyed, "spoiled" baby was a canard and a serious misreading. Yet in the book's first revision, in 1956, Spock felt compelled to address the question of permissiveness while steadfastly maintaining his advocacy of parental instinct over any theory.

In fact, it was not his theories on child raising that really nettled his critics, but his politics. The son of a Hoover Republican, Spock had become a New Deal Democrat. In 1960, he was a vocal supporter of John F. Kennedy's bid for the presidency, and he made campaign appearances on television alongside Jacqueline Kennedy, who said, "Dr. Spock is for my husband and my husband is for Dr. Spock."[3]

Having devoted his adult life to nurturing the world's children, Spock took a sharp turn in 1962 when he sensed grave danger in Kennedy's decision to resume atmospheric testing of nuclear weapons. He subsequently joined the National Committee for a Sane Nuclear Policy (SANE), lobbying vigorously for a nuclear test ban. There was also a new threat on the horizon in an almost unheard of corner of Southeast Asia. So when Lyndon Johnson ran for the presidency in 1964 on a promise not to involve the country in Vietnam, Spock became a solid supporter, fearing the jingoism and war talk of Republican Barry Goldwater. After Johnson's landslide victory, however, he broke that promise. Feeling betrayed, Spock thrust himself even more forcefully into the emerging peace movement. It was only 1965, and his was not yet the popular stand.

By this time, Spock had become a figure of national prominence whose fame, born with the book, now exceeded simple questions of child rearing. His articles and a column, "Ask Dr. Spock," appeared in *Redbook* and were read by millions. Unscrupulous advertisers had often tried to link his name with their products, but he refused to give any endorsements. He later had to battle Pocket Books when it attempted to place advertising for baby products inside his book.

Then he began his crusade. He marched to Washington and led antiwar rallies. In 1965, Spock campaigned for peace candidates across the country, and after retiring from his professorship at Western Reserve University in 1967, he devoted full time to the peace movement. But his outcry did little to prevent the escalation of the war and with it the death of children he had helped raise.

In 1967 he suggested the wording and was one of the original signers of a document entitled "A Call to Resist Illegitimate Authority." It declared that young men who had resisted induction into the army were serving their country with high patriotism. Enraged by its inability to silence Spock and other critics railing against the war with increasing volume and numbers, the government went on the offensive. Spock and four others, including Yale chaplain William Sloane Coffin, were indicted for conspiracy to subvert the draft laws. The pride of Lyndon Johnson and Lieutenant General Lewis B. Hershey of the Selective Service System would be defended. As the case went to trial, *Dr. Benjamin Spock on Vietnam,* an original paperback, was published. In it, Spock wrote, "During the Nuremberg trials following World War II, our government maintained that a person who is given orders which entail crimes against humanity is obliged — legally as well as morally — to disobey those orders and disobey his government. We believe that we are not guilty because our government is committing crimes against humanity in Vietnam. It is the war which is illegal."[4]

Appearing before eighty-five-year-old Judge Francis Ford, Spock and the others were spotlighted in a trial that dominated front-page headlines for weeks. Ford ran the courtroom in the manner of a Grand Inquisitor: his statements and rulings clearly indicated his prejudice. The verdict was guilty, "as charged by the judge," as one juror put it. The conviction was later reversed by the U.S. Court of Appeals for the First Circuit.[5]

But the damage had been done. Spock's reputation had been tarnished by critics of his antiwar activism and by the trial. His influence and the sales of his book began to wane. Although a UPI survey in the wake of the conviction found that there was no letup in confidence in Dr. Spock among American mothers — one said, "Give up Dr. Spock? I'd rather give up my husband" — it was during this period that the charges that Spock was a high priest of permissiveness became most vociferous. Spock's methods of child rearing, said his detractors, were responsible for the disaffection and rebelliousness of American youth in the 1960s. Prior to the indictment, Spock's book had been selling almost one million copies a year. After the trial, he claims, sales dropped sharply, a turn for which Spock later blamed, among others, Norman Vincent Peale.

> Right after I was indicted, he preached a sermon saying that all the irresponsibility and lack of discipline in young people, by which he meant their opposition to the war, was because when they were babies I told their parents to give them instant gratification. Well, there's nothing like instant gratification in the book. This was just the distress of Peale and other supporters of Richard Nixon over what they thought of as lack of patriotism in young people and older people who gave them any kind of moral support. Peale got this flashing idea, "That old reprobate Spock has told parents to indulge these kids, so now they won't even stand up for their country." Right after Peale preached this

sermon, I got clippings of editorials from all over the United States. Bushel baskets full of clippings — people sending things saying "That's right, Spock has ruined this younger generation." I blame Peale for starting it and Spiro Agnew for going all over the country saying "Spock is the trouble with the youth."

Dr. Spock would have other critics as well. There was feminist criticism, for instance, which derided the book as sexist and responsible for fostering the notion of women locked in as mothers. Others said it promoted the American obsession for youth and novelty. And there were those who claimed that the book placed too much emphasis on grooming the "perfect" child at the expense of the child's own nature and the parents' guilt when these children failed to grow into ideal people. In their book *The Fifties: The Way We Really Were*, Douglas Miller and Marion Nowak fault Spock's "subtle totalitarianism," claiming that the "mission to create a near-perfect being was one more instance of American product orientation."[6]

Spock answered many of his critics in subsequent editions of the book, which was revised to keep pace with changing fashions and trends — such as the movement toward natural childbirth and breast-feeding — and new medical knowledge. The third revision, for instance, was altered to eliminate the "sexist biases of the sort that help create and perpetuate discrimination against girls and women." Despite these changes, Spock's basic message remained the same: reassurance to parents, encouragement to trust instinctive reactions, cautioning against slavish adherence to abstract rules established by doctors on one hand and old wives on the other.

If a real connection exists between Dr. Spock's thinking and the generation that was linked with his name, it may lie in the sense of self-assurance, independence, and idealism that his ideas fostered. We need "idealistic children," he wrote. "Our only realistic hope as I see it is to bring up our children with a feeling that they are in this world not for their own satisfaction *but primarily to serve others*. [Emphasis added.] Children are proud to think they can be useful and will rise to the challenge."

This was the liberal spirit underpinning the book, hardly a call for "instant gratification." Perhaps this thinking played some part in forging a youthful group that resoundingly said "Hell, no" to a war that it found immoral, distasteful, and criminal and a racial division it found unfair and un-American. In his book Spock pointed out that Americans, unlike people in other nations and cultures, raised their children not to serve God and nation but to be individual and independent. If a Me Generation of spoiled children did exist, it may have resulted from distortion of the notion that "self-fulfillment" was a legitimate birthright. It was not the result of a Spockian call for unrestrained self-aggrandizement.

Spock has never given up the cause for which he was hounded. Since his retirement, he has continued to lecture on the university circuit about the need for radical political action. In 1972, he ran for president as the candidate of the quixotic People's Party, and in 1976 he was their vice-presidential choice. Twenty years after he had first joined the ranks of those opposed to nuclear weapons, millions of "his children" were joining the crusade for disarmament. He continues to rally his troops, testifying to the dangers of radiation, lecturing and writing. In a book about the hazards of radiation, Spock wrote an introduction in which he said, "I feel particularly strongly about radiation because children are much more vulnerable than adults — not only to the likelihood of developing leukemia and cancer, but also of being born with physical or mental defects. And once mutations have been produced in genes, they will be passed down forever. What right do we have to threaten with deformity or death those who are too young to protest or those still unborn?"[7]

Perhaps diminished by his run-ins with the Establishment, Spock has never quite regained the lofty profile he once held. Yet his book goes on. Its sales have passed the thirty-million-copy mark; it has been translated into twenty-six languages; and it is still the leading seller in the child-care field according to surveys of the American Booksellers Association. Now the book serves the children of the first parents to use it. Soon it will serve their children's children. Its power was simply the force of an idea whose time had come. Yet the book's success was indisputably linked with another idea whose time had come: the paperback.

TWO

Complete and Unabridged

I N THE CHRONICLES of world history, 1939 marks one of those turning points, like 1066 or 1492, a date that separates one era from another. As Europe waited under the darkening war clouds in that fateful year, Americans watched the gathering storm with anxiety and considerable despair. The wounds of the Great Depression were still open, and visions of an earlier war "over there" were fresh in the minds of many. There were some Americans, like Charles Lindbergh, who spoke admiringly of the Führer and the new order in Germany. Most Americans, however, who heard Hitler's ranting speeches over the wireless or read about him in the dispatches of correspondent William Shirer, thought Adolf Hitler was a frightening madman. But he was Europe's problem. Even in September, when Poland was blitzed and Europe was once again at war.

Although it seems pale in comparison to the world-shattering affairs in Europe, another turning point that would transform modern America was reached in 1939. In June of that year, Robert Fair de Graff, a dignified, patrician, and somewhat tightfisted publisher of Dutch descent, created a new company called Pocket Books that would mass-produce paperbound books. Like Hollywood and television, this undertaking was another amalgam of that peculiar American genius for combining culture, commerce, and a little technology. After 1939, the world of books — like the world itself — would never be the same.

Robert de Graff's initial plans for Pocket Books were modest. He started off with a list of ten books, to be sold on an experimental basis only in New York City. For openers, he planned cautious printings of no more than ten thousand copies per title. The editorial thrust of his initial selections was also conservative. He chose proven sellers from a number of areas, trying to discern exactly what the public was interested in reading and then publishing to those tastes. To remove the doubts of skeptical readers who might be wary of the small books and their twenty-five-cent price, each cover carried the guarantee "Complete and Unabridged." (When Pocket Books first appeared, they were 4¼ by 6½ inches, smaller than the current paperback, which measures 4¼ by 7 inches.) By mixing a little commercial appeal with a dash of literary aplomb, de Graff assembled his initial list of ten titles:

1. *Lost Horizon* by James Hilton, a hardcover best seller in 1935.
2. *Wake Up and Live* by Dorothea Brande, a 1936 best seller on self-improvement, the first of many such paperbacks.
3. *Five Great Tragedies* by Shakespeare, a 476-page loss leader that included *Macbeth, King Lear, Hamlet, Julius Caesar,* and *Romeo and Juliet,* with introductions by John Masefield.
4. *Topper* by Thorne Smith, a 1926 title that eventually sold a million hardcover copies and was the basis for a 1937 Cary Grant film and a later television series.
5. *The Murder of Roger Ackroyd* by Agatha Christie, to test the mystery market waters.
6. *Enough Rope* by Dorothy Parker, poems by the Algonquin wit for the "smart set."
7. *Wuthering Heights,* the first "movie tie-in," set for release along with the Olivier film version.
8. *The Way of All Flesh* by Samuel Butler, to impress the literary types.
9. *The Bridge of San Luis Rey* by Thornton Wilder, winner of the Pulitzer Prize for fiction and best-selling novel of 1928.
10. *Bambi* by Felix Salten, already a children's classic although the Disney version was still years away.

The overnight and overwhelming success of the Pocket Books venture in New York was unprecedented in American publishing history. These twenty-five-cent paperbound books, with their plas-

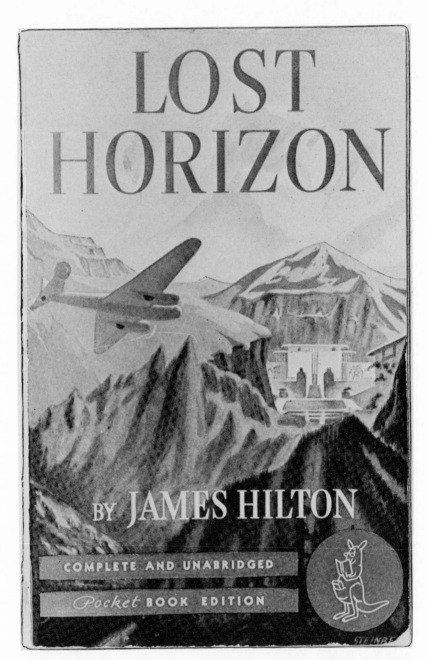

Lost Horizon was the first Pocket Book. (Photo courtesy of Jean Peters; by permission of Pocket Books, a division of Simon & Schuster, Inc.)

tic-laminated covers and bright red endpapers, took New York City by storm. The rest of the country was soon to follow. *The Publishers' Weekly* (now simply *Publishers Weekly*), the trade journal of the book business, immediately began to track the sales of Pocket Books:

- "As this is written, we can only report the first signs of promise. The first reorders came from a bookstore in Doubleday's Grand Central Shop. Concord Books, which has always catered to a public not ordinarily reached by bookstores, has reordered 1000 copies. A little cigar stand near the office of Pocket Books sold 110 copies in the first day and a half. Macy's sold 695 copies in the first day, before its window display was put in."[1]
- "The BMT and IRT [subway] newsstands have asked to carry the books and they will be tried out on 25 stands. So far, twice as many reorders have come from newsstands as from bookshops, which is taken as an encouraging sign that the books are reaching a new market." (A chart showed newsstands that had initially ordered 8150 copies reordered 15,285 more books; drugstores that had taken 2980 books immediately came back for an additional 10,500.)[2]
- "Mr. de Graff tells us that it has been impossible to refuse the requests of out of town dealers who have deluged his office with letters, telegrams and telephone calls."[3]
- A Pocket Books advertisement in *The Publishers' Weekly* claimed that 107,000 books had been sold in the first three weeks in New York City.
- "The first reports from department stores and bookstores indicate that the books are going over in a big way in other cities. . . . So far since publication in June, Pocket Books have sold 325,000 books with reorders now averaging 12,000 to 15,000 copies a day. There has been no distribution north of Boston, west of Chicago or south of Washington."[4]

The first shots in the Paperback Revolution had been fired.

For anyone born after 1939, it is difficult to imagine life without paperbacks and what the arrival of Pocket Books meant to the literary landscape of America. Fortunately, a precise profile of the American publishing and bookselling scene before the advent of mass market paperbacks does exist. In 1931, a landmark survey of publishing practices, costing more than $40,000, was made by Orin H. Cheney, a respected Irving Trust bank official, at the request and expense of the National Association of Book Publishers. It became known as the Cheney Report, and it caused about as much surprise and controversy on Publishers' Row as the Kinsey Report would several years later in American society at large.

Essentially, Cheney and his colleagues issued a scathing denunciation of publishing practices of the day. Editorial, distribution, management, economic, and promotional procedures were criticized as unorganized and inadequate; waste was unnecessarily high. Cheney cited these explanations as popular considerations in making editorial acquisitions:

- "We need this book to balance our list."
- "We've had an option on this for two years."
- "This author isn't so good, but his friend is a comer, and our man will get him for us."
- "It's a great name for our list."
- "You ought to see the picture."
- "Our sales manager read the first two pages of the manuscript and he liked it."
- "We had to get a book on this subject while it was still hot in the newspapers."
- "Two other publishers are going to put out books on the same subject and we can beat them to it."
- "Everybody's playing 'post office' and we have to have a small book of official rules by an expert."[5]

This "selection process" had led to a situation in which the sale of books was roughly parallel to the sales of such luxury items as jewelry, cut flowers, and automobiles. This was due, in part, to the distribution machinery and number of outlets for books. In the entire country, there were only some four thousand places where a book could be purchased, and most of these were gift shops and stationery stores that carried only a few popular novels. In reality, there were but five hundred or so legitimate bookstores that warranted regular visits from publishers' salesmen (and in 1931 they were all men). Of these five hundred, most were refined, old-fashioned "carriage trade" stores catering to an elite clientele in the nation's twelve largest cities. In two-thirds of America's counties, there were no bookstores at all. Thus only half of the books produced by American book publishers sold more than twenty-five hundred copies.

The Book-of-the-Month Club, founded in 1926, and other book

clubs took up some of the slack and could reach hundreds of thousands of readers. But in the early days of the book clubs, only one book per month was offered and they were still as expensive as other hardcover books.

It was into this vast literary wasteland that Robert de Graff came like a breath of fresh air, bringing with him an idea that was neither original, new, nor untried in America. The difference was that he made it work. For de Graff, the success of Pocket Books was the fulfillment of what had practically become a sacred mission. Familiar with Cheney's work and its implications, de Graff had been toying with various methods of selling cheap books since he had entered the publishing field in 1922 as a salesman for the company run by his cousin, Nelson Doubleday. Ironically, the man who reshaped America's reading habits was never much of a reader himself. In fact, he had never finished high school. Born in 1895 in Plainfield, New Jersey, de Graff had attended the Hotchkiss School in Connecticut and then went back to New Jersey and repaired cars. With the outbreak of World War I, he served with the army's Mobile Ordnance Shop.

After the war, de Graff joined his cousin's firm in Garden City, Long Island — then called Doubleday, Page and Company — as a salesman. In 1925, he became president of a Doubleday subsidiary, Garden City Publishing Company, which featured a line called Star Dollar Reprints, inexpensive hardcover reprints that sold millions of copies. He continued to run that company for almost fifteen years, until he set up Blue Ribbon Books with its Triangle line, which sold for thirty-nine cents in the Woolworth's chain. But de Graff believed that price must come down further still and availability be increased through broader distribution. One Pocket Books legend has it that de Graff hit upon twenty-five cents as the ideal price for a book when he tossed a quarter into the toll booth at Jones Beach State Park and mused that nobody misses a quarter.[6] Others maintain that de Graff suggested a higher price and that the twenty-five cents idea belonged to one of his eventual partners, Richard Simon of Simon & Schuster. Whatever the source of the cover price, de Graff's inspiration had come from Europe.

Although paperbacks had been published in America since colonial times, it was in Europe that books bound in paper covers had seen their longest and most illustrious history. In France, books had almost always been published in a paper cover. But the model for

TAUCHNITZ EDITION

COLLECTION OF BRITISH AND AMERICAN AUTHORS

VOL. 3700

ADVENTURES OF GERARD

BY

A. CONAN DOYLE

IN ONE VOLUME

LEIPZIG: BERNHARD TAUCHNITZ

PARIS: LIBRAIRIE HENRI GAULON, 39, RUE MADAME

The Copyright of this Collection is purchased for Continental Circulation only, and the volumes may therefore not be introduced into Great Britain or her Colonies. (See also pp. 3–6 of Large Catalogue.)

EACH VOLUME SOLD SEPARATELY

Tauchnitz Editions were the forerunners of the modern American paperback. (Photo by Jerome Frank)

future generations of paperbacks was born in Germany. Introduced in 1837 by Christian Bernhard (later Baron) von Tauchnitz, the Tauchnitz Editions were conceived as a series of paper-covered books in English, reprinting the works of the most popular British and American writers of the day. Sold exclusively on the Continent by contract with the original publishers, these books were aimed at Europeans who wanted to improve their English and keep pace with British trends, as well as at British and American travelers.

Respecting the rights of authors, Tauchnitz paid royalties despite the absence of an international copyright law, and in time, inclusion in the Tauchnitz Editions catalogue became a badge of honor for writers. Among the most prominent authors of the early volumes were Charles Dickens and Arthur Conan Doyle.

In 1867, an even more successful operation was started by Philip Reclam in Leipzig, an old printing center. Called Reclam's Universal Bibliothek, these were primarily public domain titles, published in a slightly smaller format than the pocket-sized Tauchnitz books. They cost twenty pfennigs, approximately ten cents, and within fifty years, Reclam's list of German-language titles had grown to six thousand volumes and sales totals included 18 million copies of the German classics; 8.5 million copies of the Greek and Roman classics; and 5 million copies of philosophical literature, including 790,000 copies of Kant. The firm's best-selling title was Schiller's *Wilhelm Tell.*[7]

Though Reclam's books actually outsold the Tauchnitz Editions, the Tauchnitz formula for a uniform series of reprints published on a regular schedule exerted far more influence over American publishers who discovered them while traveling through Europe or came across copies spirited back to the United States in steamer trunks. Even though World War I interrupted production of Tauchnitz Editions, the series returned again in 1919, when the price rose from about thirty-eight cents to roughly fifty cents. After the resumption of production, each edition carried an apologetic note: "The usual quality of paper will again be used as soon as possible." By this time, the Tauchnitz list had grown to more than five thousand volumes and included such titles as *A Bit o' Love and Other Plays* by John Galsworthy; *Paris Nights, Hugo,* and *The City of Pleasure* by Arnold Bennet; *Three Plays for Puritans* and another collection including *Pygmalion* by George Bernard Shaw; *The Last of the Mohicans* by James Fenimore Cooper; and *The Conduct of Life* by Ralph Waldo Emerson.

But postwar conditions in Germany and a large, unwieldy list of titles began to plague the Tauchnitz operation. Many of the books had become outdated, and the design was resolutely nineteenth-century. By 1930, Tauchnitz Editions was foundering as a viable operation. Its death knell was sounded in 1932 when a competing company was set up by three men with the financial backing of British industrialist Edmond Davis. The three were British publisher John Holroyd-Reece, former Tauchnitz Editions editor Max Christian Wegner, and German publisher Kurt Enoch. Of these three, Kurt Enoch was destined to make an enormous contribution to American paperback publishing.

Born in Hamburg in 1895, Kurt Enoch was the son of Oscar Enoch, who with his brother was a distributor of books and magazines and a book publisher on a small scale. During World War I, Kurt Enoch served with distinction in the German army on the Western Front. Decorated three times, he moved up through the ranks to officer's standing despite the antipathy toward Jews endemic to the old German Imperial Army. At the war's end, he returned to Hamburg, a member of the Lost Generation who had given up their innocence to the war and were now deeply disillusioned with the world. It was a turbulent moment in German history, and Hamburg was a hotbed of labor radicalism. Uncertain of what course his future should take, Enoch decided to complete his studies at the University of Hamburg. He flirted briefly with a variety of studies before settling on political economics. In 1922, he earned his doctorate, graduating with honors.

At the same time that Kurt Enoch was finishing his schooling, Oscar Enoch's health had begun to fail seriously, and son eventually succeeded father as head of the family firms. It was not the best of times to be attempting a start in business. Postwar Germany was in ruins. The coal- and steel-producing areas along the Ruhr basin had been lost to the French, and the burden of a long, costly war and the impossible reparation demands dictated by the Treaty of Versailles had crippled the German economy. German currency became practically worthless overnight as inflation raged, setting up an economic no man's land on which the newly born National Socialist and Communist parties were readying for battle.

Against this rather desperate background, Enoch took up the reins at the family publishing and distributing concerns. With a loan from his first wife's uncle, he nursed the company through the worst of times and managed to maintain solvency until conditions began to improve after 1924, when the German economy was bolstered by an influx of foreign investment. With it came the political stabilization and cultural halcyon of the Weimar Republic — and near extinction for the Nazi party. Enoch set out on a program of expansion, ambitiously seeking to become the publisher of the new young writers of his own generation. Among these, he published the early novels and poetry of Klaus Mann, the son of Thomas Mann. (Although overshadowed by his father's, the younger Mann's reputation was recently enhanced in this country with the release of *Mephisto*, winner of the Academy Award in 1982 for Best Foreign Film, which was based on Mann's novel of the same title.)

With the Crash of '29, however, all was changed. The foreign capital that had been flowing into Germany and was responsible for the German economic revival came to a screeching halt. The worldwide Great Depression again brought political upheaval inside Germany as the split between right- and left-wing camps grew into open street fighting. Germany was ripe for the comeback of Hitler, and as the Nazis' power increased, a shadow fell over the Jews of Germany. Those with foresight began to view the situation with alarm. Recognizing the sensitivity of his position as a Jewish publisher, Enoch became cautious, concentrating on a less visible publishing program and on strengthening his distributing business. It was Enoch's position as a distributor that attracted the interest of his two future colleagues, Wegner and Holroyd-Reece. They sought someone who could contribute to the development of a competitor to Tauchnitz Editions, now almost a hundred years old and growing senile as a publishing enterprise. Enoch could offer production know-how, a distribution apparatus that spanned the Continent, and a small share of capital. The trio's concept was for a modernized version of Tauchnitz, controlled by the British interests, an increasingly critical point as Hitler's power grew and restraints were placed upon German publishers. For the same reason, the editorial offices were established in Paris under the direction of Wegner. Holroyd-Reece operated out of London as a sort of roving ambassador and liaison with authors, agents, and publishers. Production, distribution, and promotion were controlled by Enoch in Hamburg. To emphasize its contemporary tilt and international flavor, the firm was christened the Albatross Modern Continental Library. Holroyd-Reece had chosen the albatross because it was traditionally the good luck symbol of English seafarers. Adopting the Tauchnitz formula of reprinting books on a regular schedule, the newcomers made several significant changes. The width of the book was reduced slightly to a more convenient 4½-by-7¼-inch pocket-sized format. The design was altered to give the Albatross paperbacks a more modern and hardcover-like appearance, complete with paper dust jackets. The Albatross design was the work of Giovanni Marder-steig, one of Europe's best-known type designers and production director of Mondadori, the large Italian printer. Another innovation was the use of a color code for the various types of books: red covers were stories of adventure and crime; blue were love stories; green designated biographies and historical novels; yellow was for psycho-logical novels and essays; orange were tales and short stories, humor, and satirical works; and grey signified plays, poetry, and collections. The books also featured descriptive blurbs in English, French, and German, printed on the inside covers, to facilitate sales by booksellers — and to readers — whose English may have been limited.

The editorial thrust of Albatross books also tilted toward the new. The first list of Albatross books typified the modernity and literary standards of the new imprint.

1. *Dubliners* by James Joyce.
2. *Gioconda Smile*, a collection of short stories by Aldous Huxley.
3. *Mantrap* by Sinclair Lewis.
4. *Bridge of Desire* by Warwick Deeping, a popular British novelist of the 1930s.
5. *Rogue Herries* by Hugh Walpole, the first book in a family saga that rivaled Galsworthy's Forsytes in popularity.
6. *Night in the Hotel* by E. Crawshay-Williams, a first novel about a day in the life of the guests in a small Riviera hotel.
7. *To the Lighthouse* by Virginia Woolf.
8. *Two People* by A. A. Milne, the first novel by the author of the Winnie-the-Pooh books.
9. *The Man at The Carlton* by Edgar Wallace, a popular detective-story and mystery writer.
10. *Dodsworth* by Sinclair Lewis.
11. *Gauntlet* by Lord Gorel, another well-known writer of mysteries.
12. *Buttercups and Daisies* by Compton Mackenzie, a very successful British novelist of the 1920s.
13. *The Limestone Tree* by Joseph Hergesheimer, a historical novel set in Kentucky.

14. *The Golden Vase/Roman Summer* by Ludwig Lewisohn, two
    novellas by a widely admired writer of the period.
15. *The Magic Island* by W. B. Seabrook, a nonfictional account of
    Haitian voodoo.
16. *The Brothers* by L.A.G. Strong, a novel.
17. *The Love of Julie Borel* by Kathleen Norris, the best-selling
    writer of women's romances before the 1920s.
18. *The Bishop Murder Case* by S. S. Van Dine, a best seller
    featuring Philo Vance, the great amateur detective.
19. *Ambrose Holt and Family* by Susan Glaspell, a popular novelist
    of the period.
20. *The Maltese Falcon* by Dashiell Hammett.

Later volumes would include James M. Cain's *The Postman Al-ways Rings Twice;* Lloyd C. Douglas's *Magnificent Obsession;* E. M. Forster's *A Passage to India;* Kenneth Grahame's *The Wind in the Willows;* Robert Graves's *I, Claudius* and *Claudius the God;* Aldous Huxley's *Antic Hay, Brave New World,* and *Crome Yellow;* D. H. Lawrence's *Apocalypse, The Plumed Serpent, The Rainbow,* and *The Virgin and the Gypsy;* Eugene O'Neill's *Strange Interlude;* mysteries by Ellery Queen; Dorothy L. Sayers's *The Nine Tailors;* Evelyn Waugh's *A Handful of Dust;* Edith Wharton's *Human Nature* and *Ethan Frome;* Thornton Wilder's *The Bridge of San Luis Rey;* and Virginia Woolf's *The Waves.*

From the debut of Albatross in 1932, response to the new venture was enthusiastic. The titles were desirable, the format vigorous and attractive — although by contemporary standards, the unillus-trated, type-only jackets might seem unexciting — and the European book trade soon provided ample space for a shelf devoted exclusively to Albatross books, an honor once reserved only for Tauchnitz Editions. It was not long before Tauchnitz, which had repelled the repeated attempts of other competitors to enter the reprint field, began to wither under the pressure of this new paper-back company. The Tauchnitz management, heirs to the baron, put out feelers to the Albatross trio through a printer used by both firms. Would Albatross be interested in buying up Tauchnitz Editions? Confident that the purchase would consolidate their hold on the market for paperbacks in Europe, Enoch and his partners promptly agreed, but the German government ruled otherwise. They did not want to see this established and traditional German firm in the hands of foreign owners. To circumvent this roadblock,

I, Claudius

by
ROBERT GRAVES

THE ALBATROSS

COPYRIGHT EDITION

NOT TO BE INTRODUCED INTO THE BRITISH EMPIRE OR THE U. S. A.

Designed by Giovanni Mardersteig, Albatross paperbacks were strikingly modern when published in 1932. (Photo by Jerome Frank)

the Albatross partners quietly provided the funds for the printer —
who was only concerned with keeping his business with both companies — who bought Tauchnitz Editions in 1934 and turned over
the management of the firm to the Albatross men.

For a time things went well and the Albatross-Tauchnitz pairing
prospered. Old titles were pared from the Tauchnitz list, some titles
were moved over to the Albatross list, and certain Albatross titles
were likewise moved to Tauchnitz Editions. Enoch traveled often,
meeting with publishers in London and Paris and occasionally making use of the villa maintained by Holroyd-Reece on the Côte
d'Azur. Then his carefully ordered world fell apart. Within a short
space of time, his father and his wife died. With Hitler's accession
to power as Reich Chancellor in 1933, the rule of the Nazis was
growing absolute. Despite his military career and distinguished service record, Enoch knew that his days in Germany were numbered.
Accordingly, he sold out his interest in the Hamburg distribution
and publishing firms and planned a move to Paris, where he would
establish a new distribution company, Continenta, to handle the
Albatross sales outside Germany. Most of the revenue from the sale
of his Hamburg companies went to pay for the exorbitant exit visas
required to leave Germany and toward the purchase of an inventory
of Albatross and Tauchnitz books, since he could remove no capital
from Germany under the strict currency laws in place. In August
1936, he left Germany for Paris, but not before he had undergone
several long and excruciating searches by the Gestapo.

At just about the time that Enoch was making his plans to leave
Germany and start a new life, another ambitious publisher was
formulating the concept for a new paperback series that would have
even more far-reaching effects on the world of books. His name was
Allen Lane, and his idea would become Penguin Books.

Born Allen Williams (his father later changed the family name to
Williams-Lane), the man who founded Penguin Books left grammar
school in 1919 at age sixteen and went to work in the publishing
house run by a distant cousin who was nonetheless called "Uncle"
John Lane. Some thirty years earlier, John Lane had launched his
own book publishing firm, John Lane The Bodley Head, and made a
name for himself in London literary circles as a publisher of origi-
nality and considerable daring. Among his accomplishments were
the publication of Anatole France and Oscar Wilde and the founding
of a literary journal, *The Yellow Book*, that was to be of great influ-

ence. When Allen Lane came to the firm, however, his uncle was in poor health and the company was in the early stages of a decline. Starting out as an office boy, Allen soon learned the business and editorial ropes and then became a traveling salesman for the firm. In 1924, Allen Lane was promoted to The Bodley Head's board of directors; a few weeks later, Uncle John died.

Although once considered one of the most lively of British publishing houses, The Bodley Head was deeply troubled when Allen Lane took the helm. Even the successful British publication of Joyce's *Ulysses* in 1936 — the rights had been purchased from Random House, which had won the landmark 1933 decision clearing the book of obscenity charges in America — was not enough to restore the firm to its former position of vitality. Lane's solution was to turn The Bodley Head in a new direction — paper-covered reprints that could be sold profitably for only sixpence. As Lane's colleague and biographer J. P. Morpurgo put it, "In a sense Allen dreamed up Penguin to save The Bodley Head. . . . Those who knew him when he was at the height of his success have no difficulty in accepting as history that Penguin was the child of necessity and impulse, conceived on a railway platform."[8]

According to Penguin mythology, Lane was returning from a weekend spent in Devon at the home of his friends Agatha Christie and her husband Max Mallowan. Stuck in the train station with nothing to read except the glossy magazines and trashy reprints sold in railway bookstalls, Lane hit upon the notion of publishing a new series of quality fiction and nonfiction reprints in attractive covers to be sold in places that did not specialize in bookselling as well as in the traditional bookstore market.

With his brothers, Richard and John, who were his colleagues at The Bodley Head, Lane drew up and refined his plan for Penguin Books. Despite the skepticism and occasional antagonism of rival British hardcover publishers, a list of ten titles was selected.

1. *Ariel* by André Maurois, a biography of Shelley.
2. *A Farewell to Arms* by Ernest Hemingway.
3. *Poet's Pub*, a novel by Eric Linklater, a popular British writer.
4. *Madame Claire* by Susan Ertz, a popular novelist of the 1920s.
5. *The Unpleasantness at the Bellona Club* by Dorothy L. Sayers.
6. *The Murder on the Links* by Agatha Christie. (Although listed as title No. 6, this Christie was postponed and its place in the original list was taken by *The Mysterious Affair at Styles*, No. 61.

As No. 6, *The Murder on the Links* finally appeared in March 1936.)

7. *Twenty-Five* by Beverly Nichols.
8. *Gone to Earth* by Mary Webb.
9. *Carnival* by Compton Mackenzie, which had to be withdrawn after publication because of copyright difficulties.
10. *South Wind* by Norman Douglas.

Another legend that grew up around the Penguin empire involved Lane's initial efforts to sell the Penguin idea to the booksellers. Using a dummy composed of a section of Penguin No. 3, Linklater's *Poet's Pub*, the three Lane brothers began soliciting sales: Allen in the country meeting booksellers he had first encountered as a young salesman for The Bodley Head, Dick in London, and John corresponding with booksellers in the four corners of the British Empire. The lackluster greeting encountered by the trio seemingly doomed the project. Until, that is, Allen's mythical odyssey to the Olympus of British retailing, Woolworth's. The tale has often been told and embroidered upon of how Lane presented the list of the books to the chain's buyer, Mr. Prescott, who was supposedly unimpressed with their "severe" design — no illustrations, only type. Enter Mrs. Prescott, who had been waiting for her husband. After examining the titles, she signaled her approval of the price and the selection of books and said she would give them a try even though she was unfamiliar with some of the books. Bowing to his wife's wisdom, Prescott then placed a token order. However, he later called Lane with a large consignment order that meant Penguin Books would be sold in every Woolworth store in Britain. Penguin was saved from an early death. Like most myths, this one had some basis in truth, but Lane's biographer has deflated it. According to Morpurgo, Prescott was in fact impressed with the books and had only shown them to his wife as a nicety. In addition, by this point booksellers had begun to come around, and the advance orders were flowing in at a steady rate.[9]

The first ten Penguin Books appeared on July 30, 1935. Success was immediate. Booksellers soon found themselves in the unprecedented situation of having customers lined up outside their doors to buy the books. But although this reception might have been a novelty, paperbacks in England were not. There had been numerous paper-covered books produced in England, going back as far as a series called British Poets, published by John Bell in the 1700s.

During the nineteenth century and the early part of the twentieth, a number of cheap fiction series had been available at railway book-stalls. There were also several series of classics bound in paper, including the perhaps best known one, the Everyman Library, which first appeared in 1906.

Lane was also obviously acquainted with his European predecessors, Tauchnitz Editions and the Albatross Modern Continental Library, already three years old by the time Penguin Books made their debut. The size, design, and scheduling of the Penguins reflected the direct influence of the German paperbacks. Penguin also adapted the Albatross color-coding scheme. In the Penguin rainbow, orange was for fiction, green for mysteries, dark blue for biography, and so on. But there were some key differences between the two, and the greatest of these was price. At sixpence, Penguin Books were vastly cheaper than Albatross books, principally because of larger print runs, which enabled Lane to keep his unit cost low. This price differential later became significant when Lane took Penguin Books to the Continent in a head-to-head confrontation with Albatross and Tauchnitz Editions. Penguins had the additional advantage of reach, with the Woolworth stores alone expanding their potential marketplace; Albatross had no such nonbookstore outlets. In addition, the traditional British export market extended across the Commonwealth to Canada, Australia, Africa, and Asia, the key factor in making Penguins synonymous with paperbacks to the literate world.

Not coincidentally, the paths of Lane and Enoch crossed in 1938. Then living in Paris, where he directed the sales of Albatross and Tauchnitz outside Germany, Enoch had also prepared a series of French-language classics in paperback that featured blurbs in English and were sold in England for sixpence. Knowing Enoch by reputation, Lane met with him in London, and the two men discussed a proposal for establishing a French Penguin. But the times were not in their favor, and a relationship that would have certainly grown to be a clash of two indomitable wills was aborted by the onset of the war. This was not their last meeting, however. Their paths later crossed again, with far-reaching consequences.

Meanwhile, with his Penguins successfully launched, Lane began to expand his concept. Another imprint, Pelican Books, was added for serious nonfiction; George Bernard Shaw's *Intelligent Woman's Guide to Socialism, Capitalism and Sovietism* (in two volumes) was the first book in the new series. Lane also made the unprecedented leap of commissioning original works to be published in the series. Later, a complete works of Shakespeare was compiled under the Pelican banner. A new translation of Homer's *Odyssey* by E. V. Rieu was commissioned to inaugurate the Penguin Classics series and then went on to become Penguin's best-selling title. Puffin Books, a line for children, later appeared. With John Lehman, a leading British literary figure, Lane launched *Penguin New Writing*, a literary journal in the paperback format that became one of the most influential vehicles for British writers during the 1940s.

But perhaps the most significant Penguin accomplishment of the early years was the introduction of the Penguin Specials, books that generally dealt with some current problem and were usually written on short notice. Obviously, the most pressing problem faced by the British in the late 1930s was the growing power of Hitler's Germany. A devoted anti-Fascist, Lane turned the Penguin Specials into a powerful and effective propaganda tool in the war of words against Hitler. The first Special, *Germany Sets Back the Clock*, set the tone for the series; later volumes included *New Ways of War* (a handbook of guerrilla war tactics), *Poland*, *The Air Defence of Britain*, and *The Attack from Within*. Jaroslav Hasek's classic novel of a malingering Czech soldier, *The Good Soldier Schweik*, and Arnold Haskell's *Ballet* were Specials that didn't exactly fit the mold, and they were later moved into more appropriate spots on the Penguin lists. But for the first time in the history of paperback publishing, the Specials had demonstrated the paperback's value as a significant means of educating and informing in a world on the edge of war. Often produced on a schedule that was three times faster than the norm, Specials gave a new legitimacy to the paperback book as a means of mass communication.

The war, when it finally came to England, also had a profound influence on Penguin's fortunes. Paper rationing went into effect, and publishers found their paper allotments based on their use during the previous year. Fortunately for Lane, the prior year had seen an unusual number of Specials, inflating Penguin's paper usage and guaranteeing a larger than usual allotment. This meant that for a time Penguin had comfortable supplies while effectively eliminating the chances for any competitor to get a start in the paperback business. In effect, Penguin became a monopoly. In just three years, more than twenty-five million Penguin Books had been sold, far beyond the wildest expectations of anyone connected with the British book business and certainly beyond Lane's own imaginings.

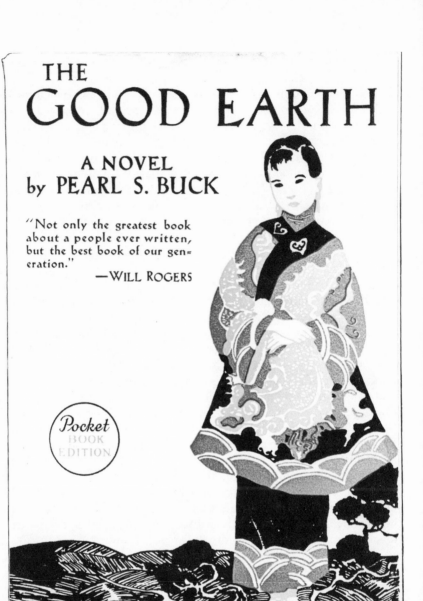

THE
GOOD EARTH

A NOVEL
by PEARL S. BUCK

"Not only the greatest book about a people ever written, but the best book of our generation."
—WILL ROGERS

Pocket BOOK EDITION

COMPLETE & UNABRIDGED

The Good Earth was used as a test of the Pocket Books concept and became Pocket Book 11. (Photo courtesy of Jean Peters; by permission of Pocket Books, a division of Simon & Schuster, Inc.)

THREE

Winning Friends and Influencing People

Do this and you'll be welcome everywhere.
— Dale Carnegie,
How to Win Friends and Influence People (1936)

ALLEN LANE'S BONANZA with Penguin Books, as well as Kurt Enoch's earlier success with Albatross/Tauchnitz, did not go unnoticed on this side of the Atlantic, but skeptics said that what had worked in Europe would never work in America. Robert de Graff thought otherwise. He had cast an admiring eye on the astonishing results achieved by the German and British paperback publishers; after founding Blue Ribbon Books in 1937, de Graff left the firm in 1938 to concentrate on a primitive market survey, a concept fairly foreign to publishing then and now. In an attempt to gauge what people actually wanted to read, de Graff prepared a questionnaire listing a wide selection of titles, and sent it out to forty thousand people. With two thousand of the surveys, he included a sample book, Pearl Buck's *The Good Earth*. It was an easy choice; the novel had been the best-selling fiction title in both 1931 and 1932. Identical in every way — except for cover material — to the Pocket Books that would follow it, the sample book later became Pocket Book 11.

One day over lunch with fellow publisher Richard Simon of the upstart firm Simon & Schuster, de Graff set forth his idea for an inexpensive paperback series. Simon, who had been to Europe often and was familiar with the success of Penguin, was already toying with the notion of a paperback line of his own, a series he planned to call the Twentieth-Century Library. It was fitting that de Graff had come to Simon & Schuster with his plan. Richard Simon and M. (for Max) Lincoln Schuster had started out in the 1920s as publishers without any books. On the day they moved into their offices, a painter had just finished lettering their door SIMON & SCHUSTER, PUBLISHERS when a friend who stopped by added a hand-lettered note, "Of what?" The pair made their first successes with crossword puzzle books; they later picked up Will Durant's *Story of Philosophy*, which had first appeared as a series of pamphlets published by the Little Blue Books of Emanuel Haldeman-Julius. The young firm quickly garnered a reputation for creating new books and finding someone to write them rather than waiting for agents to offer manuscripts. After a few years of highly successful commercial publishing, however, agents began to find their way to the Simon & Schuster offices. The two men represented the perfect partners for de Graff. They were not afraid to try something new, unlike many of the starchy traditionalists found elsewhere in publishing during that period, a group which belonged more to the nineteenth century than the twentieth. Simon and Schuster were both interested in expanding book readership. It was also somewhat ironic that de Graff, a relative of the WASP bastion called Doubleday, turned to Simon, Schuster, and their treasurer, Leon Shimkin. These were still the days when many New York clubs — including those that catered to the publishing world — were closed to Jews.

After subsequent negotiations and discussions between de Graff and Simon, Schuster, and Shimkin (the "third S"), an agreement for a partnership was struck. But de Graff, somewhat possessive of the Pocket Books idea and fearful that an alignment with Simon & Schuster would damage his relations with the other hardcover publishers with whom he had to deal for books, was reticent. Shimkin, a man with a reputation as one of the smartest business minds in publishing, proposed a simple solution. Although de Graff and Simon & Schuster would each provide a share of the capital, de Graff would have a 51 percent share in the corporation so that he could legitimately call himself the principal shareholder when negotiating with other publishers. (De Graff's share of the capitalization was $22,950 for 459 shares; Simon, Schuster, and Shimkin split 441 shares and each put in $7350 for a total of $22,050.) Despite de Graff's majority holding, though, Shimkin made certain that Simon & Schuster's vote was equal to that of de Graff's.

With the corporation set and the titles procured, the name Pocket Books was chosen by de Graff (to the woe of his later competitors, who discovered that for years all paperbacks would be called "pocket books"), and the company's symbol was created. Gertrude, the kangaroo with the Harold Lloyd spectacles, holding one book while carrying another in her pouch, was the invention of artist Frank Lieberman, who claimed to have named the kangaroo after his mother-in-law. (Gertrude would go through a long evolution. One later version would be the work of Walt Disney. Then the eyeglasses were dropped, out of fear that people would think that paperbacks caused eye strain. The most recent version is the work of illustrator Milton Glaser.)

All that was left to do was to get the word out. Other publishers, of course, were aware of the plan. Some had agreed to sell de Graff reprint rights. Others scoffed. One anonymous skeptic told *Time*, "We are cooperating because of all the agitation for cheap books and the success of cheap books in Europe. We feel we ought to give it a chance — to show it won't work here. If we thought it would really go, we would hesitate much longer about letting them have our plates."[1]

To start the publicity ball rolling, de Graff wrote an innocent sounding letter to *The Publishers' Weekly*. He must have been grinning like the cat who ate the canary when he asked, just two months before Pocket Books appeared, "Has anyone considered publishing a cheap edition for this market which people would buy instead of lend, that would not interfere with the sale of the regular edition? It seems to me that might offer some solution, for then the author and the publisher through the sale of their cheap edition would get a revenue, however small, from each person who reads the book."[2]

The question of revenues — "however small" — was crucial. While many publishers thought that book-buying Americans simply didn't want paperback books and that the American masses were not readers — an elitist conviction that pervaded the industry — others were skeptical for reasons of pure economy. It simply appeared impossible to make a reasonable profit on a book that sold for only twenty-five cents. There was strong evidence to support this conviction: others had tried and failed. The history of American publishing was littered with the failures of paperback experiments of the past. Just as there had been earlier attempts to publish paperbound books in Europe, the United States had seen a succession of paperback movements during the nineteenth century. In 1829, a high-minded group of Bostonians called the Society for the Diffusion of Useful Knowledge started what they called the American Library of Useful Knowledge, intent on printing inexpensive books in "all the important branches of learning." As it turned out, the public was not too keen on *Discourses Before the Boston Mechanic's Society* or *Universal History,* two of their early titles. The fruits of this noble experiment withered on the vine.

With the advent of machine-made paper, mechanical typesetting, and improved presses, a number of shrewd publishers attempted paperback publishing in the 1830s. Two young journalists, Park Benjamin and Rufus W. Griswold, conceived the notion of publishing serialized fiction in a tabloid newspaper format. They called their brain child "Brother Jonathan," and it served primarily as a vehicle for pirating popular British fiction, including the novels of Charles Dickens. When new owners took over "Brother Jonathan" and forced out Griswold and Benjamin, they retaliated by launching "The New World" in 1840, again printing in the form of newspaper supplements called Extras. A period of cutthroat competition ensued as the rival publishers stole material outright from each other. A number of other competitors entered the fray, and soon unbound paperback books were being hawked by newsboys on the street corners. Their content was "borrowed" from Balzac and Hugo — no royalties were paid — and the books sold for twelve and a half cents apiece. Among the early publications was Poe's *Murders in the Rue Morgue,* the first modern detective story. This "great revolution in American publishing," as it was then called, came to an abrupt end when the Post Office ruled that these Extras must be charged at book rate rather than the less expensive newspaper rate.

Dime novels, mostly romanticized tales of the American West and the forerunner of Western novels, carried the paperback torch through the Civil War years and after. But in the 1870s, there was a large-scale revival of paperback books spawned by the "cheap libraries." Spurred by the invention of inexpensive groundwood paper, popular interest in English and French novels, and the absence of an international copyright law to protect foreign writers, a boom-time market for paperbacks was created. First out of the chute was the *New York Tribune,* which offered its Tribune Extras and Tribune Novels for ten and twenty cents. Soon the Chicago firm of Donnelley, Gasette and Lloyd joined in with its Lakeside Library. The Harper Brothers, Henry Holt and Company, Dodd, Mead & Company, and Funk & Wagnalls all followed suit, churning out dozens of popular books sold through newsdealers, small bookstores, and dry goods stores. The success of these cheap books reached such heights that by 1885, almost fifteen hundred out of the forty-five hundred titles published that year were in paperback. This paperback tidal wave was bound to crash as competition, increasing costs, and the exhaustion of sources of reprints pounded away at the business. The death blow came with the Copyright Act of 1891, which extended copyright protections to foreign authors, ending a century of unscrupulous piracy and with it the first battles in the Paperback Revolution.

But the paperback idea wouldn't die. Magazine publishers began to produce more pulp magazines, the successors to the dime novels of the mid nineteenth century. And several enterprising publishers kept the notion of paperbound books alive. One of the most significant and curious projects was the Little Blue Books, first published in 1919 by Emanuel Haldeman-Julius, a socialist operating out of an unlikely base in Girard, Kansas. His pamphlet-style five- and ten-cent paperbacks were sold largely through a flamboyant newspaper campaign aimed at winning subscribers to the series. A radical in his day, Haldeman-Julius published everything from the *Rubaiyat of Omar Khayyam* and Shakespeare to a series of tracts on such taboo subjects as sex, psychoanalysis, birth control, and socialism. By 1949, the firm had sold more than 300 million Little Blue Books and they had become something of an underground institution, although the newspaper ads run by Haldeman-Julius raised the ire of his fellow publishers, who called them deceptive. A tax evasion charge against Haldeman-Julius (allegedly politically motivated) and his death in 1951, along with the rise of Pocket Books and its competitors, signaled the company's demise.

In 1929, another valiant attempt at serious publishing in paper covers was launched by Charles Boni, onetime partner in the firm of Boni & Liveright, founders of the famous Modern Library. Also a vigorous prophet of paperbound books, Boni called his pet project Boni Paper Books. They were books of seriousness, bound in paper covers and designed and illustrated by Rockwell Kent. Like the Little Blue Books, the Boni Books were to be sold on a subscription scheme, but they were priced at fifty cents. The plan succumbed to

LITTLE BLUE BOOK NO. 159
Edited by E. Haldeman-Julius

A Guide to Plato

Will Durant, Ph. D.

Durant's *Story of Philosophy* began as a lecture series in the Little Blue Books. (Photo by Jerome Frank)

distribution difficulties and folded after two years. During the 1930s, under the Borzoi imprint, Alfred Knopf attempted a few paperback editions modeled on the Tauchnitz / Albatross design; among them was an edition of *The Postman Always Rings Twice* by James M. Cain, but this scheme was also dropped. The thirties also saw the introduction of the Mercury Mysteries, published by Lawrence E. Spivak, and Hillman Novels.

Perhaps the most ambitious experiment at viable paperback publishing for the bookstore market came with the introduction of Modern Age Books in 1937. The Modern Age concept was for both reprints and original works, often published in dual cloth and paperback editions, under three separate imprints: Blue Seal for new books, at twenty-five cents; Gold Seal for longer books and illustrated works, at thirty-five cents; and Red Seal for reprints, at twenty-five cents. Modern Age even anticipated the Pocket Books strategy for selling books through newsstands and drugstores. With a left-of-center political slant, Modern Age published such titles as *The Daring Young Man on the Flying Trapeze* by William Saroyan, E. M. Forster's *A Passage to India, From Spanish Trenches* by Marcel Acier, and *Men Who Lead Labor* by Bruce Minton and John Stuart. But problems of distribution also plagued Modern Age from the outset, and its failure to succeed in the mass market outlets spelled doom for the company. After two years, Modern Age shifted to hardcover production. In an article in *The Publishers' Weekly*, Louis P. Birk, the firm's vice president, wrote of the company's inability to publish books profitably at a retail price of twenty-five or even thirty cents. He included a sample cost statement:

Completed book cost	7.5 cents
Overhead	3.
Discount to dealer	15.
Advertising	1.5
Royalty	3.
Total	30.

Asking, "Where is the publisher's profit?" Birk went on to wish Pocket Books well.[3]

Based on these figures, the industry's coolness toward de Graff's idea seemed well founded. Without drastically altering the economics of paperback publishing, the notion of twenty-five-cent books seemed a hopeless cause. Nonetheless, de Graff was adamant

The Return of the
HERO
DARRELL FIGGIS

Charles Boni **PAPER BOOKS** *New York*

The short-lived Boni Paper Books featured cover illustrations by Rockwell Kent. (Photo courtesy of Jean Peters)

when, without publicly acknowledging his relationship with Simon & Schuster, he officially notified the world of the Pocket Books plan. His press release demonstrated his stiff resolve, what some called Dutch stubbornness.

> For years, visitors returning from Europe have asked the publishers of America why good books could not be issued at lower prices. Several experiments in this direction have been tried, but they have never concentrated on issuing literally the best books. In the past, it has been maintained that Americans will not buy paperbound books the way Europeans have been doing for years. It has also been assumed that cheap books — for the 25 cent market — must be of a low common denominator — the sort that will compete with the "pulp" and "trash" market and magazines of vast circulation. I venture to question those traditional beliefs, and am prepared to make this conscientious and thorough-going experiment to prove my faith in the pent-up American demand for genuinely good and enduring books at irresistibly low prices, with almost universal distribution.[4]

Robert de Graff's optimism sprang from his strategy to overcome the fatal flaws in the economics of Modern Age and other paperback predecessors. He simply planned to reduce costs and increase volume. Both objectives were easier said than done. In attacking costs, de Graff first sliced the royalty paid to the author and the originating hardcover house. This money, called subsidiary rights income by hardcover publishers though it is anything but subsidiary, was split between author and original publisher on a fifty-fifty basis. Never one to be called generous when it came to paying for reprint rights, de Graff got publishers and authors who were certain that it would never amount to much to agree to a 4 percent royalty instead of the 10 percent that Modern Age had been paying. More significantly, he reduced the discounts to dealers from the standard 40 percent or 50 percent to 36 percent for wholesalers and just 20 percent for booksellers. He also reduced the production costs by borrowing the original publishers' plates whenever possible, reducing the size of the book to a purse-sized 4¼ by 6½ inches (slightly smaller than today's version of the mass market paperback, which measures 4¼ by 7 inches), and using the "perfect binding," an incongruously named gluing process that is vastly cheaper than the regular stitched binding of hardcover books. But the most important factor in dropping costs was the increase in print runs to ten times the size of a typical hardcover run. Greater economies would come later when print runs moved into the hundred-thousand-copy range, further reducing the unit cost of a paperback book. All of this, however, hinged on slim profit margins, as little as a half cent per book, a margin that would only prove profitable if those large print-ings sold in sufficient quantities.

To keep overhead down, the Pocket Books staff — quartered on Fourth Avenue, the old Publishers' Row — was also limited in the beginning. Besides de Graff, there was an editorial staff consisting of Dr. Morris E. Speare, who consulted on the creation of original anthologies, and Louise Crittenden, an editorial assistant who also handled publicity. In addition, there were a few people in sales, bookkeeping, publicity, and production, as well as a receptionist and an office boy. Initially, de Graff handled most of the negotia-tions with other publishers for reprints. Partner Leon Shimkin later recalled de Graff's selection process. "He would look over the *New York Times Book Review* best-seller list and endeavor to buy, as soon as he could, the rights to each and every one of those books." It was a task made easier by the fact that de Graff as yet had no competition. He was soon joined on editorial matters by an old publishing hand, Philip Van Doren Stern, Simon & Schuster's man-ufacturing director, who became Pocket Books' editorial consultant and was responsible for creating some of the early Pocket Book original or "made" books, usually anthologies of humor, short sto-ries, or verse, such as *The Pocket Reader.*

The key addition to the staff was Wallis E. "Pete" Howe, Jr., one of the best-known advertising salesmen in the business. Howe had started out as a sportswriter for the Boston *Herald* and then moved on to selling advertising for the *Atlantic Monthly,* where he inau-gurated the *Atlantic* Bookshelf. He jumped to a succession of New York newspapers before joining Pocket Books in 1939, where he was responsible for creating a sales department. His first stop was Macy's. As he later told it:

> I called on the personable Peggy Byrnes, buyer. In my briefcase were the first ten samples, so hot off the presses the covers were still agi-tated and curled. I gave them a quick shuffle and piled them one on top of another. . . . Miss Byrnes spread them out in a row and, like a West Point guard room when the Colonel enters unexpectedly, the covers rose to attention. Miss Byrnes laughed. "Junior, how much of an order were you expecting?" "Well, I kind of hoped for five thousand assorted." Every salesman knows that means I expected 2500, and was

prepared to retreat gracefully. "Wrong again, Junior." She winked so I didn't abandon all hope. "We'll take 10,000 assorted and we'll advertise them at our own expense."[5]

It was that easy in the beginning. From day one of the experiment in New York, Pocket Books practically sold themselves. Aided by an enthusiastic reception in newspapers and magazines across the country, de Graff and company did not have to go to the mountain because the mountain was coming to them. The electric rapidity of sales also meant that capital was no problem. Their real headache was printing books fast enough to meet the demand. The first Pocket Books had been printed at the small Colonial Press in Clinton, Massachusetts, after de Graff found that none of the larger book manufacturers wanted to take the risk of disturbing their press schedules with an experimental shift from hardcover to paperback production. But Pocket quickly outgrew the small company, and with the paperback established, they later turned to W. F. Hall, the large Chicago printer that produced the Montgomery Ward mail-order catalogue, and then to Arcata in Buffalo, New York.

Editorially, de Graff continued to experiment, publishing in a range of areas, constantly trying to fine-tune his sense of what the public wanted. In a letter to Frederic Melcher, editor of *The Publishers' Weekly*, de Graff confided:

> I had hoped to learn more about the public wishes from the first lot than I have so far. Shakespeare, apparently, did not have the bargain appeal that I thought it might; so I have learned that. I think that four tragedies would have been better, as the book is a little bulky and it is not worth the extra cost. Some titles that started out fairly slowly have since picked up, like *Bambi* and *The Bridge of San Luis Rey*. To date, it has been really hard to see any definite preference for a type, so I am trying to stick to a wide variety.[6]

Over the next few months, Pocket Books added classics like *A Tale of Two Cities, A Christmas Carol, The Hunchback of Notre Dame* (in two volumes), *The House of the Seven Gables,* and *Pride and Prejudice;* currently popular novels like *Show Boat, Green Mansions,* and *Appointment in Samarra;* mysteries (which didn't seem to go over at first); and a smattering of nonfiction, humor, anthologies, and plays.

But the first Pocket Books million-seller was the result of an experiment made about one year after the debut of the line. From the outset, de Graff had argued against the notion that a paperback edition would hurt the sales of the original hardcover edition of a book, a belief that was commonly held by traditionalists in the publishing industry such as Cass Canfield of Harper & Row, who refused de Graff's request to reprint Harper titles.[7] To this thinking, one bookseller tartly replied, "Does the sale of lollipops hurt the sale of Louis Sherry candy?" However, to put his theory to the acid test, de Graff and his partners at Simon & Schuster chose one of the firm's best sellers, Dale Carnegie's *How to Win Friends and Influence People*, the first in a long line of books on self-improvement and success strategies. The book had experienced a strange birth, coming from Leon Shimkin, usually the business-minded member of the Simon & Schuster troika. Shimkin had been invited to meet Carnegie, who was known for his success in teaching public speaking at YMCAs in the New York area. Shimkin heard Carnegie lecture and found him inspiring. But when he suggested that Carnegie write a book for Simon & Schuster, Carnegie was furious. He told Shimkin that he had sent two book proposals to the company and had gotten no response to either. Undaunted, Shimkin asked for permission to have a stenographer take down Carnegie's lecture verbatim. Shimkin sent the transcript to Carnegie, who was enormously pleased with himself, and a deal for a book based on the speeches was struck. It appeared in hardcover in 1936 and very quickly topped the extraordinary million-seller mark. Later Shimkin would say, "Every time I get up in the morning, I face the east and thank Allah that he came into my life." (One of Shimkin's few other editorial notions was for a tax preparation guide, and he enlisted J. K. Lasser to write it.)

Limiting their test to Texas — at that time considered a poor book state — Pocket Books issued Carnegie's inspirational self-improvement guide in a twenty-five-cent edition while the hardcover edition was still selling some 800 copies per week at $1.96. Without interfering with the sale of the hardcover edition, the paperback sold 34,000 copies in two months. Convinced that de Graff was correct about the coexistence of hardcover and paperback markets, Simon & Schuster allowed Pocket Books to go ahead with national release, and *How to Win Friends and Influence People* sold 700,000 paperback copies in six months. By April 1941, the sales had reached 1.3 million copies.

Part homily, part pep talk, Carnegie's book simply codified the twin American needs for being liked and succeeding in business, goals that occasionally could be mutually exclusive. They were tenets that George Babbitt could have embraced. Carnegie preached such bromides as, "Don't criticize, condemn, or complain." "Give honest and sincere appreciation." "Arouse in the other person an eager want." The book was filled with cheery anecdotes, quotes and quips from the famous and successful — Carnegie had interviewed such notables as Thomas Edison, FDR, Clark Gable, and Mary Pickford to get their secrets to success — and inspiring tales of men who had triumphed and others who had failed. Yet behind Carnegie's Horatio Alger–ish tales of rags-to-riches wonder boys, there was the grasping, crass materialism that was hardly new to America. Despite the homey admonitions to smile, there was an odor of manipulation about Carnegie's strategies for success. In this respect, Carnegie can be seen as the godfather to a long line of success purveyors, ranging from Norman Vincent Peale to the latter-day saints of success such as Robert Ringer, Michael Korda, and Dr. Wayne Dyer.

In addition to the Carnegie windfall, Pocket Books was racking up other big sales successes. In early 1941, the company released some selected sales figures:

Lost Horizon	239,000
Wuthering Heights	302,000
The Pocket Book of	
Short Stories	100,000 (in four months)
The Philadelphia Story	72,000 (in six weeks)
Five Tragedies	141,000 (after being withdrawn and later re-released)
The Good Earth	154,000

By the spring of 1941, Pocket Books' total sales had reached 8.5 million copies. The only discouraging word at this point was the first appearance of paperback censorship. After *Appointment in Samarra* and *The Werewolf of Paris* provoked complaints, Pocket Books withdrew both books from circulation rather than upset dealers at this early stage. Bigger battles lay ahead.

The pace of sales eventually called for a legitimate sales force, particularly if de Graff intended to fulfill his promise of universal distribution. Before the first year was out, Pocket Books had a group of ten salesmen calling on bookstores, department stores, chain stores, and stationery stores. In addition, six sales groups totaling seventy salesmen who sold a variety of merchandise exclusively to drugstore chains were recruited. Soon Pocket Books were being sold through 47 drugstore chains with 892 outlets and an additional 800 independent drugstores. They were also being displayed in six of the five-and-dime variety store chains with another 480 outlets.

But the major stumbling block to expansion was newsstands, the ripest area for widening paperback distribution. At first, Pocket Books attempted to reach the newsstands through the American News Company, a New York–based firm with a virtual monopoly on distribution to newsstands. American News acted as the exclusive national distributor for most major magazines. In addition to its magazine wholesaling operation, American News also owned the Union News Company, which operated stands in prime locations inside train stations, bus terminals, airports, hotels, and office buildings across the country. Initially sending books through the American News Company's periodical department (it also had hardcover book and stationery departments), Pocket Books released boxes containing one copy of each of its ten titles. The best sellers were often gone on the first day, but the slower titles remained on the racks because American News lacked the capabilities for recalling unsold titles. This arrangement quickly faltered, and Pocket Books told the American News Company to call in all the books. Individual newsstands began to make their own arrangements with Pocket Books, but this system was totally inefficient. A better one had to be devised, and when it was, it marked the launching of the most explosive phase of the Paperback Revolution — and with it the demise of the American News Company.

Without starting from scratch and creating a sales organization capable of effectively reaching the tens of thousands of newsstands across the country, Pocket Books soon discovered the only alternative means of selling books to this vast network past which almost every American walked each day. The discovery was made early in 1941 in a Denver, Colorado, barroom where Pete Howe encountered Joe Morton, owner of the Rocky Mountain News Company — an independent magazine distributor. Morton was one of more than eight hundred existing independent wholesalers who were struggling to compete against the American News Company. Most of them were the children of newsboys who had literally fought with their fists for a street corner from which they could hawk newspapers. A street corner grew into a city, a city into a territory. For the most part, they were two-fisted, hard-hitting, hard-drinking men. It was not a little ironic that the vaunted Paperback Revolution that transformed America's reading habits and literary tastes was soon to be in the hands of a group of men who were often barely literate and, at their worst, criminals, thugs, and gangsters, some of whom had won their territories as bootleggers.

Since the American News Company held a practical monopoly on the distribution of the major national magazines such as *Look*, *Life*, and *Time*, the independents often based their business on the distribution of local newspapers and racetrack tip sheets, the product of the national betting wire that linked bookmakers across the country. The king of the racing wire was Moses "Moe" Annenberg, newspaper circulation man, publisher, convicted felon, and father of Walter Annenberg, the founder of *Seventeen* and *TV Guide* and eventually Richard Nixon's ambassador to England.

The child of Russian immigrants, Moe Annenberg started out in turn-of-the-century Chicago, the scene of some of the most ruthless and brutal newspaper circulation wars in the history of the American press. There were already eight newspapers in Chicago when William Randolph Hearst, the czar of yellow journalism, decided to bring in another, the *Evening American.* Moe's older brother Max, who worked for the rival *Tribune* as a circulation man and had earned a reputation as a tough enforcer, was hired away by the Hearst people to get the new paper onto the streets. Max enlisted his brother Moe as a salesman soliciting subscriptions outside Chicago. That job description sounds far more civilized than it was. "Like others in the job, he had to make sure that papers were being delivered, once customers ordered them; rival newspaper circulation men thought nothing of stealing bundles of a competitor's papers and tossing them in the river. Moe was prepared to do the same thing, just as he was ready to jump into the thick of fist fights that erupted when circulation street-corner confrontations became violent."[8]

The level of violence in Chicago rose to murderous heights in what later became known as the "Annenberg wars," but it was Max rather than Moe who was blamed for escalating the carnage to outright gangsterism. As one Hearst biography put it:

From the time Hearst's *American* first rolled off the presses in July of that year [1900], ferocious circulation and distribution wars raged between the city's competing newspapers. The biggest box of ammunition in the Hearst arsenal was Max Annenberg, the *American's* circulation director. He supervised a crew of thugs whose job it was to convince newsdealers and newsboys — with blackjacks and brass knuckles when necessary — to buy ever-increasing numbers of copies of the *American*. It was the dealers' and newsboys' problem to sell the papers; Annenberg's motto was "Sell 'em or eat 'em." Since all the newspapers in town were using strong-arm distribution tactics, the encounters often turned bloody. From 1910 to 1912, when the circulation wars were at a peak, twenty-seven newsdealers were killed, while additional fatalities were recorded among the circulation crews of the various newspapers.[9]

Moe had in the meantime moved his operation to Milwaukee, where he set up a distribution agency that handled the sale of Chicago newspapers in that territory on an exclusive basis. His success led to the establishment of a group of agencies. Although his tactics were apparently not as deadly as those used by brother Max in Chicago, Moe Annenberg earned a reputation for toughness, adapting to the demands of the business. One paperback publisher later recalled Moe Annenberg's "tire iron boys," as in, "If you don't take fifty copies, we'll put a tire iron through your window."

Annenberg also surrounded himself with a group of youngsters who were cut from the same cloth as he was. They started out as newsboys, and if they proved their mettle, as Joe Ottenstein did, they were rewarded. Ottenstein was eventually granted an agency of his own by Annenberg, and he added to that until he was one of the most powerful independent distributors, with agencies in Milwaukee, Washington, D.C., and Norfolk, Virginia. Ottenstein became a power in the paperback industry by virtue of his enormous distribution empire, and he went on to become one of the founders of the Council for Independent Distribution (CID), a trade group that started out to accumulate a war chest with which to battle the American News Company. (Today it is the Council for Periodical Distributors Associations and serves as a marketing and lobbying resource for the independent distributors.)

At the time of its greatest strength, the American News Company, headquartered on Varick Street in Lower Manhattan, had more than four hundred branches, each the equivalent of a single independent agency. From its position of near-dictatorial strength, the American News Company had decreed that magazines must use the facilities of the American News Company exclusively or not at all. In that policy lay the seeds of its ultimate demise. The publishers were not happy with being told how their magazines could be distributed. But they had to swallow hard and accept it if they wanted to appear on the newsstands. There were some magazine publishers, however, who were not so willing to roll over. Gradually several of these magazine publishers, seeking to improve their sales, decided that the independent distributors could do a better job of serving local newsstands and other outlets. The independent was often a mom-and-pop operation working out of a garage or living room with a single truck for deliveries. On the other hand, the branches of the American News Company were run by salaried managers with little incentive to increase business or improve service. The Hearst organization was the first major magazine company to switch from the American News Company to independent distribution. Other magazines soon followed, setting off a pitched battle between the American News Company and the independents. The magazine publishers had learned, as Pocket Books quickly discovered, that although the American News Company was biggest, it wasn't necessarily the best. As Leon Shimkin of Pocket Books said, "We found that the independent wholesaler could get there fastest with the mostest."

By making this switch at the very moment that these strong-willed and occasionally violent men were challenging the supremacy of the American News Company, Pocket Books took the eventful step that would catapult it from its already successful beginnings to heights never before imagined by American publishers. The marriage of paperback books to the magazine distribution system opened the way for the Paperback Revolution. Books were being sold in more places than ever before in American book history. Within a few years' time, Pocket Books had more than six hundred of the independent distributors across the country and in Canada moving its books through a pipeline that eventually reached more than a hundred thousand outlets in newsstands; cigar, stationery, and food stores; and just about anywhere else one of the racks could be squeezed in. In a short time, 75 to 80 percent of Pocket Books' business was going through the magazine wholesalers. It was the beginning of a long-lasting relationship that would alter the course of the paperback's development. Like all marriages of convenience, the pact with the independent distributors (or IDs as they are called) demanded some sort of tradeoff. The paperback business was going to reach the true mass market, but the payback came in the form of power sharing with the men who controlled the sales outlets. Perhaps de Graff and company did not realize it, but they had exchanged a portion of their role as publishers for the pot of gold held out to them by the independents.

At the same time, in leaving the American News Company, Pocket Books had created a vaccuum for that firm. The managers of the Union News Company stores — the retail arm of the American News Company — could see the public demand for paperbacks. The so-called quarter books — every Pocket Book cost twenty-five cents — were good for business and the managers wanted to sell them. But under Pocket Books' agreement with the independents, the American News Company was shut out. Convinced that if they couldn't get Pocket Books, they would do the next best thing, the American News Company set out to find an imitation.

In their search for a competitor to Pocket Books, the American News Company settled upon Joseph Meyers, who had founded Illustrated Editions Company in 1929, a very successful firm that published a series of elegantly bound illustrated classics at thirty-nine cents, as well as a group of other imprints, such as the ninety-eight-cent Macy Classics and Cameo Classics, both series of inexpensive hardcover reprints. Along with his partner, Edna B. Williams, Meyers had also bought the J. S. Ogilvie Publications Company, a producer of pulp magazines. With the backing of the American News Company, Meyers signed up his first list of twelve books, paying between $250 and $500 for reprint rights.

Elmer Gantry by Sinclair Lewis.
The Rubaiyat of Omar Khayyam with illustrations.
The Big Four by Agatha Christie.
Ill Wind by James Hilton.
Dr. Priestley Investigates by John Rhode.
The Haunted Hotel and 25 Other Ghost Stories.
The Plague Court Murders by Carter Dickson.
The Corpse in the Green Pajamas by R.A.J. Walling.
Willful and Premeditated by Freeman Wills Crofts.
Dr. Thorndyke's Discovery by R. Austin Freeman.
Count Bruga by Ben Hecht.
Mosquitoes by William Faulkner.

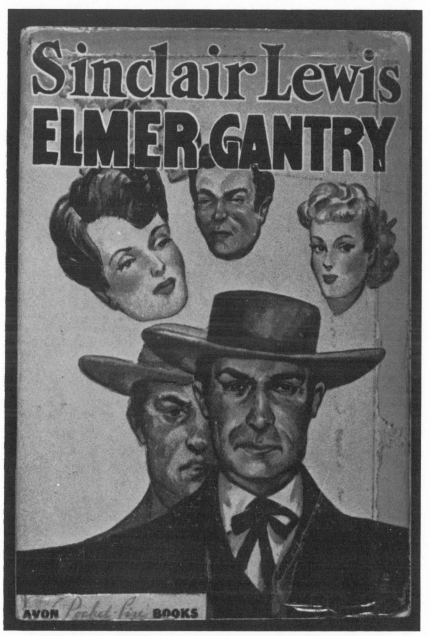

A mild illustration by Avon's standards. A judge ruled that Avon must remove the words "Pocket-Size" from its covers. (Photo by Kevin Hancer)

Christened Avon Pocket Size Books, they were released on November 21, 1941. Two weeks later, Pocket Books filed suit against Meyers, charging Avon with appropriating the Pocket Books style and format. They had a good case. It would take a long hard look to discern the difference between an early Avon Book and a Pocket Book; one difference was the Avon logo, a badly drawn head of Shakespeare. During the next two years, the case went back and forth from court to court like a tennis ball. One court favored Avon Books and then an appeal decision went to Pocket Books and a later ruling overturned that. In the end, Avon was enjoined from using the word *pocket* on its covers and it could no longer stain the edges of its books red, as Pocket Books did. However, the court ruled that Avon could continue to publish because people wanted to read books regardless of who had published them.

Despite their similarity in appearance to Pocket Books, Avon Books were different in a very significant way. Unlike de Graff, who approached editorial selection with the seriousness and convictions of a missionary out to convert the world, Meyers was not guided by any vision of raising the literary tastes of America. He was more interested in paying as little as possible for reprint contracts, and the American News Company, his financial backer, was only interested in sales. For the most part, as the first list demonstrated, Avon Books stuck to mysteries — later they would add Westerns and other genre books — not unlike the pulp magazines Meyers published under the Ogilvie label. That Sinclair Lewis and William Faulkner were on the list probably had less to do with their critical standing than with their controversial aspects: *Elmer Gantry* was a fictional portrait of a religious huckster, and Faulkner, of course, was then perceived as a "dirty writer." This divergence in editorial approach between Pocket Books and Avon would become even more apparent as new paperback houses entered the competition. On one hand, companies like Pocket Books that had their roots in the traditional hardcover book business would maintain a strong editorial sense. On the other hand, Avon and the others that followed it from the magazine and distribution side of the business were influenced by their impressions of what people read in magazines. For years, there would be a tangible and significant disparity between the quality of books on either side of this split.

Avon was not the only competition attempting to break Pocket Books' hold on the market. Allen Lane of Penguin Books had for years longed for a piece of the American market. He had often visited America, was well known in New York publishing circles, and had the ambition of one day becoming as successful an American publisher as he was a British publisher. In fact, he made a couple of false starts in the United States, trying as early as 1937 to find a satisfactory distributor for Penguin Books in America. There were, however, several major stumbling blocks. Under copyright restrictions, Lane could not import into the States those books protected under U.S. copyright, effectively locking out many of his Penguin titles. More important, he was unable to find the right person to whom he could entrust the task of developing the United States market for Penguin. An impulsive man, Lane often made such decisions based on feeling rather than verifiable assets such as experience.

His choice for an American manager must have come as something of a surprise. Ian Ballantine was a twenty-two-year-old graduate of Columbia University who had gone to study at the London School of Economics. While in England, Ballantine had come to Lane's attention with a paper he had written on the Modern Age experiment. Later known as one of the best salesmen in the business, Ballantine had undoubtedly done a solid job of selling himself to Lane. Having worked out a copyright solution, Ballantine acquired a minority share of the American branch and was appointed American manager despite the fact that he had no professional experience in either producing or selling books. But he did have a keen theoretical mind, a single-mindedness about paperback books, and an uncanny ability to promote his ideas. Also commending him was a connection to publishing through his uncle Saxe Commins, a major influence on Ballantine and a highly respected editor first at Liveright and later at Random House, where he was responsible for the famous Modern Library Editions. Ballantine had other illustrious family as well: his mother's aunt was "Red" Emma Goldman, the notorious anarchist whose views had replaced Judaism as the family orthodoxy.

Rumors of the impending move of Penguin Books into New York had reached de Graff just weeks after the Pocket Books operation got under way. In a letter to Frederic Melcher of *The Publishers' Weekly*, he wrote, "I understand the Penguins are starting off in this country with 80 titles, but so far I have been unable to get a complete list of them. If you have any additional information, I

These early Avons were typical of the firm's reliance on mysteries and thrillers. (Photos courtesy of Avon)

would be very interested in having it. I am delighted that they are starting for I think that the more of them that do come in, the more it will call cheap books to the attention of the public." His letter was dated August 14, 1939. He would not have to wait long for an answer. The Penguin list was announced the following day.

With a loan from his father, a somewhat bohemian Scottish actor who had immigrated to the United States, Ballantine set up shop on East Seventeenth Street with the help of his eighteen-year-old bride, Betty, whom he had married in England. She was the daughter of a British colonial officer, born and raised in India. Their first headquarters was a tiny office with a couple of secondhand desks and lots of cartons of unopened books. To get the fledgling Penguin outpost off the ground, Ballantine also enlisted the support of Walter Pitkin, Jr., a classmate from Columbia and son of the best-selling writer of *Life Begins at Forty*. Pitkin had worked briefly as an editor at Prentice-Hall, and after graduating from Columbia, he edited a magazine called *The School Executive*. He and his wife, Susan, later shared an apartment with the Ballantines, and every evening and on weekends they would all troop down to the office to clip the 6*d*. prices off the covers of the imported Penguin Books as they were unpacked.

While still working for the magazine, Pitkin also saw part-time duty as a salesman for Penguin, and his experience on one occasion was typical of bookstore reaction to paperback salesmen. Toting a briefcase full of Penguins, he went off to Boston with the intention of introducing the books into that city. He visited thirty or forty bookstores in the Boston area, including the landmark Old Corner Bookstore, at the time one of the largest in the country. The buyer there, a man notorious with publishers' salesmen, was the aptly named Mr. Dragon. Pitkin had an appointment to see him and was ushered upstairs to a hard wooden bench in a narrow corridor. All around him were little cubbyholes where other salesmen were also waiting for Mr. Dragon. He would see one salesman in one of these cubbyholes and then move on to the next. Pitkin had been rehearsing his sales spiel because everybody had told him that if he could sell the Old Corner, he would have it made. But he never got the chance. Mr. Dragon came in and immediately did all the talking, telling Pitkin about how long he had been in the business and of all the novelties he had seen. Then he said, "Now you think these books are important or going somewhere? Well, I'm going to tell you something. They'll be dead and gone in five years." With that, Pitkin was dismissed and told to return the next day. When Pitkin went back, Dragon told him that it was store policy to keep all books in stock and he was therefore going to buy all the titles, one of each, and keep them under the counter. They may have been second-class citizens in the world of books, but the Penguins had arrived.

Gradually, Penguin hired a team of commissioned salesmen who carried the books to the trade around the country. But the Penguins faced serious difficulties from the start. Within a month of the opening of the New York office, England was at war with Germany. Paper rationing and the Nazi blockade severely limited the importation of books to America. Soon the quality of paper started to deteriorate, until by a certain point, as Pitkin said, "The paper got to be the same color as the ink. That was acceptable in England, because you read what you could, but it was not acceptable here." Finances were also a concern because Allen Lane was unable to send any capital out of England to finance American expansion. And even if he had been able to underwrite American production, there was still no one on hand in the New York office with production experience. For the first two years of its existence, the New York branch of Penguin Books was essentially in a holding pattern, selling whatever imports managed to slip through. They could only watch as Pocket Books sold at a phenomenal rate and Avon Pocket Size Books were introduced.

December 7, 1941, would change everything.

FOUR

They Were Expendable

Books are weapons in the war of ideas.
— motto of the
Council on Books in Wartime

WAR, as Allen Lane of Penguin Books had learned, was truly hell. Just as every British family faced the loss of sons, husbands, and fathers, the men and women of Penguin Books had to confront the loss of young men who had once worked beside them.* There were also the disruptions — paper rationing, currency controls, shipments destroyed in bombings, warehouses requisitioned by the military, exports sent to the bottom of the ocean. But Lane found that war carried with it some blessings as well. Opportunities were created that the paperback book was uniquely suited to fill. First, there was the crushing need of the various armed services for inexpensive portable books of all kinds for educational and entertainment purposes. In a stroke of good fortune, a single Penguin Book fit exactly into a pocket of a soldier's uniform that had been designed to carry an entrenching tool. This serendipitous bit of tailoring made Penguin many lifelong friends among soldiers who carried their books to the front. There was also an increase in the demand for books by those on the home front whose outlets for entertainment had been curtailed by blackouts and bombings. And finally, as Lane had proven with the Penguin

*Among the casualties was Allen Lane's brother John, whose ship was sunk in November 1942.

Specials, there was a new urgency for books about wartime events that could be written and produced quickly and then widely distributed. So it was during these years of conflict that Lane built an army of readers who depended upon Penguins to help them cope with the deprivations of the war.

These were lessons that both Pocket Books and the New York office of Penguin Books were going to learn very soon. Without suggesting that either firm reacted to the war like black marketeers exploiting the national emergency, it is fair to say that during the war both companies improved their own positions and radically increased the potential audience for paperback books. In the process, they were able to perform functions useful to the war effort.

Before Pearl Harbor, Pocket Books was already doing a healthy business with the army through wholesalers who sold merchandise directly to the Post Exchanges. For instance, in April 1941, Fort Dix in New Jersey ordered one thousand assorted titles and in a few days reordered a thousand more, specifying that they wanted mostly mysteries.[1] With the declaration of war and the rush to enlist, the demand for books by the separate branches was going to soar. The impact that the war would have on the paperback business became immediately apparent. In his minutes of an editorial meeting held on December 17, 1941 — ten days after the bombing of Pearl Harbor — Robert de Graff noted:

> General discussion of a book on instructions for conduct during an air attack. This was suggested to Phil Stern by the War Department who would stamp such a book with their official seal of approval. Material would consist of silhouettes of American and enemy aircraft for use by air spotters, blackout instructions, etc. War Department would furnish all materials. Book would be published under Pocket Books imprint but could not be profitmaking. Any profits would be given to a specific organization. Unanimously approved. Everyone felt that the publicity would be of great value. . . . Suggestion was made that a complete King James Version of the New Testament be published for use in army and navy. Plates and other editions are being investigated. . . . WEH [Wallis Howe] said that we are going to put an all out push on _You Can't Do Business With Hitler._ A _Life_ ad, truck posters, window streamers and posters are all on the way. . . . Mr. Schuster's suggestion of a book of episodes from the war met with approval.[2]

What de Graff and company could not guess was that perhaps for the first time they were going to be beaten to the punch by a com-

petitor. The American office of Penguin Books already had the inside track on a book of aircraft silhouettes and they would have it
on the stands in less than two months.

Between the British entry into the war and Pearl Harbor, the
American office of Penguin had been limping along steadfastly but
without any measure of the success of its British parent. Books that
trickled in from England trickled out again to the bookstores. Unlike Pocket Books, Penguin had no powerful distribution force and
little to sell anyway. On several occasions, Lane had dispatched
both of his brothers to the United States and made several expedi-
tions himself in an attempt to stimulate a bona fide publishing
program in New York that could compete on an equal footing with
Pocket Books. According to Morpurgo, he was confounded by currency restrictions that prevented him from transferring the capital
needed to establish American production of Penguins and by the
lack of someone experienced with production in New York.

The solution to Lane's problems in America arrived in the person
of Kurt Enoch, the German publisher who had created Albatross in
Germany and who reappeared suddenly in New York as a refugee.
Enoch's exploits in escaping France after the country fell were the
stuff of adventure tales. Separated from his young second wife, his
two teenage daughters from his first marriage, his sister, and his
seventy-two-year-old mother, Enoch was briefly interned by the
French as an enemy alien after the Germans invaded Poland and the
French declared war. He was released after three months and returned to Paris. With his business of distributing exported books all
but ruined by the war, Enoch then decided to join the Prestataire, a
special branch of the French army for foreigners. After another long
period of separation from his family, during which time Enoch was
in a remote military camp, France was invaded and the supposedly
invincible Maginot line, a system of defenses, cracked like an egg
before the Nazi blitz. With his unit in chaos, Enoch attempted to
return to Paris, but the German advance made that impossible.

Uncertain of the whereabouts of his family — one of his daughters and his sister had been interned by the Vichy government in
his absence — Enoch began to head south. Unbeknownst to him,
his wife Marga, his youngest daughter, and his aging mother had
also begun the trek south, part of a long column of refugees fleeing
Paris before the Nazis arrived. Miraculously, the women were reunited with the other daughter and sister, although Enoch's mother

was separated in the chaos and had returned to Paris, only to make her escape later. A second miracle came about when a soldier holding a slip of paper with the women's whereabouts encountered Enoch by chance in a post office line when he heard Enoch's name called out. The entire family was reunited.

Through the intervention of Eleanor Roosevelt, temporary visas were being granted to refugee Jews in the United States consular office in Marseilles, and Enoch was able to obtain visas for his entire family. Then began a harrowing and dangerous journey across the Pyrenees, most of it by foot, without proper documents. After crossing through Fascist Spain, the group made its way to Lisbon and boarded the Greek liner *Nea Hellas* for passage to America. With little more than the clothing they wore, the Enochs docked at Hoboken in October 1940. Later, the refugee publisher would recall the intensely emotional dockside scene when his fellow passenger Heinrich Mann was reunited with his brother Thomas, who had helped make the arrangements for the trip.

With halting English and a small allowance from his brother Otto, who had arrived in America earlier, Enoch cast about New York for what he knew best — a publishing venture. He quickly renewed acquaintances with a group of European refugees who had also reached New York, men like Fritz Landshoff, Maurice Dekker, Dr. Eric Proskauer, and Henry Koppell, who would all make their mark in the American publishing scene. Enoch was beginning to make contacts and the possibility of a publishing project with one of these men seemed imminent when he received a summons from Allen Lane during one of the British paperback king's 1941 New York forays. Lane explained to Enoch his problems in New York, concluding with the gloomy assessment that he would be forced to shut down the operation there if matters did not improve. Enoch suggested that the obvious solution to Lane's dilemma was American production, but Lane said he lacked anyone to oversee an American program. As Enoch recalled, "I asked Lane whether he would be interested in an American publishing initiative if I made myself available, joined forces with him and Ballantine, and succeeded to raise at least a modest start-up in capital — which I thought I might be able to obtain by way of loans from acquaintances among some reasonably well-to-do immigrants. His answer was a quick and decisive 'Yes,' which left me with the impression that this was an idea in the back of his mind when he called me up."

After meeting with Ballantine, whom Enoch recalled as being "a polite, serious young gentleman with whom I would be able to establish a good working and sympathetic personal relationship," the émigré publisher agreed to a plan under which he would become vice-president of the firm and receive a 5 percent share in the operation after the war, provided he could raise the necessary capital. Fortunately, another refugee German publisher, Kurt Wolff, had arrived in New York and was planning to establish a publishing enterprise of his own in America, financed by still another German publisher, Curt von Faber, and his stepson Kyrill Schabert. As the Wolff plan was only in the preliminary stages, the capital earmarked for this venture was idle and Wolff and his partners agreed to grant Enoch temporary loans that were sufficient to finance the first American-produced Penguin titles.[3]

In the meantime, Ballantine had turned to his friend Walter Pitkin, Jr., and asked him to join the firm as an editor at twenty dollars a week. Pitkin's first job, however, would be to write a book. While Enoch was negotiating with Lane and arranging for the loan, Ballantine had entered into talks with Colonel Joseph I. Greene, head of the *Infantry Journal*, a quasi-official magazine for the army. Greene wanted Penguin to produce paperbacks that could be distributed in basic kits to new recruits. In addition, Penguin would be given any surplus books for general distribution as well as a substantial paper quota with which to produce other books that Colonel Greene deemed "useful to the war effort."

Allen Lane had already published in England a book called *Aircraft Recognition*, a spotter's guide to German, Italian, and British airplanes that eventually sold an extraordinary three million copies. Although this book was available through the New York office, it failed to include Japanese planes, and in the wake of the attack on Pearl Harbor and with constant rumors of a German super plane — a long-range bomber capable of striking the eastern coast of the United States — the need for an American edition intensified. Published as a "Fighting Forces–Penguin Special" under the joint imprint of the *Infantry Journal* and Penguin Books, the book was called *What's That Plane*, written by Pitkin, and available on the racks by the end of February 1942. In it, all warplanes were divided into four basic types, and three views of each — front or rear, side and top or bottom — were illustrated. In addition to the photographs, drawings, and technical information, *What's That Plane*

A wartime success for the American branch of Penguin, *What's That Plane* was an original conceived and created by Penguin. (Photo by Jerome Frank)

contained a gallant dash of such red-blooded American cheerleading as, "The 'Helldiver' is one of the U.S. planes which, before the war is over, is going to make Hitler & Co. wish they had never started a vogue for dive bombing."

The necessary silhouettes for the book had come from the British Information Service on the same day they were delivered to the Pentagon. According to Pitkin, the army censors refused the firm's requests for any materials the military could provide. Not only did these censors keep this information from Penguin, but they even failed to allow the silhouettes to go out to American servicemen. As Pitkin later recalled, "One day I was in my office and the secretary ran in and said there was a man in a glorious uniform to see me. He was the chief petty officer on the *Marblehead* — a heavy cruiser, I think — and the ship had been savaged in a battle. As soon as it docked in New York for repairs, the first thing this officer had done was look me up because he said that in this battle the only reference they had on Japanese planes was our book. He was being shipped out again and said he wanted the absolute latest information before he sailed."

How real was the fear of being bombed by the enemy? In New York City, it was real enough that Kurt Enoch and his family were able to rent inexpensively a deluxe penthouse apartment. The living quarters came so cheap because of the widespread belief that a top-floor apartment was more vulnerable to a direct hit. Another hot rumor was that the Japanese and Germans would attack Alaska and come into the United States over the Rockies. There was no doubt that the fear of attack was real. The hundreds of thousands who joined civil defense groups as airplane spotters attested to that. In such an atmosphere, factual books like *What's That Plane* provided a realistic means of coping with the misinformation that created rumors — however ludicrous they may seem with the benefit of hindsight. After going through two editions and ten printings, *What's That Plane* eventually sold four hundred thousand copies.

With this and other military-related titles, including *The New Soldier's Handbook, How the Jap Army Fights, Psychology for the Fighting Man*, and the *Handbook for Army Wives and Mothers*, the New York office of Penguin Books had come into its own. Ian Ballantine oversaw the sales and distribution responsibilities, including the still available stocks of imports; Pitkin acted as editor; and Enoch handled design, manufacturing, relations with suppliers, and the economics of the operation. A further addition to the staff was Sidney B. Kramer, as accountant-treasurer. As Enoch remembered the setup, "Everybody helped everybody, when and where needed. And with personal relationships warming up between us and our families, a good spirit of teamwork and of common purpose developed and had been maintained throughout the difficult war years. Especially in the beginning, when money and staff were at a minimum, Ballantine, myself, and others joined to pack, ship, or do other menial jobs until late into the night in order to get the work done or to save money."

With the *Infantry Journal* agreement in place, Penguin had what it needed for survival: titles and paper. In addition to the monthly "war books" that had a direct bearing on the war effort, Pitkin was free to extend his hand in selecting books for reprint. Along with eyewitness reports on the war like *Thirty Seconds Over Tokyo* and *Guadalcanal Diary* — both hardcover best sellers — Penguin Books was also able to reprint with its own paper supplies such general interest titles as *The Ox-Bow Incident,* Harold Lamb's *Ghengis Khan,* A. J. Liebling's *Telephone Booth Indian,* and an edition of Whitman's *Leaves of Grass* with commentary commissioned by Pitkin for the series. Within the space of a year, Penguin Books in New York was not only on its feet but had reversed its situation dramatically. In spite of their success, the Penguin people could only look at Pocket Books in admiration. It would be a long time before Penguin — or anyone else, for that matter — could equal or surpass the success Pocket Books was having.

For de Graff and his Simon & Schuster partners, the loss of the aircraft-recognition book that they had contemplated was insignificant. There were larger and more important problems to contend with. None was more worrisome than where to get enough paper to satisfy the unexpected appetite of both troops and civilians for more paperback books. Pocket Books' 1941 sales had reached twelve million copies. Wallis Howe expected them to reach twenty million in 1942. All that was holding them back was the War Board's Paper Limitation Order, which allotted paper according to prior use. Pocket Books would be entitled to a portion of its use in the previous year, but at a time when its growth curve was shooting off the charts, that amounted to a serious blow to expansion.

By the middle of 1942, sales of Pocket Books to the services had reached the level of 250,000 copies per month. Attempting to gauge

General interest books complemented Penguin's war-related books. (Photo by Jerome Frank)

what the soldiers were reading, Pocket Books surveyed the whole-salers who sold books directly to military camps and compiled the following army camp best-seller list:

1. *The Pocket Dictionary and Vocabulary Builder.*
2. *Nana* by Émile Zola.
3. *Believe It or Not* by Robert Ripley.
4. *The Pocket Book of Boners* (light humor by Dr. Seuss).
5. *The Pocket Quiz Book* by Rosejeanne Silfer and Louise Crittenden, two Pocket Books editorial staffers.
6. *The Pocket Book of Verse,* edited by M. E. Speare.
7. *The Pocket Book of Short Stories,* edited by M. E. Speare.
8. *How to Win Friends and Influence People* by Dale Carnegie.
9. *Lost Horizon* by James Hilton.
10. *The Art of Thinking* by Ernest Dimnet.
11. *Wuthering Heights* by Emily Brontë.
12. *The Best of Damon Runyon.*
13. *The Pocket Reader,* edited by Philip Van Doren Stern.
14. *Microbe Hunters* by Paul de Kruif.
15. *The Pocket Book of Mystery Stories,* edited by Lee Wright.

With the exception of the leading title, *The Pocket Dictionary and Vocabulary Builder* (which presumably was popular among soldiers who found themselves forced to write letters home for the first time in their lives), Pocket Books found that this list of army best sellers reflected the Pocket Books best sellers in general. The list also failed to include mystery titles, which were growing in popularity, particularly those by Ellery Queen and Erle Stanley Gardner. A trend was also developing, as *The Publishers' Weekly* pointed out: mysteries sold even better if the title sounded slightly sexier, as in *The Case of the Lucky Legs.* The same appeal worked for a Dorothy Parker book, *After Such Pleasures,* which was not tampered with but was thought to have sold in paperback on the strength of its suggestive title alone.[4]

From the onset of the war, Pocket Books also began a vigorous campaign, similar in spirit to the *Infantry Journal*–Penguin Books collaboration, of publishing books that were directly related to the war effort. Each month, Pocket Books released one title aimed, as Pocket Books put it, "at helping in the national emergency." The first of these was Douglas Miller's *You Can't Do Business with Hitler: What a Nazi Victory Would Mean to Every American.* Promoted as "must reading" with the recommendation of Wendell

Willkie and William Shirer, the hardcover edition had been the fifth-best-selling nonfiction book of 1941, a year that saw a large number of war books reach best-sellerdom. Besides Miller's book, the others included *Berlin Diary* by Shirer; *The White Cliffs*, a narrative poem that formed the basis for the song and movie; *Out of the Night* by Jan Valtin, a book about the underground versus the Gestapo; *Blood, Sweat and Tears*, the collected speeches of Winston Churchill; and *My Sister and I*, the story of a Dutch refugee boy.

For its updated edition of *You Can't Do Business with Hitler*, Pocket Books launched what was then a major publicity campaign to promote the book. As a Pocket Books ad explaining why Little, Brown and Company made a current best seller available for paperback reprint put it: "They could render an important service to American wartime morale by securing the widest possible distribution for this vital book." To push the book, Pocket Books committed itself to an all-out promotion — the 1942 version of hype — by sending out posters and window stickers to dealers, and banners for the trucks of the magazine wholesalers. By January 1942, Pocket Books had delivered 300,000 copies of the book to the pipeline and had another 100,000 ready for distribution, a total at least four times as great as the sales of the hardcover edition.

Other titles followed in the Pocket Books war series. Among them were *The Pocket Book of the War*, an original book of articles by leading foreign correspondents around the world, edited by Quincy Howe; *Defense Will Not Win the War* by W. F. Kernan ("Everyone with eyes to see should get a copy of this book," said the *New York Times*); and James Reston's *Prelude to Victory*. In an ad in *The Publishers' Weekly* of November 28, 1942, the Writers' War Board — members included Rex Stout, Pearl S. Buck, Clifton Fadiman, Paul Gallico, William Shirer, and John P. Marquand — issued a plea to American booksellers:

> In our opinion, *Prelude to Victory* is one of the very few books now current that hits hard at the stupidities, weaknesses, blindnesses in us — *in all of us* — that will certainly lose us the peace, if not the war — unless we get rid of them. . . . Because when you have read it and pondered it and digested it and said to yourself, "I guess this guy means me," you're a better American, better armed, better equipped to fight this war and fight for a decent peace after the war. So, if you can help get some of those Americans to part with a quarter and read *Prelude to Victory*, you will have done something toward winning the war and the peace.

Not everything that Pocket Books published about the war was quite so somber. As a morale-boosting effort, light humor about the war was also produced and became extremely popular. Random House publisher Bennett Cerf, well known as a raconteur, became a best-selling paperback author by editing a series of original humor books for Pocket Books. The first of these was called *The Pocket Book of War Humor*, and it sold half a million copies in six months. Later he compiled *The Pocket Book of Cartoons* and *The Pocket Book of Anecdotes*. But the most astonishing wartime humor success was not one of these originals but a reprint of a hardcover book that had been the best-selling nonfiction title in 1942, with sales of about 350,000 copies. The light-hearted adventures of a hardly war-like rookie soldier as he learned about army life, Marion Hargrove's *See Here, Private Hargrove* was offered to Pocket Books while still a hardcover success by its publisher, Henry Holt & Company, so that the book could secure an even wider audience. The paperback edition hit the million-seller mark in less than a month and sold another half-million copies by July 1943. It quickly surpassed the Pocket Books leader, *How to Win Friends and Influence People*, which had sold 1.4 million copies by September 1943, and became the first Pocket Book to sell more than 2 million copies.

By the fall of 1943, however, the war was exacting an escalating price on the publishing industry. The scarcity of paper, transportation difficulties, and manpower shortages were all taking a heavy toll. Pocket Books had instituted strict shipping quotas early in 1942 after the Paper Limitation Order went into effect, and by early 1943 the company announced that it was reducing its publication schedule from five to four new titles per month. On existing titles, there were no new printings as available stocks were used up. Under the quota system, Pocket Books guaranteed that all orders for the armed forces would be completely filled, but any unusually large trade orders would be cut by 10 percent to discourage hoarding by wholesalers and dealers. In addition, Pocket Books said it would favor its oldest customers and place a moratorium on orders from new accounts. Wallis Howe said that Pocket Books could easily have sold thirty-five million books in 1943 if the paper had been available. In order to economize on its paper ration, Pocket Books began to reset some of its books in smaller type and to drop other longer books in favor of shorter novels. (To circumvent rationing, it was not uncommon for some publishing houses to buy up smaller companies simply to receive their paper quotas.)

Despite both their intentions and ambitions, Pocket Books and Penguin Books together simply could not satisfy the various services' enormous appetite for books after the quotas has been placed upon their paper use. Neither firm had the paper to mount an unlimited publishing program that could bring books to the ten million men in uniform who had shown a greater interest in reading than anyone had dreamed possible. Nor did they have the distribution mechanism capable of reaching large numbers of troops. Basically limited to serving those soldiers and sailors on U.S. bases, the two firms had no systematic method for getting books to men stationed overseas, on ships, or in field hospitals. For these soldiers and sailors, books became a commodity as scarce as cigarettes and hot meals. The American fighting man had shown that he wanted to read, and paperbacks could play an important role in informing and entertaining the troops.

The army's Library Service, responsible for meeting the book needs of the military, was well aware of this and wasted no time in making large paperback purchases. According to Library Service historian John Jamieson:

> The Library Section began to make large purchases of paperbound books as soon as the troops began to go overseas. . . . These collections of paperbound books were sent overseas at first in the original publishers' containers. . . . Perhaps three million were sent overseas between 1941 and the end of 1943, not to mention several million more purchased by the Red Cross or by unit officers or mailed by civilians to friends overseas. But there were grave impediments to the use of this material. Distribution was haphazard and irregular and duplication was heavy. . . . Pocket Books and Penguin published a few titles principally for army distribution but they could not afford to produce a large variety of titles solely for the army.[5]

The solution to the logistical problems of supplying the army with a variety of inexpensive paperback books would prove to be one of the most ambitious — and ultimately successful — combined military-civilian operations undertaken during the war. The project was Editions for the Armed Services, and its overwhelming success was not only a boon to the soldier but proved to a still dubious publishing industry that Americans not only would read paperbacks, they would read them by the millions. This was a lesson that would completely change the face of the publishing industry in the postwar period.

The idea for the Armed Services Editions, as they were called, came from Colonel Ray Trautman, chief of the Army Library Service, who had wanted to buy a large quantity of a British title called *Combined Operations: The Official Story*. But he would only consent to the purchase if the American publisher agreed to print the book in an inexpensive paperback edition. When the publisher proved to be unable to meet this demand, Trautman turned to H. Stahley Thompson, the graphic arts specialist of the Information Branch of the Special Services Division, who suggested producing the book in a 6½-by-9-inch format and printing it on the large rotary presses used by catalogue houses, underutilized at the time because of the falloff in wartime business. Thompson believed this could be accomplished at a cost of less than ten cents per unit. Although that plan never materialized, Trautman and Thompson were intrigued by the notion of the rotary press and the possibilities it opened up. Because these presses were idle, using them for book production would not interfere with the press schedules of the book industry's usual manufacturers. So they took their idea to Malcolm Johnson of Doubleday, Doran & Company, the president of the Book Publishers Bureau and also one of the members of a committee that created the Council on Books in Wartime.[6]

The council was the result of one of the publishing industry's few moments of concerted action. A group of strong-willed and highly individualistic people, publishers had rarely found anything upon which they could agree. A good example had been the 1931 Cheney Report, which they had paid for but quickly dismissed and disregarded. However, following the entry of the United States into the war, Melvin Minton and Clarence Boutell of Putnam's had approached Malcolm Johnson with a plan for mobilizing the publishing industry behind the war effort. They gathered together a group of publishers, booksellers, writers, and newspapermen and on March 17, 1942, announced the formation of the Council on Books in Wartime, taking as their slogan "Books are Weapons in the War of Ideas." Sanctioned by the government and incorporated, the council stated its aims:

> To achieve the widest possible use of books contributing to the war effort of the United People —
> By the use of books in the building and maintenance of the will to win;
> By the use of books to expose the true nature of the enemy;

By the use of technical information in books on the training, the fighting, the production and the home fronts;

By the use of books to sustain morale through relaxation and inspiration;

By the use of books to clarify our war aims and the problems of peace.[7]

At first, the council's efforts were little more than public relations devices. Lectures were given on the importance of books, and Stephen Vincent Benét, the writer, gave a radio talk called "The Night They Burned the Books" about the Nazi book burnings. But the council's first concrete plan to promote war-related books proved a failure despite a promising beginning. The council announced that it would label certain books "Imperative" and that these titles would then be broadly promoted by all segments of the book business. A committee of prominent writers and critics was named to select these "Imperative" books, and the first of them was W. L. White's *They Were Expendable.* One of the first accounts of Americans in combat, the book told the story of the early Philippine campaign and General MacArthur's withdrawal, what White called "America's Little Dunkirk." Its choice as an "Imperative" was laudable in view of the fact that this was not a simplistic, flag-waving morale booster. The grim realities of the war and the sacrifices it would demand were made clear from the start. In his foreword, White said, "We are a democracy running a war. If our mistakes are concealed from us, they can never be corrected. Facts are frequently and properly withheld in a war, because the enemy would take advantage of our weakness if he knew them. But this story can now safely be told because the sad chapter is ended."[8]

The book then started out with a young soldier's description of a captain's orders to "hold a position." " 'For how long?' you ask. 'Never mind,' he answers, 'just hold it.' Then you know you're expendable. In a war, anything can be expendable — money or gasoline or equipment or most usually men." After this, another serviceman, one of four survivors from a torpedo boat squadron, added, "Never mind about that. People don't like to hear about that."[9]

But he was wrong. They did. With its "Imperative" status, *They Were Expendable* became the seventh-best-selling nonfiction book of the year 1942. In addition, Penguin Books issued a paperback edition of it as a "Fighting Forces Special" in 1944.

That was the beginning and end of the success of the "Imperative" program. It was, as publishing historian John Tebbel wrote, "torpedoed by a single word, 'Imperative,' which in the always individualistic book industry became immediately a matter of opinion. Inevitably, some publishers thought their books were more 'imperative' than others."[10]

Despite this failure, the council's other major effort more than compensated for it. The object of the plan was simple: the mass production of paperbound books at low cost for distribution to soldiers and sailors overseas. But carrying out this plan was not so simple. It required the agreement of publishers who had demonstrated that even in the midst of the national emergency they could be expected to put their own interests first, as some had in the "Imperatives" plan. After several months of negotiating and planning, the council finally announced an agreement with the army in May 1943. The plan of operation, as outlined by John Jamieson, worked along the lines of the existing paperback industry. "An advisory committee on selection would select approximately fifty books a month for reprinting, from lists provided by publishers concerned. Royalties of one cent would be paid — ½ cent to the publisher, ½ cent to the author. The books would be popular novels; books about the war and other nonfiction; books of humor; occasional classics; and 'made' books — that is, specially prepared anthologies of stories and verse. The contract would contain an agreement that the books were to be kept out of the civilian market."[11] This last point had been the critical stumbling block. Many publishers retained black memories of a flood of books that the army had purchased during the First World War flowing back into the consumer market at cut-rate prices, crippling a number of publishers. This time the books would be printed on inexpensive paper and simply stapled together, to ensure their eventual destruction after so many readings. In other words, they were expendable.

The dictates of size and portability and the requirements of the presses that would be conscripted for production of the Armed Services Editions called for a major change in the design of the books. Using five printing firms — the Cuneo Press, Street & Smith, W. F. Hall, the Rumford Press (printer of *Reader's Digest*), and the Western Printing and Lithographing Company — the books were printed "two-up," or in pairs joined like Siamese twins at their feet. The pair of books was then separated by a horizontal cut and bound by staples. Since the five printers used two different-sized printing presses, there were two book sizes. The digest presses — Hall, Western, and Rumford — printed books of shorter length that measured 5½ by 3⅞ inches; the pulp presses — Cuneo and Street & Smith — handled longer books, with a 6½-by-4½-inch format. In both sizes, however, the books were printed in two columns of type per page with the staple binding along the shorter side. The use of staples instead of glue proved to be not only cheaper but actually more durable in the tropical South Pacific. As one officer later reported, "Insects eat the glue, sewed backs molder, but your stapled books hold up real well."

Once the horse-trading over the terms of the agreement with the publishers was completed, the organization of the Armed Services Editions was a model of efficiency. Credit for the project's smooth operation belonged chiefly to one man, Philip Van Doren Stern. A veteran publishing man, Stern had the advantage of both hardcover and paperback experience, having been a charter member of the Pocket Books organization. Before joining the ASE staff, Stern had spent two years with the Office of War Information (OWI), a propaganda unit that had been the wartime home to a number of publishing men and women who put their talents to use in the military (among them Victor Weybright and Oscar Dystel). Taking over the day-to-day functions of the ASE in the summer of 1943 while maintaining his office at Pocket Books, Stern had a paid staff of ten people who were responsible for planning, manufacturing, and delivering thirty titles per month, approximately the output of a large, modern paperback house. To accomplish this, the staff first had to make a character count of each book — a physical tally of the number of letters, punctuation, and spaces in a book. Books of approximately equal length were then paired off, type was set for both books, and printing plates were made. The plates were then sent off to one of the five printing plants on a tightly structured schedule; the covers were all prepared at a separate plant. After printing, covering, and stapling, the books were sent to the Army Library Service's distribution points where they were shipped to outfits stationed around the world. In terms of numbers alone, the operation was a mammoth success. "Between the fall of 1943 and the fall of 1947, 1322 titles were printed, and a total of 122,951,031 volumes were delivered to the army and navy at an average cost to the government of 6.09 cents per volume."[12]

The selection of titles fell to a committee of volunteers. Mrs. Stephen Vincent Benét was the first of these, and she was later

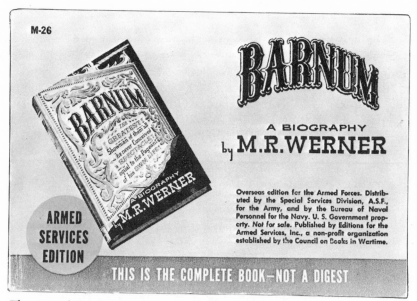

The Armed Services Editions were responsible for the creation of a large paperback audience. (Photo courtesy of Jean Peters)

joined by Louis Untermeyer, the writer and anthologist, and a group of writers and booksellers. All choices were then screened by army and navy representatives, who were inclined to favor books that were already proven successes. Nonetheless, the list of books finally published was broad and often challenging. With few exceptions, the books were complete and unabridged — in some cases, authors made their own abridgments and others waived their royalties — and said so on their covers. The first list of titles, designated the "A" list and delivered to the army in September 1943, included these books:

The Education of H-y-m-a-n K-a-p-l-a-n by Leonard Q. Ross (Leo Rosten).
Report From Tokyo by Joseph C. Grew.
Oliver Twist by Charles Dickens (abridged).
Tortilla Flat by John Steinbeck.
The Human Comedy by William Saroyan.
The Unvanquished by Howard Fast.
The Ministry of Fear by Graham Greene.
Typee by Herman Melville.
Lord Jim by Joseph Conrad.
The Fireside Book of Dog Stories, edited by Jack Goodman.

The spectrum of authors ranged from Henry Adams to Stefan Zweig. Other prominent authors published by the Armed Services Editions were Louis Bromfield, James M. Cain, Erskine Caldwell, Willa Cather, Thomas Chastain, A. J. Cronin, Isak Dinesen, Daphne du Maurier, C. S. Forester, James Hilton, A. E. Housman, MacKinlay Kantor, Ring Lardner, Jack London, J. P. Marquand, Ogden Nash, John O'Hara, Marjorie Kinnan Rawlings, Rafael Sabatini, Lillian Smith, Rex Stout, Lytton Strachey, James Thurber, Mark Twain, H. G. Wells, and Thomas Wolfe.

By subject classification, the Armed Services Editions titles broke down this way:

> Contemporary fiction: 246
> Westerns: 160
> Humor: 130
> Mysteries: 122
> Historical novels: 92
> Biographies: 86

There were also smaller numbers of adventures, aviation stories, classics, cartoons, travel books, current affairs, drama, fantasy, history, music and the arts, nature, poetry, science, sea stories, self-help books, and sports stories.

If simple numbers are any indication, the most popular authors were the Western writers, starting with Max Brand and Ernest Haycox, each of whom had eighteen books reprinted in the series, and Zane Grey with eight (although *Riders of the Purple Sage* was excluded because it was judged by the army committee to be anti-Mormon). Other contemporary novelists whose work was frequently reprinted included J. P. Marquand (seven titles); John Steinbeck (eight titles); Thorne Smith (seven titles, including *Topper*); and C. S. Forester (eight titles, including the Horatio Hornblower books and *The African Queen*).

It would be impossible to judge which titles were actually most read by the men because the books were passed on until they literally fell apart or, as was often the case, were deliberately pulled apart. According to one veteran of the war in the South Pacific, a planeload of men was flying toward a parachute drop, all hunched on the floor because the seats had been removed. They had with them a single Armed Services Edition and so, to kill time, it was passed around, page by page, with the faster readers urging the slower readers to hurry up. That was the experience of Knox Burger, who returned from the war to become an editor at *Collier's* magazine and later a key personality in the paperback world, editing books at Dell First Editions and later at Fawcett Gold Medal Books. Today he is a prominent literary agent.

Another indication of popularity were those books that reappeared in the series. The first of these were *The Robe* by Lloyd C. Douglas and Betty Smith's *A Tree Grows in Brooklyn,* both of which first appeared on the "D" (or fourth) list and again on the "K" (eleventh) list. Other books that merited encore appearances included *My World and Welcome To It* by James Thurber; *Peace Marshal,* a Western by Frank Gruber; Marjorie Kinnan Rawlings's *The Yearling;* MacKinlay Kantor's *Gentle Annie; White Fang* by Jack London; Steinbeck's *The Grapes of Wrath; Selected Stories* by Edgar Allan Poe; *Mrs. Parkington* by Louis Bromfield; *Payment Deferred* by C. S. Forester; Bram Stoker's *Dracula;* Marquand's *Wickford Point;* Somerset Maugham's *The Razor's Edge; Strange Fruit* by Lillian Smith; Zane Grey's *The Heritage of the Desert; Is Sex Necessary?* by James Thurber and E. B. White; *The Postman Always Rings Twice* by James M. Cain; Carl Sandburg's *Selected Poems;* O'Hara's *Pal Joey;* and *The Ox-Bow Incident* by Walter Van Tilburg Clark.

But far more important than the simple vogue of some writers or the success of particular titles was the meaning of the books to the men in the field. After a tour of bases in the South Pacific, Colonel L. C. Frederick of the Army Air Force told a meeting of the Council on Books in Wartime in February 1944:

> These books of yours came as a godsend to book-hungry Americans. . . . While I was at Tarawa, Apamama and Nonema, in the Gilberts, I had the pleasure of seeing three cases of your books arrive. The sight of these rugged, tropicalized American soldiers, marines and Seabees walking away from the head of a long Council book distribution line, and enthusiastically going over their new attractively-bound books, praising them, fitting them into their pockets, already bargaining with their comrades — if you had been there, I am sure you too would have had a little lump in your throat. . . .[13]

Reports from the soldiers themselves were also filtering back to the States. One reader, writing from "Somewhere in Hawaii," told *The Publishers' Weekly:*

Being an avid reader, I appreciate these small handy volumes since
they can be easily carried around in one's field bag or mashed into
one's pocket. It is only since I have come overseas and utilized these
editions have I had the opportunity of reading more books than I had
while stationed in the continental United States. I think the finest
book in the "A" series was the biography by Rackham Holt of George
Washington Carver. This is by far one of the best biographies I have
ever read.[14]

One young marine, on board a ship that was taking him to the
battle of Okinawa, later recalled, "In their bunks, some of the guys
read armed service double-columned editions of the classics." That
was the recollection of William Manchester as he recounted his
experiences in the Pacific war in *Goodbye Darkness.*

In November 1944, the *New York Post* reported the experience of
another officer:

I was gratified when I saw a GI lying in the shade of a bomber reading
Huckleberry Finn. Somehow I knew that this particular GI's mind
wasn't dwelling in the mud and mire this war had placed him in, but
rather he was floating down the Mississippi on a raft with Tom and
Huck. My discovery of this soldier wasn't accidental. I saw men in
chowlines reading worn copies of *Moby Dick, The Robe* and dozens of
other good books. . . . I wish I could find words to tell the American
public that their sons — and daughters too — are becoming the best-
read army in our history. I remember watching a tense volley-ball
game in New Guinea. Suddenly the call "books" split the game in two
and each player made a beeline for the recreation hut where the books
were being given out. . . . Just a few days ago we received a letter from
a colonel commanding an artillery unit in France. He recounted how a
single copy of *A Tree Grows in Brooklyn* had passed from hand to hand
until it reached him. "I can't express how much that book meant to
me. Instead of thinking only of the German gunfire while waiting for
the next flash, I thought about the people in the book," he wrote.
    Once in India, I came upon a bearded top sergeant, deep in Walter
Lippmann's *Foreign Policy.* I asked him his views on our foreign policy. "Sorry, sir," he said, "I haven't got any just now. But will you wait
until I finish this book?"[15]

The project was hailed by all involved — publishers, army and
navy librarians, soldiers. But it was unable to survive the war without controversy. In 1943, Michigan congressman George Dondero
denounced the books as "communistic propaganda" because of pas-

sages in Louis Adamic's 1934 book *Native's Return* recommending that America adopt a semicommunist form of government. This attack came at a time when there was already great fear — long before "Tailgunner" Joe McCarthy got going — of communists in the military. An examination of the book revealed that the author had removed the offending paragraph himself in a 1938 edition. But Dondero's assault captured public attention and thereafter all the Armed Services Editions selections had to be scrutinized more carefully. Also prohibited were books that supported any political position, under the provisions of the Soldier Voting Law, which censored all political materials that might be seen by soldiers.

The war record of the Armed Services Editions did not end on V-J Day in 1945. With the fighting over, Stern departed the ASE operation and returned to his full-time post as a vice president at Pocket Books. He was replaced as manager of the ASE project by H. Stahley Thompson, the man who had initially proposed the notion of using the paperback format. After serving overseas with *Yank*, the army weekly newspaper, Thompson had returned to oversee the postwar ASE project. It was the army's decision to maintain the program because of the large number of men still serving as occupation troops. The format of the books was altered to resemble the typical paperback size used by Pocket, Penguin, and others. The number of titles published each month was reduced, and printings were cut to 25,000 copies. Even so, another 3,056,798 books were shipped out between October 1946 and September 1947, when the program, like an old soldier, faded away.

It is difficult to pinpoint exactly what the Armed Services Editions accomplished in a few brief years. Did they make converts of nonreaders? Did they alter the literacy rate within the armed forces? Did they change the lives of the men and women who read them? Did they help win the war? The reports of the officers and men in the field leave little doubt that the Armed Services Editions were a significant morale booster for millions of men preparing for or wearied from combat as well as those lying wounded in army hospitals. Most veterans say that the army means waiting — waiting for food, waiting for orders, waiting for action. The Armed Services Editions helped with the waiting.

A more tangible measure of the books' impact came from the letters written by servicemen to the authors of many of the reprinted books. Fifty of the writers represented on the ASE list were surveyed after the war about their wartime fan mail. Betty Smith, author of *A Tree Grows in Brooklyn*, reportedly got the most mail, mainly letters from men thanking her for giving them a little piece of home. H. Allen Smith, a now all but forgotten writer whose books dealt humorously with newspaper life, said he received more than five thousand letters. About a quarter of the men who wrote to him said they were going to take up writing after the war. Of his mail, James Thurber said, "About 75 per cent of the men who wrote encountered my books for the first time. Almost all of the letters were hugely favorable, particularly those from boys who picked up my books in hospitals or managed to get hold of one on a ship or in some far off place, and a great number of the boys mentioned the fact that the books had helped their loneliness and it helped remind them of home. One letter from the South Pacific, signed by five privates, asked me to explain what *Is Sex Necessary?* meant." Iconoclastic H. L. Mencken, whose *Heathen Days* and *Happy Days* were reprinted, reported, "At least nine tenths of these letters are friendly. I recall, however, one or two notes from pious fellows who did not like my attitude." Six hundred men wrote to Katherine Anne Porter, whose *Selected Short Stories* was a "made" book selected especially for the ASE. Said Porter, "One of my pleasantest occupations was answering these letters, for they were all without exception, friendly, sensible, sincere and some very good letter writers among them too. . . . A few of them were young writers who wanted to discuss technique and ideas, but all the others were simply men who read the book somewhere in isolation, boredom or danger and wrote to thank me. This is a very treasurable memory."[16]

The books had done their job. The armed services had been provided with inexpensive books given free to the men in large numbers. Few of the books ever reached the United States, to the enormous relief of the publishers, although Armed Services Editions did become a valuable commodity on the European black market. And American publishers were also certain that the books would pay a handsome dividend in new readers. The common thinking was that the ASE had created a large pool of readers who would return to lift the American publishing industry to new heights. Despite the problems created by the war, the publishing business had come through the turmoil with record-setting years. The prospect of millions of men, now confirmed readers, returning to America and picking up where they left off had some publishers drooling. Others were more cautious, thinking it unwise to assume that men who had received free books under extreme conditions were going to behave in the same fashion once they had to go out to a bookshop and pay for the book they wanted. In addition, there were added the distractions of the radio, cars and plenty of gasoline, and something new on the horizon called television.

These concerns didn't faze the paperback publishers, particularly Robert de Graff and Pocket Books. First of all, they knew these men had been reading not just books but *paperback books* during the war. The Armed Services Editions had gone a long way in conditioning the younger generation to be perfectly at home with books in paper covers. In addition, Pocket Books had no worries about how to lure these men into bookshops. Paperbacks could now be found, thanks to independent magazine distribution, on almost every street corner and in every drugstore in America. There would be little chance that the former readers of Armed Services Editions wouldn't be willing to plunk down twenty-five cents. With his partners from Simon & Schuster, de Graff had every right to look to the future with great optimism.

They also had reason to be pleased with their track record. In spite of the problems brought on by the war, Pocket Books was selling more than forty million books per year by the end of the war. Leading those sales was a long list of million-sellers that had piled up during the company's first five and a half years. At the top of the list, of course, was the wartime wonder *See Here, Private Hargrove*, which had reached 2,170,841 copies by November 1945.

POCKET BOOK BEST SELLERS TO NOVEMBER 15, 1945:

How to Win Friends and Influence People (Dale Carnegie)	1,876,587
The Pocket Dictionary	1,774,024
The Pocket Book of Cartoons (Bennett Cerf)	1,414,775
The Pocket Book of War Humor (Bennett Cerf)	1,391,222
The Pocket Book of Boners (Dr. Seuss)	1,344,438
The Pocket Book of Short Stories (M. E. Speare, ed.)	1,306,355
The Case of the Curious Bride (Erle Stanley Gardner)	1,270,074
Lost Horizon (Pocket Book #1)	1,269,492
Believe It or Not (Robert Ripley)	1,227,987
Damon Runyon Favorites	1,180,283
The Pocket Book of Verse (M. E. Speare, ed.)	1,175,365

The Case of the Lame Canary (Erle Stanley Gardner)	1,152,262
The Best of Damon Runyon	1,106,813
The Pocket Entertainer (Shirley Cunningham)	1,079,450
The Case of the Counterfeit Eye (Erle Stanley Gardner)	1,078,386
Singing Guns (Max Brand)	1,060,453
New Adventures of Ellery Queen	1,054,059
The Thin Man (Dashiell Hammett)	1,047,178
The Case of the Stuttering Bishop (Erle Stanley Gardner)	1,033,692
The Case of the Substitute Face (Erle Stanley Gardner)	1,010,405
Topper (Thorne Smith)	999,861

SALES OF OTHER SELECTED POCKET BOOKS:

Farewell My Lovely (Raymond Chandler)	852,969
Five Great Tragedies (William Shakespeare)	717,010
The Maltese Falcon (Dashiell Hammett)	620,273
Nana (Émile Zola)	586,374
The Good Earth (Pearl S. Buck)	530,994
The Pocket History of the United States (Allan Nevins and Henry Steele Commager)	499,968

While failing to yield any best sellers, Pocket Books' wartime program of publishing significant books relating to the war effort had garnered some impressive sales:

You Can't Do Business with Hitler	415,794
Tarawa	221,522
The Pocket Book of the War	219,423
Defense Will Not Win the War	179,347
The Coming Battle of Germany	183,240
Lend-Lease	157,686

Not everything worked so well. There were failures, too. Anything that sold less than a hundred thousand copies had to be considered, in the Pocket Books scheme, a major disappointment. Among the worst-selling Pocket Books of those early years: *Swiss Family Robinson, The House of the Seven Gables, A Christmas Carol, Treasure Island, Gulliver's Travels, National Velvet, The Three Musketeers, The Hunchback of Notre Dame, Heidi,* and *Little Men* (*Little Women,* on the other hand, was a success; did the title make the difference?).

Looking at these lists, Pocket Books could already discern some emerging patterns in their paperback sales. The large number of what Pocket Books called "made books," also known as paperback originals, that had sold a million copies or more showed that paperbacks did not necessarily need the benefit of hardcover acclaim to succeed. This was a lesson later forgotten when the pressure of competition started a mad scramble for reprint rights and ultimately brought about the phenomenon known as the paperback auction. Only in recent years have paperback publishers rediscovered the advantages of original paperback publishing. For the most part, Pocket Books could also see that their meat and potatoes was light nonfiction rather than "blockbuster" novels. This would hasten Pocket Books' move into cornering the areas of paperback self-help, how-to, and humor books. It would also create Dr. Spock.

On the debit side, Pocket Books was also learning what did not work. Other than a few Max Brands and Zane Greys, Pocket Books failed to make a real dent with the Western market, and accordingly steered away from the category, leaving the field wide open to competitors who would follow. Neither did they have much success with classics or children's books. There were two reasons for this. The paperback had not yet become an educational tool; until the publishers figured out how to break into this market, they would have to wait on classics. The other reason was the continuing success of hardcover reprinters like Grosset & Dunlap and the Modern Library that produced inexpensive hardcover editions of children's books and the classics.

Pocket Books also shied away from "high-brow" fiction. There was no Faulkner, Joyce, Hemingway, or O'Hara here (except for the aborted attempt to reprint *Appointment in Samarra*). In the same vein, Pocket Books avoided the sort of serious nonfiction that found a home in Penguin's Pelican list. Accordingly, Pelican was to publish such prominent and prestigious works as Walter Lippmann's *Public Opinion*, Ruth Benedict's *Patterns of Culture*, *The Birth and Death of the Sun* by George Gamow, and *The Story of Human Birth* by Alan Guttmacher, effectively staking out Penguin's position as *the* publisher of serious nonfiction in paperback.

But Pocket Books could lay claim to other achievements. Two of the most striking of these came in the last days of the war and were much akin to Allen Lane's Penguin Specials in their dealing with current affairs. Six days after Franklin D. Roosevelt died in 1945, Pocket Books produced a book called *FDR: A Memorial*. Written by Pocket Books editor Donald Porter Geddes — the man who later approached Dr. Spock about writing a book on child care — the book was a tribute in words and pictures to the leader who had guided America through the Depression and the Second World War, the republic's most trying years since the Civil War. The first true "instant book," as these quickly produced paperbacks have come to be called, *FDR* sold 465,853 copies in a few months' time. Pocket Books duplicated this "instant" feat in August 1945 after the first atomic bomb was dropped on Hiroshima. Within a few weeks, *The Atomic Age Opens*, a layman's introduction to atomic power, also written by the resourceful Geddes, was available as a Pocket Book. Between August and November, Pocket Books sold 265,935 copies of it.

The war was over but the battles were just about to begin. The unfettered success of Pocket Books in the paperback field was going to draw new money and fresh competition to the paperback business like flies to honey. With wartime restriction on paper lifted, millions of men and women demobilized, and America's coming prosperity, the stage was set for the period of awesome expansion and dramatic growth that would take the paperback from the novelty that few thought would last to a position of dominance in America's publishing industry. Even those publishers who had looked upon the paperback as a bastard child unworthy of their attention would follow the pack that was now moving toward "two-bit" books. For better or for worse, the paperback stood at the entrance to a new realm — of power, profits, and influence unlike anything seen before in American publishing history.

FIVE

The Case of the Mysterious Millions

"And here's a toast, Della, to the greatest courtroom strategist of them all."
— Erle Stanley Gardner,
The Case of the Negligent Nymph (1950)

T HE PUBLISHING TRADE has always suffered from an uneasy dual personality. Is it an art that requires a businesslike structure, or is it a business that demands the artist's sensitivity? That question has long plagued publishers. Right after the Second World War, however, the book trade entered a period of heated debate over that dilemma when many of the "artisan" publishers detected the creeping influence of Big Business on the book business and balked at the intrusion. One man sparked the controversy during the postwar period: millionaire department-store magnate Marshall Field III. His arrival on the book scene helped change the face of the book industry in the second half of the century, particularly the paperback end of the business. Already an influential newspaper publisher who owned the Chicago *Sun*, the liberal New York paper *PM*, and a string of radio stations, Field purchased both Simon & Schuster and Pocket Books in 1944, marking the arrival of the great upheaval in the structure of book publishing.

Until this time, the twenty-five-cent paperback had been tolerated by some hardcover publishers, ignored or dismissed by others, and resented by quite a few of the sherry-and-biscuit boys of the old school. Field's purchase of Pocket Books was a clear signal to these skeptics that not only was the paperback here to stay, it was where the money was. The stakes had risen enormously and paperbacks were bound to attract more attention. The five-year-old industry had crossed its Rubicon. The old guard was suddenly confronted with the twentieth-century phenomenon of the paperbound book, not simply as a fact of life but as a factor in their own economic survival. The old world was rapidly changing, and they would have to change with it or get out of the way.

As is true of many publishing milestones, an apocryphal tale sprang up around Field's purchase of the two publishing properties. Perhaps fostered by Field himself, it is quaint but probably inaccurate. According to the legend, Field was strolling through New York's Grand Central Terminal when he happened to notice a rack of paperbacks. Asking the newsstand clerk what they were, Field was told that they were the new Pocket Books. Struck like Paul on the Road to Damascus, Field had a revelation. He was so taken with the idea of "pocket books," he decided to call Robert de Graff and buy the company.

"Nonsense," said Field's biographer Stephen Becker. Calling this a "cute and not very bright little story," Becker pointed out, "Field had been haunting bookshops on and off since 1936; it is hardly likely that he had put five or six years into noticing the existence of paperbacks. What he noticed in 1944 was that he needed to buy up a few profitable enterprises. He was obviously not averse to combining that need with cultural improvement, and even those who criticized the intellectual level of many paperbacks admitted that it was something just to get so many books into the hands of so many people."[1]

There was other evidence against the Grand Central story. Field had previously hired Freeman Lewis, a veteran of the inexpensive book market, as a consultant. In addition, Field was already well acquainted with Max Schuster, a backer and board member of *PM*. Leon Shimkin was also known to Field because he had written a memo in 1940 saying that the *PM* experiment would not succeed. (Although Field ignored the astute Shimkin's forecast, the prophecy was fulfilled and *PM* folded after suffering heavy losses, most of which Field absorbed himself.)

Initially, de Graff resisted the sale of Pocket Books, as did Simon and Schuster, who felt that selling the company was akin to selling a child. Field assured each of the men that management of the firms would remain in their hands — a pledge that was basically adhered to, to the benefit of all involved. Leon Shimkin worked out a complex arrangement with Field's representative John Wharton that called for a twenty-year transfer plan with the purchase price tied to profits; management would remain intact and the profits would be split. On October 1, 1944, the deal was announced and the two firms became the centerpiece of Field Enterprises.

The announcement set off howls in the trade. Field's possession of Pocket Books and S&S, along with his none too secret appetite for Grosset & Dunlap, the leading reprinter of inexpensive hardcovers, set alarms ringing. For the first time since J. P. Morgan had become interested in publishing in the 1920s, the book industry found its laundry being aired on the financial pages instead of in the book reviews.

The first reports of battle came from *Time,* which observed that the industry was a "bedlam of deals, counterdeals and rumors."[2] The next shots fired in this war came from inside the industry when a small but extremely powerful cartel consisting of Random House, Harper & Brothers, Charles Scribner & Sons, the Book-of-the-Month Club, and Little, Brown & Company stole a march on Field and bought Grosset & Dunlap out from under his nose. According to Bennett Cerf, the publisher and co-founder of Random House, the papers that would have made Grosset & Dunlap a fiefdom in the Field domain were waiting to be signed when Donald Grosset, son of the firm's founder, called Cerf, entreating him to be the white knight who could rescue Grosset before Leon Shimkin could close the deal for Field.

Cerf commented, "The thought of one firm, Simon & Schuster, controlled by Field, having the original publishing unit, the hardbound reprint and the paperback too, was frightening. They could go to an author and say, 'Not only can we publish your book, we can guarantee you the hardbound reprint and the paperback.' That would be a package deal no other publisher could match."[3] Random House was unable to afford Grosset alone, so Cerf quickly rounded up the other partners and made the deal. The cost was about $2.5 million. Great repercussions would soon be felt in the paperback field when this cartel backed a new company called Bantam Books.

When the dust had cleared after the battle for Grosset & Dunlap and Field's purchase of Pocket Books and Simon & Schuster, the industry was ready to survey the damages. The first disgruntled voice belonged to Lovell Thompson of the old Boston house Houghton Mifflin. He wrote in *The Publishers' Weekly* in November 1944:

For the first time, book publishing has crashed the "Business and Finance" section of *Time* magazine. They do not realize, I assume, that there is nothing either businesslike or financial about publishing. According to their statement, Marshall Field is a victim of the same illusion. . . . The result is that the book business is suddenly beginning to behave like the oil business in the teens, or the car business in the twenties or the movies in the thirties. There is a strange tendency for the cheerful, disorganized, ne'er do well publishing industry to combine vertically in the familiar pattern of big American business. . . .[4]

Going on to remind his colleagues of what publishing "really" is, Thompson — like some temperance preacher railing against demon gin — cautioned about the dangers of low-priced publishing, thundering the old publisher's rule that in the low-price world, "the worst books sell best."

Thompson's fusillade against both business outsiders and reprinters quickly drew return fire from the opposing camp. Speaking for the paperback world, Pocket Books editor Donald Porter Geddes wrote:

The best books apparently have the greatest appeal to the greatest number of people. [A] mass market publisher markets many more dictionaries and Bibles than he does individual detective stories. It would seem that readers by the million prefer poetry, good poetry — in fact, the best poetry. It would seem that they prefer Shakespeare to a most popular current best-selling novel of some substance. In fact, it would seem as though the intellectual composition of this large mass market is not proportionately different from the intellectual composition of the smaller — very much smaller — original book market that buys new books at higher prices. The larger American public need no longer suffer from the delusion that it is intellectually inferior, or, from a literary point of view, lacking in any aspect in good taste, judgment and appetite.

As to Thompson's complaint about books and high finance, Geddes continued:

Finance can organize adjuncts to the book business that will put books in every single home and do so on a basis that will be increasingly profitable not only to the original publisher but also to the author. A great American author will then not just be a person who has been read by one hundred or two hundred or five hundred thousand or possibly a million Americans, but one who will have been read by as many as twenty-five million Americans.[5]

It was ironic that the fear of robber barons invading book territory was raised by so beneficent a figure as Marshall Field III. A true liberal and staunch supporter of FDR, he had devoted time and resources to social improvement and was once quoted as saying that he wanted to put his money to work constructively.[6] Thus the democratization of reading and literature implicit in inexpensive books appealed to him not only for the return on investment they brought but because he sincerely believed that the paperback could be a force for good. As he said in a prepared release at the time he bought the company, "I am happy to associate myself in this way with a group of publishers who have pioneered in democratizing the creation and distribution of good books in America. All of them believe in making good books conveniently and widely available by exacting editorial and production standards, intensive promotion and bold experiments in developing new outlets."

Although continuity of management had been promised by Field when the deal was struck, one significant change was made immediately at Pocket Books. Before buying the two firms, Field had enlisted as a consultant Freeman Lewis, who had been beating the drums for inexpensive hardcover books in chain and variety stores while he was with Doubleday's New Home Library and Triangle Books. A frustrated writer and the nephew of Sinclair Lewis, he had previously worked with de Graff as executive vice president of Blue Ribbon Books. His move into Pocket Books signaled that the company was embarking on the next stage of its development, and Lewis, who was named executive vice president at Pocket Books, was to emerge as one of the central characters in the paperback industry. With de Graff as president, Shimkin as treasurer, Simon and Schuster still sitting on the board of directors, and Freeman Lewis, known throughout the trade as Doc, essentially responsible for operations, Pocket Books was well prepared to graduate to the next level of paperback publishing.

The company that Field now owned was piling record atop record, and sales manager Pete Howe reported volume at forty million copies in 1945. Pointing to a widening pool of distribution that he said included drugstores, variety stores, cigar stores and newsstands, general merchandise chains (Sears Roebuck, Montgomery Ward, J. C. Penney), bookstores, and half a million food stores, Howe dreamily envisioned eight hundred thousand potential outlets for books of all kinds.[7]

With new ownership and all the paper it needed after rationing was lifted, Pocket Books shifted into high gear in a postwar expansion drive. In order to compete with the magazines on newsstands, the books were redesigned. Gordon Aymar, a top art director, was brought in to oversee art and design. Dropping the familiar two-color frame and rounded panel that had been Pocket's "look," a solid color running across the cover was substituted, while across the top of the books, a white strip was added saying, "Pocket Book. More than 132,000,000 Pocket Books have been sold." (This number was raised with each month's new releases.) Eventually a machine was designed that would number each Pocket Book as it came off the presses. And the Perma-Gloss covers, dropped during the war, were back. Gertrude also received a postwar facelift. Her glasses were dropped and the little kangaroo in her pouch was replaced with a book.

The Pocket Books that Field had acquired for about three million dollars was the undoubted king of the growing ranks of paperback publishers. And the jewel in the company's crown was Erle Stanley Gardner, creator of Perry Mason. By the end of the war, Pocket Books had published eight Gardner mysteries featuring the lawyer-sleuth Mason, his trusty secretary Della Street, and the loyal private eye Paul Drake. (They were, in order of sales figures at the time, *The Case of the Lucky Legs, The Case of the Curious Bride, The Case of the Counterfeit Eye, The Case of the Howling Dog, The Case of the Velvet Claws, The Case of the Sulky Girl, The Case of the Dangerous Dowager,* and *The Case of the Shoplifter's Shoe.*) Of these, five had already topped the million-seller mark. A ninth book, *The Case of the Baited Hook,* was published in January 1946.

The perpetrator of this extraordinary output was a self-proclaimed "one-man fiction factory." Born in Malden, Massachusetts, in 1889, Erle Stanley Gardner was the son of a mining engineer; his father's occupation kept the family on the move, and they finally ended up in California. Gardner's first brush with the law came when he worked as a typist in a Willows, California, law office. He went to study law at Valparaiso University in Indiana but was forced to leave in a hurry after a run-in with a professor turned into a bottle-throwing fracas and a warrant was issued for his arrest. Heading west, Gardner laid low by working in an Oregon railroad construction camp before making his way back to California. Taking up once more in a law office, he learned enough to pass the California bar exam in 1911. By 1923, he was putting his courtroom experience to work in stories written for such pulp detective magazines as *Black Mask*. After a few years, Gardner was being paid handsomely for his work, but he continued to practice law into the thirties and had developed a reputation as an advocate for the downtrodden. As Gardner wrote his father, "I have built up a law practice in which I am dealing with large numbers of clients of all classes — except the upper and middle class." According to one report, he had become the champion of the Chinese in California, at the time a cut below even the Mexicans in California society.[8]

His courtroom experience, along with a fascination for legal quirks and unusual precedents, provided much of the fodder for the Perry Mason stories, the first of which was *The Case of the Velvet Claws*, written in 1933 and reportedly dictated to Gardner's secretary in three and a half days. Despite his success in the pulp field, Gardner submitted the book to several disinterested publishers before he found a patron in Thayer Hobson, president of William Morrow. Gardner later credited Hobson as his discoverer, and it was Hobson who was responsible for convincing Gardner to stick to a single character rather than try to create new ones. *The Case of the Velvet Claws*, appearing in a market clogged with mysteries, sold thirty-two hundred copies in a few months — a respectable sale for a hardcover mystery in those days, but certainly no indication of what was to come. Perhaps Thayer Hobson knew something that the rest of the world would take a while to find out. He wrote the copy line for the jacket on *The Case of the Velvet Claws:* "Perry Mason — criminal lawyer. Remember that name. You'll meet him again. He is going to be famous."

When Gardner's work first appeared, the mystery world was split into two basic camps. On one side were the purists. Descended from Edgar Allan Poe (whose *The Murders in the Rue Morgue* was the first modern detective story) and Arthur Conan Doyle, the line continued with Agatha Christie, S. S. Van Dine, and Dorothy L. Sayers. Born of an age that worshiped at the new altar of Science, these mysteries placed the accent on the purely deductive abilities (Poe's "ratiocination") of a super sleuth whose intellectual prowess overcame brute violence. For the most part, these classical purists operated in an upper-crust milieu worlds apart from the average paperback reader. The solution came as order was restored to a world of privilege temporarily thrown into chaos. As fine as the writing sometimes was, it was escapist entertainment.

Then came Dashiell Hammett. First appearing in *Black Mask* in

1922, Hammett sired a new style of mystery. Realistic, often violent, and set on the sleazier side of the tracks or in high places that
were façades for a corrupt society, Hammett's books were summed
up in a new word: hard-boiled. It was a style suited to the times.
The revolution in Russia had changed the place of the aristocrat.
The world had been through a war that revealed mass death in a
previously unseen light. Through the twenties and thirties, and into
the forties, when America experienced the economic mayhem of
the Great Depression, the gangsterism and corruption fostered by
Prohibition, and another world war that gave new meaning to the
concept of man's capability for evil, the niceties of civilized death
in the classic mystery no longer corresponded to the harsh reality
of the modern age.

Just as Gardner drew on his courtroom experience for Perry Mason's cases, Hammett could rely on his years spent as a detective
for Pinkerton, America's most famous private detective agency. In
his earliest stories, he introduced the anonymous Continental Op,
the first in a string of now mythical American private eyes that
included Sam Spade and Nick Charles. Besides creating a new style
and giving a new voice — a distinctly American one — to the mystery, Hammett was raising the genre to literary heights never before
attempted and unequaled since. Along with his contemporaries
James M. Cain and John O'Hara, who were taking the hard-boiled
style in separate directions, Hammett moved the American novel
into a new arena that combined social concern and literary realism
with politics, a new sexual frankness, and an extremely bleak view
of human nature.

Unlike the purists' work, Hammett's books didn't rise to a carefully calculated climax and tidy dénouement in which justice and
the social order were restored intact. Instead, they exposed greed,
guilt, and corruption on all sides, a condition that Hammett saw as
an outgrowth of the American system, a system capable of creating
a city like Personville, or, as it was pronounced, "Poisonville," in
his 1929 novel *Red Harvest:*

> Since then the smelters whose brick stacks stuck up against a gloomy
> mountain to the south had yellow-smoked everything into uniform
> dinginess. The result was an ugly city of forty-thousand people, set in
> an ugly notch between two ugly mountains that had been all dirtied
> up by mining. Spread over this was a grimy sky that looked as if it had
> come out of the smelter's stacks.

Like many other writers and intellectuals of the period, Hammett was attracted to leftist causes, became a Marxist, and joined the Communist party. He was to pay for that choice. When he refused to name names during the "red scare" days, Hammett was convicted of contempt of court and jailed for six months. Already in poor health, he left prison at the end of 1951 desperately sick. Blacklisted and hounded by a hostile government that was seizing his royalties, Hammett died in 1961. His books were few — six novels, including *The Dain Curse, The Maltese Falcon,* and *The Thin Man,* and a collection of stories, *The Continental Op* — and his career lasted but ten years, after which the creative juices stopped flowing. Perhaps he was giving too much of himself to another writer, Lillian Hellman, whose career as a playwright was taking off as Hammett's waned. But no mystery writer — and few writers in general — who followed Hammett could deny his influence or impact.

When the first Perry Mason appeared in 1933, the comparisons to Hammett were inevitable, but Gardner did not take kindly to the reviewers who called attention to the fact. He tried to distance himself, and soon the hard-boiled Perry Mason of *Velvet Claws* developed into the smooth, sophisticated lawyer who belonged far more to the purist school of detection. There was little overt violence, frank sex, or societal corruption in Gardner's books. He had no contempt for the system. In his books, it always worked in his hero's favor. Justice triumphed and innocence was preserved. Whatever the style, Gardner had obviously struck a chord. As he once told an interviewer, "I'm the product of the paperback revolution. Ordinary readers see in me somebody they can identify with. I'm for the underdog. The average man is always in a state of supreme suspense because life is all complications with no conclusion. In my books, he sees people get out of trouble."[9]

How deep a chord he struck soon became apparent. Gardner joined the Pocket Books list in 1940 when Lee Wright, Simon & Schuster's mystery editor who had gone over to work for Pocket Books, signed up *Velvet Claws* as Pocket Book No. 73. It was the company's fifteenth mystery, and although mysteries had become a profitable category, none of the eleven other mystery novelists approached the raging success that Gardner's books were going to produce. The sales figures were awesome. In 1952, Pocket Books reported that the *million-copy* first printing of *The Case of the Lonely Heiress* would bring Gardner's total Pocket Books in print to fifty million copies. "Unless I am mistaken," said Doc Lewis, "this is the highest copy sales figure ever attained by any author while he is still alive."[10] By 1958, Perry Mason's twenty-fifth anniversary year, Gardner's books had reached the hundred-million mark. These included fifty-five Perry Masons, some travel books, and the pseudonymous Bertha Cool–Donald Lam mysteries by A. A. Fair. Gardner was frequently serialized in the *Saturday Evening Post* and his books had been translated into more than twenty languages. Ten years later, when he was lauded by Charles W. Morton in a gushing article in the *Atlantic Monthly*, the totals had reached 165 million books sold, 130 titles published, and sales worldwide of 20,000 copies per day. In addition, there was the television series created, owned, and supervised by Gardner that ran for nine years and 292 episodes. *Variety* estimated that Raymond Burr, the actor famed as Mason, was earning about one million dollars per year for the role — an indication of the rewards Gardner was collecting.[11]

Why the success? What was the secret? In the *Atlantic Monthly* article, Charles Morton simply stated, "Intrinsic quality is a perfectly good reason for the success of Gardner's books." But were they really that good? Part of their appeal undoubtedly lay in the perfectly realized formula, which Gardner had developed to nearly scientific precision: Mason gets a client who is so embroiled in legal difficulties that his or her guilt seems assured and conviction a mere formality. Mason himself is also put in jeopardy, by either threatened arrest as an accessory or possible disbarment. The story then builds to a trick ending reversing the circumstances, invariably in a packed courtroom with Mason displaying his dazzling legalistic fireworks.

Cleverly plotted and always with the gimmick of the unusual legal trick, the books were no more clever than those of other purists like Agatha Christie or Dorothy L. Sayers, whose books were in fact far more unique, witty, and original. And the characters populating Gardner's dramas accurately reflected the amount of time he spent on them — no more than four days with a Dictaphone. This dictation system, involving three secretaries — sisters — allowed Gardner to set himself a yearly quota of 1.2 million words. It also led to the frequent charge that the "word factory" was exactly that — that Gardner was guilty of employing ghostwriters. In response to these rumors, Thayer Hobson of Morrow once offered a $100,000 reward to anyone who could prove that Gardner worked with either a ghostwriter or a collaborator. "It would be worth $100,000 and a lot more just to find someone who could write like Gardner," said Hobson. "Scores of writers have tried to imitate him. No one has ever put it over."[12]

Obviously, Gardner was no Georges Simenon or G. K. Chesterton, and today his early books are badly dated. Hammett and James M. Cain, on the other hand, still seem fresh; their best writing is as dynamic and sensational as it was when it was first published during the 1930s. But it is Gardner who is, according to Guinness, the best-selling novelist of all time. Perhaps the explanation is simple. He provided reliable entertainment consistently, like television soap operas or movie serials. They didn't challenge the reader — except perhaps to beat Mason to the punch — or leave questions unanswered. They were popcorn: hard to stop eating once you start but not very filling. For people who were looking for a way to escape life's "complications with no conclusion," as Gardner put it, a twenty-five-cent Perry Mason was an easy way out.

Despite the sales of Erle Stanley Gardner and the success in general of Pocket Books, all was not well at the end of the war for the paperback industry. The business Marshall Field III found himself in was vastly different from the one that existed when Robert de Graff set out in 1939. Besides Joseph Meyer's Avon Books and the revitalized Penguin Books, two more competitors had cropped up during the war years. The continuing growth of Pocket Books seemed to be ample proof that there was still plenty of room for expansion. But the paperback racks were beginning to grow a bit more crowded. The appearance of Popular Library, launched late in 1942, and Dell Books, which followed in 1943, signaled to the book trade that the paperback wars were beginning to heat up.

Like Avon, the two new companies got their start with the blessing of the American News Company. Popular Library was the child of Ned L. Pines, who had started out in Brooklyn by publishing a small newspaper and graduated into the field of pulps (including *Thrilling Wonder Stories, Thrilling Western Stories,* and *Future Science Fiction*) and magazines such as *Screenland* and *Silver Screen.* His editor was Charles Heckleman, also a writer of Western novels. Reflecting its magazine heritage, Popular Library stuck pretty much to what it knew — mysteries and Westerns.

A far more formidable foe for Pocket Books was Dell Books, an outgrowth of the vast magazine empire owned by George T. Delacorte, who had begun building his business in 1921 with magazines and pulp fiction. Buying and selling magazines as they grew profitable, he had owned more than two hundred different publications by 1945. They included *Modern Screen, Modern Romance,* and *Inside Detective.* In the 1930s, he began to amass a comic book line-up of staggering proportions. In addition to licensing all the Walt Disney characters for comic book use, Dell could boast of its Flash Gordon, Looney Tunes, and Little Lulu comic books. At one point, the company was selling 300 million comic books per year in addition to 160 million magazines. Most of these were going through the American News Company, and in 1942 Dell was the ANC's single largest supplier of newsstand materials.

Alongside these vast holdings, Delacorte had another asset, a young woman named Helen Meyer. Meyer had joined the Dell organization when she was sixteen after working as an adjustment clerk handling complaints at Select Distributing, a company set up by *McCall's* and *Popular Science.* When a girlfriend told Meyer there was a job open at Dell, she went over and was interviewed by George Delacorte himself. Meyer took the job at a starting salary of twenty dollars per week. By the time Dell Books was set up in 1942, Helen Meyer had become George Delacorte's "right-hand man," overseeing editorial and business details. Later described as "shrewd" by some and "a man-eater" by one male colleague, Meyer certainly must have been a tough lady to make it in the man's world of magazines and paperbacks circa 1942. As an illustration of that world, she once described going with Delacorte to meet an important buyer at the Commodore Hotel and being told to wait in the lobby because the man would not permit a woman in his room.

Delacorte claimed that he had been considering paperbacks ever since he had visited Europe, where he — like de Graff and others — had seen the success of Tauchnitz, Albatross, and Penguin. He even said he had approached Simon & Schuster with the idea of a paperback series before de Graff had. But Delacorte, an iconoclastic individualist, preferred to go it alone. Later, however, when the American News Company approached him with the proposal to distribute paperbacks, Delacorte went along with them. With the profits provided by magazines and comic books and the distribution available to him through the American News Company, Delacorte finally made his move after reaching an agreement with the Western Printing & Lithographing Company of Racine, Wisconsin, to acquire, edit, and produce the books. Western, a large printing company founded in 1907, was producing children's books, playing cards, and notions as well as all of Dell's comic books. Besides their book production experience, Western could provide the final link in the chain with a supply of surplus paper it held during the wartime rationing days.

Through its magazine and pulp experience, Dell knew what it could do best. Accordingly, the Dell lists were to be dominated almost exclusively by one category, mysteries. To set Dell Books apart, they carried the Dell mystery logo, a keyhole with an eye peering through it. The other distinctive features were a four-color "mystery map," showing the details of the scene of the crime, and a list of characters in the story. The first Dell Books appeared in 1943; by 1945 the company had eighty titles on its list and was publishing four new titles per month until rationing forced a cutback to two releases, usually in print runs of two hundred thousand copies.

Like Avon before it, neither Popular Library nor Dell showed any inclination toward improving the intellectual atmosphere in America's heartland. In fact, Dell's editorial and cover decisions essentially were left to Western. The releases from all three companies owed more to their pulp magazine notions of the mass market than to any considerations of literary value. Mirroring their magazines, all three companies produced lists weighted heavily toward mysteries. The first lists of Popular Library and Dell Books are representative of where they would continue to focus their publishing efforts:

POPULAR LIBRARY

1. *Saint Overboard* by Leslie Charteris.
2. *Danger in the Dark* by Mignon G. Eberhart.
3. *Crime of Violence* by Rufus King.
4. *Murder in the Madhouse* by Jonathan Latimer.
5. *Miss Pinkerton* by Mary Roberts Rinehart.
6. *Three Bright Pebbles* by Leslie Ford.
7. *Death Demands an Audience* by Helen Reilly.
8. *Death for Dear Clara* by Q. Patrick.
9. *The Eel Pie Murders* by David Frome.
10. *To Wake the Dead* by John Dickson Carr.

DELL BOOKS

1. *Death in the Library* by Philip Ketchum.
2. *Dead or Alive* by Patricia Wentworth.
3. *Murder-on-Hudson* by Jennifer Jones.
4. *The American Gun Mystery* by Ellery Queen.
5. *Four Frightened Women* by George Harmon Coxe.
6. *Ill Met by Moonlight* by Leslie Ford.
7. *See You at the Morgue* by Lawrence G. Blochman.
8. *The Tuesday Club Murders* by Agatha Christie.
9. *Double for Death* by Rex Stout.
10. *The Lone Wolf* by Louis Joseph Vance.

At the same time, Avon was steering a roughly parallel course. One difference was that Avon could at least point to an occasional novel by Somerset Maugham, John O'Hara, Booth Tarkington, and even D. H. Lawrence, although it is likely that *The Virgin and the Gypsy* was published for the value of its title and Lawrence's prurient reputation rather than for its literary merits. The disparity in quality between what was being published by Avon, Popular Library, and Dell and the books coming from Pocket Books and Penguin — each with stronger roots in traditional book publishing — was becoming more evident. One result of this disparity was the attitude taken toward backlist books, titles that had a life span longer than a few months in the marketplace. The three magazine-oriented publishers were accustomed to sending out "product" each month, selling it, and that was it; a new batch followed right behind. In this short-term thinking, little planning was made for building a list of books that could deliver consistent sales. But in the scheme of both Pocket Books and Penguin — and later Bantam Books and New American Library — books that could be assured of sales year after year were part of each company's stock in trade.

The major uncertainty was which direction the industry would take. Obviously, companies on both sides of the fence could point to their success. What followed was going to be a battle for the heart and mind of the paperback business. Max Schuster understood this conflict and laid out the lines of battle as far back as 1942 when he wrote in a memo to his partners in Pocket Books:

> We cannot stress too much the life and death importance of the content of the books and the basic editorial appeal in all its varied forms

Dell Book Number 1, featuring the distinctive keyhole with peeping eye. (Photo by Kevin Hancer)

Avon was banking on Lawrence's reputation as a "dirty writer" when it published *The Virgin and the Gypsy*. (Photo by Kevin Hancer)

— recent best sellers, mysteries, practical books, the home library classics, anthologies, humor, etc., etc. . . . Dick [Simon] and I feel most strongly that we must continue to merit such faith and enthusiasm [from readers]. We must continue to overwhelm not only the wholesalers and distributors, but the ultimate consumer — the reader — with the excellent and superior content of the books. We must surprise them and astonish them with the seemingly impossible.

As a long term trend, I'd advocate concentration on books which other competitors cannot even approach in quality. If we do more books like *The Office Wife* [by Faith Baldwin] or the movie types like *Claudia*, the Avons and Delacortes will meet this by doing the *Chickies* and other Broadway box office hits. If we compete in terms of lowest common denominator, they will cut lower; if we compete in terms of discounts and price advantages, they will try to cut our throats, but if we give the readers the world's best books in unimpeachable form — the Shakespeares and the Bibles, the world's great short stories, the world's great poems — in addition to the mysteries and recent best sellers — we'll build so invulnerable a good will that we will, to a great degree, be impervious to competition.[13]

Schuster's point was astute and prescient. For years to come, Pocket Books was without a real challenger to its position atop the paperback market. Although Dell had become by 1945 the second-largest paperback house, it was a distinction without real meaning and one that would not last long. For example, it was not until 1957 that Dell had its first million-selling title. The quest to equal or surpass Pocket Books would fuel the ambition of other publishers and spark the next rounds in the Paperback Revolution. The scene of the battle was Penguin Books, Inc., the American outpost of Allen Lane's worldwide Penguin empire, then under the direction of Ian Ballantine and Kurt Enoch.

During the war, Penguin had made steady if unspectacular gains. Although it could boast of no million-sellers on the order of Pocket Books, the Penguin name was taken seriously by the book trade and had won the respect of booksellers, authors, and other publishers. Its war book publishing programs in association with *Infantry Journal* and the Military Services Publishing Company had been successful, and the company had been awarded the Navy "E" in 1945, a certificate of achievement for its support of the war production program. But as the war wound down and peace treaties ending it were negotiated, battle lines within the company were being drawn in a prelude to a series of splits that would end, as one participant put it, "with blood on the floor." The ultimate result of what started out as a palace revolt against Allen Lane would be the creation of Bantam Books and New American Library, two of the most powerful and influential paperback houses to take their places alongside Pocket Books just as the Paperback Revolution was gathering a full head of steam.

SIX

Penguin Hatches Twins

Rooster or Capon?
— 1950 Bantam ad claiming all its books were uncut
Good Reading for the Millions
— slogan of New American Library

THROUGH THE war years, Allen Lane had been forced — though not happily so — to leave Penguin's American operation be. He had little choice in the matter bacause the war kept him from exerting direct control over the New York operation. Lane could neither dictate editorial policy across the Atlantic nor wield a financial stick. However, he must have felt reasonably secure with the veteran Enoch in place. Certainly the company's limited success was paying dividends; if nothing else, the American company was able to export books back to England. But with the war nearly over, Lane could again turn his sights back toward America. Though pleased with the fruits borne by the colonial seeds he had planted, Lane knew the American operation was no Eden. The colony had gained a measure of independence from the sovereign and, in Lane's eyes, needed to be brought back under more stringent controls. As Ballantine remarked about the situation, "It was a case of the tail wagging the dog."

In Lane's view, the American branch had begun to take steps in a distinctly distasteful direction. The most outwardly visible of these was the appearance of illustrations on the covers of Penguins, which the Americans had begun to employ in 1943. Although modest and practically primitive by later standards, these covers were anathema to Lane. But the cover crisis was only a symptom of a wider split within the company. Ian Ballantine, the brash youth of a few years earlier who had started up the New York operation with Lane's blessing, a few cartons of books, and little else, believed Penguin was in a position to challenge Pocket Books. His certainty was founded on the basis of his securing the services of the Curtis Circulating Company as a national distributor for Penguin in the latter years of the war. This was the distribution arm of the Curtis Publishing Company, which published the *Saturday Evening Post* and *Ladies' Home Journal*, two of the most widely read popular magazines in the country. With the backing of the Curtis sales organization and its powerful force of salesman who sold books to the independent distributors, Ballantine had what he believed was the machinery to propel Penguin into the front ranks of the paperback business. This meant opting to compete in the true "mass market" where Pocket Books and Dell were strongest. To do so meant steering a more popular course. Lane, with his own very British views of what Penguin should publish in America and how they should do so, would have none of it.

Whether their disagreements were so fundamental as to preclude any compromise is academic. Far more significant than their theories of paperbacking were personalities. In Lane, Ballantine, and Enoch (whose feelings were more closely aligned with Lane's) were three emphatic actors, none of whom seemed suited for a supporting role. Each in his own way was single-minded, enterprising, visionary, ambitious, and possessed a strong ego. In short — as one of the popular Westerns might put it — the town wasn't big enough for all of them. What followed was the shoot-out at the Penguin corral. When the dust had settled, Ballantine was gone, taking with him editor Pitkin, accountant-lawyer Kramer, most of the office staff, and the agreements with *Infantry Journal*, the Military Services Publishing Company, and Curtis Circulating Company.

Setting up briefly as Ballantine and Company, the firm published important originals such as *Island Victory* and *Psychology for the Returning Serviceman*, along with a few more reprints under the Military Services Company/Superior Reprints imprint, among them Liam O'Flaherty's *The Informer*. But Ballantine had much bigger plans in the offing. Ballantine approached Random House publisher Bennett Cerf with the proposal that he finance a paperback house backed by Curtis, certain that it could challenge Pocket Books' sovereignty. Fresh from his maneuverings to obtain Grosset & Dunlap, Cerf was hesitant. As he later recalled, "We knew that to start a rival to Pocket Books would take at least one million dollars and we didn't have it. So I sent Ian to Grosset."[1]

Impressed with Ballantine's connection to the Curtis organization, Grosset president John O'Connor supported the young man's proposal. But the blessings of the other publishers who owned Grosset were still required, and that was no small doing. Particularly reluctant was Charles Scribner, a crusty publishing traditionalist who was known to be tight with a dollar. He wanted no part of paperbacks. Bennett Cerf later related that the most convincing argument in favor of the move came from an unlikely quarter — Robert de Graff himself. "When Bob came as a 'friend' to give us a talk about why we shouldn't go into the business we figured it must be a damned good idea."[2]

The company that emerged was a force to be reckoned with. Grosset & Dunlap and Curtis Publishing each held 42.5 percent of the stock, Ballantine held 9 percent, and Pitkin and Kramer each got 3 percent. The company's board of directors was composed of some of the most august and powerful men in publishing: Cass Canfield of Harper & Brothers; Charles Scribner; Meredith Wood of the Book-of-the-Month Club; Cerf of Random House; Grosset president O'Connor; and four Curtis executives. Ballantine was installed as president, Pitkin as vice president, and Kramer as treasurer and secretary.

"Just saying Curtis was our distributor was enough for people to believe in us," said Ballantine. "Combined with the prestige of the other publishers, we were clearly going to be a major house."

Like Albatross and Penguin, the new "major house" took on the wings of a bird. At the suggestion of a young Grosset editor named Bernard Geis — who would later make his own name well known — the company was christened Bantam Books and took as its symbol a feisty rooster.

On July 28, 1945, an advertisement in *The Publishers' Weekly* announced "the establishment of a new series of 25¢ paper-bound books." The ad went on to say, "Bantam Books, Inc., will be an independent neutral channel for the mass publishing and distribution of reprints of novels, detective, mystery and western stories, non-fiction, humor, short stories, poetry, anthologies; in short, books appealing to every reading taste and within the reach of every buyer."

A far more impressive-looking ad appeared in *PW* on the cover of the December 1, 1945, issue. Running for six pages as well as on the inside and outside back cover, the promotion extolled Bantam Books as "an example of the best in the fine art of quarter book-making." The ad clearly showed that the new firm had classy blood-lines and was going to be a top-notch operation with tremendous impact on the paperback scene. The firm's exclusive pedigree showed in its list of twenty initial titles, released on December 15, 1945:

1. *Life on the Mississippi* by Mark Twain.
2. *The Gift Horse* by Frank Gruber (mystery).
3. *Nevada* by Zane Grey (Western).
4. *Evidence of Things Seen* by Elizabeth Daly (mystery).
5. *Scaramouche* by Rafael Sabatini (historical novel).
6. *A Murder by Marriage* by Robert G. Dean (mystery).
7. *The Grapes of Wrath* by John Steinbeck, the best-selling, Pulitzer Prize–winning novel of 1940.
8. *The Great Gatsby* by F. Scott Fitzgerald.
9. *Rogue Male* by Geoffrey Household (espionage).
10. *South Moon Under* by Marjorie Kinnan Rawlings (novel).
11. *Mr. and Mrs. Cugat* by Isabel Scott Rorick, a 1941 best-selling novel.
12. *Then There Were Three* by Geoffrey Homes (mystery).
13. *The Last Time I Saw Paris* by Elliot Paul, a nostalgic prewar portrait of Paris and a 1941 nonfiction best seller.
14. *Wind, Sand and Stars* by Antoine de Saint-Exupéry, a 1939 nonfiction best seller.
15. *Meet Me in St. Louis* by Sally Benson, the novel on which the musical film was based.
16. *The Town Cried Murder* by Leslie Ford (mystery).
17. *Seventeen* by Booth Tarkington, a favorite since it was published in 1916 and became a best seller.
18. *What Makes Sammy Run?* by Budd Schulberg (novel).
19. *One More Spring* by Robert Nathan (novel).
20. *Oil for the Lamps of China* by Alice Tisdale Hobart, a 1934 best-selling novel.

The first list was something of a guide to the company's future direction. Ever the theoretician, Ballantine liked statistics and sur-veys. One figure that impressed him showed that 60 percent of the top-selling books in the previous fifty years had been novels, out-selling mysteries many times over. Unlike Pocket Books, with

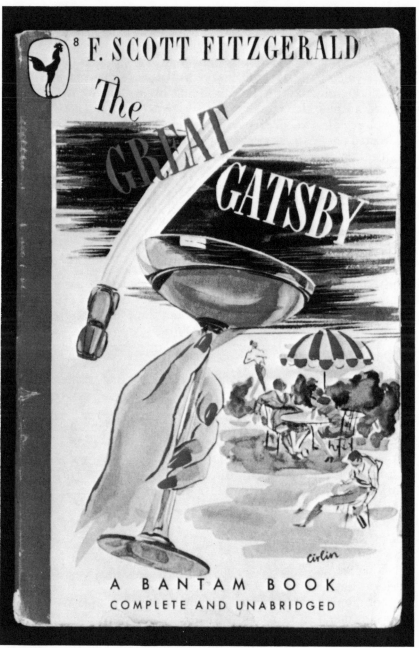

Fitzgerald's *Gatsby* was Bantam Number 8. (Photo by Jerome Frank)

about 50 percent mysteries on its list, and the other competitors, Avon, Dell, and Popular Library, Bantam shied away from the mystery. While they had their place on the Bantam Books list, mysteries did not dominate. The six on the first list would correspond with the company's plan to publish approximately 25 percent mysteries. Bantam came to concentrate far more on Westerns and eventually corralled the market, printing as many as four hundred thousand copies of a good Western. There was also an obvious move made in the direction of best-selling novels, historical novels, and more "literary" fiction, even if it was questionably packaged on occasion. For instance, the blurb on *The Great Gatsby* read, "A story of love and adventure on Long Island." Publishing better books was sometimes a matter of prestige rather than profits. Quality novels, like *The Grapes of Wrath*, were usually longer than the average "category" or "genre" book. One reason so many mysteries were published — besides their apparent popularity — was their length. To be profitable as paperbacks, books could be no longer than 190 pages. Mysteries were usually kept at least that short by their hardcover publishers. Another way around the long book problem was to build up a surplus in a "page bank" by doing shorter books. Or you simply took a loss, as Bantam did with *The Grapes of Wrath*. "We lost money on every copy," Ian Ballantine later recalled of the 576-page book. "But it was important to have a book of that stature on that first list. Steinbeck had plenty of short books. By throwing his longest work into our first list of twenty titles, we established Bantam as his publisher."

To back up the books, Bantam relied on the strength of the Curtis Circulating Company, with three hundred men in the field. In addition, the company spent half a million dollars in its first six months on free racks for the dealers, racks that were supposedly just for Bantam Books. The practice at the time was for books to be displayed by publisher rather than category. A large, handsome rack covered with Bantam emblems would go a long way toward ensuring that Bantam Books were on display. One of these racks (No. 60), designed by Ballantine, was a three-tiered, wooden-sided rack with a protruding, bosomy upper shelf, nicknamed the Mae West. Print runs on major titles ran in the 400,000 to 500,000 copy range. By February 1947, *PW* could report: "Strong reordering by wholesale distributors characterized the close of Bantam Books' first year of 25¢ reprint publishing." The best-selling titles were *Murder by Mar-*

riage ("a rough-tough whodunit"), *The Grapes of Wrath,* and Zane Grey's *Nevada.*[3]

Finding good novels to reprint created no strains for Bantam in the beginning. The intensely competitive auctions and bidding that have characterized the paperback business in more recent years were as yet unheard of. Even more significant was the advantage the new company had gained through its ownership. In the hard-cover houses that owned it, Bantam Books found not only a reliable source of current best sellers but a rich lode of prominent books from years past. As Ballantine commented, "In our hurry to get into production, we tended to go to the hardcover houses who owned us for reprint rights. Doing so created no hardships. In the beginning, we were stuck trying to choose between Hemingway and Faulk-ner." (For the record, Bantam never reprinted Faulkner, and the first Hemingway title was not published until *A Farewell to Arms* — No. 467 — appeared in 1948.)

The luxury of this relationship was not without its drawbacks. Such power is rarely attained without a tradeoff. Bantam's cage, while golden, was nonetheless a cage. With such powerful backers as Curtis, with its extremely effective sales force, and the collection of publishing power brokers who sat on the Bantam board, the rel-atively inexperienced Ballantine and Pitkin would have enormous pressure applied to them. Although Ballantine maintained that he was never pressed to accept ill-considered suggestions, Walter Pit-kin, Jr., later explained:

> There was a great deal of tugging and hauling on the part of the direc-tors quite early, and it proceeded in a way that was quite difficult for management. Different directors — differently motivated — would recommend titles. And I think that Ian Ballantine would have liked to have all of those titles work out for Bantam.
>
> What he picked up from the Curtis people was different in nature. It was an enormous organization, powerful, rich, strong. Mostly their input was by category. "Do more Westerns." "Try romances." "Mys-teries aren't so hot." "More mysteries." Depending on how the wind was blowing.
>
> I would say Bantam always responded very positively to this input insofar as it related to categories. That's a very important thing be-cause it came to represent a lot of the program. Because of that input and input on particular titles from publisher-owners, the amount of input from outside was enormous. And this finally affected my role.

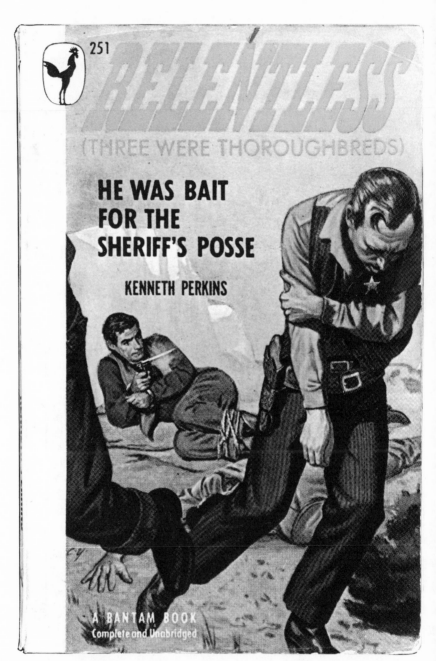

251

RELENTLESS

(THREE WERE THOROUGHBREDS)

HE WAS BAIT
FOR THE
SHERIFF'S POSSE

KENNETH PERKINS

A BANTAM BOOK
Complete and Unabridged

Bantam soon specialized in the Western genre. (Photo courtesy of Jean Peters)

My role as arbiter of titles was far greater under Penguin than it was at Bantam. My specific title input was enormously reduced from what it had been previously because there had not been this political game to play. We had moved from the earlier age into the modern age. This was publishing by consensus as opposed to publishing by enthusiasm and inspiration. . . . Of course, we didn't realize that we'd lost our innocence; however, in a very real sense we sold out our different careers for a different kind of career.

Ian Ballantine had serious run-ins with the directors, and looking back at it in a true light, I see that Ian was very determined to hold to his way of publishing through enthusiasm and not to buckle under to the machinery which had grown around the decisions. . . . There wasn't a hell of a lot of room left for personal enthusiasm anymore. Curtis would raise hell if something didn't have a sales figure above a certain level on a ten day checkup. The directors found they were responding affirmatively to the Curtis reaction. But it was essentially a non–book publishing input.

The pressures were evident in other ways. Most ominous was the trend in covers. In order to compete with the other publishers in the mass market — notably Avon, Dell, and Popular Library — as well as the magazines displayed on the newsstands, the Bantam cover design began to move toward pictorial and increasingly realistic styles designed for mass appeal. This road was no primrose path, and soon Bantam, along with most of the other paperback houses, would be taking dangerous steps in a direction that would cause great problems for the industry.

Meanwhile, back at Penguin Books, Inc., where Enoch had cast his lot with Allen Lane when Ballantine departed, the situation was rather grim. Enoch's decision was no doubt an outgrowth of Lane's earlier pledge that Enoch would receive a share in the company. In the wake of the splintering, Enoch had convinced Lane that a major reorganization was required and he wanted 40 percent of the company, a demand to which Lane acquiesced. But survival was going to require a major overhaul, the outcome of which was certainly not assured. Ballantine's departure had left Enoch without experienced editors, an office staff, or a distributor, although Curtis agreed to maintain Penguin's distribution on a temporary basis. Left with only a production assistant and sales manager Phillip Album, Enoch and Penguin Books, Inc., teetered on the brink.

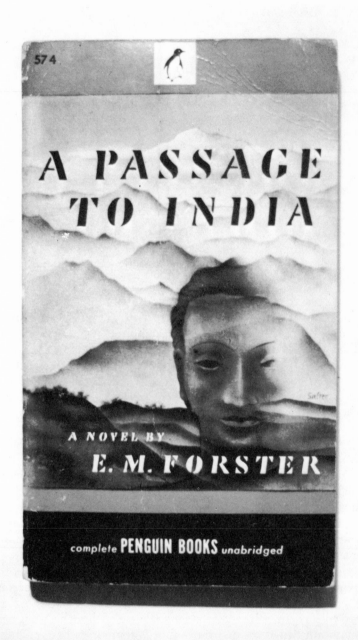

A Passage to India was one of the Penguins of the postwar period. Allen Lane objected to illustrations of any sort on the American books. (Photo by Jerome Frank)

But if Kurt Enoch had proven one thing in his life, it was his capacity for survival. Through two world wars and a series of calamitous uprootings, he had managed to land on his feet. As he faced this new crisis, his greatest asset was the respect he had won from suppliers, particularly the printer W. F. Hall in Chicago, which extended a line of credit at a time when capital was still a problem for Penguin Books, Inc. Nonetheless, his English was perfunctory at best, and although he was acquainted with American literature and was a well-educated and cultivated European, he had no grasp of current American writers, tastes, or trends and only passing knowledge of the ins and outs of American publishing. Consequently, his most pressing need — besides finding new distribution — was for editorial expertise.

As a stopgap measure, Allen Lane dispatched Eunice Frost, a close and trusted aide, to New York in an attempt to shore up Enoch's position and keep things afloat. Although she was able and efficient and understood that the American operation must be allowed to move in directions that Lane opposed, Frost had no expectations of making the posting a permanent one, and she suffered from the same unfamiliarity with American literary tastes and writers that Enoch did. Yet she was able to begin building an editorial staff by bringing in the first new editors, Donald Demarest and Arabel J. Porter, a Swarthmore graduate who had previously worked at Dutton's Everyman Library (a series of inexpensive classics) and later came to be known as the "Bohemian Quaker." Eunice Frost also began to choose the first of the American Pelican books, *Public Opinion* by Walter Lippmann and Ruth Benedict's *Patterns of Culture* among them. In addition, the new American-procured fiction reprinted under the Penguin imprint included D. H. Lawrence's *The Lovely Lady*, E. M. Forster's *A Passage to India*, and Georges Simenon's *The Patience of Maigret*.

The uncertainty of the situation in New York was resolved with the arrival of Victor Weybright. Stationed at the U.S. Embassy in London with the Office of War Information (OWI) during the war, Weybright had developed a close acquaintanceship with Allen Lane and was godfather to Lane's daughter. Lane had a way of making promises of positions with Penguin to friends, and he had done so with Weybright. Without informing Enoch, Lane told Weybright to introduce himself to the German now in charge of Penguin Books, Inc., in New York. It was part of a scheme that Lane had devised, according to his biographer, J. P. Morpurgo:

It suited Allen to be vague with Weybright and secretive with Enoch; though he was convinced that Weybright's knowledge of the American literary scene might be useful to Penguin Books Inc., he knew also that Weybright had no business experience. He thought it best to leave Enoch the responsibility for accepting or rejecting his services. . . . So when Weybright arrived in Enoch's offices, though as a stranger and though the suggestion that he put forward as from Allen was couched in the vaguest terms — nothing more definite than that he might join Penguin Books Inc. in some executive capacity — his arrival was well-timed. And so, in all probability just as Allen Lane had planned, Enoch and Weybright came to work together.[4]

Though surprised and annoyed by the lack of communication from Lane, Enoch heard Weybright out, was impressed with his credentials and connections with the world of writers, publishers, and scholars, and found him amiable. In addition, as he later recalled, "I expected that Victor's friendship with Allen Lane would be useful in our dealings with our British partners."

A more unlikely pairing than Enoch and Weybright would be difficult to imagine. Enoch was the lean, ascetic, methodical European. More Prussian than German Jew, he had the bearing and reserve of an aristocrat, a mien traceable to his roots in Hamburg, a city well known for its citizens' air of superiority. Some took Enoch's reserve for coldness, perhaps because of his uncertain English. Weybright, on the other hand, was a rotund — later obese — boyish-faced bon vivant. Something of a social butterfly, he had become a cross between an Oxford don and an English country squire, even to the extent of carrying a rolled umbrella and affecting a British accent during his stay in London. Born a Maryland farmboy, he attended the University of Pennsylvania and the University of Chicago. In Chicago he lived at Jane Addams's Hull House, serving as a secretary there. At the time, the famous settlement house was an intellectual and academic nexus, where Carl Sandburg, Vachel Lindsay, or Clarence Darrow might appear for a visit. Weybright became the managing editor of *Survey Graphics*, a progressive magazine, and later came to New York as an editor at Butterick Publishing, where he became familiar with the New York literary scene. In addition, he was an editorial adviser to the *Reader's Digest* and had written *Spangled Banner*, a biography of Francis Scott Key. During the war, Weybright had been responsible for establishing the London branch of the OWI, taking a special interest in the promotion of American books abroad, a role that won him the friendship of many American publishers.[5]

About the only thing Enoch and Weybright shared visibly was their pipe-smoking habit. That and something unseen but far more significant. Different as they were in temperament and personality, the two men both believed in the existence of a mass market for quality paperback books of nonfiction and fiction, even though they could publish highly commercial books of the most dubious merit. That view was the glue that cemented their relationship, a partnership that would catapult the pair to the pinnacle of the paperback industry but that would ultimately end years later in bitterness.

As soon as Weybright settled in — having been offered half of Enoch's promised equity in Penguin Books, Inc. — he set out aggressively to build the Penguin American list. One innovation was the establishment of a special editorial advisory board that would provide counsel and recommendations for both the Penguin and Pelican lines. The first two members of this panel were Judge Jerome Frank and Dr. Eduard C. Lindeman. Frank, a distinguished jurist, was a judge of the U.S. Circuit Court of Appeals and the author of articles and books, including *If Men Were Angels* and *Law and the Modern Mind*. Lindeman was a leader in the adult education field, a professor of social philosophy at Columbia since 1924, and for many years a contributing editor of the *New Republic*.

Opting for many of the writers that were feared as too scandalous or highbrow by other paperback publishers (particularly Pocket and Bantam), Weybright acquired *Pal Joey* by John O'Hara, *Bread and Wine* by Ignazio Silone, *Manhattan Transfer* by John Dos Passos, *Serenade* by James M. Cain, as well as books by William Faulkner and Erskine Caldwell.

Allen Lane undoubtedly recognized the talents of the two men he had brought together to run the American operation. But in their selection was his undoing. Neither Enoch nor Weybright could ever be comfortable working for someone else, just as Lane himself could never dance to another man's tune. To succeed in America, Penguin needed men of vision, ambition, and innovation who were attuned to the Penguin tradition — men who could combine "commerce and conscience" as one of Lane's colleagues put it. But such men need to control their own destinies, and Lane's failure to grasp this cost him dearly. The friction between Enoch and Lane came quickly. Although he had been promised a 40 percent share in the

American company — half of which he had pledged to sell to Weybright — Enoch was dismayed at Lane's failure to carry out the
agreement. Faced with the threat of Enoch's resignation and suit,
Lane finally resolved the situation late in 1946. However, the dis-
agreement had done its damage. Enoch later recalled, "The experience of the whole affair and its handling by Allen did leave its scars.
It put me on guard and raised doubts with regard to Allen's personal
reliability and credibility."

This was only the first of several sore points that soon developed
between Lane and his American colleagues. Another was Lane's
displeasure with the American system under which books were sold
to wholesalers and retailers on a returnable basis, unlike the British
system of outright sale. Nor did he have much stomach for the
illustrated covers, thinking them crass and tasteless, an opinion
shared by Eunice Frost. This was so despite the fact that — as his
own advisers had tried to convince him — the American edition of
a book outsold the same book in a British edition when they competed in the open marketplace, even though the American book
was more costly. The seriousness of this rift was made clear in a
two-page "My dear Allen" letter from Weybright to Lane on October 10, 1946. Responding to Eunice Frost's contention that Penguin
Books Limited (the British parent) would be embarrassed by the
covers and production values of certain Penguin Books, Inc., titles,
Weybright wrote:

> If this is actually the situation, it is serious. As time runs on, PBL will
> undoubtedly be embarrassed as British travelers on the Continent re-
> turn to England with American Penguins in probably greater numbers
> than would ever be imported directly to England. We are so proud of
> our intimate link with PBL that I had begun to feel that the converse
> was true and that the emerging quality of PBI editorially and produc-
> tion-wise was something which you would be increasingly proud to
> acknowledge as a legitimate product of your own genius.
>
> I am convinced more than ever that if we want to attract the Amer-
> ican masses to good literature, we have got to display on our covers
> more than a beautiful bit of typography, no matter how distinguished
> it might be. Frostie thought, and still thinks, otherwise. . . . Pocket
> Books have imitated the magazines and Bantam Books have imitated
> Pocket Books. We struck out, imitating no one, to meet the necessities
> of display with as much style and dignity as possible.
>
> We couldn't imitate the PBL format any more than the *New Yorker*

could have imitated *Punch*. The general intention of our covers is to attract Americans, who, more elementary than the Britishers, are schooled from infancy to disdain even the best product unless it is smoothly packaged and merchandised. . . . I suspect that what may annoy you about the PBI cover designs is not the covers themselves so much as the American ethos which requires a special adaptation, not necessarily a compromise, in the whole business of luring the public to better and better literature. . . ."

However, these grievances were just preliminaries to the main bout. Lane's chief complaint was the company's emerging editorial direction. In choosing such writers as James M. Cain, James T. Farrell, William Faulkner, and especially Erskine Caldwell, Weybright prompted Lane to suggest that a new imprint would be needed — Porno Books. As J. P. Morpurgo put it:

Allen regarded Penguin Books Inc. as no more than an extension of the home firm. His instincts were not tuned to American needs and he was nervous lest excesses in the program might waft a bad odour back across the Atlantic. He was not well-informed about recent developments in American fiction and his British editorial advisors were either too busy or themselves without the interest that would have persuaded them to enlighten him.[6]

These differences, it soon became clear, placed the two camps on a collision course. After long and eventually unpleasant negotiations, the association between the British parent and the American subsidiary was severed as of January 1948, and Enoch and Weybright acquired Lane's interest in the American operation, dividing it equally between themselves. Out of the breach emerged a new company, the New. American Library of World Literature, or, as it came to be known, NAL. Although there was a period of one year during which a dual imprint was used, Penguin and Pelican were eventually dropped in favor of New American Library's Signet (for fiction) and Mentor (for nonfiction) imprints.

Enoch later said that he and Weybright regretted the split. In retrospect, Lane's colleague Morpurgo termed the breakup one of Lane's major errors, considering the subsequent success of New American Library. Lane had lost the American beachhead from which he could realize his long-held hope of becoming an American publisher on a par with his standing in England. But Enoch thought otherwise:

Without the autonomy which we gained, we would not have been able
to play the innovative role in our industry. On the contrary, the denials
and the impediments to which we were subjected . . . would have
made it impossible to successfully create an American Penguin as
distinguished and powerful among its competitors as British Penguin
was in its homeland — which was Allen's ambition and inspiration.

In the short time between the marriage of Weybright's editorial
sense and voracious reading appetite to Enoch's business and production expertise and the separation from Allen Lane, the company
had made impressive gains, in terms of both sales and the quality
of the books it was publishing. In addition to Farrell and Faulkner,
Penguin Books, Inc., had reprinted the works of other major American novelists including Thomas Wolfe, Edna Ferber, Sherwood Anderson, Richard Wright, and Lillian Smith. The firm was also
publishing the works of such distinguished foreign writers as Alberto Moravia, James Joyce, Virginia Woolf, and Ignazio Silone. In
November 1946 they brought to the United States — following the
British lead — the series of classics that included the *Iliad* and the
Odyssey (translated by E. V. Rieu), Dante's *Inferno*, three plays by
Chekhov and three by Ibsen, Ovid's *Metamorphoses*, Voltaire's
Candide, Turgenev's *On the Eve*, Gorki's *Childhood*, and a selec-
tion of short stories by Maupassant. An edition of three plays by
George Bernard Shaw sold three hundred thousand copies in about
one month's time.

In the nonfiction arena, the American Pelicans were hailed as the
best in paperback and greeted with surprising success. In their first
year, about a million Pelicans were sold, despite the intransigence
of dealers who were responsible for seeing that the books found
their way into the racks, a job that often fell to some high school
student who worked part-time in the corner drugstore. The independent magazine wholesalers, who controlled the hundred thousand or so outlets — the mass market — had little interest in what
they sold, only in how fast it sold, or "turned." All too often, specialized books got lost among the multitudes of titles, a deadly
problem for more serious works that depended on long-term consistent sales rather than quick turnover. To improve the chances for
Pelican's (and later Mentor's) survival, Enoch and Weybright became missionary-educators, preaching the gospel of displaying the
Pelican/Mentor books in the paperback racks to wholesalers, key
booksellers, professors, and educators. Their efforts paid off.

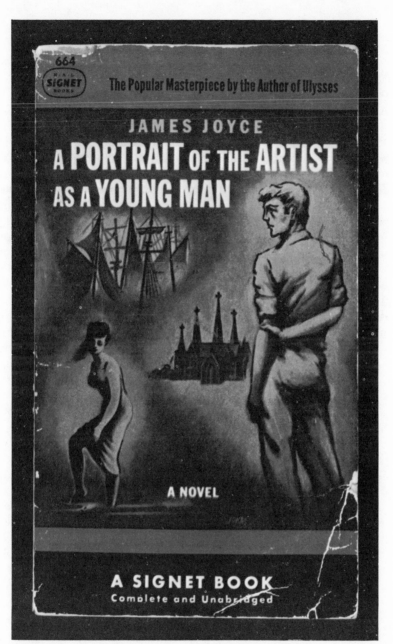

NAL's Signet imprint, the successor to Penguin, became the leading paperback publisher of outstanding literature. (Photo by Jerome Frank)

The line gradually expanded to include such works as *The Physiology of Sex* by Kenneth Walker, *Religion and the Rise of Capitalism* by R. H. Tawney, *America's Role in the World Economy* by Alvin H. Hansen, *Philosophy in a New Key* by Susan Langer, and *An Introduction to Modern Architecture* by J. M. Richards and Elizabeth Mock. The Pelicans had also crossed an important bridge when the price of the entire series was raised on September 1, 1947, to thirty-five cents, a result of the lower print runs and better production qualities required for these titles. The list had also produced a best seller of sorts in Ruth Benedict's *Patterns of Culture.* First published in 1934 by Houghton Mifflin, the book — an introduction to cultural anthropology involving the study of three sharply contrasting cultures — had sold a few hundred copies in hardcover and was as much as out of print when the Pelican edition was issued in November 1945. It sold 90,000 copies at twenty-five cents in its first year, dropped off to 45,000 copies in 1947, and hovered between 50,000 and 60,000 copies per year until it approached the million-copy mark in 1960. For its 1958 Mentor edition, NAL commissioned a preface by anthropologist Margaret Mead (also an NAL best-selling author with *Coming of Age in Samoa,* reprinted in 1949 as Mentor No. 44). In it, Mead wrote of the book's lasting impact:

> For a quarter of a century, Ruth Benedict's *Patterns of Culture* has provided a felicitous and provocative introduction to the understanding of anthropology. . . . *Patterns of Culture* has helped to knit the sciences and the humanities together during a period when they had drawn very far apart.
> When Ruth Benedict began her work in anthropology in 1921, the term "culture," as we use it today for the systematic body of learned behavior which is transmitted from parents to children, was part of the vocabulary of a small and technical group of professional anthropologists. That today the modern world is on such easy terms with the concept of culture, that the words "in our culture" slip easily from the lips of educated men and women almost as effortlessly as do the phrases that refer to period and to place, is in very great part due to this book.[7]

The success of this and other serious works in the fields of science, archeology, economics, history, and philosophy was undoubtedly an encouragement to the partners. But it was the work of one novelist that made Penguin (and later NAL) a serious competitor to Pocket Books with its superstar Erle Stanley Gardner. That writer was Erskine Caldwell. *God's Little Acre,* his 1933 novel, was not only the firm's first million-seller, but it became a cause célèbre throughout America as it gained a reputation as one of the most censored books in the country during the 1940s and 1950s. Issued as Penguin No. 581 in March 1946, *God's Little Acre* had sold 3.5 million copies in paperback by January 1948. An additional four Caldwell titles (*Tobacco Road, Tragic Ground, Journeyman,* and *Trouble in July*) reprinted by Penguin were approaching sales of one million copies each at the time of the split with Allen Lane. Indeed, the presence of Erskine Caldwell — despite his impressive paperback sales — was one of the thorns in Allen Lane's side. Lane saw no place for a writer of Caldwell's scandalous reputation in the Penguin pantheon.

Caldwell was a Georgia boy. Born in 1903 in Coweta County, the son of a minister, he attended Erskine College, the University of Virginia, and the University of Pennsylvania and had worked as a reporter for the *Atlanta Journal.* With the coming of the Depression, he struck out on the road, traveling the South and working as a mill laborer, cotton picker, cook, waiter, taxicab driver, farm hand, soda jerk, football player, bodyguard, stagehand in a burlesque house, and crewman on a gunrunner mixed up in a Central American revolt.

In his autobiographical book *Call It Experience: The Years of Learning How to Write* (1951), Caldwell recalled that he was living in Maine when he received a letter from Maxwell Perkins, the legendary Scribner's editor who had worked with Fitzgerald, Hemingway, and Thomas Wolfe. Perkins had been alerted to Caldwell's short stories by F. Scott Fitzgerald and invited him to submit his work to Scribner's. After a series of rejected stories, Perkins finally informed Caldwell that *Scribner's Magazine,* the Olympus for young writers, would accept two of his stories and pay him "two-fifty," if that was acceptable. Caldwell was taken aback by the offer and Perkins raised it to "three-fifty."

"I guess that's all right," said Caldwell. "I thought I'd get a little more than three dollars and a half, though, for both of them." Perkins quickly assured the fledgling writer that he had meant three hundred and fifty dollars.

Scribner's published the first collection of Caldwell stories, *American Earth,* in 1931. The book sold fewer than a thousand copies. A little less than a year later, his first novel, *Tobacco Road,* was released. The critics' response was generally cool, as was the

The Birth and Death of the Sun was typical of the seriousness of the Pelicans, predecessors to the Mentor books. (Photo by Jerome Frank)

book buyers' reaction. Perkins rejected Caldwell's next book, prompting the writer's agent to take him to Viking, where he was offered a contract with an option to see his next three books. They also turned down the book Perkins had rejected but published Caldwell's subsequent book, *God's Little Acre*. It appeared just as a stage version of *Tobacco Road* (adapted by Jack Kirkland) began a record-setting seven-year run on Broadway. Despite its notoriety, the trade edition of *God's Little Acre* sold only eight thousand copies by 1949, although it was reported to be one of the most popular titles released in the Armed Services Editions. Between 1946 and 1949 the Penguin and Signet paperback editions sold 4.5 million copies.

Caldwell wrote from experience and those experiences had shaped his politics. Like other Depression-era writers including Dos Passos, Sherwood Anderson, Upton Sinclair, Lincoln Steffens, and Dashiell Hammett, Caldwell openly espoused communism. And like other writers of the period — realists like Farrell, O'Hara, James M. Cain, and Dos Passos — he wrote out of the American tradition of naturalism, a school shaped by writers from Crane and Dreiser down to Hemingway. His most successful works were his southern novels, what Alfred Kazin called "comic grotesques" in his landmark study of American fiction, *On Native Grounds* (1942). They were written, commented Kazin, "with his hands and feet and any bludgeon within reach."

The most famous of these were *Tobacco Road* and *God's Little Acre*, stories about southern "poor white trash." Of the two, *God's Little Acre* was more popular. Caldwell later told an interviewer that this was probably because it was less pessimistic and depressing than *Tobacco Road*, adding, "And maybe it's a better book."[8]

God's Little Acre is a modern fable. The story follows the misadventures of the Walden family, led by father Ty Ty, whose only ambition is to find gold on his dirt-poor Georgia land. Rather than farm, Ty Ty and his two sons and two black sharecroppers spend most of their time digging huge holes. Part of the property has been set aside as "God's Little Acre," and anything produced on this land is given over to the church. Of course, "God's Little Acre" is conveniently shifted whenever it threatens to interfere with the prospecting. Alongside this almost burlesque scene with its savaging of southern religiosity is the labor battle being waged in a neighboring mill town where Ty Ty's son-in-law Will is pressing the locked-out workers to take over the mill. However, when the workers march on the factory and turn the power back on, Will is shot down, a martyr for the struggling workers. Against these blatantly Marxist underpinnings, *God's Little Acre* was also pushing — and breaking — contemporary limits of permissiveness. Although Will, the hero-worker, is married to Ty Ty's daughter Rosa, he seduces Darlin' Jill, Ty Ty's seductive nymphet daughter, and Griselda, the wife of Ty Ty's son Buck, in a steamy scene of cunnilingus in front of the other women.

Although the hardcover edition had been censored and cleared in court, the paperback edition was subject to a furious wave of banning almost from its first appearance. It is not a little ironic that it was the book's "salaciousness" and not Caldwell's politics that caused him trouble. Through the late 1940s and into the 1950s — the height of the anti-Communist period — Caldwell, an outspoken leftist, was America's most popular novelist. While other writers of the left were blacklisted or jailed, Caldwell went unscathed and sold record numbers of books. Undoubtedly, the frank — and brutal — sexuality of his books, though innocuous by contemporary standards, was partly responsible for his success. But a few suggestive passages don't sell millions of books. It was easy to find far more erotic material "under the counter" at the corner drugstore or newsstand.

Caldwell's popularity went beyond that. Like most best-selling writers, he was first and foremost a storyteller. His deceptively simple plots and style were accessible and told with a fable-like quality. He had no pretensions to literary greatness and thought of himself as a teller of tales, an heir to the South's "oral tradition," real or imagined. As he told Carvel Collins in the *Atlantic Monthly:*

> I think you must remember that a writer is a simple-minded person to start with and go on that basis. He's not a great mind, he's not a great thinker, he's not a great philosopher, he's a story teller. I mean that's the field I belong in; there are, of course, great writers who have great minds, but I don't pretend to. I can't take the responsibility of saying that I know anything that anybody else doesn't know, because I don't.[9]

Caldwell was not without critical detractors. Most condemned the language, frankness, and brutality of his work. But he also had his champions. In *Time* magazine in February 1957, William Faulkner ranked Caldwell behind only Thomas Wolfe, himself, and Dos Passos (and ahead of Hemingway) as a novelist. In *On Native*

Grounds, Alfred Kazin named Caldwell and James T. Farrell "the two most formidable left-wing naturalists." Wrote Kazin, they "brought a zest to their documentation of 'capitalistic decay' that was strangely irrelevant to Socialism, but actually the very secret of their power."[10]

But Caldwell's greatest cheerleader was none other than Victor Weybright, who campaigned long and hard for greater critical recognition for him. In 1954, Weybright was lobbying among his academic friends for honorary degrees for his best-selling writer — "in atonement for the creation, however mistakenly, of a critical impression that popularity means shoddiness." In 1957, Weybright set his sights on loftier distinctions, such as the Nobel Prize.

No such distinctions were forthcoming. Although compared favorably and often to Hemingway, Faulkner, and Steinbeck, Caldwell won no literary prizes. But his output did not abate. He produced more than thirty volumes, mostly novels and story collections but some nonfiction as well, including four books in collaboration with *Life* photographer Margaret Bourke-White, whom he married in 1939 and divorced three years later. Among these were *Have You Seen Their Faces* (1937) and *Say, Is This the U.S.A.?* (1941), which were compared to *Let Us Now Praise Famous Men,* Walker Evans and James Agee's classic photo-documentary. But toward the end of his active writing career Caldwell had fallen into self-imitation if not self-parody, and the critics began to decry his repetitiousness. His reputation in disrepair, Caldwell was briefly bolstered in 1965 with the publication of *In Search of Bisco,* a well-received nonfiction account of his return to the South in search of the black boy with whom he had played as a child (as fictionalized in *Georgia Boy,* 1943). Nonetheless, by 1961, NAL had sold more than sixty-four million Caldwells around the world, and he had been translated into more than thirty languages.

When Penguin first published *God's Little Acre* in 1946, the book's success provided more than just a hot best seller. It helped pull the company through the industry's first serious downturn. The growth at Penguin, the addition of Bantam Books, and the expansion of postwar programs at Pocket Books, Avon, Dell, and Popular Library meant that the paperback racks were becoming overcrowded. Wholesalers' warehouses were filled with slow-moving titles. One of Freeman Lewis's first acts after he arrived at Pocket Books was to institute a recall of books, because the bottleneck in the distribution system threatened to damage new releases. His action was imitated by the other houses, and millions of books were returned in 1946, the first in a series of up-and-down years that would continue to haunt the industry.

Before that time, unsold books had posed no serious problems for the paperback houses. The few books that were not sold could simply be exchanged for new titles, and they were shipped elsewhere to meet demand. Bud Egbert, a long-time Pocket Books executive who worked his way up through the sales ranks, was then working with his father, who operated a "galley," or reship distributor, in the Southwest that sent books by mail to dealers who were not serviced by an independent wholesaler. During the war years, Egbert recalled, "Every book that was printed was sold. If anybody made a return, you called them up and asked what was wrong. You even threatened that if they continued to do that you would have to give the books to someone else. Basically you gave the books to your friends because supplies were short. By 1949, that was over."

The problems caused by overproduction did not end with the 1946 callback. Returns became a perennial plague on the paperback industry. In the late 1940s, the paperback houses tried to increase their sales by publishing more titles rather than increasing unit sales on fewer titles. Bantam, for instance, went from four to six books per month in 1947 and to eight titles per month in 1948. The excesses in production, spurred by the renewed availability of paper stocks and reduced costs, meant more books were flowing into the distribution pipeline. Yet while total book sales were on the rise, the universe of outlets was not expanding rapidly enough to absorb the increased output of titles. By the mid-1950s, the problem was epidemic, and for relief the wholesalers demanded and got a shift to the magazine industry's system of returning only the cover of the book instead of the complete book; the body of the book would be either destroyed or shredded and sold for pulp. When production costs were as low as they were at this time, it was an efficient, if somewhat dismaying, solution.

But the publishers were looking for new methods of control along with improving the efficiency of returning books. Pocket Books began testing titles in selected cities before their release in an effort to predetermine realistic print runs. Bantam also attempted a testing method. Employing the Curtis Circulating Company's field men, Bantam based its back-to-press reprints on ten-day checkups of titles in selected cities. Ian Ballantine maintained that an accurate sales curve could be predicted, enabling the company to reprint books more efficiently. With this system, Bantam claimed to be keeping its returns to the unlikely figure of 1 percent. Pocket Books also made the first experiments in "selective distribution." Until 1946, all Pocket Book titles were printed in roughly equivalent quantities and indiscriminately shipped out to the wholesalers, regardless of the book's potential sales. In October 1947, they switched instead to a system in which books were given a ranking — 1, 2, 3, or 4 — based on anticipated sales. A No. 1 title was given an initial printing of 400,000 copies and full-scale distribution. This was soon increased to 500,000 copies, with 100,000 copies held in reserve to meet the demand for reorders; on unusually major titles, such as an Erle Stanley Gardner, initial printings of 750,000 to one million copies were not unheard of. Books in groups 2, 3, and 4 varied from 150,000 to 250,000 initial copies, with their distribution proportionate to their anticipated sales rankings. But another flaw in the system went unreformed; the publishers still decided how many books a wholesaler would receive and "force-fed" those books to the wholesalers without realistically determining their ability to sell them.

Paperback houses were also looking for new opportunities for sales and revenues. Pocket and Bantam both experimented with the first use of advertising in their books in 1947, although the ads were limited at first to the Book-of-the-Month Club and other book clubs; no general space advertising was accepted — yet. Another new direction was the educational field, and in 1945, Pocket Books began the Teen-Age Book Show under the direction of Martha Huddleston. The show brought books to children in 229 cities. In 1946, Pocket Books and Huddleston formed the Teen-Age Book Club, which brought paperbacks to students. In 1948, *Scholastic* magazine shared sponsorship of the club, which grew to include other publishers' books. In 1947, Bantam also started a separate imprint, Scholastic Bantams, in association with the magazine, using twenty-six of the titles already on their list — which they withdrew from the marketplace temporarily — as well as new titles aimed just at the school market. The first of these was *Twenty Grand Short Stories*, a collection of American short stories *Scholastic* had published as *Here We Are*.

A far more significant educational market was opening up at the college level. College enrollment after the war boomed, urged on by the Servicemen's Readjustment Act of 1944. Through its financial assistance to veterans, the GI Bill meant that a college education, once the birthright of the wealthy, would be open to millions of ex-servicemen who otherwise would have gone directly into the work force. According to the Veterans Administration, 2.3 million veterans studied in colleges and universities under the GI Bill. New American Library was in the best position to exploit this new market and meet the demand for college-level books in paperback. With its Mentor list of serious nonfiction and the Signet list of quality fiction, NAL gained admission to the college market through a force of college travelers who went to the university bookstores and won classroom adoptions for Mentor and Signet titles.

The GI Bill was also responsible in part for another social tidal wave. Those veterans making up for lost time with their wives had less fear about paying for a family: the GI Bill provided. Thus began the baby boom, starting in 1946. It was the boom that gave Dr. Spock an immediate audience and made his name a household word overnight.

Other changes were afoot as the 1940s began to fade. They could be seen in what America was reading. During the war years, the most popular novels had been religious epics like *The Keys of the Kingdom* (1941), *The Song of Bernadette* (1942), *The Robe* (1943), and *The Miracle of the Bells* (1947). No doubt their inspirational value was behind their success in the uncertain days of the war. But by 1948, Americans were ready to examine the war, and they had two novels from which to choose; both ended up as best sellers. Norman Mailer's *The Naked and the Dead*, with its tough barracks language (Mailer's use of *fug* in place of *fuck* was suggested by his cousin, attorney Charles Rembar, who pointed out that it was a simple way to avoid the censors and more accurately reproduce the soldiers' pronunciation), and Irwin Shaw's *The Young Lions* painted new portraits of the American fighting man. Both were critical and popular successes. Mailer's first novel, *The Naked and the Dead* made him an overnight sensation and sold a little under 200,000 copies that year. Shaw's book, also a first novel after his success with story writing, sold 78,050 copies in 1948. Both books would find much larger audiences when NAL reprinted them a few years later.

While these novels presented a darker picture of Americans at war, there were other unsettling shadows on the landscape. In 1947, Jackie Robinson broke professional baseball's color line. The race question had been broached in two best sellers: *Strange Fruit* (1944), Lillian Smith's first novel, told of blacks and whites in the South. (It was the surprise fiction leader that year.) *Black Boy* (1945), Richard Wright's stark autobiography, sold half a million copies (including book club sales). Both of these books would also be reprinted by NAL.

In Washington, a rising young man with a bright political future, Alger Hiss, was accused of passing secrets to the Communists. Russia had the Bomb. And the Communists had China. The new threat called cold war turned hot when the Russians blockaded Berlin, forcing the famous airlift that kept the western sector of the city alive. What William Manchester called the Age of Suspicion had dawned.

It was also an age of new fears created by the mushroom cloud that now hung on the horizon. The power of the atomic bomb was an abstraction to most people after its first use against Japan. But all that changed with a 1946 article in *The New Yorker*, which Knopf published in book form and Bantam reprinted in March 1948. The thin volume was John Hersey's *Hiroshima*, a masterpiece of contemporary reporting. It did more to open eyes to the destructive power that man had unleashed than anything before it or anything since. In 1982, as the antinuclear movement gained momentum around the world, *The New Yorker* once again issued an article on the nuclear issue, which Knopf once again published in book form. Jonathan Schell's *The Fate of the Earth* was then published in paperback by Avon Books, which had paid a guarantee of $375,000 for the reprint rights. Schell's book, a scientific, political, and metaphysical treatise on the effects of a nuclear war — in brief, the end of humanity — was one of the most widely discussed and influential books of the year. Yet for sheer emotional impact and the power of humanizing the destructive power of the atomic bomb, *Hiroshima* remains unsurpassed.

Born in Tientsin, China, in 1914, John Hersey was the son of missionaries and went on to school at Yale and Cambridge before returning to China as a correspondent for *Time* magazine. He became a favorite of *Time*'s owner Henry Luce, also born in China, and was one of the magazine's star attractions. While in China,

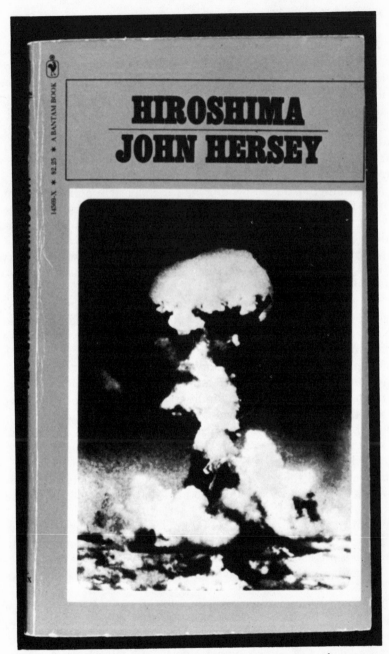

A later edition of *Hiroshima*, John Hersey's masterpiece of reportage and a multimillion-seller for Bantam. (Photo by Jerome Frank)

Hersey also brought Theodore H. White in as a *Time* stringer. During the war, Hersey was a combat correspondent for *Time* and *Life* and wrote two nonfiction accounts of the war. One of these, *Into the Valley*, was the second of the Council on Books in Wartime "Imperative" books. Another of his articles in *The New Yorker* made a hero out of a young navy officer named Kennedy for his exploits aboard *PT-109*. In 1944, his first novel, *A Bell for Adano*, about an American officer's problems in occupied Italy, won the Pulitzer Prize, was a best seller and was reprinted by Bantam.

On his way back from postwar China, where he had been reporting for *Life*, Hersey went to Japan, where, as the Bantam Books copy later put it, the "ashes were still warm." There he interviewed survivors of the Hiroshima blast and submitted the report to *The New Yorker* instead of *Life*. Luce was furious and Hersey was gone from Time, Inc., but only after he told Luce that there was as much truthful reporting in *Pravda* as there was in *Time*.[11]

Although *Hiroshima* had had considerable impact as an article and hardcover book, it was certainly no best seller. Realizing the difficulty of publishing a book so sympathetic to the Japanese in the postwar years, Bantam played its cards cautiously, if somewhat misleadingly. The cover of the first paperback edition showed a man and woman, looking anything but Oriental, walking away from a bright light. The woman wore completely Western clothing and neither she nor the man was tattered or injured. The copy read: "Six Survived to Tell What Happened." This cover approach had been tested and approved for Bantam by the Gallup organization. If the cover was deceptive, it was — to Ian Ballantine at least — a practical necessity. "We thought the book was important. We wanted people to read it. We couldn't very well just say 'wipeout.'" The Bantam edition went through five printings during the next seven years, and became a staple of the Bantam backlist and assigned reading for most American students. By 1980, there were more than four million copies of the paperback edition.

This was not Bantam's only plunge into the area. In 1949, the company reprinted Dr. David Bradley's *No Place to Hide*, a "layman's guide" to atomic bombs, written by a Columbia professor and witness to the atomic testing at the Bikini Atoll. Telling Americans that "one bomb could destroy a big city" and that the "bomb could be easily smuggled into a town," the book did not make any best-seller lists. But this was Ian Ballantine at his best, publishing topical books with full enthusiasm, something he had learned from his mentor Allen Lane.

As if Communists and the Bomb were not enough to worry about, America also had to face a new revelation that struck closer to home. The shock was delivered by a book that forced Americans to look at themselves in a new light. It came from an unexpected quarter, the University of Indiana at Bloomington, where Dr. Alfred Kinsey, who had previously confined his interests to the sex life of insects, had discovered that men and women knew very little about their own sex lives. Using a two-and-a-half hour, 300- to 500-question interview, Kinsey and his associates compiled more than twelve thousand case histories. Confining their research to no group in particular, the team uncovered patterns of sexual behavior among Americans from all walks of life that completely shattered the myth of American innocence. Sex may not have been talked about among "decent" Americans, but actions — as reported by Kinsey — spoke thunderously. It was as if Kinsey had unearthed some secret society. Among his revelations:

- 85 percent of all married men had engaged in sexual intercourse before marriage.
- 50 percent of all American husbands committed adultery.
- The average unmarried male had three or four orgasms per week.
- One male in three — and one female in seven — had some adolescent homosexual experience.

Word of Kinsey's research began to filter out of Bloomington. When Lawrence Saunders of the W. B. Saunders Company, a Philadelphia medical text publisher, heard Kinsey speak, he signed the sex researcher to a contract. They planned a 10,000-copy first printing of *Sexual Behavior in the Human Male* but advance interest pushed that figure to 25,000. Within ten days of its release, it was reprinted six times, for a total of 185,000 copies. Needless to say, W. B. Saunders had never had a best seller before. The book eventually sold 225,000 copies to readers who were probably disappointed to be confronted by a ponderous research work complete with statistical charts and graphs. It has been suggested that *Sexual Behavior and the Human Male* was one of the most unread best sellers of all time.

While the lengthy book never found a paperback publisher, two paperback houses moved quickly to respond to public interest in the subject, once again proving the paperback's ability to publish topically — and do it well. Although not "instant" books, two serious studies of the Kinsey Report by New American Library and Bantam were soon available in the paperback racks. An original paperback, *About the Kinsey Report,* a Signet Special, was released on May 29, 1948, in a 750,000-copy printing. The book was a compilation of eleven essays by a group of doctors, social scientists, economists, theologians, and educators that included Erich Fromm and Ashley Montagu. The editor of the project was none other than Donald Porter Geddes, who had departed from Pocket Books in 1945 after he had brought Dr. Spock to the company. For the volume, Geddes wrote an introductory essay, "New Light on Sexual Knowledge," which used many of the original graphs published in the Saunders edition and commented upon the major social impact that Kinsey's Report was creating:

> While each of these [eleven] persons has a different reason for thinking the Kinsey Report important, they all add up to the same thing — they think that the world will be a happier, more peaceful place, that there will be more justice in it, and that individuals properly educated in terms of sexuality will make better children, more law-abiding citizens, happier, better — much better — parents, when our knowledge of human nature has been augmented and implemented by a scientific knowledge of the sex drive.[12]

NAL reported one month later that the book had not only outsold the original Kinsey Report but that it had sold faster, NAL believed, than any other book in American publishing history. The first printing of 750,000 copies was exhausted within ten days of publication, and a second printing of 750,000 copies was ordered. Newsstands accounted for 95 percent of the total sales, and although it was packaged tastefully, with a symbolic male figure and a statistical graph on the cover (by artist Robert Jonas), the book undoubtedly appealed to the curious who expected a cheap thrill. They would be disappointed. Another interesting fact about the NAL edition was the review attention — practically unheard of for twenty-five-cent paperbacks — it received. (It was, however, ignored by the *New York Times,* which refused to review or accept advertising for the original Kinsey Report despite the fact the book was on the newspaper's own best-seller list.)

The second Kinsey-related paperback was a reprint of *American*

Sexual Behavior and the Kinsey Report, originally published by Greystone Press in May 1948 and released by Bantam as its leading title in July of that year. The book was a simplified version of the Kinsey Report, but it was no slapdash affair. It was co-authored by David Loth and Morris Ernst, who was already well known as a champion of liberal causes and most famous for his defense of *Ulysses* in the landmark case finding Joyce's masterpiece not obscene.

With these endeavors, some paperback houses were making an effort to establish their legitimacy as publishers. While the mystery / detective thrillers, Westerns, and romances constituted about one-third of all paperbacks being published by the late 1940s, titles of lasting impact were also coming to the surface. They were being originated or revived as well as reprinted by Bantam, New American Library, and Pocket Books. Even the category houses, such as Popular Library, were trying to upgrade their image with an occasional serious novel.

KEY POSTWAR PAPERBACK RELEASES

1946

Georgia Boy by Erskine Caldwell (Avon).

Babbitt by Sinclair Lewis (Bantam).

Only Yesterday by Frederick Lewis Allen (Bantam. Ian Ballantine commented that this book, a study of the 1920s, was especially timely because it suggested parallels between postwar troubles in the 1940s and those of 1919 and 1920).

Public Opinion by Walter Lippmann (Pelican).

Patterns of Culture by Ruth Benedict (Pelican).

An Enemy of the People: Anti-Semitism by James Parkes (Pelican).

God's Little Acre by Erskine Caldwell (Penguin).

The Pocket Book of Baby and Child Care by Dr. Benjamin Spock (Pocket Books).

The Atomic Age Opens by Donald Porter Geddes (Pocket Books).

1947

Duel in the Sun by Niven Busch (Popular Library. The basis for the Gregory Peck–Jennifer Jones hit movie, this became Popular Library's first multimillion-seller and further attested to the pull of the Hollywood-paperback connection).

A Tree Grows in Brooklyn by Betty Smith (Bantam).

The Pearl by John Steinbeck (Bantam. Released as a simultaneous hardcover-paperback edition and as a movie tie-in).

Citizen Tom Paine by Howard Fast (Bantam).

Young Lonigan by James T. Farrell (Penguin-Signet).

Short Stories by Thomas Wolfe (Penguin).

Journeyman by Erskine Caldwell (Penguin).

Uncle Tom's Children by Richard Wright (Penguin. Five stories by the author of *Native Son* and *Black Boy*).

A Portrait of the Artist as a Young Man by James Joyce (Penguin. The cover line read, "The Popular Masterpiece by the author of *Ulysses*").

Introduction to Modern Architecture by J. M. Richards and Elizabeth B. Mock (A Pelican paperback original).

Good Reading, edited by the Committee on College Reading (Pelican. An original-paperback bibliography of the world's great literature).

1948

Hiroshima by John Hersey (Bantam).

American Sexual Behavior and the Kinsey Report by David Loth and Morris Ernst (Bantam).

About the Kinsey Report by Donald Porter Geddes and Enid Curie (Signet).

The Wild Palms by William Faulkner (Penguin-Signet).

Tragic Ground by Erskine Caldwell (Penguin-Signet).

Philosophy in a New Key by Susan Langer (Pelican-Mentor).

100 American Poems, edited by Selden Rodman (Penguin-Signet).

Strange Fruit by Lillian Smith (Penguin-Signet).

Christ Stopped at Eboli by Carlo Levi (Penguin-Signet).

They Shoot Horses, Don't They? by Horace McCoy (Signet).

Darkness at Noon by Arthur Koestler (Penguin-Signet).

The Snake Pit by Mary Jane Ward (Signet).

Look Homeward, Angel by Thomas Wolfe (Signet).

I, the Jury by Mickey Spillane (Signet).

Tales from the Decameron by Boccaccio (Pocket. Included ten pages of two-color illustrations, a major departure for paperbacks).

Tales of the South Pacific by James Michener (Pocket).

Anna Karenina by Leo Tolstoy (Pocket. A movie tie-in edition, it was called "streamlined" — in other words, abridged).

1949

The Amboy Dukes by Irving Shulman (Avon. First of the "gang novel" genre).

A Farewell to Arms by Ernest Hemingway (Bantam).

No Place to Hide by Dr. David Bradley (Bantam).

Other Voices, Other Rooms by Truman Capote (NAL-Signet).

Intruder in the Dust by William Faulkner (NAL-Signet).

If He Hollers, Let Him Go by Chester Himes (NAL-Signet).

The Age of Jackson by Arthur M. Schlesinger, Jr. (NAL-Mentor. 1946 Pulitzer Prize winner for history).

The Iliad, translated by W. D. Rouse (NAL-Mentor).

While this sampling represented the effort being made to publish good books for the paperback market, competition was creating a more disturbing trend. Just as Max Schuster had warned back in 1942, the lowest-common-denominator approach was attracting the attention of paperback houses with increasingly dismal results. Part of the problem was the rush of small fly-by-night operations that wanted to exploit the growing success of twenty-five-cent books. Among them were such short-lived imprints as Green Dragon Books, Handi-Books, Pony Books, Bonded Mysteries, Hip Books, Graphic Books, and Checkerbooks. Few lasted more than a year or two.

To the wholesalers, for whom turnover was all, the mysteries, thrillers, hard-boiled novels, and "sexy books" seemed to turn faster in the mass market racks, even if their success was fleeting. Early on, pressure began to be applied for more of these, and the publishers, particularly those who had come from the magazine side of the business, responded readily. The shift in the mass market by the end of the 1940s was disturbing enough to merit a warning from Frederic Melcher of *The Publishers' Weekly*, a long-time advocate of inexpensive books, in an editorial called "A Cycle That Can End in Vulgarity." Reminding his readers of the paperbacks' shady nineteenth-century past, Melcher pointed out that the earlier generation of paperbound books "started with melodrama, wild west and detective stories, and tended toward a vulgarity which brought about their end, when flashiness could go no further." He continued:

> We are sending memory back over this nineteenth century record because there can be danger that our present cycle might run over the same route, and we hope it will not. The present era has been extended by a half dozen major imprints, and again bases its wide acceptance on the popular appetite for mysteries, westerns and romance. The readers have not changed too much in their interest from seventy-five years ago. But more than before, the publishers of paper-covered books have done an important piece of work for the spread of reading, by planning all sorts of compendiums, anthologies, and the like, which had no counterpart in the output of the earlier publishers mentioned.
>
> On the trail of the wide distribution of books of adventure and romance, a vulgarity has sometimes appeared which, as at the end of the dime novel period, can spread an unhappy aura over the whole area of paper-covered series. This reaching out for more readers by following the earlier lead of the pulps as to covers and text is as unfortunate as

would be a trend towards copying the comics in their experiments with the themes of crime and passion. . . . In less than ten years, the paper book market has become a matter of importance in book trade decisions. The new market has been built up by the appeal of titles and jackets, and can be lost by copying the worst appeals of pulps and comics, which are on simultaneous display. It is important that quality be kept up.[13]

Unfortunately, Melcher's plea fell on deaf ears. By the turn of the 1950s, the lure of quick profits meant that paperback houses were rushing to see who could be more bold than the others. It was bringing out the worst in even the best of the paperback houses. The trend toward lowest-common-denominator appeal manifested itself in several areas: cover illustrations and cover copy, retitling, abridgments, and editorial selection.

Through the industry's first five years, covers were almost primitively simple; often symbolic rather than realistic, they were frequently whimsical and hardly daring. But dramatic changes came in the years after the war. The paperback houses, imitating the worst magazines, pulps, and comics, discovered that sex sells. Soon, new books were testing the limits of propriety on local newsstands. Old books were given new covers, classics were misrepresented, and a passage in a book that contained the slightest suggestive connotation became the passage that was illustrated on the front cover. A book that did not feature a woman in some state of undress — and preferably reclining — was difficult to find.

Nothing was sacred. The 1944 Pocket Books edition of *The Maltese Falcon*, for instance, had a cover showing three hands reaching toward the falcon statuette; the copy read simply, "Sam Spade and the Black Bird." For a reissue in 1947, however, a new illustration appeared. This one showed a woman getting undressed while a man sat on the other side of a sheer curtain fingering a high-heeled shoe, a pair of panties draped across his leg. The copy now read, "Sam Spade searched each article of the girl's clothing." One of the few cases of Marshall Field's direct involvement in a Pocket Books decision came over a cover. A planned illustration for *Lust for Life*, Irving Stone's novel about van Gogh, depicted a nude. Field vetoed the cover, not because of moral grounds but because he argued that van Gogh had never painted a nude.

Bantam, which had started off with tasteful art and excellent design work, soon fell into the trap of dishonest blurbs and sugges-

The changes in covers on the Pocket Books edition of *The Maltese Falcon* illustrate the changing trend in cover art. (Photos by Kevin Hancer; by permission of Pocket Books, a division of Simon & Schuster, Inc.)

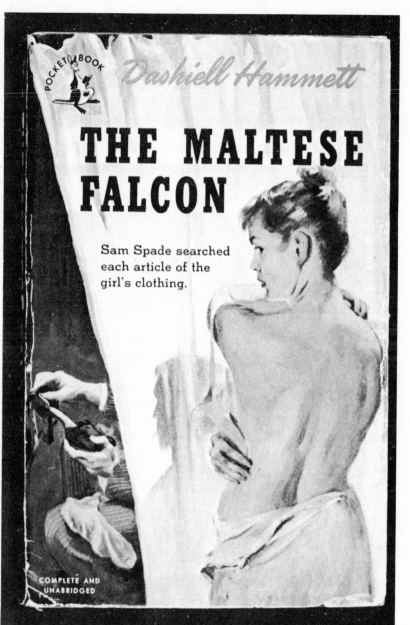

Dashiell Hammett

THE MALTESE FALCON

Sam Spade searched
each article of the
girl's clothing.

tive covers. Sinclair Lewis's novel *Babbitt* was first released with a simple drawing of a man looking up at the title. For a later reissue, a highly realistic cover was used. In it, Babbitt walked arm in arm with his wife while a woman in a tight skirt leered at him. The copy read, "What did this man want?" In a legendary case of re-titling, a Bantam book called *Five Days* sold better as *Five Nights*. Theater and film critic Stanley Kauffmann, who was a Bantam editor, recalled, "I chose a good novel by Shirley Jackson, a very delicate book. In the course of the story, a woman can't sleep and goes out for a walk. The copy read, 'A married woman prowls the back streets.' At least I didn't write that one. But I wouldn't say I never wrote anything kissing kin to it. It's not really news that sex sells. We're using the word *sex* in the 1949 context, which is a very long way from the 1981 context. A woman in a gauzy nightgown you could vaguely see was a sexy 1949 cover." In 1948, Bantam produced the first "beefcake" cover, a picture of a naked man climbing out of the water, a scene from *The African Queen* by C. S. Forester.

While Bantam, Pocket, and NAL were all guilty of moving in the direction of superrealistic covers emphasizing sex, the leaders in bad taste were still the pulp-oriented publishers, and Popular Library probably deserved the crown of worst offender. One of the most famous of the company's covers was for *The Private Life of Helen of Troy*, a 1925 best seller by John Erskine. Popular Library's 1948 cover showed a statuesque woman whose nipples could plainly be seen through her sheer toga. Known as the "nipple cover," it was unusual because few illustrations went so far and the artist got away with it here supposedly because Helen was a figure from classical antiquity.[14] By 1950, Popular Library was trumpeting its revealing covers as a selling point to the trade. An ad in *PW* shouted, "HERE ARE THE BARE FACTS! It's the cover that reaches out and gets attention first — and Popular Library covers are eye-dazzlers!"

On the plus side, there were good covers being drawn as well, and the highest artistic standards were those set at NAL with its two stars, Robert Jonas and James Avati. A European whose work was influenced by the Bauhaus school, Jonas was first employed by Kurt Enoch, who gave a sympathetic ear to Jonas's notions of design. He gave the Mentors their singular look. Many of his covers employed arrangements of geometric shapes and representative art rather than starkly realistic illustrations. His most famous illustration was

A Nobel Prize did not protect an author's work from being misrepresented. (Photo by Kevin Hancer)

Popular Library's famous "nipple cover." (Photo by Kevin Hancer)

probably a Penguin edition of *God's Little Acre* in which he first used the "peephole" format that became a basic element in all the Signet Caldwell books until later editions employed new covers. In it, a board fence is depicted and a knothole in the boards allows the reader to peer into the Walden family farm.

James Avati's work was far more realistic but with an almost romantic softness, as in his cover for D. H. Lawrence's *Sons and Lovers*. One of Avati's most famous — or notorious — covers was the one for J. D. Salinger's *The Catcher in the Rye*, a most inoffensive cover that the author nonetheless detested and was partly responsible for Salinger's decision to seek a new paperback publisher when the license on the book expired a few years later. Together, Jonas and Avati set standards for paperback illustration that were rarely equalled by their frequent imitators.

Yet even NAL was seeing its way to sexier covers, although the company never quite sank to the extreme depths of many of their competitors. But by the beginning of the 1950s, the sensational cover had taken over the paperback racks. Sadly, at the moment that the paperback book was beginning to win praise for its contribution in improving literacy and spreading the market for writers, the trend toward exploitation blackened the industry's image. Competition had sent the business down the low road. The 1950s started out with growing sales potential for paperback books, but their reputation had been badly soiled. Critics who called them junk or trash had legitimate reasons. And the debate over quality in the paperback business would dominate the next few years of its history.

Three covers by Robert Jonas, including the "peephole" effect on Truman Capote's *Other Voices, Other Rooms.* (Photo by Jerome Frank)

A typical James Avati cover for New American Library. (Photo by Jerome Frank)

1001

J. D. SALINGER

The Catcher in the Rye

This unusual book may shock you, will make you laugh, and may break your heart—but you will never forget it

A SIGNET BOOK
Complete and Unabridged

James Avati's most notorious cover eventually cost NAL the rights to Salinger's work. (Photo by Jerome Frank)

SEVEN

Two-Bit Culture: The Great Contradiction

They were Commies. . . . They were red sons of bitches who should have died long ago. . . . They never thought there were people like me in this country.
— Mickey Spillane, *One Lonely Night* (1951)

If our publication can expedite the flow of international literature, it will fulfill its most important purpose.
— Introduction to *New World Writing* No. 1 (1952)

DURING THE first ten years of its existence, the mass market paperback had been the subject of frequent arguments and controversy, but most of the discussion took place within the publishing industry. Trade publishers either liked or didn't like what the paperback houses produced and treated them accordingly. Some trade houses still refused to sell rights to the reprinters. Among the others who did, there were those who handled the reprinters gingerly, like dead fish, at arm's length. Often they assigned a secretary the task of carrying out reprint arrangements. (Ironically, that strategy placed many women in key roles just as subsidiary rights flowered in importance to hardcover publishers.) However, the option of ignoring the paperback grew less viable as the reprint was increasingly viewed as a source of income. Reprint royalties were once thought of as icing on the cake of regular trade and book-club sales. But this income was beginning to mount as paperback sales grew, more titles were reprinted, and prices, led by Mentors and Dr. Spock, crept up to thirty-five cents. By the fifties, some hardcover publishers had already turned to the practice of lining up paperback guarantees before signing contracts with the author for a book. Economically at least, the paperback had come of age.

Soon the rest of the world was sitting up and taking notice of this precocious ten-year-old. To be sure, much of the discussion centered on those (gasp! ugh!) covers. And a great deal of the press coverage accorded to paperbacks treated them as a sort of novelty, a late-1940s version of the Hula-Hoop or Pac-Man. With the coming of the fifties, there was a fundamental change in attitude. Previously, all talk of a Paperback Revolution had been limited to Publishers' Row. But as the sales figures climbed at a seemingly geometric rate, the serious journals, pulse takers, and opinion makers realized it was time to turn this flat rock over and see what crawled out. In the process, they would decide exactly what it all meant for the Republic. Some liked what they found; others thought they had uncovered evidence of the decline of Western civilization. Predictably, there was little agreement. It was the dawn of the great debate over paperback books.

One of the first critics to take a serious look at paperbacks and what they meant was Harvey Swados. Writing in the *Nation* in 1951, Swados outlined the essence of the disaccord that lay ahead:

> Last year, the stupefying total of 214,000,000 paper-bound books was published in this country, as compared with 3,000,000 in 1939. Most of them were sold and the probability is that a larger proportion of them was read than of hard-cover books, many of which are bought as unwanted gifts or as book-club prestige items for the coffee table. Whether this revolution in the reading habits of the American public means that we are being inundated by a flood of trash which will debase farther the popular taste, or that we shall now have available cheap editions of an ever-increasing list of classics, is a question of basic importance to our social and cultural development.[1]

The business that Swados was examining with such gravity was in a state of flux, a rapidly changing period of transition from newborn industry to one in healthy adolescence, complete with growing pains, as new companies seemed to come and go almost overnight. Paperback sales were moving forward, and each year after 1946 brought increases in production and sales. As 1950 began, *The Pub-*

lishers' Weekly reported that a large increase in paperback production was planned for the year, and it told of caution and concern among the reprinters who recalled the overproduction and devastating returns of 1946. Nevertheless, most paperback publishers were reporting steady sales gains that went as high as 40 percent over previous years.[2] By year's end, a survey of the industry estimated 1950 paperback sales at 200 million copies (compared with 147 million in 1948 and 184 million in 1949), with some eight hundred titles issued, worth about $46 million in revenue. A breakdown of production by individual firm gave an indication of Pocket Books' size and relative strength: Pocket, 50 million books; Bantam, 38 million; New American Library, 30 million; Dell, 25 million; Avon, 15 million; Popular Library, 15 million.[3]

Another indication of the changing face of the paperback business was the upward movement in cover prices. For ten years, twenty-five cents had been an inviolable barrier, with two exceptions: Penguin had pushed the price of the nonfiction Pelicans (later NAL's Mentors) to thirty-five cents, and Pocket Books had done likewise with *The Pocket Book of Baby and Child Care,* which had already become the company's fastest and best-selling book. But fiction was still universally priced at twenty-five cents in paperback. Then, in June 1950, New American Library shook the industry by announcing its plans to publish longer novels at thirty-five and fifty cents. In order to get customers to shell out the extra dime, NAL called the thirty-five cent books Signet Giants. (Allen Lane had already used a similar strategy in England with Penguin Giants.)

The first book in the thirty-five-cent series was Richard Wright's *Native Son.* Wright was born outside Natchez, Mississippi, in 1908, the son of a sharecropper who deserted the family when Wright was five. After a childhood of roving from one foster home to the next, he ended up in Chicago in 1927, living on odd jobs and going on relief when the Depression hit. He joined the Communist party in 1934 and turned his talent to writing Marxist publications, later working for the Federal Writers' Project. In 1936, after moving to New York, he wrote the *WPA Guide to Harlem,* and in 1938 he won a prize from *Story* magazine for his novelette "Uncle Tom's Children," which became the title story in a collection published that same year. Living in Brooklyn on a Guggenheim Fellowship, he wrote his first novel, *Native Son* (1940). It was a brutally violent story of a young black man in Chicago whose frustrated circumstances force him to commit murder. Highly naturalistic, the novel established Wright as a major talent. A stage version followed and then a film in which Wright himself played the lead. In 1945, he added *Black Boy*, an autobiographical account of his first seventeen years, to his accomplishments. It became a best seller that year, a rather extraordinary achievement for a black writer in a still over-whelmingly racist society.

When NAL published *Native Son* in 1950, the company had es-tablished itself as the only mass market reprinter willing to consis-tently handle serious work by black writers or about blacks. In addition to Wright's work, NAL (Penguin before it) had published Chester Himes's *If He Hollers, Let Him Go* and Lillian Smith's *Strange Fruit*, a 1944 best seller about racial relations in the South that had been banned in Boston in a notorious First Amendment case. Later NAL would publish Wright's *Black Boy* and Ralph Elli-son's *Invisible Man*.

The company's plan for fifty-cent books required a subtle decep-tion, and it is unlikely that anyone was actually fooled by it. Kurt Enoch devised what he called a double spine, printed in two colors on which the book's title appeared twice, giving the appearance of two books in one. The first of the Signet Double Volumes were Willard Motley's *Knock on Any Door*, Kathleen Winsor's *Forever Amber*, Irwin Shaw's *The Young Lions*, and Norman Mailer's *The Naked and the Dead*. The increase in cover price was more than simply a way to make more money. The rise was unavoidable be-cause of two factors. With a twenty-five-cent ceiling, longer books could not be profitably published without abridgments or conden-sations. This kept many major writers and books from being re-printed. More significant was the fact that the new cover prices reflected an increasing intensity in the competition for desirable reprint properties. The success of Pocket Books' rivals, specifically NAL and Bantam, meant that jockeying for rights to major novels was becoming more fierce.

The system of acquiring paperback reprints had evolved out of the formula established by the dollar hardcover reprinters like Gros-set & Dunlap during the 1930s. The paperback publisher licensed for a limited time the right to issue a paperbound edition of a book at a certain price in English and to sell it in certain specified parts of the world. The paperback publisher guaranteed a stated amount of money (the advance), whether the book earned back the money

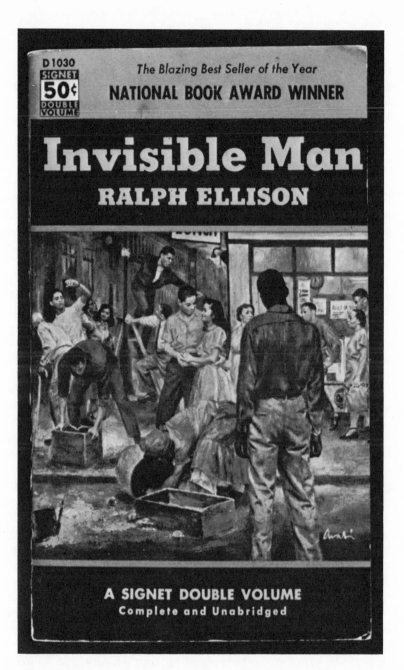

An early Double Volume, this edition of *Invisible Man* featured an Avati cover that pulsed with street energy. (Photo by Jerome Frank)

or not. In the early years, this royalty rate was one cent on the first 150,000 copies and one and a half cents on sales thereafter; if the retail price was higher, the royalty was proportionately increased. The paperback royalties were then split fifty-fifty between author and original hardcover publisher.

The method of acquiring reprint rights involved a simple sealed-bid auction. The winner was the publisher who offered the largest advance without knowledge of what his competitors were proposing. Such modern paperback auction techniques as "floors" (minimums), "topping privileges," and round-robin auctions in which successive bids are solicited by the auctioneer were all creatures of the future. But the auction was where explosive changes were already beginning to transform the paperback and upset the traditional balance of publishing power. By 1952, Doc Lewis of Pocket Books cautioned, "Increasingly, the amount of money required to secure a reprint contract is reaching a level above the amount which is being earned by sales. I would estimate that of the 'big bid' books of the past two years, that is, titles which were acquired by guarantees of *$15,000 or more* [Emphasis added], less than five will ever earn out their minimum guarantees."[4]

The "big bid" books to which Lewis referred undoubtedly included the four titles NAL had issued as Double Volumes. Victor Weybright, in a sort of mad shopping spree, purchased all four books in one week in February 1950, paying $30,000 for *Forever Amber*, $30,000 for *The Naked and the Dead*, $25,000 for *The Young Lions*, and $25,000 for *Knock on Any Door*. With the exception of Willard Motley's *Knock on Any Door*, each book had been a best seller a few years earlier. Mailer's novel had almost reached 200,000 combined bookstore–book-club sales in 1948 and *The Young Lions* had sold around 75,000 copies. Kathleen Winsor's *Forever Amber* was a historical romance with an emphasis on the bawdy, set during the Restoration period. It became the number-four fiction best seller in 1944, was banned in Boston, and then became the number-one seller in 1945, selling 868,630 copies that year alone. Miss Winsor, very photogenic and highly publicized by her hardcover publisher, might have fit in nicely on the television talk show circuit if one had existed in 1945. She looked pretty, could draw a crowd, and yet had little to say. On a promotional tour for Victory bonds during the war, Winsor traveled with Bennett Cerf, MacKinlay Kantor, and Carl Van Doren. Cerf later said of her, "Kathleen Winsor was an amateur speaker at the time and she never learned her speech by heart. She'd come out on stage and fish in her bag, which had everything in it but a live seal, and she'd finally come up with a piece of paper, which she'd carefully unfold. She then read in a colorless monotone."[5]

For New American Library, Miss Winsor and the other Double Volume gambles paid off, at least temporarily disproving Lewis's dire prediction of the failure to meet guarantees. Appearing on the newsstands in August 1950, *Knock on Any Door* sold out its first printing of 250,000 copies in two weeks. *Forever Amber*, spiced with the "Banned in Boston" imprimatur, sold out its 410,000-copy initial printing in less than a month after it appeared in September, as did the first printing of *The Young Lions*. But of those first four, *The Naked and the Dead* was destined for the greatest success in paperback. The book had been greeted with great fervor when it was initially published. It was also obviously very controversial, presenting a view of the American boy in combat totally at odds with the widely accepted notions that Hollywood had fostered in countless wartime propaganda films starring the likes of Errol Flynn and John Wayne. Mailer, the new enfant terrible of American letters, launched his career amid controversy and mixed critical appraisal. Though the hardcover had been a success, the paperback edition, released in January 1951, had sold one million copies by the following October.

The next two Double Volumes were Kathleen Winsor's *Star Money*, a novel about a successful young writer that had little of the impact of its predecessor, and Louis Bromfield's novel of India, *The Rains Came*. When the plan for Double Volumes at fifty cents had been announced, most other publishers were skeptical, if not convinced that it was doomed. The assumption was that the public was too conditioned by "quarter books" and would balk at the 100 percent price increase. But the Double Volumes were soon outstripping the sales of the regular Signet editions. NAL had taken a key step in breaking down the barrier of price resistance, an ill-defined psychic roadblock that publishers still argue over the way judges used to deal with obscenity: they couldn't say exactly what it was, but they knew it when they saw it. In the wake of NAL's success, other paperback houses naturally followed suit with their own thirty-five- and fifty-cent editions. Bantam countered with Bantam Giants at thirty-five cents and Bantam Fifties. Pocket Books pro-

Winner of the National Book Award

FROM HERE TO ETERNITY

James Jones

A SIGNET TRIPLE VOLUME
Complete and Unabridged

The first book auctioned to a paperback house for $100,000, *From Here to Eternity* became an early Triple Volume, priced at seventy-five cents. (Photo by Jerome Frank)

duced Cardinal Books at thirty-five cents and Cardinal Giants at fifty cents. In the meantime, NAL went a step further in 1952 with seventy-five-cent Signet Triples, the first of these being Ayn Rand's *The Fountainhead*; then came James Jones's *From Here to Eternity*, which set a new advance record when Weybright paid $102,000 in one of the first competitive auctions.

The heightened competition for reprints and the surging advances it created, along with the doubling of cover prices and the prolifer-ation of new houses, indicated that the industry was on the move. Before 1950, two more houses that were to survive more than a year were launched. Pyramid Books was the creation of Matthew Hutt-ner and Alfred R. Plaine. In 1949, their first list of mysteries and love stories also included an abridged edition of Wilkie Collins's *The Moonstone.* In that same year, Doubleday launched a hybrid of the hardcover and paperback called Permabooks, rack-sized books bound in laminated board covers. In 1951, Permabooks were shifted over to true paperback covers. At first, Permabooks were mostly anthologies and light nonfiction of the type popularized by Pocket Books, including how-to, self-help, and inspirational books, such as the company's best-selling *The Greatest Story Ever Told* by Fulton Oursler. As the list grew, fiction was later added.

A third new paperback house, launched in 1950, represented a much more portentous branching-out for the paperback business — into the area of original paperbacks. The concept was the child of the Fawcett family and was called Gold Medal Books. Like several of the paperback imprints that preceded it, Gold Medal had its roots planted firmly in the magazine business. When Pocket Books turned to independent distribution in 1941 to get its paperbacks into the mass market, the magazine world quickly exploited this potential new profit maker. Among the magazine publishers, the Fawcett family was prospering during the heyday of the American magazine — the days before radio, television, and cut-rate subscrip-tions when magazines were sold almost exclusively on the news-stands. The company's story was a classic rags-to-riches success cut from the Horatio Alger mold. After World War I, Wilford H. "Cap-tain Billy" Fawcett returned to his home in Minnesota where he began producing a small bulletin of barracks humor and chatter for disabled servicemen in a veterans' hospital. A local wholesaler eventually started putting copies of the little magazine in hotel lobbies and drugstores. From this came *Captain Billy's Whiz Bang.*

Although the sexual innuendo of the title was intentional, the name came from a notorious World War I artillery shell.

Within a short time, the magazine was circulating half a million copies per month and the company flourished. So did the Fawcett clan. In addition to Captain Billy, there was a brother, Roscoe (who died in 1946), and four sons, Wilford, Jr., Roger, Roscoe, and Gordon, who ran the business following Captain Billy's death in 1940 after the company had been brought east to Greenwich, Connecticut. Though perhaps not an influential giant like Luce's Time, Inc., empire or the powerful Curtis-published *Saturday Evening Post*, Fawcett built a large, successful magazine line with *True, Cavalier*, and *Mechanix Illustrated* for the male market and *True Confessions* and *Motion Picture* for women and teenage girls. The jewel in the family crown, *Woman's Day*, was added in 1948.

While Avon, Dell, and Popular Library had used their magazine experience and the power of the American News Company to join Pocket Books and Penguin before the war, the Fawcetts did not gain their toehold in the paperback industry until 1945 when Ian Ballantine left Penguin to set up Bantam, taking Curtis Circulating with him. Kurt Enoch turned to the Fawcetts as Penguin's national distributor to the independent magazine wholesalers, and two years later, when Weybright and Enoch formed New American Library, Fawcett came along as distributor of the new line.

Encouraged by NAL's seemingly easy success and the apparent license to print money called paperbacks, the Fawcetts soon decided that they wanted a piece of the pie. However, under their contract with NAL, they were forbidden to compete for reprints. So they settled for the next bext thing: an all-original paperback line. Following test runs with *The Best of True Magazine* and *What Today's Woman Should Know About Marriage and Sex* — both adapted from Fawcett magazines — the company launched its Gold Medal line in January 1950. Overseeing the company's editorial direction was Ralph Daigh, who had worked for Captain Billy since 1925. The first editor of the books was Jim Bishop, a *Collier's* magazine editor who later became known for his best sellers *The Day Lincoln Was Shot, The Day Christ Died*, and *The Day Kennedy Was Shot*. Bishop departed after a year and was replaced by William Lengle, a veteran editor at Fawcett magazines. Also to pass through Gold Medal's doors was a Radcliffe graduate named Rona Jaffe, who joined the company in 1952 and left in 1955 to pursue a writing career after being described by _Good Housekeeping_ as "Miss Brilliant Promise of the Year." She turned her Fawcett experiences to good use in her first novel, _The Best of Everything_ (1958), an "insider's" account of working girls at a large magazine and paperback publishing company obviously modeled on Fawcett.

With initial print runs of two hundred thousand copies, the Gold Medal Books were primarily "category" originals in the Western, mystery, and thriller genres aimed at the male adventure reader. Authors were paid $2000 per book, advances that were based not on sales but on print runs. When the initial printings were increased to three hundred thousand copies, the advance rose to $3000. That was not a bad piece of change for a writer in 1950. If Gold Medal's literary achievements fell short of candidacy for the Pulitzer, the company could lay claim to introducing into paperback two of the giants of the mass market field. John D. MacDonald, chronicler of the corrupt in golden Florida with his Travis McGee mysteries, made his debut with _The Brass Cupcake_ (1950). Louis L'Amour, successor to Max Brand as the best-selling Western writer, wrote _Hondo_ (1953), which was released in conjunction with the John Wayne film of the same title. The company was also producing original novels by established writers like Sax Rohmer and Mac-Kinlay Kantor, along with works by John (William's brother) Faulkner and Howard Hunt (who later came to fame for his role in Watergate). One of the company's biggest and most notorious best sellers was written by a woman — or so it seemed. _Women's Barracks_, an account of a group of French women soldiers stationed in England during the Occupation, had strong lesbian undertones and a cover showing women in a locker room as they stripped down. The book was ostensibly written by Tereska Torres, but Ralph Daigh later revealed it had been translated by Meyer Levin, not yet known as a best-selling writer. Levin was also Tereska Torres's husband.

A congressional committee damned them, censors yanked them from newsstand racks, and critics sniffed lightly and quickly passed them off as trash — not an unfair assessment in the main. But Gold Medal Books sold. By November 1951, the firm had produced more than nine million books, going back to press with most of the titles and reissuing several of them as many as three or four times.

Although Gold Medal had started the trend toward original publishing in 1950 and the company created a stir over the implications

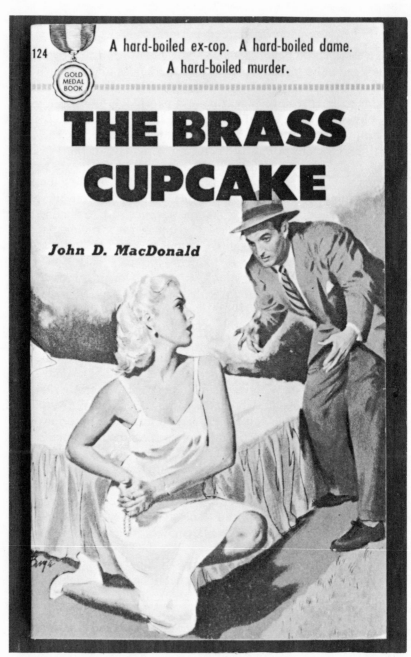

GOLD MEDAL BOOK

A hard-boiled ex-cop. A hard-boiled dame. A hard-boiled murder.

THE BRASS CUPCAKE

John D. MacDonald

John D. MacDonald's first appearance in paperback for the Gold Medal series of originals. (Photo by Kevin Hancer)

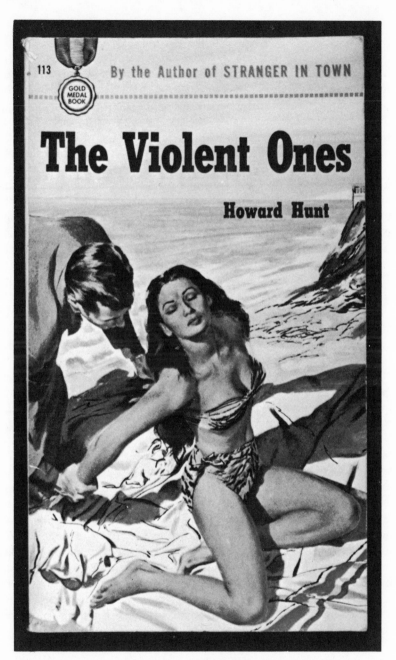

By the Author of STRANGER IN TOWN

The Violent Ones

Howard Hunt

Howard Hunt wrote spy thrillers for Gold Medal long before his involvement in Watergate. (Photo by Kevin Hancer)

of paperback originals for the industry, the line did not cause the industrywide fear and trembling that accompanied the announcement of still another new firm in early 1952. The plan behind this new company called for a daring concept that went beyond simple original paperback publishing. It was the brain child of Ian Ballantine, with twelve years of experience now an old-timer in the paperback business. Ballantine proposed publishing simultaneous hardcover-paperback editions of new books in cooperation with regular trade houses, thereby circumventing the established reprinting system and turning the industry on its collective ear. Although the idea has become increasingly common practice in contemporary publishing (in 1982, for instance, it was done with *Pinball* by Jerzy Kosinski and Thomas McGuane's *Nobody's Angel*), it was not the case in 1952. In fact, it was downright subversive, like advocating Communism before the House Un-American Activities Committee.

But Ballantine had proven himself no stranger to controversy and conflict. In fact, they seemed to follow him. He had lived through one great upheaval when he split away from Penguin Books to form Bantam in 1945. The end of his days at Bantam proved to be no less stormy, and he left the company early in 1952. Although he had proven himself an astute student of the art and science of paperback publishing, Ballantine had less facility for the ins and outs of boardroom politics and bottom-line management. He was also thought to be headstrong and unbending. But the board of directors at Bantam was no trifling bunch. The heavy hitters from the publishers who owned Grosset & Dunlap — which in turn owned half of Bantam — were joined by their man John O'Connor, Grosset's president and Ballantine's immediate superior, as well as the men from Curtis Circulating. In other words, it was a formidable line-up. If nothing else, Ballantine prided himself as an innovator, an experimenter. Businessmen often have little truck with such types. Ballantine wanted to do things other paperback houses were not doing. But he was under tremendous pressure from the directors, who wanted to do just that, direct. They also didn't want to tamper with a sure thing. Theater and film critic Stanley Kauffmann, who joined Bantam in 1949 as an editor, was watching from the sidelines as Ballantine took the field. "There was a struggle between Ian Ballantine and the ownership. He had ambitions to seriousness that they didn't share. They had a goose that was pouring out golden eggs.

They didn't want to monkey with it. There was a power struggle and he lost."

One of the first battles in this struggle came over book prices. Like others in the paperback field, Ballantine saw the necessity for higher prices because twenty-five cents was a constraint on the reprinter. There was simply no way to introduce longer novels and serious nonfiction without raising prices or making condensations and abridgments (which many reprinters did without qualms). In this, Ballantine was opposed by his superiors. The first battle came over Ballantine's desire to reprint a book called *Roosevelt and Hopkins: An Intimate History* by Robert E. Sherwood, a major work about FDR and his most trusted and powerful lieutenant, Harry Hopkins. Originally published in 1948 by Harper & Brothers, the book had been a nonfiction best seller that year. In April 1950, Harper reissued the book in a revised edition. In July, Bantam announced that it would publish the book on an experimental basis, in two volumes at thirty-five cents each. In addition, the book would be available for only 120 days. At the time of the paperback's release, Ballantine said of the plan, "A low cost edition published at the right time can create tremendous word-of-mouth recommendations for the right book through hundreds of thousands of new readers. . . . Because *Roosevelt and Hopkins* is one of the most interesting and most important books of the last ten years, we believe that the reading public will prove that this technique of publishing a limited edition, at the lowest possible price, will shape a new pattern and a greater market for fine books."[6]

Ballantine believed that the book had passed the peak of its hardcover performance and that a paperback edition could successfully revive it. In other words, his interest went beyond profiting from the sale of a reprint and into creating new life cycles for books deserving a wider market and a longer life. This penchant for toying with the accepted relationship between one edition of a book and another was to become a driving force in Ballantine's long career in publishing. Sometimes they were a great notion; in other cases, they fell by the wayside. Unfortunately, the latter was the case with *Roosevelt and Hopkins.* Although Ballantine asserts that the book was a success, the record is less certain. Walter Pitkin, then Bantam's editor in chief, called it "a dismal failure" and later commented, "Ian did succeed in publishing through enthusiasm. *Roosevelt and Hopkins* was a case of that. It involved enormous difficulties because of the amount of the investment and the judgment that it was likely to turn out to be a 'dog,' as the Curtis people would say. It was a very complex and unhappy kind of thing, really over the protests of the directors. Ian, being the publisher, finally insisted, 'I want to do this,' and we did it."

While the book's failure might have proved, first, that two-volume paperbacks were dead before they left the warehouse and, second, that *Roosevelt and Hopkins* was not the right title for the mass market, the thirty-five-cent cover price was not held to blame. NAL had already gone ahead with its plan for thirty-five-cent Giants and fifty-cent Double Volumes. Bantam and Pocket Books also made plans to launch thirty-five-cent books. For Bantam, the first of these was Taylor Caldwell's *This Side of Innocence.*

The second of Ballantine's battles was far more serious and ended in his departure from Bantam. In 1951, Ballantine had set his sights on expanding into the British market and established a British subsidiary, Transworld, to publish paperbacks in England under the Corgi imprint for the British Commonwealth markets. Contractual agreements kept American books from being exported directly into these markets. Without the approval of the executive committee of the board of directors, Ballantine lent Transworld some much-needed cash. The board members were either outraged by this relatively minor offense or saw in it a way to rid themselves of a boat rocker. In his memoirs, Bennett Cerf commented on the affair:

> He was forced out of the business he had brought to us. I think this was shameful, but the others overruled me. Ballantine was a very difficult fellow to handle. He didn't know what diplomacy meant and he didn't realize he was dealing with some very successful gentlemen who liked their prerogatives respected. . . . They forced him to resign. I was outraged and demanded another hearing. Ian had been foolish enough to confront these strong publishing men without a lawyer. They made up their minds even before he could plead his case.[7]

After the close of business on February 5, 1952, Ballantine was gone.

It did not take him long to resurface. In May 1952, *PW* carried news of Ballantine's plan for a new company that would simultaneously publish hardcover and paperback editions of selected books. The idea set the world of publishing abuzz. Simply, the Ballantine notion was to publish a hardcover edition for the bookstore trade that would also gain review attention while a paperback edition would reach the mass market. Theoretically, the advantage of this system meant the hardcover house could undercut existing cover prices from the average of $3 down to $1.50 or $2 through shared plant costs and other production efficiencies while gaining review attention as well as the widest possible distribution. As Ballantine pointed out, his plan was not meant for well-known, best-selling authors who would not necessarily benefit from such a strategy but for lesser-known writers who needed exposure. A key element of the scheme was the increase in the author's royalty to 8 percent, with the entire paperback royalty going to the author instead of being split with the publisher.

The concept of simultaneous editions was not without precedent. Ballantine had himself used it at Penguin during the war, with *Iwo Jima* and *Tank Fighter Team*, two Fighting Forces Specials published in conjunction with Dial Press and *Infantry Journal*; in 1943, Simon & Schuster had published Wendell Willkie's *One World*, an extremely influential book that sold millions of copies that year through newsstands and drugstores in a large-sized paperback edition as well as several thousand copies in hardcover through bookstores; Pocket Books had done the same with Dr. Spock, turning the hardcover edition over to Duell, Sloan & Pearce; and NAL had done some co-publishing with a number of publishers on illustrated books about wildflowers and birds.

At the heart of the plan was Ballantine's contention that the paperback was the best way to reach the mass audience. Not only would the paperback edition sell by itself, but Ballantine believed that the word of mouth generated by the paperback would spur greater interest in the hardcover, thereby creating a mutually beneficial relationship. The plan was also tacit recognition of the immense power wielded by the distributors in editorial matters. At Bantam, Ballantine had witnessed this firsthand with the Curtis organization. He saw his idea as a means of balancing the magazine distributor's voice with that of the trade publisher, who might otherwise lose all influence over what was being produced for the paperback market. In theory, the plan meant a smaller percentage of profit for the publisher. But to Ballantine that was as it should be. He was saying that the author should be profiting from his book, a subversive idea if ever one was spoken by a publisher.

This was the most controversial aspect of the Ballantine concept

because it represented a new alignment in the hardened relationship between authors and publishers, radically altering the traditional roles played by each. For all its supposed liberalism, the
publishing industry was extremely resistant to change. Nowhere
were attitudes more rock-solid among publishers than in matters
relating to writers. Ballantine took his case before such writers
groups as the Authors' Guild, the Authors' League, and the Mystery
Writers of America. The reaction was somewhat mixed; to the writers it sounded too good. Where was the catch? Why did a publisher
want to give them more? Nonetheless, the leaders of the Guild
endorsed the plan.

By September, Ballantine Books announced its staff and first titles. In addition to Ballantine and his wife, Betty, who served as
corporate secretary and was also growing in stature as an editor, the
editorial staff included Bernard Shir-Cliff, a young Columbia graduate who had been hired by Ballantine while he was still at Bantam,
and Stanley Kauffmann, then a novelist of some note.[8] The firm's
first office was Ballantine's apartment in London Terrace off West
Twenty-fourth Street in Manhattan, though it was soon moved to
404 Fifth Avenue. As a national distributor to the magazine wholesalers, Ballantine enlisted the Hearst Corporation's International
Circulation Distributors. Two hardcover publishers, Houghton Mifflin and Farrar, Straus & Young, announced their interest in the
concept and planned to participate on a title-by-title basis. The first
book on the list was *Executive Suite,* a first novel by Cameron
Hawley, a businessman who had written short stories for the *Saturday Evening Post.* Along with it were *The Golden Spike,* a novel
of juvenile delinquency by Hal Ellson, whose earlier books in this
genre were the very successful *Duke* and *Tomboy; All My Enemies,*
a novel by Stanley Baron about a Communist agent on a secret
mission in America; and *Saddle by Starlight,* a Luke Short Western
published in hardcover by Houghton Mifflin. For books not published by another trade house, Ballantine set up his own hardcover
operation; *The Golden Spike* was the first of these.

By the end of 1953, the results of Ballantine's first year of operation were encouraging. *Executive Suite,* the first title, which had
been released in hardcover by Houghton Mifflin, had been well
reviewed by the media. A story of corporate boardroom intrigues, it
even won a favorable nod from the dean of reviewers, Orville Prescott of the *New York Times.* In eight months, the hardcover had

sold a respectable 22,000 copies and the simultaneous paperback went over the 475,000 mark. The book was also sold to MGM and was made into a film with William Holden, Barbara Stanwyck, Walter Pidgeon, and other big names. Luke Short's Western sold more than 200,000 copies in paper without damaging sales of the $1.50 hardcover. Ironically, Houghton Mifflin's Lovell Thompson, the man who had earlier berated "low-price publishing," talked about the advantage of the Ballantine plan. He cited the example of Ruth Park, an Australian novelist who, despite excellent sales abroad and fine reviews, had not sold well in the United States and was passed over by reprinters. Houghton Mifflin "simul-published" her third book, *Witch's Thorn*, to considerable success in both editions. Another critical success was the original publication of *The City of Anger*, a novel of political corruption and the numbers game and the first work of fiction by William Manchester, then known for his biography of Mencken. The biggest commercial success was *The Burl Ives Song Book*, which Ballantine published in both editions. A color-illustrated songbook, it sold tens of thousands of copies as a popular Christmas gift just as the folk music craze was beginning to gather force.

In addition to Westerns, mysteries, war books (which followed Ballantine from Penguin to Bantam and then to Ballantine Books) and other novels, Ballantine soon began to publish books that stood outside the existing categories. Just as the entire Ballantine Books concept was unconventional, the Ballantine list began to acquire an offbeat appeal. One new category was a type of nonfiction different from the academic-oriented Mentors or the how-to Pocket Books. It was a brand of contemporary reportage best exemplified by the work of reporter John Bartlow Martin, a well-known journalist, in such books as *Why Did They Kill?* — a predecessor of sorts to *In Cold Blood* — and *Break Down the Walls*, a serious inquiry into the American penal system. The genre later took a more political tone when Ballantine began to publish the controversial writings of C. Wright Mills. Far less distinguished was a brand of sensationalist nonfiction, often historical in nature, such as *Those About to Die* by Daniel Mannix, a book about the excesses of the Roman circuses.

Another much more successful new area was offbeat humor. Until that point, paperback humor books had been limited to borrowings from the *Saturday Evening Post*, joke books, and Bennett Cerf's anecdotes. But in 1954, Ballantine published *The Mad*

Reader by Harvey Kurtzman, the first in a series of enormously popular *Mad* paperbacks. Taken from the fledgling *Mad* magazine, which was just beginning to style its own form of unconventional humor and exaggerated illustration — as well as its 1950s archetype, Alfred E. "What Me Worry" Neuman — the typical *Mad* humor was, if not subversive, at least nonconformist. Parents found it sick; but it appealed to kids unlike anything appearing in mainstream comics. It was irreverent, anti-authoritarian, and iconoclastic. It spoke to a younger generation that would, in a few years, be taking over the campuses. In fact, the initial printing of *The Mad Reader* even contained an attack on Senator Joseph McCarthy; Ballantine later said that around the time of the eighteenth printing, it was time to drop that feature because kids no longer had any idea who McCarthy was. *The Mad Reader* was brought in to Ballantine by Bernard Shir-Cliff, who was given the magazines by one of the Ballantine salesmen whose son was a *Mad* fanatic. While Ballantine was still at Bantam, his uncle Saxe Commins called to say that he had a very good student in his publishing course at Columbia University and that Ballantine should make a job for him. Bernard Shir-Cliff came to Bantam in a make-work position of gathering statistics about paperback books. He eventually was made a junior editor, and when Ballantine left Bantam, Shir-Cliff went along with him as a full-fledged editor at Ballantine Books.

The *Mad* books provided the groundwork on which Ballantine built a collection of irreverent humor books that poked a stick in the eye of contemporary styles and shibboleths, such as *The Power of Negative Thinking*, a Shir-Cliff–inspired riposte to Norman Vincent Peale. Another notorious example came a few years later when Ballantine published *I, Libertine* in response to a hoax. Late-night radio host Jean Shepherd, famed for his program on WOR and its audience of "Night People," enlisted his listeners in a conspiracy against the smug, conservative "Day People" by creating demand for a product that did not exist — a book called *I, Libertine*. Advertisements for the nonexistent book were taken out, an entry for the book was placed into the Philadelphia Public Library's card catalog, an airline pilot urged his colleagues to harass bookshops across the country for the book, and another disc jockey produced an interview with the "author," Frederick Ewing. Ballantine soon heard that booksellers were frantically asking for a book that did not exist. So he commissioned the book. Tracking Shepherd down, he signed

Concocted by Ballantine in response to a prank, *I, Libertine* was the
work of Jean Shepherd and science fiction writer Theodore Sturgeon.
(Photo by Kevin Hancer)

him to write it in collaboration with Theodore Sturgeon, the science fiction writer. The result was a send-up of the eighteenth-century historical novel popularized by *Forever Amber.* The copy touted the book as "Turbulent! Turgid! Tempestuous!" — and according to Ballantine, the cover was also a trick, containing twenty-four visual errors such as light coming from the wrong direction. The book prompted an editorial in *Life* and was soon the most widely publicized book of the day. Ballantine published a modest 180,000-copy printing, and Shepherd and Sturgeon did full-blast publicity events in keeping with the spirit of the book. They held an autographing party in a Liggett drugstore in Times Square, a favorite spot for the "Night People," after Shepherd initially requested that the party be held in a remainder bookstore in order to "eliminate the middleman."

While Ballantine Books employed this type of humor to good publicity effect, it was not the core of the company's program. Very quickly, the genre that became almost synonymous with Ballantine Books was science fiction. Until this point, science fiction had no significant place in paperback publishing. In fact, it barely existed in book form at all. It was viewed by publishers as a sort of fringe genre that they knew or cared little about. The field belonged principally to the magazine and pulp publishers who flourished from the 1920s through the 1940s, and from which writers like Heinlein, Asimov, Bradbury, and del Rey drew their sustenance. With the exception of novels by Jules Verne and H. G. Wells and Shelley's *Frankenstein* — which were considered "classics" rather than science fiction — and more recent works like C. S. Lewis's trilogy commencing with *Out of the Silent Planet* (1939) — actually religious allegory — or Huxley's *Brave New World* (1932) and Orwell's *1984* (1949) — political and social allegories in a science fiction guise — book form science fiction before 1950 was limited to a few anthologies of magazine short fiction.

In 1943, for instance, Pocket Books had published the first science fiction paperback, *The Pocket Book of Science Fiction*, an anthology edited by Donald A. Wollheim, a veteran editor of science fiction magazines and later a dominant figure in paperback science fiction publishing. The following year, Penguin produced an anthology called *Out of This World,* edited by Julius Fast, brother of Howard and later the author of successful pop psychology books including *Body Language.* In 1950, Bantam also published a collection called

A Shot in the Dark, science fiction stories thinly disguised as mysteries. However, before 1952, no paperback publisher could lay claim to what can be called a science fiction program.

Ballantine radically changed that. On the company's early lists were not only collections of science fiction from the magazines but an impressive line-up of full-length novels that became classics of the genre and books that ultimately transcended the category. The first full-fledged science fiction novel on the list was a collaboration between Fred Pohl and C. M. Kornbluth, a first novel by a pair of veterans who had collaborated previously on short fiction. Serialized in *Galaxy* magazine as "Gravy Planet," the completed novel was retitled *The Space Merchants* by its editor, Stanley Kauffmann. Not a simple story of rockets, robots, and cosmic damsels in distress — the recycled elements of the Western in futuristic garb known as the "space opera" — *The Space Merchants,* if not high art, was a social satire. In the story, an overcrowded future Earth is controlled by advertising agencies, and Congress consists of representatives of large corporations (as in the "Honorable Senator from Yummy Cola"). The plot involves an ad agency's plan to control Venus by luring "consumers" — as average people are called — to join the first colony there. In the background, a subversive group called "Consies," short for conservationists, fights as outlaws to prevent the destruction of natural resources. This satirization of contemporary culture in futuristic guise had its predecessors — *Gulliver's Travels* is arguably a tale of science fiction — but it became typical of the style in science fiction pioneered by Ballantine Books. Ian Ballantine called the books he published "adult science fiction." "Adult" not in the sense of "For Adults Only" movies, but in their thematic seriousness, relative sophistication, and literary ambitions.

An even greater example of this style came through in another Ballantine Book brought in by Kauffmann. As he recalled, "The idea of Ballantine's methods struck a chord in Don Congdon, Ray Bradbury's agent, and he relayed it to Bradbury. We got a manuscript and I did some work on it. Then he got the galleys and wouldn't let go of them. He was fussing with them. So I had to fly out to California and work with him for a week out there." The finished novel, an extension of a *Galaxy* story called "The Fireman," appeared in 1953 as Ballantine Book No. 41, *Fahrenheit 451* — the "temperature at which book paper catches fire and burns."

Ray Bradbury's classic about book burning was published at the height of the anti-Communist era. (Photo by Kevin Hancer)

The historical context in which Bradbury's book appeared is more than a little significant. The House investigations into un-American activities and Senator Joseph McCarthy were on the rampage. Communist writers were being suppressed. Paperback books were under fire by local censors, and late in 1952, the Gathings committee — a congressional investigation into the paperback business — was empowered (see chapter 8). In other words, Bradbury's jeremiad about a future dystopia in which books are burned and the people anesthetized by a vacuous, omnipresent television soap opera was no fantasist's vision. In 1953, in a famous speech at Dartmouth College, President Eisenhower had warned, "Don't join the book burners," a rebuke aimed at McCarthyism. *Fahrenheit 451* was informed and shaped by the culture that Bradbury was observing, including the growing threat of a nuclear cataclysm, an event with which the book ends, unlike the pale Truffaut film version. Other memorable science fiction novels from the early Ballantine period include the Arthur C. Clarke classic *Childhood's End*, John Wyndham's *The Midwich Cuckoos*, and other works by Pohl, Kornbluth, and Sturgeon. All of these received the unique stamp of illustration by Richard G. Powers, surrealistic Dali-esque imagery and geometric abstractions that were in marked contrast to the pulpish semiclad space maidens with metallic cones on their breasts who were always in the clutches of an invading monster. Ballantine's unique science fiction cover treatment even extended to Gore Vidal's novel *Messiah*. Although it seems unlikely, the packaging of a Gore Vidal novel as science fiction was not a misunderstanding of Vidal but a measure of the seriousness with which the category was viewed. The recurrent themes in Ballantine science fiction — serious overcrowding of the earth, dread of nuclear catastrophe, a dwindling food supply, ecological insanity, excessive government control — were all part of a pattern of concerns that later emerged on the Ballantine list in the form of serious nonfiction, including the work of C. Wright Mills, Paul Ehrlich's *The Population Bomb*, *Diet for a Small Planet*, or the nature books published in association with the Sierra Club and Friends of the Earth.

The fact that science fiction had arrived as a potential category for paperback publishers was underscored later in 1952 with the arrival of another paperback house that became known primarily for its publishing in the science fiction field. Ace Books was the creation of Aaron A. Wynn, who had been in the confessional mag-

The cover art for *Out of the Deeps* was typical of the singular look Richard Powers gave to Ballantine science fiction. (Photo by Kevin Hancer)

azine business for seventeen years when, in 1945, he started a book line called Current Books. In 1946, he acquired the L. B. Fischer Publishing Corporation, which had been started by two German refugees, Gottfried Berman-Fischer and Fritz Landshoff. Wynn merged these two operations into A. A. Wynn, Inc. His paperback operation had a gimmick conceived by Walter Zacharius; it would publish two paperback novels bound back to back and call them Double Novels, priced at thirty-five cents. The appeal to the reader was obvious. They were getting two novels for a little more than the price of one. In fact, the two "novels" were often novelettes or long short stories rather than full-length novels. But the plan appealed to readers and the sight of the Ace Double Novels, with the back cover "upside-down" in the racks, became a familiar one.

Generally the two books printed together were of the same category, principally, at the outset, two mysteries or Westerns. The first mystery package included *The Grinning Gringo* by Samuel W. Taylor, a reprint of a book originally published by A. A. Wynn, Inc., and *Too Hot for Hell* by Keith Vining, an original. The first Western duo was *Bad Man's Return* by William Colt MacDonald, a reprint, coupled with *Bloody Hoofs*, an original by Edward J. Leithead. Without a doubt the most famous of the Ace Double Novels was Ace D 15, the combination of *Narcotics Agent*, a typical genre thriller by Maurice Helbrant, with *Junkie*, "Confessions of an Unredeemed Drug Addict," by "William Lee" who in fact was William S. Burroughs. Ace felt it necessary to include a glossary, in a vain bid to make Burroughs comprehensible. Ace came by the book through Wynn's nephew Carl Solomon, who worked for his uncle as an editor but happened to have been a poet and Allen Ginsberg's compatriot in a psychiatric hospital. Ginsberg passed *Junkie* to Solomon, who gave it to Wynn, and it was published by Ace.[9]

One feature of the Ace Double Novel was that it allowed Ace to combine an unknown (cheaper) writer's work with that of a better-known author. This strategy was put to good effect by the series editor, Donald A. Wollheim, who was the leading promoter of the genre and a guru to the growing legions of science fiction fans. Wollheim got good mileage out of the Double Novels as he launched new writers in the format, moving Ace more heavily toward that genre until it pulled alongside Ballantine and the two companies began to dominate the field. By 1954, Ace had also branched out into the business of twenty-five-cent editions of single

These Avon covers were far more typical of science fiction artwork done by other paperback houses. (*Science Fiction Reader* photo by Kevin Hancer; *Perelandra* photo courtesy of Avon)

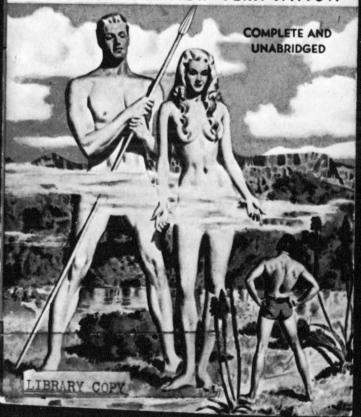

by the author of *OUT OF THE SILENT PLANET*

C.S. LEWIS

PERELANDRA

WORLD OF THE NEW TEMPTATION

COMPLETE AND
UNABRIDGED

novels in paperback. In order to concentrate on Ace paperbacks, Wynn sold off his hardcover operation in 1956 to two of his executives, Lawrence Hill and Arthur W. Wang, who formed Hill & Wang.

The introduction of Ballantine and Ace was only a part of the growth spurt that made 1952 something of a momentous year in the paperback's development. Another major surge was under way at Dell Books. After its strong beginnings in 1942, Dell had slipped out of contention as a meaningful competitor to Pocket Books when Bantam and New American Library vaulted ahead on the basis of more imaginative, diversified editorial programs featuring best-selling books and noteworthy fiction. Fawcett's Gold Medal had also been an instant success, and Dell was soon floundering at the bottom of the heap with Avon and Popular Library. The principal reason for their situation was that Dell was still essentially oriented toward comic books and magazines. Books were an afterthought at Dell, and no one in the Dell hierarchy had developed into a competent book publisher. The Dell list was composed almost entirely of category fiction, an editorial policy dictated by the demands of the American News Company. Western Printing in Racine, Wisconsin, was responsible for selecting and producing the books for Dell, but there was no strong central editorial figure there either. In 1952, however, the company's status took a sharp upward turn with the overhaul of the Western editorial staff. That year Western hired Frank Taylor to oversee Dell's reprints, and having seen Gold Medal reap impressive rewards, George Delacorte brought in Knox Burger to establish a series of originals called Dell First Editions.

The addition of these two editors marked a major turning point in Dell's fortunes. Taylor was a literary man, through and through. He had worked in advertising sales at *Saturday Review* before joining the young but, in Taylor's words, "terribly exciting" firm of Reynal and Hitchcock in 1941. He soon rose to editor and vice president there, bringing into the firm Lillian Smith's *Strange Fruit* in 1944 and after the war heading for England, where he signed on Stephen Spender, V. S. Pritchett, and other prominent British writers. When Reynal and Hitchcock dissolved in 1947 after Curtice Hitchcock's death, Taylor moved on to Random House as a roving editor and was responsible for initiating the publication of Ralph Ellison's *Invisible Man*. He left Random House for three years to work as a producer in Hollywood but returned to New York un-

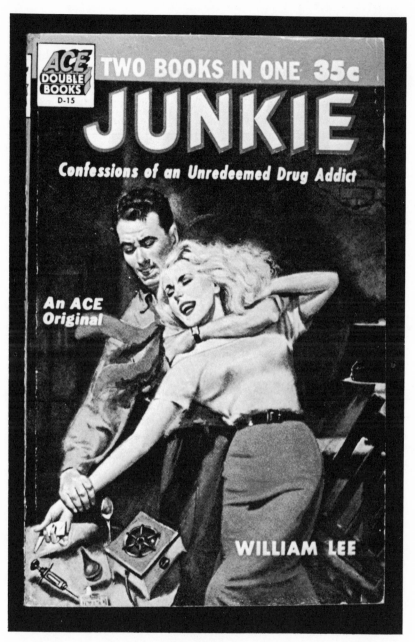

A first edition of *Junkie* by William Lee (William S. Burroughs) is highly prized by collectors of old paperbacks. (Photo by Kevin Hancer; courtesy of the Berkley Publishing Group.)

happy with West Coast movie life. He asked Bennett Cerf, his former boss, what he might do. Taylor recalled, "Bennett told me the Paperback Revolution had occurred in my absence and said, 'My advice to you is get in it.' I was very snobby about it because for years I had been the discoverer and finder — there is excitement in finding new writers. The idea of reprinting was not appealing to me." Nonetheless, Taylor took the job of overseeing the Dell reprints at Western. He found that Dell Books came in three flavors — romance, Western, and mystery. The endpapers of the romances were printed with hearts, the Westerns with steer horns, and the mysteries with skull and crossbones. He also learned that a large part of his job involved "educating," as he put it, the Dell organization about books.

Taylor also found some assets when he arrived. The most important of these was a young editor named Allan Barnard, a holdover from the previous Western staff. As Taylor put it, "Allan had tentacles and enormous sensitivity to what sells." The other boon was the fact that there was no shortage of funds at either Dell or Western, which were both cash rich. Taylor immediately set out to employ these funds. He took Allan Barnard off the tether and encouraged him to follow his instincts. Taylor himself set about charting a fresh editorial direction for the company. One of his first exercises was to go through lists of authors and see who was not being reprinted. His initial find was Evelyn Waugh, and Taylor spent a rather hefty $41,000 to acquire all nine of Waugh's novels from Little, Brown. He also discovered Mary McCarthy just "kicking around," and added her to the Dell list.

At the same time that Taylor was revitalizing the Dell reprint list, Knox Burger was preparing to put together an all-originals program. Burger came to Dell from *Collier's* magazine, where he had developed a solid reputation as a young fiction editor. His contacts with writers from *Collier's* were powerful, and he would bring many of these writers to First Editions, including John D. Mac-Donald and Kurt Vonnegut. He also started to beef up his own editorial department. As his second in command, Burger brought in Donald Fine, formerly with Doubleday, and hired as a receptionist / reader Arlene Donovan, who had been a baby sitter for Burger's children and who quickly rose to an editor's position.

Dell First Editions established itself by aggressively acquiring books, although still staying close to the mystery, suspense, and adventure vein that Gold Medal had successfully mined. The emphasis was on bringing in good writers. Burger published some John D. MacDonald, who had already done several of his Travis McGee mysteries for Gold Medal. Fine discovered the Australian novelist Morris West, then a radio announcer, whose first American book was Dell's *Kundu*, a story of lycanthropy set in New Guinea. West later wrote for Dell First Editions under the pseudonym Michael East. When Dell turned down one of West's mysteries set in Rome, the writer took it to William Morrow, which published it in hardcover. The next book after that was *The Devil's Advocate*. Fine later said about Dell First Editions, "We conducted business like a fine, traditional hardcover publishing house. Tremendous time was lavished on editing and back and forth with authors. We wouldn't publish anything unless we were terribly pleased with it. That's what we cared about." It was commonly acknowledged that a rivalry existed between the two divisions, reprints and originals; Arlene Donovan later called it a "polite cold war." But with Burger, Fine, and Donovan on one side and Taylor and Barnard on the other, Dell now had an editorial staff that combined commercial instincts with literary sensibilities, and a strong "hands-on" editorial expertise. It was a team that compared favorably with any in the industry, reprint or hardcover.

Perhaps because paperbacks could supply economic incentives greater than those at hardcover houses, the paperback business was increasingly drawing editorial talent that would be welcome in any trade house. At NAL, Victor Weybright had supplemented his staff with Arabel Porter and Marc Jaffe, who came from *Argosy* magazine and was as at home with Westerns and mysteries as he was with William Styron or Peter Mathiessen, both of whom he encountered in Paris while scouting around Europe. At Pocket Books, Doc Lewis's staff had grown to include Herbert Alexander, a former advertising man who knew what sold, and Lawrence Hughes, later the head of William Morrow. Ballantine could boast of Stanley Kauffmann and Bernard Shir-Cliff. At Bantam, Saul David and Grace Bechtold were establishing themselves. Though hardcover publishers still behaved condescendingly or patronizingly toward the paperback houses that were increasingly buttering their bread, it was clear that the paperback publishers' marketing strength was now being buttressed by solid editorial expertise. These editors, who all surely could have found places in trade publishing, were going to push the paperback in new and more interesting directions.

It was also becoming clear that the paperback was a growing force on the American cultural scene. The surging growth in sales, the proliferation of new companies and imprints, the phenomenon of paperback originals, the flurry of controversy over Ballantine's plan, and the rising advances and cover prices all heightened the paperback's visibility in literary and intellectual circles. Among writers and critics, the paperback had its cheerleaders, who believed that inexpensive paperback books were democratizing American literature, taking it out of the hands of the select few and putting it before the masses. On the other hand were the critics who said trash in any guise still smells like trash; and the paperback was trash. Others worried that the paperback meant the death of the hardcover and wondered what it would mean for writers. At the extreme were those people who saw paperbacks as nothing but a pox on the land, a plot to subvert American morality and fit only to be wiped clean from the newsstands and drugstore racks.

This emerging debate underlined the growing schizophrenia of the paperback industry. It was the Great Contradiction between the lowest of lowbrow fiction on one end of the scale and serious nonfiction and literature on the other. *New York Times Book Review* editor David Dempsey, writing in the *Atlantic Monthly* in January 1953, characterized this duality.

> There are today about twenty paperback houses in the field. Seven of these account for approximately 85 per cent of the total business. Their product is a highly competitive melange of serious literature and trash, of self-help and pseudo-science, of sex and inspiration. Never before has American publishing put forth such a nicely homogenized product, with the cream of letters so palatably disseminated in the total output. This explains why Edith Hamilton's *The Greek Way* and the novels of Kathleen Winsor can be sold bust by jowl on drug counters. It accounts for the fact that Faulkner's *The Wild Palms* has been made available, if not necessarily comprehensible, to a million rank-and-file buyers. It has suddenly made the books of Flaubert, Hawthorne, and D. H. Lawrence contemporary with Steinbeck. If the reprints have done nothing else, they have taken the classics away from the protective custody of the pedants.[10]

While writers and critics like Professor Eduard C. Lindeman and Malcolm Cowley were taking sides in such magazines as the *New Republic, Harper's,* and *Saturday Review* — and as Ashley Montagu put forward the suggestion that paperbacks should be the "standard book while all other books remain the luxuries they have become" — the debate over the paperback's rightful place in America's cultural hierarchy came to a head in 1954. Kurt Enoch wrote an extensive essay about the paperback for the *Library Quarterly* in June 1954. In it he related the history and workings of the paperback business and then turned his sights on the social role of the paperback. Characterizing the paperback as part of the mass media, Enoch explained that paperbound books were different because they were free from the pressures of government or advertisers. Stated Enoch, "There has been a sort of law: the wider the audience, the less provocative or disturbing to established ideas and taboos the medium has to be. The fundamental problem . . . is thus to achieve a mass audience while preserving the special virtues of books. . . . We offer predominantly contemporary American literature, without neglecting to make available a good cross-section of the best or most important foreign writing. Informative or scholarly nonfiction is steadily increasing. . . ." In Enoch's eyes, the paperback was fulfilling a specific — and uniquely American — function by achieving, "in matters of the mind and arts, as we have already achieved in the economic area, the broad and general distribution of goods that are a vital factor in the dynamic expansion of a free society."[11]

Shortly afterward, from his spot in "The Easy Chair" at *Harper's* magazine, Bernard DeVoto wrote "Culture at Two Bits," an acerbic rejoinder to Enoch's article and the sentiments it expressed, which DeVoto called "a mossy stone." His criticism centered on the fact that while "important" books — many of which Enoch had listed — were being reprinted, they were rarely available. "If you are quick on your feet, you can get or could have got Machiavelli, Benvenuto Cellini, Crane Brinton, Aaron Copland, George Kennan and much more substantial stuff at the corner newsstand." But DeVoto told of walking into every cigar stand, drugstore, and newsstand he could find, looking for the products of the cultural revolution, without any luck. "Tripe," he wrote, "always has been the basis of the publishing business, and in the two bit book it is performing the functions of all popular literature in all ages. At worst it is preventing boredom, assisting digestion and peristalsis, feeding people's appetites for daydreams, giving the imagination something to work on and taking the reader out of a momentarily unsatisfactory life into a momentarily more enjoyable one. At best, or so the theory of revolution holds, it is plowing, harrowing and seeding the soil." DeVoto completed his critique by suggesting that unless more good books were published alongside the awful ones, "the tripe merchants" should stop talking about their cultural service to a "dynamically expanding free society."[12]

It was fitting that Kurt Enoch should be the object of DeVoto's scorn. No firm was more clearly a symbol of the Janus-faced paperback industry than Enoch and Weybright's New American Library. The home of Mentor Books — the only line of paperbacks besides Pocket Books that had developed any brand-name recognition — and the publisher of Faulkner, Caldwell, Silone, Moravia, Farrell, Joyce, Tennessee Williams, Lawrence, Woolf, Ralph Ellison, and a host of the other leading contemporary novelists, NAL claimed as its best-selling writer Mickey Spillane.

Frank Morrison Spillane was born on March 9, 1918, in Brooklyn and raised, as he later said, "in a very tough neighborhood in Elizabeth, New Jersey." If he had a motto as a writer, it might well have been, "You can keep all your awards. All I want is a fat check."

For Spillane, fat checks were never a problem. In 1947, E. P. Dutton published his first book, *I, the Jury*. It sold a modest few thousand copies but was picked up for reprint by Victor Weybright, and in January 1948 New American Library published it at twenty-five cents. In a little more than two years, paperback sales of *I, the Jury* had surpassed 2 million copies. In the meantime, Spillane had written three more books, all published by Dutton in 7500-copy first printings and reprinted by NAL. By the end of 1951, NAL had sold more than 5 million of Spillane's Mike Hammer thrillers. In December 1951, the company issued a 2.5-million-copy first printing — the largest one at that point in paperback history — of his fifth book, *The Big Kill*. After *I, the Jury* Spillane wrote six more Mike Hammer novels: *Vengeance Is Mine* (1950), *My Gun Is Quick* (1950), *One Lonely Night* (1951), *The Big Kill* (1951), *The Long Wait* (1951), and *Kiss Me, Deadly* (1952). Spillane was estimated to be earning about $80,000 per book in that early period. By 1953, Spillane's first six novels had topped 17 million copies sold, and Mike Hammer's creator had pulled past Erskine Caldwell and was now in second place as the best-selling author behind Erle Stanley Gardner. Yet in 1952, at the peak of his sales and without explanation, Spillane stopped writing and took a nine-year break. Although he returned in 1961, popularity undiminished, Spillane is best known for those early titles.

Mickey Spillane broke into the business by writing for the comic books, and the techniques of that genre informed his literary style. Spillane had to be taken as seriously as Superman. His characters were one-dimensional grotesques yanked from the garish pages of the popular comic books of the period. Leading the parade was Mike Hammer, the two-fisted, craggy-faced (not handsome; that was an effeminate trait) private dick with a crew cut; his voluptuous secretary, Velda, always trying to get Mike to tie the knot; and Pat Chambers, the beleaguered homicide detective and pal of Hammer's who vainly tries to keep the private eye from taking the law into his own hands. Spillane surely did not take himself seriously. His tough-guy act before the press and cameras, right down to his own regulation skinhead haircut, was all bluff, a play to the grandstands. The sublime contradiction in Spillane was his devout religious conviction following a 1952 conversion to the Jehovah's Witnesses. He handed out tracts and participated in baptisms by immersion. Victor Weybright once told of arranging a meeting between Spillane and some Catholic priests, among his most vociferous critics. The expected confrontation over Spillane's books never materialized because the meeting turned into a theological discussion of the precepts of the Jehovah's Witnesses. There was also the suggestion that Spillane's nine-year sabbatical was the result of his conversion, although later, in typically tough-guy fashion, he laughed that off, asserting he had come back to make some more money — the only reason he ever wrote anything.

By stretching things a bit, Spillane's Jehovah could be seen as the active principle in his books. Mike Hammer — the Hammer of God? — was his fictional avatar, an angel of death incarnate, wreaking almighty vengeance upon the immoral, corrupt, criminal, and godless. If Dashiell Hammett had created the hard-boiled private eye, Spillane perverted him. In many ways, Sam Spade was the model for Hammer. But Mike Hammer was a Frankenstein, Sam Spade gone haywire. (Often Spade seemed more than just a model. In a scene in *Kiss Me, Deadly*, Hammer disarms a would-be assassin the same way Spade handles Wilmer Cook, the "gunsel" who has been following him in *The Maltese Falcon*.) But it would be difficult to find two writers more diametrically opposed: Hammett, the leftist whose heroes were no heroes at all but lonely, somewhat seedy men who asked more questions than they answered; Spillane, the anti-Communist crusader whose comic book hero Mike Hammer shot first and asked questions later.

Spillane's books were the obvious products of their times. He took his plots from the headlines. In 1951, these included the investigations into organized crime launched by Senator Estes Kefauver of Tennessee. Kefauver's hearings went public, and mobster Frank Costello was grilled on live television, outdrawing the World Series in those days of television's infancy. The Kefauver hearings put organized crime on the front pages. (Not coincidentally, Kefauver was readying for a run at the Democratic presidential nomination.) Organized crime thus became the chief bugaboo in several Spillane plots. Tales of call-girl rings, the narcotics trade, and murder rings — now out in the open — became grist for Spillane's mill. When Senator McCarthy emerged, Spillane found himself a new model and a new villain. Mike Hammer switched to fighting Communists (*One Lonely Night* was Spillane's first anti-Communist book) and became the ultimate cold warrior, an *Übermensch* for frightened Americans who had heard tales of baby-eating Stalinists. Hammer's methods went beyond loyalty oaths, smears, and blacklisting. The evil of the Communists was battled with the only weapons Hammer possessed: a blast from his forty-five, a kick that shattered bone on impact, strangulation by Hammer's meaty hands.

Spillane's Hammer was a creature of his times. But was he more? Was Mike Hammer an archetype, a metaphor for a darkly violent animus within the millions who bought the books? If Spillane was laughing in his cuff, did his readers take him seriously? There was more than simply sex and violence in his novels. Hammer embodied many perverse notions that seemed to represent the male Zeitgeist of the fifties. The first of the Hammer books, *I, the Jury* — the all-time best seller of the group — was typical of the series; it contained the rage that was seething beneath the supposed civility of American life in the early 1950s. The book introduced war veteran Mike Hammer as a private investigator who chose his profession over police work because the cops are tied down by the rules and regulations imposed by a "pansy" bureaucracy. Hammer sets himself above the law because of the "right-ness" of what he does. The law and order cant of modern conservatives in 1950 was no different than it is today. When Hammer's war buddy is murdered by a heroin ring, Hammer vows vengeance; he will become cop, judge, jury, and executioner. Not even the state's worst threat — hanging or "frying" — is justice enough for Hammer; he must exact an eye for an eye.

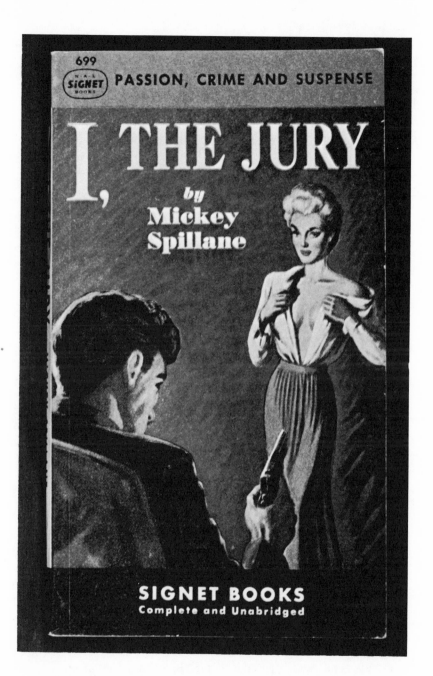

Mickey Spillane's first paperback edition launched his career as one
of the most successful writers of all time. (Photo by Kevin Hancer)

In the course of his search, Hammer encounters the beautiful psychiatrist Charlotte Manning, who like all women is overcome by Hammer's sheer maleness. She quickly accepts Hammer's marriage proposal, sacrificing her career without hesitation. He will not, of course, even consider the possibility that his wife will hold a job. All women in Hammer's world are purely sexual objects, and most of them are criminals as well. Sex is primitively animal; Hammer doesn't make love — he ruts. Yet though he is constantly brought to the peak of arousal by Charlotte, Hammer will not succumb because she is to be his bride, a streak of perverse Victorian chasteness within Spillane. Of course, Charlotte turns out to be the leader of a heroin ring run from her psychiatry practice. Charlotte is a woman, an intellectual, a criminal. Ergo she must die and does, at the hands of Hammer on the last page, as do so many women in Spillane's books.

Hammer stood for, in no special order, sexism, racism (blacks are either shuffling genetic defectives or pimps and pushers), anti-intellectualism, homophobia, and a brand of jackbooted fascist vigilantism in the guise of preserving order. Though he is a war veteran, Mike Hammer evidences no vitriol toward the Nazis. Indeed, a beautiful woman is often described as a Nordic or a Viking. His disdain is reserved for women, professionals, homosexuals or "pansies" (lesbians are twice cursed), and the criminal class — often ethnics. If Spillane was diagramming the psyche of the American male circa 1952, the picture was a disturbing one. Or was he merely playing out a fantasy and, in doing so, defusing the furies that Mike Hammer represented. Was Hammer simply Walter Mitty with two fists and a forty-five? In their book *The Fifties*, Douglas Miller and Marion Nowak comment, "Hammer was popular because he enacted a daydream. He catered to the politically disarmed and sexually insecure, the ambiguous American who needed a powerful dose of artifice and reassurance."[13]

Other contemporary critics did not look upon Spillane with much delight. In their view, he was not only a bad writer but a bad habit for Americans. And more, he stood for the threat that paperback books presented. Critic Dwight Macdonald wrote:

The kind of detective fiction which might be called the "classic style" ... has been overshadowed by the rank noxious growth of works in the sensational style ... enormously stepped up in voltage by Mickey

Spillane. . . . The sensationalists use what for the classicists was the point — the uncovering of a criminal — as a mere excuse for the minute description of scenes of bloodshed, brutality and alcoholism. . . . A decade ago, the late George Orwell showed how the brutalization of the genre mirrors the general degeneration from the 19th century standards. What he would have written had Mickey Spillane's works then been in existence, I find it hard to imagine.[14]

Inveighing against both Spillane and the publishers who brought him forth to the masses, critic Bernard Rosenberg commented, "What makes mass culture so tantalizing is the implication of effortlessness. Shakespeare is dumped on the market along with Mickey Spillane and publishers are rightly confident that their audience will not feel obliged to make any greater preparation for the master of world literature than for the latest lickspittle."[15]

Spillane found a somewhat less harsh critic in Charles Rolo, who at Victor Weybright's behest wrote an article comparing Spillane to Georges Simenon, the French novelist who was then Europe's best-selling writer and the master of using the mystery to explore the psychology of character. While glorifying neither Spillane's technique nor the sophistication of his plots, Rolo found something in Spillane and Simenon — in fact, in most modern mysteries — that previous commentators had passed over. Rolo declared that the mystery was the twentieth-century version of the Passion play. The murderer is Everyman; the murder, the imperfection in all mankind. Wrote Rolo, "They allow us to play, vicariously, the role of different kinds of Savior."[16]

While Rolo's metaphysical musings seemed to wander pretty far afield — did Spillane really see Hammer as a "parfit gentile knight"? — his essay served as a counterpoint to critics of the reprinters, who asked, "Can anything good come out of the paperback?" Spillane, because of his extraordinary successes and excesses, had become a lightning rod for criticism of paperbacks. In him, all of the sins of the paperback reprinters were gathered. But the adventures of Mike Hammer were far from the only example of how low the paperback could sink. Many of the Gold Medal originals, for instance, were drawing the ire of censors who found the covers pornographic and the contents immoral. Ace, Avon, and Dell were not far behind, and a score of lesser reprints that came and went stuck to the low road. After Spillane, however, perhaps the most infamous group of paperbacks was the surge of urban gang novels that emerged in the late forties and early fifties. Juvenile delinquency was increasing at the beginning of the 1950s — or at least it was getting more attention. "More discipline" was already being preached from the pulpits. Ennui, the beginnings of affluence, and the atmosphere of fear and repression that characterized the American fifties probably all played their part. Perhaps it was the beginning of the restlessness that found full expression in the Beat Generation and their flower children successors. Parents and preachers began to link their children's unruly behavior with the rude new music called rock and roll, so wild and frenzied compared with the gentler tones of Liberace, Patti Page, Perry Como, and Pat Boone. Whatever the cause, the unsettling specter of an angry young generation began to appear in movies and books.

In an attempt to "expose" the craziness of the young, Hollywood produced the generation's first cult gods in *Rebel Without a Cause* (1955), with James Dean, and *The Wild One* (1954), with Marlon Brando. ("Whatcha rebelling against, Johnny?" "Whaddya got?") The trend was also visible in novels like Irving Shulman's *The Amboy Dukes* (Avon), which sold more than four million copies, and Hal Ellson's *Duke* (Popular Library), *Tomboy* (Bantam), and *The Golden Spike* (simultaneous Ballantine hardcover/paperback). Another of the most famous of this teen gang genre — one of the first books to be passed around by kids who "indexed" the good pages — was *The Blackboard Jungle* (1954), Evan Hunter's first novel. The book was especially well thumbed for two reasons: the scene in which a teacher is assaulted and an early appearance in paperback of the word *fuck* (until that time, it had been deleted, bowdlerized, or printed as "f--k"). Bud Egbert, then a Pocket Books salesman who had joined the home office at the time the book was released, later recalled, "A wholesaler sent a wire to our office and said under no circumstances would he put this book out, and if we had any questions, see page so-and-so. That sent all our little secretaries dashing to find the book. And there it was." Although it was successful in paperback, *The Blackboard Jungle* had an even greater impact as a film. In the screen version, Bill Haley and the Comets sang "Rock Around the Clock," and rock and roll was here to stay. Parents now had irrefutable evidence that rock and roll and juvenile delinquency went hand in hand.

While Mickey Spillane and the teen gangs seemed to be taking control of the paperback racks in the heartland, their domination was not complete. Like a wildflower struggling up through the ash heap, better books were pushing through to the marketplace and surviving. Despite DeVoto's contention that good books in paperback were impossible to find, quality — as subjective a term as any — was finding its way through the cracks. The promise of the Paperback Revolution was that all books would find their audience, given the opportunity. If the reprinters were guilty of bringing forth the worst that the mass culture in the 1950s was capable of producing, they were also responsible for some of its finer moments. At its best the paperback could offer, as NAL's slogan neatly put it, "Good Reading for the Millions," and this was the Great Contradiction, echoed in the comment of critic David Dempsey. "As for the horrendous Spillane — perhaps he is the price we must pay in a democratic culture, for being able to buy *A Passage to India* for 25 cents. As bargains go, it is not so bad."[17]

Key Paperbacks: 1950–1955

1950

This Side of Innocence	Taylor Caldwell (Bantam; first 35¢ Giant)
Laura	Vera Caspary (Popular Library; movie tie-in)
Knight's Gambit	William Faulkner (Signet)
The Revolt of the Masses	José Ortega y Gasset (Mentor)
The First Lady Chatterley	D. H. Lawrence (Avon)
Reflections in a Golden Eye	Carson McCullers (Bantam)
Sex and Temperament	Margaret Mead (Mentor)
Focus	Arthur Miller (Popular Library)
The Young Lions	Irwin Shaw (Signet Double)
Forever Amber	Kathleen Winsor (Signet Double)
How to Survive an Atomic Bomb	Adapted from the government's "The Effect of Atomic Weapons" (Bantam)

1951

The Man with the Golden Arm	Nelson Algren (Pocket)
Judgment Day	James T. Farrell (Signet)
Tender Is the Night	F. Scott Fitzgerald (Bantam Giant)
The Man Who Sold the Moon	Robert Heinlein (Signet)
For Whom the Bell Tolls	Ernest Hemingway (Bantam Giant)

The Naked and the Dead	Norman Mailer (Signet Double)
1984	George Orwell (Signet)
A Rage to Live	John O'Hara (Bantam Fifty)
All Quiet on the Western Front	Erich Maria Remarque (Lion)
The Snow Was Black	Georges Simenon (Signet)
A Streetcar Named Desire	Tennessee Williams (Signet)

1952

When Worlds Collide	Edwin Balmer and Philip Wylie (Dell)
What to Listen for in Music	Aaron Copland (Mentor)
The 42nd Parallel	John Dos Passos (Pocket)
The Story of Philosophy	Will Durant (Pocket)
A General Introduction to Psychoanalysis	Sigmund Freud (Perma Special)
The Way West	A. B. Guthrie (Pocket)
Brave New World	Aldous Huxley (Bantam)
A Documentary History of the United States	Richard D. Heffner (Mentor original)
Buddenbrooks	Thomas Mann (Pocket)
The Greatest Story Ever Told	Fulton Oursler (Perma)
Burmese Days	George Orwell (Popular Library)
Fountainhead	Ayn Rand (Signet; first Triple Volume, 75¢)
Lie Down in Darkness	William Styron (Signet Double)
Only the Dead Know Brooklyn	Thomas Wolfe (Signet)
New World Writing No. 1	(Mentor)

1953

Fahrenheit 451	Ray Bradbury (Ballantine simultaneous original)
The Shaping of the Modern Mind	Crane Brinton (Mentor)
Out of My Life and Thought	Albert Einstein (Mentor)
Invisible Man	Ralph Ellison (Signet Double)
Mosquitoes	William Faulkner (Dell)
Sartoris	William Faulkner (Signet)
The Diary of a Young Girl	Anne Frank (Pocket)
Mythology	Edith Hamilton (Mentor)
Kon Tiki	Thor Heyerdahl (Perma)
New Poems by American Poets	Rolf Humphries, ed. (Ballantine original)

The Night Has a Thousand Eyes	William Irish (pseudonym of Cornell Woolrich) (Dell First Edition)
From Here to Eternity	James Jones (Signet Triple Volume)
The Imitation of Christ	Thomas à Kempis (Pocket)
Studies in Classic American Literature	D. H. Lawrence (Anchor)
Growing Up in New Guinea	Margaret Mead (Mentor)
The Lonely Crowd (abridged edition)	David Riesman (Anchor)
A Stone for Danny Fisher	Harold Robbins (Pocket)
The Catcher in the Rye	J. D. Salinger (Signet)
The Day of the Locust	Nathaniel West (Bantam)
I Thought of Daisy	Edmund Wilson (Ballantine; reissue of a 25-year-old novel with negligible original sale)
The Theory of the Leisure Class	Thorstein Veblen (Mentor)
discovery No. 1	Vance Bourjaily and John W. Aldridge, eds. (Pocket)
New Voices: American Writing Today	(Perma)
7 Arts (reprinted arts criticism)	(Perma)
Junkie	William Lee (William S. Burroughs) (Ace)
Lady Chatterley's Lover (abridged)	D. H. Lawrence (Signet)
Sons and Lovers	D. H. Lawrence (Signet)

1954

Go Tell It on the Mountain	James Baldwin (Signet)
The Sea Around Us	Rachel Carson (Mentor)
The Long Goodbye	Raymond Chandler (Pocket)
The Body Snatchers	Jack Finney (Dell First Edition original)
An Analysis of the Kinsey Reports on Sexual Behavior	Donald Geddes, ed. (Mentor)
The Wall	John Hersey (Pocket/Cardinal Giant)
The Song of God: The Bhagavad-Gita	Christopher Isherwood, translator (Mentor original)
Daisy Miller and *The Turn of the Screw*	Henry James (Dell)

The Mad Reader	Harvey Kurtzman (Ballantine original)
Philosophy in a New Key	Susanne Langer (Mentor)
Down and Out in Paris and London	George Orwell (Perma)
The Meaning of the Glorious Koran	Marmaduke Pickthall, translator (Mentor simultaneous original)
Never Leave Me	Harold Robbins (Avon original)
Nine Stories	J. D. Salinger (Signet)
East of Eden	John Steinbeck (Bantam)
Messiah	Gore Vidal (Ballantine)
Utopia-14 (Player Piano)	Kurt Vonnegut (Bantam)
The Outsider	Richard Wright (Signet)

1955

The Age of Enlightenment	Isaiah Berlin (Mentor original)
You Asked for It (Casino Royale)	Ian Fleming (Popular Library)
The Age of Belief	Anne Freemantle (Mentor original)
The Blackboard Jungle	Evan Hunter (Pocket/Cardinal)
The Fires of Spring	James Michener (Bantam)
Sayonara	James Michener (Bantam)
The Red Pony	John Steinbeck (Bantam)

Just as the much-vilified Spillane was gaining his full stride in the paperback market, New American Library was diverting some of its profits toward a project so at odds with everything that Mickey Spillane's novels represented that NAL's involvement in both undertakings seemed implausible. Victor Weybright's once-strong relationship with Allen Lane had soured after their bitter separation in 1947, but Weybright still looked to Lane and Penguin as the model paperback operation in many respects. And it was Weybright's translation of Penguin ideas into New American Library actions that inspired a cultural high-water mark for the paperback book during the 1950s in the *New World Writing* series. As Weybright wrote in the introduction to the first issue, "By publishing new work in these pages, we hope to give aspiring authors a respected position in a sort of literary salon amongst the eminent. . . . If our publication can expedite the flow of international literature, it will fulfill its most important purpose."

The statement was bold, if not audacious — as well as somewhat pompous. Particularly coming, as it did, from a paperback publisher, Mickey Spillane's publisher, no less. But having announced such lofty goals, the editors of *New World Writing* spent seven years in the pursuit of literary excellence. From 1952, the year in which New American Library launched the series, until 1959, when the fifteenth and final NAL issue was released, *New World Writing* represented the best and brightest in American letters ever published by an American paperback house. To a large degree, Weybright's ambitious designs were fulfilled. Among its achievements, *NWW* could count the first appearance of a segment from a biting antiwar novel then titled *Catch-18* by unknown Joseph Heller; one of the first American appearances of an obscure Irishman named Beckett, living in Paris and writing in French; and the first excerpt from an unpublished novel by another unknown named Kerouac.

The concept behind the project was simple: to combine the literary excellence and avant-gardism of small magazines like the *Kenyon Review* and *Story* with the mass market distribution machinery of the paperback book. If the experiment worked, it would attest to the existence of a large, unacknowledged American audience for serious fiction, poetry, drama, and belles-lettres. At the same time, it would prove to a disdainful literary community that the paperback wasn't all trash. It was not an idea without precedent, and Weybright readily credited the influential *Penguin New Writing* as the model. Launched in November 1940, at the nadir of Britain's war fortunes, *Penguin New Writing* had been the result of an unlikely collaboration between Allen Lane, the mastermind behind Penguin but never an intellectual or even at home with the literary elite, and John Lehmann, a Brahmin in that same elite and a partner in the Hogarth Press with Virginia and Leonard Woolf. J. E. Morpurgo later said of the project, "*Penguin New Writing* was dedicated to two gods: Literary excellence and anti-Fascism. Allen was prepared to offer devotion to both deities."[18]

Throughout the war years and after, *Penguin New Writing* served as home to some of the finest British writers of the period, including Graham Greene and George Orwell. At *New Writing*'s peak, each issue sold more than a hundred thousand copies. Wrote Morpurgo, "*Penguin New Writing* must be numbered amongst the most significant of all Penguin ventures, the voice of a literature at war, a platform for distinguished writers of the middle generation, a source of hope to their neophyte juniors and a link between writers and their dispersed audience."[19]

For Weybright and Enoch of New American Library, the link to Penguin and *New Writing* was more than inspirational. New American Library had developed out of the New York office of Penguin, and while still associated with Allen Lane, the American operation had imported the series into the United States along with other Penguin books. To Weybright, the demise of *Penguin New Writing* in 1950 offered the opportunity to plant NAL's flag in new literary territory. In a confidential memo to Rudolf Littauer, NAL's attorney and, like Kurt Enoch, a German émigré, Weybright outlined the rationale behind *New World Writing*. "The proposed journal would identify NAL at once with the important writers of the future; it would win their respect and good will; it would be an investment in our future list." In addition, Weybright said, such a project would build morale and summon up the creativity of the staff, and "it will give us a standing among critics, writers and teachers. It would establish NAL as the intangible salon of literature in New York."

Less than one year later, in April 1952, after months of extensive contacts with agents, writers, and other publishers, the first issue was ready. With an initial print run of one hundred thousand copies, the book had been designed by the prominent book designer Ernst Reichl, perhaps most famous for his work on the Random House edition of *Ulysses*. The issue also introduced the fifty-cent cover price to the Mentor series, up from thirty-five cents. On the front cover, *New World Writing: The First Mentor Selection* was billed as "An Important Cross Section of Literature and Criticism."

In an introductory note, Weybright wrote:

> It is intended to be more than just a sprightly anthology which at first glance it may appear to be. It is a Mentor Book. As a Mentor, it will benefit from widespread distribution, at home and abroad, to thousands of newsstands and bookshops no existing literary or scholarly publication reaches. . . . The intention of *New World Writing* is to provide a friendly medium through which promising, genuine and vigorous talent may be communicated to a wide and receptive audience, and also to provide an instrument for serious letters and criticism. . . .

The cover of the first issue (see accompanying photo) offered evidence that the editors had gone a long way toward reaching their goal. The line-up was, as promised, a mingling of the established

The cover of the first *New World Writing* lists the contents. (Photo by Jerome Frank)

with the newcomers. Isherwood, Williams, Auchincloss, Vidal, and Merton were familiar to both the literary community and a wider audience. Isherwood's *Berlin Stories* had already made him something of a cause célèbre. Williams was internationally famous for *A Streetcar Named Desire.* Auchincloss and Vidal were both young darlings of the literati. Merton's *Seven Storey Mountain* had been a hardcover best seller in 1949. But among the other names — some of which later gained fame — were some newcomers whose published works had been limited to the small magazines. Flannery O'Connor had published only in the *Sewanee Review* and the *Partisan Review*, although *Wise Blood*, her first novel, from which her contribution was excerpted, was about to be published. Shelby Foote had written three books, and the excerpt that appeared was from his concurrently published Civil War novel, *Shiloh;* his piece reads with as much power and immediacy thirty years later as when it first appeared. William Gaddis — whose selection was the most avant-garde piece in the first collection — was at the time unpublished, his novel *The Recognition* not yet complete. Giuseppe Berto, whose novels had been published by New Directions, was a young Italian writer-journalist who began to write while a prisoner of war in Texas during World War II, and his contribution was set in a prison camp.

Upon publication, *New World Writing* garnered an enthusiastic reception. Calling it a "consciously high-brow but eclectic anthology of avant-garde writing," George Mayberry of the *New York Times* wrote, "The overall worth of the volume certainly outweighs the inadequacy and ineptitude of a good many of the writers included. [He liked Isherwood, Locke, Foote, Morris, Macauley, and Seide; he disliked Gaddis, Williams, and Alice Dennis.] It is salutary that, at a time when the paperback book field is largely dominated by private eyes and cowboys, the publishers of Mickey Spillane have seen fit to bring this experiment, and frequently exciting volumes, to the newspaper stands and railway terminals." Critic Carlos Baker wrote to Weybright, "It strikes me as a superior piece of sampling of the present new writing." Publisher William Targ commented, "The best 50 cents worth of reading in this or any other year." Northrop Frye said in a letter to Weybright, "It seems to me not only an excellent selection in itself but an ingenious and admirable publishing idea. I have often thought that something like this was the only way of getting good new writing across, as bound volumes don't sell and little magazines fold." However, not all the responses came from the literary world. A reader in Brookline, Massachusetts, wrote to NAL, "I read with keen interest the first volumes in your *NWW* series and I am moved to express my admiration for you for publishing them. It is refreshing to find a publisher who does not share the views of Hollywood producers, Broadway producers and most magazine publishers and who believes that intelligence and creativity are not incompatible with wide circulation. The trend which you have started may well be the beginning of a sweeping change of attitude among the businessmen who are engaged in presenting the arts to the people in this country." And from a housewife in Alexandria, Virginia: "Your *NWW* is a joy to me. It is lonesome to be a 36 year old housewife living on love, PTA, seed catalogues and a lousy library. The little book gives me a lot of new thought — new names to look for — new things to see. I hope you continue the selection."

Though the series was helpful to careers and boosted morale among the contributors, it did not make any of them rich. The payment rate was two and a half cents per word, whether you were unknown William Gaddis or celebrated Tennessee Williams (except in cases where pieces were specially commissioned). For the first issue, for instance, Louis Auchincloss received $142.43 on the first printing and an additional $16.09 when the issue went back to press. Flannery O'Connor got $83.08 plus $9.38. Wright Morris earned a total of $76.34. Poetry was even less profitable for the writer. James Schuyler received $7.50; Howard Moss, $11.53; Howard Nemerov, $22.50. The smallest payment, for the shortest poem, went to James Laughlin for his whimsical contribution:

> THE EGOTRON
> I think is what those science
> fellows should develop next.

NAL's executive editor, Arabel Porter, was given the job of overseeing the editorial composition of the series, coordinating submissions, commissioning articles, and contacting writers. However, it was apparent that *New World Writing* would demand the attention of the rest of the editorial staff, and the other editors as well as Weybright were pressed into service as readers. All submissions were read by the staff and selection by consensus rapidly developed. Most of the material that made it into the magazine, which was scheduled twice yearly, came from agents, by direct solicitation from writers, or from other publishers eager to place material from forthcoming novels because they realized that an appearance in *NWW* was an influential platform for their writers. However, unsolicited manuscripts came pouring in over the proverbial transom. Arabel Porter once estimated that at least fifteen hundred original manuscripts were read for each issue of *New World Writing*. While the reading alone constituted a herculean task, there were also problems of legal questions, rights clearances, and the awesome job of designing and typesetting such a wide variety of materials in an aesthetically pleasing format — a challenge further complicated when the series grew to include original artwork and photography.

A key member of NAL's editorial staff during this period was Marc Jaffe, a Harvard graduate and a Marine during the Second World War who had worked for *Argosy* magazine before joining NAL. Although he was nominally the mystery and Western editor at NAL, Jaffe became an important contributor to *New World Writing*'s editorial development. On vacation in Europe in 1952, for instance, Jaffe also did some scouting for NAL. Writing to Arabel Porter from Paris, Jaffe suggested that NAL publish something of Jean Genet's, and a portion of *The Thief's Journal* appeared in the second issue. Jaffe also wrote of having dinner there with William Styron, whose *Lie Down in Darkness* NAL published, and Peter Mathiessen, at that time organizing *The Paris Review*, who was a contributor to *New World Writing* No. 3. Jaffe also wrote, "Have you heard about Samuel Beckett, an Irishman (not young) writing in French?" That was the beginning of *New World Writing*'s courtship of the future Nobel Prize winner. Some time after his return to New York, Jaffe wrote in a memo to Porter, "I have been following developments on this author ever since my return from Europe and now we are actively interested in getting some of his work in the next *NWW*. I have been in continuous contact with his American publishers-to-be, the Grove Press, and his agent Marion Saunders. The Grove Press intends to publish his play, *En Attendant Godot*, next spring. I thought it might be advisable to get an extract from the play, but it seems that this is inadvisable due to the structure and style of the work."

Weybright's interest in Beckett was sparked, and he wrote to Porter, "What would you think of having Niall Montgomery undertake an article on Beckett? I think we could do a great turn for modern literature by an article on Beckett that described his life as well as his work and attempted to interpret his significance." Certain that *Godot* was not right for *NWW*, Jaffe instead proposed an excerpt from the novel *Molloy*. "I think it would be quite a coup to publish the *Molloy* translation. Whatever the significance of Beckett, I think we want to get him into the next *NWW* before any of our competing publications publish any of him." An excerpt from *Molloy* did indeed appear — along with an essay, "No Symbol Where None Intended" by Niall Montgomery, a vain attempt at Beckett-explicating — in *New World Writing* No. 5 (April 1954), netting Beckett $100. A second piece, *Yellow*, a short story, was published in No. 10 (November 1956), for which Beckett received $128.

Jaffe's concerns about "competing publications" were legitimate. Although *New World Writing* was first out of the gate with the idea of a "mass market small magazine," Pocket Books was readying a similar project, and in February 1953 *discovery* No. 1 was published. Unlike *New World Writing*, which was conceived and edited inside NAL, *discovery* was the child of two outsiders who brought their idea to Pocket Books: Vance Bourjaily, who had published a first novel to little success and no paperback reprint, and John Aldridge, who had written admiringly of Bourjaily in his essay "After the Lost Generation." The two met as a result of that article, and the idea for *discovery* was hatched. Bourjaily was familiar with *Penguin New Writing*, which he had read while stationed in Cairo and Beirut during the war. Like Weybright, Bourjaily cited *New Writing* as the inspiration for a similar American publication. Aldridge and Bourjaily took the idea to Pocket Books, where they got a receptive hearing from Herbert Alexander, Pocket Books' vice president and editorial director. Doc Lewis was less enthusiastic. As Bourjaily recalled, "He took the view that paperbacks were, and always would be, an adjunct to hardcover publishing. He may have changed later. But the idea that a paperback should be a reprint was being challenged at NAL by Victor Weybright. Doc never doubted that he was right, but he was willing to hedge his bets. He felt that within two years he would know who would prevail." With the prodding of Herbert Alexander, who realized that the project meant Pocket Books' editors would gain experience in handling writers, contacts with authors and agents, and advance word about books in progress, Pocket Books went ahead with the series, launching it under its thirty-five-cent Cardinal imprint.

Given an office and a borrowed secretary, Aldridge and Bourjaily edited the first issue. In their preface, they wrote, "In planning *discovery*, we began by rejecting the cynical portrait of the American reader as a juvenile oaf. We rejected the timorous assumption that pressure groups can put an honest magazine out of business. We rejected the kind of practicality which dictates that the contents of a large-circulation magazine must be inoffensively general, meeting the romantic needs of the pablum set at both ends of the human life span and leaving nothing of merit for the adults in the middle."

The magazine was dedicated to the principle of no principles. No "school" was encouraged, no trends promoted, no style rejected as unstylish. It was, as the editors said, "for its writers rather than its readers in the firm conviction that the role of literature in human history is to lead and not to follow." There were only a few unwritten general guidelines. All material was appearing for the first time; at least one new writer was introduced in each issue; a novella was published in each issue; and in marked contrast to *New World Writing*, all the contributors were to be American.

If the whole affair had the ring of "The Hardy Boys Start a Literary Revolution," the youthful enthusiasm was not misspent. In the first issue, with its Paul Klee-ish cover, were stories by Norman Mailer, Stanley Baron, Hortense Calisher, Herbert Gold, and the first appearance of William Styron's *The Long March*. Having collected all the work, Bourjaily discovered there was no nonfiction, so he wrote "Confessions of an American Marijuana Smoker" under the pseudonym U.S.D. Quincy. It was an account of seven disappointing experiences with "hemp." Bourjaily later learned of a graffiti exchange that took place in a Greenwich Village bar known for its marijuana smokers, where someone wrote "U.S.D. Quincy is a fink." Underneath was added, "U.S.D. Quincy is the editor of *discovery*." Bourjaily later commented about the essay, "That piece was important to me. It formed the core of my novel *Confessions of a Spent Youth*."

After two issues, Aldridge departed amicably and Bourjaily received more assistance from Pocket Books personnel. Future novelist Anne Bernays became his assistant, and Robert Pack took on the poetry editing. Pocket Books editors Bob Kotlowitz and Larry Hughes also had a hand in the selection, and the publisher set up Bourjaily in an office at 20 West Forty-seventh Street from which he could edit the series. Pocket Books was rewarded when *discovery* used an Evan Hunter story, later published in hardcover by Simon

& Schuster as *The Blackboard Jungle* and reprinted by Pocket Books to strong success.

A healthy rivalry between *discovery* and *New World Writing* soon developed. As Bourjaily put it: "My feeling was that there were two camps, *discovery* fans and *New World Writing* fans. There were distinctions between us. It's fair to say they weren't redundant. We did different things. We weren't pros; we thought of ourselves as writers. These were the emerging group of postwar American writers, rather than an eclectic selection of world literature." Although they competed for manuscripts, Bourjaily and Arabel Porter met and became friendly, with Porter occasionally tipping off Bourjaily to something *New World Writing* did not use. Saul Bellow's "The Gonzaga Manuscripts," which appeared in *discovery* No. 6, had been rejected by *New World Writing.* Victor Weybright was not interested in reciprocation. Bourjaily reported that Weybright said, "We won't do *discovery* rejects."

By the time the sixth issue of *discovery* rolled around, Bourjaily was already moving on, returning to his own writing. He had never intended to make *discovery* a permanent position for himself — he was a writer, not an editor — but he expected the project would continue after his departure. He was mistaken. As Bourjaily put it, "They wouldn't have missed me, but my leaving provided the occasion for Doc to say, 'If Vance isn't going to be the editor, perhaps we should discontinue.' " In addition, although *discovery* was paying for itself, it was making no "contribution to overhead." The sixth *discovery* was the last. In the meantime, others had tried similarly to make a go of it. Avon published *Modern Writing* and *New Voices* taken from the *Partisan Review,* and Permabooks put out *New Writers* and *7 Arts.* (All of these reprinted material from magazines rather than publishing original work.) But after brief life spans, these too disappeared, leaving *New World Writing* to carry the banner for mass market paperback publishers in the little-magazine area.

Through seven years and fifteen issues, it more or less succeeded. The pressures of a two-a-year schedule meant occasional unevenness in the quality, but in the main, *New World Writing*'s track record was dazzling. Not only had the most interesting emerging writers of the fifties been published — those on the cutting edge of new trends in fiction of the period — but Weybright had fulfilled his promise of internationalism by offering the contemporary work of Irish, Dutch, Japanese, Arabic, South Korean, Brazilian, Ghanaian, and Icelandic poets.

But it was for short fiction that the series was best known. Few major writers of the period were not represented. Norman Mailer, Nelson Algren, James Baldwin (an excerpt from *Go Tell It on the Mountain*), Heinrich Böll, Jorge Luis Borges, Ralph Ellison, James T. Farrell, Nadine Gordimer (a chapter from her unpublished first novel), Eugene Ionesco (*The Bald Soprano*, with illustrations by Saul Steinberg), James Jones, Nikos Kazantzakis, Seán O'Faoláin, Boris Pasternak, Ignazio Silone, Glendon Swarthout, and Dylan Thomas (*Adventures in the Skin Trade* was excerpted before publication) all appeared one or more times. There were also essays by Margaret Mead ("Sex and Censorship in Contemporary Society," commissioned by Weybright in response to the Gathings committee's investigation into obscene paperbacks); a section from Louis Armstrong's autobiography, "Storyville Days and Nights"; Erskine Caldwell's "How to Live Like an Author"; Malcolm Cowley's "The Time of the Rhetoricians"; André Gide's "On Literary Influence"; and Dan Wakefield's discussion of J. D. Salinger.

There were also the famous newcomers such as Joseph Heller, whose "Catch-18" was the first chapter of a novel in progress. When it was received from Heller's agent, one of NAL's editors, Walter Freeman, told Porter, "Of all the recommended pieces lately, this stands out. It seems like a part of a really exciting, amusing novel." Victor Weybright called it the "funniest thing we have ever had for *NWW*." The other editors agreed, and "Catch-18" was accepted. Heller received $125 for the excerpt. He wrote to Arabel Porter, "I should like to tell you at this time that it was with great delight and pride that I received news that you were interested in publishing a section of *Catch-18;* and I should like to express my thanks for the recognition implicit in your decision and the encouragement I have received from it." After the first excerpt was published, another, called "Hungry Joe," was rejected, but Arabel Porter asked Heller's agent, "Has he finished the novel? And if so, may we see it?" Unfortunately for NAL, the publication of Heller's excerpt did not give them the inside track on the novel, which was published by Simon & Schuster as *Catch-22* and reprinted by Dell.

One of the over-the-transom submissions that made the pages of *NWW* was from unknown Thomas Berger. In her comments to the other editors, Porter wrote, "I think this is an extraordinary piece of writing, a good muscular style and considerable irony. I think we should buy it." Porter asked Berger for a more arresting title than the one he had submitted, "The Advocate." He wrote back suggesting "Confession of a Giant." Published in *NWW* No. 8, the story was a piece of Berger's unfinished first novel, *Crazy in Berlin*. He was paid $217, and the story led to the novel's publication. (The money came in handy. At the time, Berger was struggling and also took on some freelance copyreading chores from Porter to help make ends meet.) *New World Writing* also launched Shirley Ann Grau ("White Girl, Fine Girl" in *NWW* No. 4 and "Isle aux Chiens" in *NWW* No. 10) and published in *NWW* No. 10 Anatole Broyard's "For He's a Jolly Good Fellow," a story that Broyard had submitted himself after earlier work had been published in *discovery*.

The other great "find" of *New World Writing* came by way of Malcolm Cowley, who suggested a manuscript recently rejected by Viking, where he was an editorial consultant. "It's a very long autobiographical novel by John Kerouac. It's about the present generation of wild boys on their travels between New York, San Francisco and Mexico City. . . . Of all the beat generation crowd, Kerouac is the only one who *can* write and the only one who doesn't get published." "Jazz of the Beat Generation" was published in *NWW* No. 7 under the pseudonym "Jean-Louis"; Kerouac received $120 for the excerpt from what came to be *On the Road*.

Despite its critical successes, *New World Writing* was barely paying its bills. The first several issues had gone to press more than once, raising unrealistic expectations that were gradually brought down to earth as print runs went up to 135,000 copies and then fell back down to 100,000 for the later issues. Although the series was covering its own expenses, it was creating an enormous drain on the editorial staff, and by 1959, after fifteen issues, New American Library was ready to call it quits. The total sales for the series had been over one million copies, but its influence on readers and writers and the contemporary literary scene far outweighed simple numbers. In the supposedly uneventful fifties, *New World Writing*, along with *discovery*, had stood for the new, the challenging — the assault on the status quo. Even if the series did not always succeed, it was not for lack of enthusiasm. At the time of its demise, Victor Weybright said, "The silver lining in the dark cloud over *NWW* is that Lippincott will carry on with the project henceforth. [It was dropped after three issues.] It has been financially successful [not so], but we are encountering arrears of energy, so I hand the torch to others so our editors can get on with the many projects facing us. Besides, we don't need *NWW* to demonstrate — as seemed important in 1952 — that paperback books are not a vulgar juggernaut."

The liveliness of these "small magazines" was testimony to the fact that this period of the 1950s was not just a stretch of eight years when Eisenhower slept. The social novelists of the 1930s — Farrell, Caldwell, O'Hara — and the reportorial novelists of the 1940s — Hersey, Michener, Wouk — were giving way to a literature of alienation in the 1950s, represented by Styron in *Lie Down in Darkness*, Ellison's *Invisible Man*, Mailer's essay "The White Negro," and later by Saul Bellow. It was a sense of disaffection peculiar to America's youth, and while some paperback publishers had exploited this disaffection with violent gang fiction, other writers were treating it more seriously. To a large extent, they were writers who appealed to the growing ranks of younger paperback readers who were discovering their deepening estrangement from mainstream, grey flannel America. It was an unease voiced by Mailer, Malamud, and Styron, and in the nonfiction of C. Wright Mills. But two novelists seemed to capture this growing separation between the old generation and the new better than anyone else. Both were published in paperback by NAL, as were Styron, Mailer, and Ellison. They were J. D. Salinger and Jack Kerouac, and they became two of the first authors deserving of a label coined years later, the "paperback literati." Although Salinger's and Kerouac's disgust with society was mutual, it took the two in opposite directions.

J. D. Salinger was born in New York City in 1919, attended public schools, a military academy, and three colleges; he served in the army from 1942 to 1946. Salinger had been writing stories since he was fifteen and was already familiar to *New Yorker* readers when *The Catcher in the Rye* was published by Little, Brown in 1951 and became a Book-of-the-Month Club selection. After winning wide — not unanimous — critical acclaim, the novel made it to the best-seller list in *The Publishers' Weekly* and stayed there for five months, although not selling well enough to make it as one of the year's ten top-selling novels. (On the best-seller list along with Salinger's novel were Herman Wouk's *The Caine Mutiny*, Nicholas Monsarrat's *The Cruel Sea*, James Jones's *From Here to Eternity*, and William Styron's *Lie Down in Darkness*.) New American Library had purchased paperback rights in advance of publication, as Victor Weybright later recounted:

One Friday afternoon I had received an advance copy of J. D. Salinger's *Catcher in the Rye*. I read it that evening and went into a cold sweat lest the reprint rights should be seized by a competitor if I waited until Monday morning. I tracked [Little, Brown publisher] Arthur Thornhill down on the telephone, made a deal and discovered later that we had beaten the field, most of whom did not receive their advance copies until [the] Monday or Tuesday following."[20]

Having propelled Weybright into such a fevered paroxysm, the slim volume about sixteen-year-old Holden Caulfield and his forty-eight-hour quixotic revolt against "phoniness" appeared in a twenty-five-cent Signet edition with a first printing of 350,000 copies in April 1953. A box on the cover read, "This unusual book may shock you, will make you laugh, and may break your heart — but *you will never forget it.*" For Signet and thirty years of readers to come, that statement was largely true. Few people were disappointed or unhappy about the book. Save one: J. D. Salinger.

Marc Jaffe (still an NAL editor at this point), who had been in communication with Salinger, recalled that the writer came to NAL's offices to discuss the book prior to its paperback appearance. "He said he would be much happier if the book had no illustrated cover at all. In fact, he would be happier if the book was distributed in mimeographed form. Of course, he had no control over the cover." Kurt Enoch, who was then responsible for covers, assigned NAL's star artist, James Avati, to paint the cover for *The Catcher in the Rye*. Avati produced a simple but effective illustration that showed Holden, wearing his famous red hunting hat turned backward and carrying his Gladstone bag, walking along a city street. He was passing in front of a nightclub that had some posters of semidressed women out front and Avati was asked to dress them up a bit, even though they were in the background. It was a most inoffensive cover, yet Salinger was dismayed by it. As Jaffe explained, "The book went on to tremendous success, but even knowing Salinger was unhappy, NAL never changed that cover. When the license came up for renewal, I was at Bantam and it became known he was unhappy." Oscar Dystel, by then the head of Bantam, recalled that Little, Brown's Arthur Thornhill (who was on the Bantam board of directors) called to tell him of Salinger's difficulties with NAL. "He asked me if I might be interested in discussing Salinger. I said, 'I'll be on the next airplane.' I dropped everything, went to Boston, and asked Arthur what he wanted. We shook hands on a two-cent-per-book royalty and Arthur then told me that Salinger had to approve the cover. I said, 'Anything he wants. We'll do it on plain brown paper.' Salinger actually sent us a swatch to show us the color he wanted. He even selected the typeface. The *J* and the *D* were set in different types. Bantam still uses that cover."

Though writing out of a similar sense of alienation, Jack Kerouac couldn't have been more different from J. D. Salinger. In temperament, public visibility, and literary styles — the beats had only disdain for anyone who wrote for the "slick" *New Yorker* — Salinger and the high priest of the beats were in different universes. Yet they spoke to the same audience. Twenty-five years after *On the Road,* Jack Kerouac and his cohorts have attained near-mythic heights, like some beat Knights of the Round Table. Biographies, memoirs, and reconsiderations of Kerouac and the beats are churned out yearly, either adding to the myth or attempting to demystify this wild bunch who were sainted by the next generation when it also took to the road.

Jack Kerouac was born in 1922 in Lowell, Massachusetts, the third and last son of French-Canadian parents. The son of a printer, Kerouac earned local fame as a high school halfback good enough to win a scholarship to Columbia University, provided he take a year of college prep at the Horace Mann School. During the Second World War, he joined the merchant marines and wrote an unpublished novel, *The Sea Is My Brother.* He returned to the city, pulled by some force of culture or circumstance to the people he came to call the beats — Allen Ginsberg, William S. Burroughs, Herbert Huncke (who introduced Kerouac to speed), John Clellon Holmes, and, finally, the low-life drifter Neal Cassady, prototype for Dean Moriarty in *On the Road.* In 1950, Kerouac published his first book, *The Town and the City,* an autobiographical novel edited by Robert Giroux and published by Harcourt, Brace. While the book was in preparation, Kerouac was on the cross-country odyssey with Cassady that inspired *On the Road.* In 1951, he wrote *On the Road* in twenty days, a furiously typed, 120,000-word paragraph written on a single roll of taped-together art paper. Giroux rejected it. Through Allen Ginsberg and Carl Solomon, whose uncle was A. A. Wynn of Ace Books, Kerouac had gotten a contract with Ace, but Ace also turned down *On the Road.* It finally reached Malcolm Cowley at Viking, now in regular typescript, but there was no enthusiasm there besides Cowley's. The critic-editor nonetheless placed an excerpt with the *Paris Review* and another with Arabel Porter in *New*

The Bible of the beats that sent a whole generation "on the road."
(Photo by Jerome Frank)

World Writing No. 7. The section that appeared in April 1955, "Jazz of the Beat Generation," was set in a San Francisco jazz club, an extended meditation on bop, written in a frenzied outpouring, a seemingly speed-induced paean to Lester Young and Charlie Parker. Kerouac insisted on using a pseudonym because he feared that his ex-wife would want the fee for child support of a daughter he claimed was not his.

On the Road, still with the support of Cowley, gained another sponsor at Viking, and they published the novel in 1957. Kerouac found a champion in Gilbert Milstein, daily book reviewer of the New York Times, who praised the novel to the skies, calling its publication a "historic occasion" and concluding, "On the Road is a major novel." The book made the New York Times best-seller list. Kerouac attained instant celebrity. In 1958, Signet issued the novel in a fifty-cent edition, to long-lasting success. (Kerouac's agent sold two other novels, Maggie Cassidy and Tristessa, to Avon as paperback originals, published respectively in 1959 and 1960.)

Although Viking accepted Kerouac's The Dharma Bums, written in 1957 and published in 1958, it rejected his other work. However, he had found a new patron in Barney Rosset of Grove Press, who published The Subterraneans in 1953. Barney Rosset had emerged out of the early 1950s as the most enthusiastic publishing advocate of the avant-garde. The son of a wealthy Jewish banker and an Irish Catholic mother, Rosset attended Swarthmore and discovered Henry Miller, about whom he wrote a college paper. On a trip to New York he purchased a sub-rosa copy of Tropic of Cancer — printed in Mexico — from Frances Steloff in the legendary Gotham Book Mart. Finding Swarthmore restrictive, he transferred to the University of Chicago. A stint in the army followed. Rosset was an admirer of the books being published by New Directions, an avant-garde house famous for its annual review. While he was studying literature at the New School after his army service, someone suggested he buy a publishing company that had put out three books but was about to fold. So, almost on a whim, he bought Grove Press. The three books were Melville's The Confidence Man, The Selected Writings of the Ingenious Aphra Behn, and The Verse in English of Richard Crashaw. Hardly a daring beginning for the man who was to be almost single-handedly responsible for the rewriting of censorship laws in this country. Rosset proved his publishing inexperience by taking the three books, which had been paperbound, and issuing them in hardcover. It was 1952. Rosset was doing the exact opposite of what several other trade houses were about to try: converting out-of-print and academic titles into inexpensive paperback editions. It was the initiation of the next major stage of the Paperback Revolution, the "quality" paperback.

The idea of the trade paperback — which is sold mainly to the bookstore trade rather than through the mass market racks serviced by the magazine wholesalers — was not a new one in 1952. Many other experiments, including the Modern Age and Boni books of the 1930s, had been tried earlier in the century. But none of them seemed to fire the imagination of booksellers, who undoubtedly saw paperback books as a threat to their sales of hardcover books. Even the success of the mass market paperbacks had done little to dent their disdain. However, Mentor Books, because of their superior quality and higher price, began to gain a toehold in university classroom adoptions and eventually in regular bookstores.

The idea of direct paperback sales to bookstores gained more currency when Allen Lane of Penguin dispatched Harry Paroissien to the United States to pick up the pieces of Penguin Books, Inc., after the split with Enoch and Weybright. Relocating the operation in Baltimore, an East Coast port city that was cheaper to do business in than New York, Paroissien, at Lane's direction, moved the Penguins away from the mass market. Working from the strength of its rich backlist of literary classics, history, and other academically oriented titles, Paroissien aimed at the growing university and college market. As an indication of its principal interest in the educational market, Penguin made an agreement for distribution with the D. C. Heath Company, one of the country's largest textbook publishers. Clinging to this specialized market, Penguin sold some six hundred thousand books in America during 1951. Its profits were important to the home office, but the U.S. Penguin fulfilled another important function by providing a convenient overflow valve for its parent, which could set larger print orders back in England with the assurance of a certain level of American sales. Although the Penguins eventually flourished in this somewhat rarefied atmosphere and the Penguin name acquired a certain cachet among the literary, the company never gained in the United States the full measure of power and influence that the name Penguin conferred elsewhere in the world.

At about the same time that Paroissien was transplanting Penguin to Baltimore, a neophyte publisher named Hayward Cirker was building a company in Lower Manhattan out of scholarly titles that had been remaindered or lay dormant and out of print. In 1951, Cirker took three of the books from his Dover list of scientific, scholarly, technical, and art books and turned them out in paper covers. The books were Unamuno's *Tragic Sense of Life*, Planck's *Thermodynamics*, and *The Handbook of Designs and Devices*. Principally known as a mail-order house, Dover did have some penetration into the bookstore trade.

However, neither Penguin nor Dover had the astonishing impact that accompanied the appearance in 1952 of Doubleday's Anchor Books. Doubleday had already attempted mass market publishing with its Permabooks line, launched in 1948 with laminated board covers — more permanent than laminated paper covers, hence Permabooks — but had switched the series into paper covers in 1951 for reasons of economy. Doubleday apparently did not have the mass market touch, and by 1952 Permabooks was on the endangered species list. But Doubleday owned presses for the Permabook line and wanted to keep those presses rolling. Enter Jason Epstein, a young Columbia University graduate who proposed reissuing out-of-print hardcover titles, specifically tailored for the needs of colleges, as paperbacks that would be more expensive and better produced than the mass market books. The break-even point for the books was set at twenty-seven thousand copies. Could Doubleday really sell twenty-seven thousand copies of *The Lonely Crowd* or *Lafcadio's Adventures*? Or *The Idea of a Theater*? Epstein reportedly said, "I don't know how many people want to read it. But I'm sure that there are at least twenty-seven thousand who *think* they want to read it."[21]

The books were rack-sized, as the Permabooks had been, many with covers by Edward Gorey, the noted and eccentric illustrator. The prices ranged from eighty-five cents up to $1.25, which was comparatively expensive even though a few mass market books had reached seventy-five cents by this time. And although they were aimed at graduate and post-graduate students, Anchor Books soon exceeded that circumscribed audience in an extraordinary fashion. In a few weeks, ten thousand copies of the first four titles had been sold. By 1954, sales were over six hundred thousand copies for the year. The reach of the books had gone beyond the university, into the bookstores and beyond. One element of this success was the fact that Anchor Books — as well as later trade paperbacks — offered a full "trade discount" of 40 percent to the bookstores instead of the 20 percent offered by mass market houses. Doubleday could also back Anchor with one of the largest and best-established groups of salesmen in the publishing business.

Aaron Asher, an editor who moved through a series of different trade paperback imprints during a distinguished career in publishing, recalled his first contact with Anchor. "I was serving in the army, stationed in Alabama between 1953 and 1955. I remember going into a stationery store in this strange southern town where they had a few newspapers and magazines. If you wanted a bookstore you had to go to Atlanta. But I was immediately struck by the first list of Anchor Books, and I was astonished to see them there. They were around ninety-five cents, which was startling then; it was still the day of the twenty-five-cent mass market book. But their covers were different and the books were completely different in nature."

By the time the Anchor series was off and running, Alfred A. Knopf soon joined in and issued its series of Vintage Books (Knopf himself is a great oenophile, and these books were the best from his "private stock"), all priced at ninety-five cents, published in rack size, and drawn from the estimable Knopf backlist, which included many of the finest writers of the preceding fifty years. Among the first Vintage titles were *The Art of Teaching* by Gilbert Highet, *The Stranger* by Albert Camus, *Death in Venice and Seven Other Stories* by Thomas Mann, and a two-volume edition of Tocqueville's *Democracy in America.*

The existence of the two new lines was unspoken testimony to the irrefutable fact that the paperback now occupied a central position in the publishing world. Anchor, Vintage, and their successors were another step in the continuum that had begun with Robert de Graff in 1939. While the mass market paperback that de Graff had brought forth helped to create a paperback readership, it had not always given that readership what it wanted. Anchor and Vintage quickly maneuvered to fill that void. As Epstein later explained, "When Anchor Books and Vintage began they tried to occupy some ground which was free at the time; that is, the mass market houses were publishing mainly books through magazine distributors while

Anchor and Vintage and the other trade paperback lines that came later found that they could distribute profitably through direct accounts. We were trying to reach a much smaller and more specific audience, mainly academic, literary, highbrow — specialized in these and other ways."[22]

The immediate widespread acceptance and success achieved by the two lines quickly inspired others to do the same. Beacon Press paperbacks, an offshoot of a Boston-based publisher, were originated by Sol Stein, and Meridian Books was launched by Arthur Cohen, co-founder with Cecil Hemley of Noonday Press; both Beacon and Meridian were among the first houses to go to a large-sized format, thus prompting the phrase "oversized paperback." Because they, like Vintage and Anchor, were primarily publishing serious nonfiction and classics and they all exhibited major improvements in design and production values over the mass market paperbacks, these books were soon christened quality paperbacks, a name that stuck for years to come. This was to the great displeasure of Enoch and Weybright at New American Library, who were properly peeved because they believed they had been publishing quality books since 1947. Another popular name for the trade paperbacks then was "egghead paperbacks," because of their intellectual qualities as well as the national prominence of "egghead" Adlai Stevenson, two-time loser to Eisenhower. Whatever they were called, by 1957 there were many more of them. R. R. Bowker, publisher of reference materials for the library and book market as well as of *The Publishers' Weekly*, began to produce a catalogue called *Paperbound Books in Print* in 1956 as a supplement to its annual *Books in Print*. The 1957 edition listed more than ninety firms issuing paperback books at that time, including the dozen or so mass market houses. (Those early issues of *Paperbound Books in Print* listed about 6000 titles, were bound in paper, and cost $2 per issue or $3 for a year's subscription to two volumes. The current edition comes in three volumes, bound in cloth, each the size of the Manhattan phone directory; it lists more than 220,000 titles and costs $69.50.)

Among this new wave of paperback publishers was Barney Rosset of Grove Press, who quickly saw the error of his ways in binding his three books in hard covers. At considerable expense, he had the bindings cut off, and the three original Grove books were once again paperbacks, the first in the Evergreen line that was launched in 1954. It took much of Rosset's considerable personal fortune to keep

Grove afloat in the early days as he published such titles as a bilingual edition of *Mid-Century French Poets*, Erich Fromm's *The Forgotten Language*, and Henry James's *The Sacred Fount*. But his reputation was shaped after a 1953 trip to Paris during which he saw *En Attendant Godot* and made the acquaintance of Samuel Beckett. Rosset brought the play back to the United States and published it in English in a hardcover edition that sold about three hundred copies at about the same time that the Broadway production with Bert Lahr mystified New York theatergoers and closed after some fifty performances. Rosset had already published some of Beckett's prose in Evergreen editions, and *Waiting for Godot* joined the list. (Rosset saved No. 33, his school football number, for *Godot*.) Although it didn't set any records, the paperback edition caught on as Beckett began to be considered more carefully in the United States. (The Evergreen edition of *Waiting for Godot*, so familiar to a generation of college students, has sold more than a million copies.) After Beckett, Rosset added the plays of Ionesco and Brecht. He was acquiring more visibility among the ranks of avant-gardists, particularly after the introduction of the *Evergreen Review*, a twice-a-year paperback magazine that was a showcase for the most experimental poets and novelists of the period, including Beckett, Burroughs, Ferlinghetti, Ginsberg, Robbe-Grillet, Camus, Henry Miller, and Günter Grass. In addition, Rosset underwrote Kerouac after Viking turned down his earlier work, and *The Subterraneans* (Evergreen 99) and *Doctor Sax* (Evergreen 160) were followed by later Kerouac work.

It was in 1959, however, that Rosset firmly fixed for himself and Grove a place in publishing and literary history. It also marked the beginning of a (somewhat) unfair image of Barney Rosset as "the dirty book man." (Writer Seymour Krim said of Rosset, "He was criticized in later years for making bucks out of porn when it was just that he was fascinated by sex in every conceivable shape and form.") Rosset, an ardent believer in the freedom to publish, decided that America was ready to read one of the great novels by one of the great novelists, *Lady Chatterley's Lover* by D. H. Lawrence. "It was part of my publishing philosophy to be against censorship," Rosset later remarked. "It was a perfect vehicle to fight censorship." With the approval of Lawrence's widow, Grove prepared an unexpurgated edition of the novel, which had been published in the United States only in an expurgated edition (in hardcover by Knopf and in paperback by NAL) because of a Post Office Department ban. To improve his case as a publisher of seriousness, Rosset enlisted the critic Mark Schorer to write an introduction, and the poet Archibald MacLeish, then Librarian of Congress, contributed a preface. Rosset's deliberate act of nose-thumbing was a signal that the sexual revolution and the massive social loosening of the 1960s were about to begin and censorship and the age of repression were on their way out.

Key Paperbacks: 1956–1959

1956

Malone Dies	Samuel Beckett (Evergreen)
Waiting for Godot	Samuel Beckett (Evergreen)
Nerves	Lester del Rey (Ballantine original)
I, Libertine	"Frederick Ewing" (pseudonym of Jean Shepherd and Theodore Sturgeon) (Ballantine original)
Why Johnny Can't Read	Rudolf Flesch (Popular Library)
The Dead Sea Scriptures	Theodore H. Gaster, translator (Anchor original)
Child Behavior	Gesell Institute (Dell)
Existentialism from Dostoevsky to Sartre	Walter Kaufmann (Meridian original)
Out of the Silent Planet	C. S. Lewis (Avon)
Listen! The Wind	Anne Morrow Lindbergh (Dell)
A Night to Remember	Walter Lord (Bantam)
The Deer Park	Norman Mailer (Signet Double)
White Collar	C. Wright Mills (Oxford/Galaxy)
A Good Man Is Hard to Find	Flannery O'Connor (Signet)
79 Park Avenue	Harold Robbins (Pocket)
Bonjour Tristesse	Françoise Sagan (Dell)
God Is My Co-Pilot	Col. Robert L. Scott (Ballantine original)
Zen Buddhism	D. T. Suzuki (Anchor original)
Best Television Plays	Gore Vidal, ed. (Ballantine original)
The Man in the Gray Flannel Suit	Sloan Wilson (Pocket)

1957

Notes of a Native Son	James Baldwin (Meridian)
James Dean: A Biography	William Bast (Ballantine original)
The Quare Fellow	Brendan Behan (Evergreen original)
The Hedgehog and the Fox	Isaiah Berlin (Mentor)
The Bridge Over the River Kwai	Pierre Boulle (Bantam)
The Anatomy of Revolution	Crane Brinton (Vintage)
Naked and Tender	R. V. Cassil (Avon original)
Tales from the White Hart	Arthur C. Clarke (Ballantine original)
The Marquis de Sade	Simone de Beauvoir (Evergreen)
The Ginger Man	J. P. Donleavy (Evergreen)
On Life and Sex	Havelock Ellis (Mentor)
The Quiet American	Graham Greene (Bantam)
Death Be Not Proud	John Gunther (Pyramid)
Goodbye, Mr. Chips	James Hilton (Bantam)
The Journey to the East	Hermann Hesse (Noonday)
Siddhartha	Hermann Hesse (New Directions)
Andersonville	MacKinlay Kantor (Signet)
Profiles in Courage	John F. Kennedy (Pocket/Cardinal)
Perelandra	C. S. Lewis (Avon)
Gift from the Sea	Anne Morrow Lindbergh (Mentor)
Tales of the South Pacific	James Michener (Pocket)
Peyton Place	Grace Metalious (Dell)
The Cruel Sea	Nicholas Monsarrat (Pocket)
The Last Hurrah	Edwin O'Connor (Bantam)
Ten North Frederick	John O'Hara (Bantam)
Life of Christ	Giovanni Papini (Dell)
Evergreen Review	Barney Rosset and Donald Allen, eds. (Evergreen original)
Lectures in America	Gertrude Stein (Beacon)
Realm of the Incas	Victor W. Von Hagen (Mentor original)
The Day of the Locust	Nathaniel West (Bantam)
The Organization Man	William H. Whyte (Anchor)
Marjorie Morningstar	Herman Wouk (NAL)

1958

After the Lost Generation	John Aldridge (Noonday)
The Second Foundation	Isaac Asimov (Avon)
Giovanni's Room	James Baldwin (Signet)
Flowers of Evil	Charles Baudelaire (New Directions)
Endgame	Samuel Beckett (Evergreen original)
The Wapshot Chronicle	John Cheever (Bantam)
A Coney Island of the Mind	Lawrence Ferlinghetti (New Directions)
Civilization and its Discontents	Sigmund Freud (Anchor)
From Russia with Love	Ian Fleming (NAL)
The Confidential Agent	Graham Greene (Bantam)
Dubliners	James Joyce (Viking/Compass)
On the Road	Jack Kerouac (Signet)
The Subterraneans	Jack Kerouac (Evergreen)
Compulsion	Meyer Levin (Pocket)
A Charmed Life	Mary McCarthy (Dell)
Mandingo	Kyle Onstott (Fawcett/Crest)
The Hidden Persuaders	Vance Packard (Pocket)
On the Beach	Nevil Shute (NAL)

1959

The James Beard Cook Book	James Beard (Dell original)
Watt	Samuel Beckett (Evergreen original)
Seize the Day	Saul Bellow (Popular Library)
The Martian Chronicles	Ray Bradbury (Bantam)
The October Country	Ray Bradbury (Ballantine original)
The Myth of Sisyphus and Other Essays	Albert Camus (Vintage)
The Edge of the Sea	Rachel Carson (Mentor)
Childhood's End	Arthur C. Clarke (Ballantine original)
By Love Possessed	James Gould Cozzens (Fawcett/Crest)
The Presentation of Self in Everyday Life	Erving Goffman (Anchor)
Lord of the Flies	William Golding (Capricorn)
Our Man in Havana	Graham Greene (Bantam)

The Worldly Philosophers	Robert Heilbroner (Simon & Schuster)
The Burl Ives Song Book	Burl Ives (Ballantine original)
Finnegan's Wake	James Joyce (Viking/Compass)
Zorba the Greek	Nikos Kazantzakis (Simon & Schuster)
The Dharma Bums	Jack Kerouac (Signet)
Maggie Cassidy	Jack Kerouac (Avon original)
Please Don't Eat the Daisies	Jean Kerr (Fawcett/Crest)
The White Negro	Norman Mailer (City Lights)
The Intimate Henry Miller	Henry Miller (Signet original)
The Causes of World War Three	C. Wright Mills (Oxford/Galaxy)
The Power Elite	C. Wright Mills (Simon & Schuster)
Atlas Shrugged	Ayn Rand (Signet)
Jealousy	Alain Robbe-Grillet (Evergreen original)
Exodus	Leon Uris (Bantam)
The Sirens of Titan	Kurt Vonnegut (Dell original)
Lady Chatterley's Lover	D. H. Lawrence (Grove)

EIGHT

The Lady
Goes to Court

Most of the publishers engaged in this sordid
competition operate in the field of cheap reprints selling
[for] from 10 to 75 cents.
> — Report of the Select Committee on Current Pornographic
> Materials (1952)

It is not so much the publisher's right to publish that
needs protection as the reader's right to read.
> — Douglas M. Black
> President, American Book Publishers Council (1952)

IN 399 B.C., SOCRATES was accused, "firstly of denying the gods recognized by the state and introducing new divinities and secondly, of corrupting the young." He was condemned to death, beginning the story of political, religious, and moral censorship in the Western world.[1]

The history of book censorship is written in legislation and legal decisions. One of the most important of these came in England in 1868, codifying obscenity statutes and establishing a basis for several generations of judicial bickering. Ruling on a challenge to the Obscene Publications Act, Lord Chief Justice Alexander Cockburn wrote in what was called the Hicklin rule: "I think the test of obscenity is this, whether the tendency of the matter is to deprave and corrupt those whose minds are open to such immoral influences and into whose hands a publication of this sort may fall." By his definition, Cockburn had implicitly ruled that obscenity was defined not so much by what it is as by who would be exposed to it. It was one of the most lasting decisions in the history of censorship.

Meanwhile, in the United States, a parallel movement was under way guided singly by a man who fought a holy war against obscenity, won convincingly, and held more official powers than any unelected man in America for the rest of his life. Anthony Comstock, a grocery clerk and — as his diaries later proved — a compulsive masturbator, began his crusade after the Civil War, abetted by a wave of clerically sponsored censorings. In 1872, Comstock founded the Committee for the Suppression of Vice and lobbied for a law that would govern obscenity. Known as the Comstock Act, it was one of the few pieces of legislation ever passed by Congress that bore the name of someone other than an elected official. Comstock's bill banned from the mails "every obscene, lewd, lascivious or filthy book, pamphlet, picture, paper, letter, writing, print or other publication of an indecent character." An amendment to the act made Comstock a special anti-obscenity agent of the Post Office with sweeping powers of search and seizure. Comstock's success soon gave rise to a wave of state anti-obscenity measures that came to be called the Comstock Load.[2]

Well into the 1930s, the Comstock laws reigned freely until the first blow for freedom was struck in 1933 with the celebrated decision in the case of James Joyce's *Ulysses*. Judge John M. Woolsey and, later, Apellate Court Judge Augustus Hand concluded that the novel was not lustful because a book must be judged as a whole. In Woolsey's decision, the sex in the book repelled rather than attracted. In Woolsey's words, *Ulysses* was "emetic, not aphrodisiac." As Charles Rembar, the noted First Amendment lawyer, commented, the judge had elevated, "into legal principle the proposition that nausea is not immoral."[3] Upholding Woolsey, Judge Hand wrote, "The erotic passages are submerged in the book as a whole and have little resultant effect." But in Rembar's view, the victory of the whole-book rule was tainted. The decisions of both judges confirmed the Hicklin rule. A great work of literature could still be found obscene if it was arousing or provocative.

The atmosphere at the time of the paperback's birth, in other words, was still highly repressive. Under then-current laws, such books as Lillian Smith's *Strange Fruit,* Theodore Dreiser's *An American Tragedy,* Edmund Wilson's *Memoirs of Hecate County,* Erskine Caldwell's *God's Little Acre,* and Kathleen Winsor's *Forever Amber* were being found obscene and banned in such supposedly progressive and enlightened states as New York and Massachusetts. For a period, paperback publishers were able to avoid controversy because they were publishing books that had already been cleared by the courts. But by the end of the 1940s, a new trend was emerging. Local censors took it upon themselves to attack paperback books. The essence of the problem was not always the book itself, but its availability. *Who* could read the book and not *what* the book contained had become the central issue. Obviously, the paperback publishers had not helped their own cause with their precipitous slide in quality.

One of the first noteworthy paperback censorship cases took place in Boston, where *God's Little Acre* (Duell, Sloan & Pearce and NAL) and James M. Cain's *Serenade* (Knopf and NAL) came under attack; the case went to trial in March 1949. Both books were labeled indecent, but there was some speculation that religious factors weighed into the complaint against *Serenade,* especially because of a steamy seduction scene set inside a church. In May, both books were cleared by the Massachusetts Superior Court. But the victory was short-lived. In August 1950, the Massachusetts Supreme Court reversed the earlier decision, and *God's Little Acre* was again banned as "obscene, indecent and impure." Even though the judges agreed with the lower court that the book was a "sincere and serious work possessing literary merit," and that it was of "value as a sociological document," they still found Caldwell's novel in the main obscene. However, *Serenade* was cleared when the same judges found that despite the sexual episodes, "they were not portrayed in a manner that would have a substantial tendency to deprave or corrupt its readers." (It should be noted that the phrase "Banned in Boston" was happily displayed by publishers who knew its potential as a sales pitch.)

At about the same time, Caldwell's books *Tragic Ground* and *Journeyman,* as well as *God's Little Acre* — in their NAL editions only — along with a Pocket Book, *Dr. Whitney's Secretary* by Dorothy P. Walker, were banned in Jersey City, New Jersey. Also in New Jersey, Vivien Connell's *The Chinese Room,* a historical novel published by Dial in 1942 that sold 2.5 million copies when Bantam reprinted it in 1948, was forced off the racks by a local prosecutor. The trickle of paperback titles coming under fire soon turned into a wave of bannings across the country. The targets of the censors were often the small newsdealers who had the books delivered by truck and placed in the racks by the magazine wholesaler's driver.

The newsstand or cigar store owner neither chose the titles he received nor was responsible for their display. But he was usually the first to be indicted or attacked and boycotted by local censors. In July 1950, in Fall River, Massachusetts, two local dealers and two chain store managers were charged with intent to sell books that were "indecent, obscene or impure, or manifestly tend to corrupt the morals of youth" to persons under eighteen years of age. Fourteen titles from six different publishers were involved in the case. They included *The Chinese Room* (Bantam), *The Dim View* (NAL), *The Girl on the Via Flamina* (Pocket Books), *Duke* (Popular Library), *The Gilded Hearse* (NAL), *A Hell of a Good Time* (a collection of short stories by James T. Farrell put out by Avon), *Beyond the Forest* (NAL), *The First Lady Chatterley* (Avon), and *Carnival of Love* (Lion Books). In Dubuque, Iowa, newsdealer James Norton of the Norton News Agency was indicted for sale of allegedly obscene publications that included books by Erle Stanley Gardner and Thorne Smith, *The Wayward Bus* by Steinbeck, *Midnight Lace* by MacKinlay Kantor, *A Stranger in Paris* by Somerset Maugham, six titles by Erskine Caldwell, and other books and magazines such as *Hit, Laff, Eve, Flirt, Eyeful,* and *Man to Man.*

Until 1952, the instances of paperback bannings were isolated and undirected. Often a local religious group would be behind the effort to force local newsdealers to yank certain titles from their racks. More often than not, these newsdealers weren't interested in taking a stand for their First Amendment rights; they only wanted to keep their businesses afloat. If caving in to the local decency association was the price, they paid it. But in May 1952, the House of Representatives authorized a probe of the paperback, magazine, and comic business to determine the extent of "immoral, obscene or otherwise offensive matter" or "improper emphasis on crime, violence and corruption." The resolutions creating the probe, called the Gathings resolutions for their sponsor, E. C. Gathings (D–Kansas), established a select committee of nine to investigate current literature. In June 1952, House Speaker Sam Rayburn appointed the committee, with three members from the Judiciary Committee, three from the Post Office Committee, and three from the House at large. Once constituted, the committee included E. C. Gathings as chairman, Emanuel Celler (D–New York), Francis E. Walter (D–Pennsylvania), Reva Beck Bosone (D–Utah), George P. Miller (D–California), Carroll D. Kearns (R–Pennsylvania), Edward H. Rees (R–Kansas),

Katherine B. St. George (R–New York), and Louis C. Graham (R–Pennsylvania).

According to committee chairman Gathings, the principal target of the committee would be "the kind of filthy sex books sold at the corner store which are affecting the youth of our country." The *Washington Post* observed editorially on May 12, 1952, that Gathings had chosen a "futile and dangerous form of attack upon a difficult problem," adding that the investigation would be "a threat to every publisher," amounting to intimidation. "There is no such thing," concluded the editorial, "as good censorship."

The House of Representatives Select Committee on Current Pornographic Materials opened its hearings on the first day of December 1952 with a statement that attacked paperbacks before a word of testimony was heard. The statement accused paperback reprinters of "the dissemination of artful appeals to sensuality, immorality, filth, perversion and degeneracy," and assailed the "lurid and daring illustrations of voluptuous young women on the covers of the books." Although a few representatives of the paperback industry would be called to testify, their reception was frosty. The committee had staked out its position early. Little that was said in the next week of hearings would sway those committee members who had come not for a hearing but for a hanging.

Most of the committee members were clearly with the likes of one of the first witnesses, the Reverend Thomas Fitzgerald, a member of the National Council of Catholic Men and director of the National Organization for Decent Literature (NODL), a group that issued a monthly list of books, magazines, and comics it considered objectionable. Fitzgerald charged that such objectionable literature resulted in "moral damage" to the young and the "loss of ideals," leading to juvenile delinquency. Contending that the issue was "not one of freedom but of license," he gave the committee a list of 274 paperback books he deemed objectionable along with a six-point recommendation for controlling such books. Fitzgerald asked for an industry code; measures toward the creation of "an informed and alert public . . . to make sure these publications are not available to our youth"; a bill for impounding mail; another for prohibiting interstate transport of obscene material; extension of a law to cover the shipment of obscene material by all methods of transportation; and establishment of a permanent committee like the Gathings group.

The committee already had a list of its own, comprising more than sixty paperbacks considered objectionable by its counsel, Ralph H. Burton. They included *Woman of Rome* by Alberto Moravia, *The Snow Is Black* by Georges Simenon, *A World I Never Made* and *Young Lonigan* by James T. Farrell, Caldwell's *God's Little Acre, I Can Get It for You Wholesale* by Jerome Weidman, *The Amboy Dukes* by Irving Shulman, *The Wayward Bus* by Steinbeck, *Dollar Cotton* by John Faulkner, and *Tomboy* by Hal Ellson.

Reverend Fitzgerald was only the first in a string of witnesses who pilloried the paperback. The deck was stacked against the publishers. The committee heard from religious leaders, police officials, school superintendents, and judges, one of whom declared that Shulman's *The Amboy Dukes* (Avon) had been responsible for two crimes brought into his court and that "such books" contributed to the problem of delinquency. One publisher, David C. Cook III, president of a religious book company based in Chicago, urged a code for the book industry similar to the one used by the motion picture industry.[4]

On the first day of the hearings, the committee did hear from two magazine wholesalers, Sam Black from Springfield, Massachusetts, and Victor Ottenstein from Washington, D.C. Neither proved to be a vigorous advocate of the freedom to read. Black asserted that wholesalers were compelled to distribute books they considered offensive. Ottenstein said his company received few complaints, and when they did, they removed the books and publishers compliantly took them back. Listening to two independent magazine distributors speak to the question of morality must have been a moment of considerable irony.

Also called on the first day was the only paperback editor to be heard from in the course of the hearings, Ralph Daigh of Fawcett's Gold Medal Books. Several Gold Medal titles had been cited as "objectionable" by the committee — meaning they would be referred to the Post Office for action. One of these was *Women's Barracks,* and it became the focus of much of the committee's attention as Daigh was questioned at length about the book. The bias of the committee was reflected in the questioning Daigh received from committee counsel Ralph H. Burton and the pugnacious Edward H. Rees, and other committee members:

These Avon books were typical of the paperbacks condemned by the
Gathings Committee. (Photos courtesy of Avon)

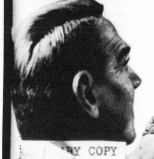

AN AVON
Special

JACK
WOODFORD

35¢

THREE
GORGEOUS
HUSSIES

THEY WERE THE COVER GIRLS
ON THE BOOK OF TEMPTATION.
THIS IS THEIR INTIMATE STORY

SPECIALLY REVISED
AND EDITED

BURTON: What type is it that sells as high as a million, on the average; that is, what titles usually run to a million?

DAIGH: Well, I would say good books; I don't think there is any type.

REES: What kind of books did you say?

DAIGH: Good books, not any particular type.

REES: How do you describe a good book?

DAIGH: A book is usually a good book if the public buys it in quantity.

BURTON: That is, good from the standpoint of sales and profits?

DAIGH: Well, that's true, but I also believe the other is true.

REES: You mean that if the public buys the book, that means it is a good book; if they don't, it is a bad book? That is the way you size it up?

DAIGH: Well, the second doesn't necessarily follow, but I do believe that when the public buys a product in the multimillion lots, that is an endorsement by the public, and it does connote that it is a good book.

BURTON: All right. Can you give me the names of some of the titles that have sold in million lots?

DAIGH: I should be able to give them quicker than I can. I know that *Women's Barracks* has sold in excess of one million.

[The committee report said, "Although *Women's Barracks* treats in large measure, and rather frankly, of homosexual relations between women, Mr. Daigh maintained that he saw nothing wrong in promoting its general distribution since it was a 'good book' because of the entertainment and education it imparts." The questioning turned to the comparison of the book to the classics and themes of murder, lust, and adultery as treated by Shakespeare and the Greeks.]

KEARNS: Isn't that a terrifically weak defense to state and mention those classics of Shakespeare to leave the door open to a book and try to place this publication in any sense of the word in the same category and with the same comparison with Shakespeare?

DAIGH: I see nothing ridiculous about it, nothing at all. I think our author is a sincerely able literary person, has written the best book in his ability, and I hope that Shakespeare did the same.

REES: You think it compares favorably with Shakespeare's books?

DAIGH: I don't think that is the question. I think both are eminently entitled to publication, exposure to the public.

GATHINGS: And the book sells for a quarter?

DAIGH: Yes, sir; and Shakespeare sells for a quarter in some editions too.

BURTON: Can you find anything in Shakespeare in equal number of pages, with as much obscene material as you find in *Women's Barracks* in the same number of pages?

DAIGH: Well; frankly, I don't know. I go along with the chairman of the committee on the difficulty of defining the word "obscene." It is an extremely hard word to define, and it varies with individuals, and if I were to make such a listing it would differ from a listing made by someone else.

In four more days of hearings, the committee heard from school officials, one of whom wanted book dealers near schools to stop selling pocket-size books that the committee found objectionable, and a New York City police official who suggested licensing all book dealers. He also made the point that his department avoided proceedings against books because the courts moved too slowly and the resultant publicity was always good for the book. Several Post Office Department officials described how the Post Office dealt with obscene material; they then pressed for legislation that would strengthen the postmaster general's hand in impounding obscene materials and any mail addressed to someone who had been charged with selling pornography by mail. (The majority report of the committee recommended enacting these measures as law.)

On the last day of the hearings, the only other representative of the paperback industry testified. He was John O'Connor, chairman of the board of Bantam Books and president of Grosset & Dunlap. Seven Bantam titles, including Steinbeck's *The Wayward Bus* and *Dollar Cotton* by John Faulkner (William's brother), had been called objectionable by the committee.

Most of O'Connor's testimony was focused on the book *Don't Touch Me* by MacKinlay Kantor, who later won the Pulitzer Prize for his Civil War novel *Andersonville*. In an atmosphere of open hostility, O'Connor was pressed to justify the propriety of publishing the book. Although it became apparent that it was not a book that he personally cared for, O'Connor made a valiant effort to defend his right to publish and distribute Kantor's novel. However, he allowed himself to be trapped when Representative Rees turned the questioning toward the issue of whether children should be allowed to read the book.

REES: I am not talking about MacKinlay Kantor; I am talking about the material in this book. Do you think it is good for folks to read?
O'CONNOR: If they wish to read it.
REES: Do you think it is good for children?
O'CONNOR: I think the only question is whether it is pornographic.
REES: That is not the only question. I am just asking you, do you think children ought to read the book?

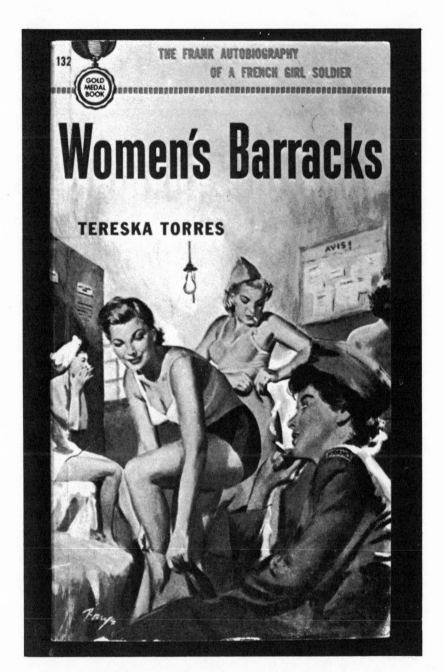

No single book was more furiously assailed by the Gathings Committee than this wartime diary. (Photo by Kevin Hancer)

O'CONNOR: I don't think I would give it to my daughter to read, for example, if that is the answer you want from me.

REES: Well, that is one answer, yes.

O'CONNOR: I don't think this particular book is one that is good for adolescents to read, no; I don't.[5]

REES: Do you think it is good for anybody to read? Do you think it is something that does a fellow good?

O'CONNOR: If a man wished to read it, why not, or a woman, an adult person.

REES: So you think it is all right to put that out?

O'CONNOR: I think so. Why not?

REES: Well, if you had read the thing you would know why not.

O'CONNOR: I have read it and I don't think . . .

REES: Do you like it?

O'CONNOR: No, I don't say I like it. I read a great many books. I read them professionally, so perhaps my opinion of a book would be different from your opinion of it as far as its . . .

REES: I am afraid it would be under those conditions. I am asking you now, do you think the book you have mentioned, *Don't Touch Me*, do you think that it is a good book to put out on the newsstands?

O'CONNOR: Would you let me make a statement of my opinion with respect to this book?

REES: Answer whether it is a good thing to put out on the newsstands for sale to the public.

O'CONNOR: For adults, why not?

REES: Because of the stuff that is in it.

O'CONNOR: Well, that is your opinion, Mr. Rees. . . . This book is published under a constitutional guarantee and it is also subject to prosecution under the pornography statutes if it is a pornographic book. If it is a pornographic book, then it should be suppressed and the publisher should be punished and the distributor should be punished.

GATHINGS: What do you think, Mr. O'Connor, this committee was formed for? Had there been such a congressional committee prior to this time?

O'CONNOR: Happily not.

GATHINGS: To ferret out this kind of trash.

REES: Did you say happily not?

O'CONNOR: Yes; because I think the testimony before this committee has been entirely one-sided.

O'Connor's testimony was lengthy, and if nothing else, he won a small measure of respect from the committee members. He added that he felt the hearings should have included testimony from social scientists, psychologists, literary experts, and legal experts. He objected to the Detroit police procedure of pressuring news dealers to remove books on the basis of a letter from a prosecutor without bringing the matter to court. He insisted that the "rule of law" must prevail in obscenity cases, arguing in favor of the whole-book principle laid down by Judges Woolsey and Hand in the *Ulysses* case and against judging by isolated passages, as the committee had done. O'Connor also pointed out that none of the seven titles issued by Bantam and cited by the committee had been the object of any legal action, nor had they been criticized on moral grounds in their original hardcover editions.

Although these samples from the testimony and from the committee majority's obviously skewed judgments point to a certain naiveté that might seem almost charming thirty years later, it is important to keep the hearings in a historical and political context. The early 1950s were a frightening period in America. A reminder of the tenor of the times in which the Gathings hearings took place came from John B. Keenan, director of public safety in Newark, New Jersey, who filed a statement with the committee but did not appear. Keenan had been warring against objectionable movies, pictures, and publications in Newark and said he was hampered in his drive by the lack of adequate laws. He wrote, "If the Communists are not behind this drive to flood the nation with obscenity, to weaken the moral fiber of our youth and debauch our adults, then it is only because the greedy business men are carrying the ball for them."

The specter of Communism might have sent a chill down more than a few spines on the committee and in the publishing industry. At the very time that the Gathings committee was relentlessly attacking the publishers on moral grounds, all of Washington was caught up in other hearings. The House Un-American Activities Committee (HUAC) was in its glory. And in February 1950, the junior senator from Wisconsin, looking for a campaign issue, held up his "list" of Communists in the State Department at a Women's Club meeting in Wheeling, West Virginia. America added "McCarthyism" to its vocabulary. The cloud of the Communist conspiracy hung over the government. And although the publishing industry was not affected by the "red hunters" to the degree Hollywood and academia were, there had been several instances of suppression. Max Lowenthal's 1951 book critical of the FBI, *The Federal Bureau of Investigation*, was the object of a smear attack by Walter Winchell, a friend of J. Edgar Hoover's. In another case, editor Angus Cameron was smeared as a sympathizer, forcing his resignation from Little, Brown in 1951.[6] Earlier, the Vanguard Press had been investigated by HUAC for publishing editions of economic and political books written by Communists. Doubleday was a target because it published Howard Fast's *The American*. Fast, an admitted Communist, was later jailed and blacklisted, although he eventually recanted his party allegiance. Nelson Doubleday, Sr., was called a Communist by Ralph Toledano, a well-known right-wing smear artist.[7]

Political fear was part of the problem, but the early fifties were also a time of almost compulsive sexual repression. Another statement to the Gathings committee reflected the paranoia of the church. Samuel Cavert of the National Council of Churches said:

> We recognize the wide circulation of publications which have had a deleterious influence on morals to be a symptom of moral laxity among our people which must be of concern not only to the churches but also to public agencies of government and education. . . .
>
> While the churches are committed to freedom of the press, I am confident that they are concerned that this freedom should not be exploited in such a way as to undermine the moral stamina of our people. . . . It is quite obvious that industries which profit by circulation of these publications should exercise more restraint and self-discipline themselves in the interest of public welfare. The hearings being conducted by the Congressional Committee are performing a service to our nation in focusing attention upon the problem.[8]

In its five days of testimony, the committee had heard from only two witnesses from the paperback industry, and one of them, O'Connor, was not involved in the day-to-day operations at Bantam. Four other paperback houses, all members of the American Book Publishers Council, had been called but then told their testimony was not required, a fact that O'Connor protested. However, Avon, Pocket Books, and New American Library each filed statements that were placed in the record to dubious effect. Avon's statement, written by editor Charles Byrne, was essentially a defense of a single title that had been battered by a stream of denunciations, Irving Shulman's *Amboy Dukes*. Byrne quoted reviews and sociologists' statements endorsing the book and presented records of orders from

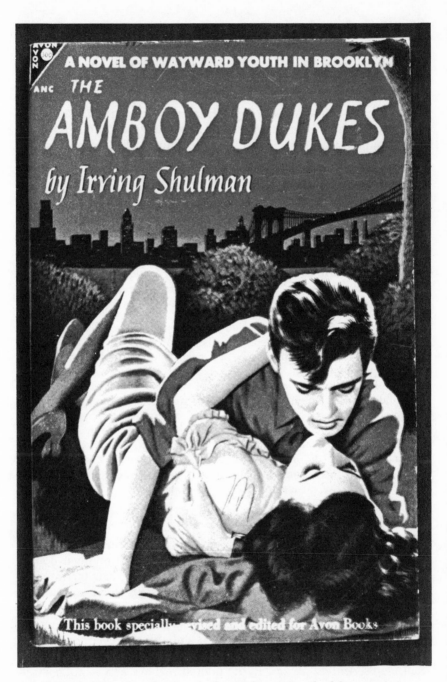

Shulman's novel was accused of provoking juvenile delinquency in the course of congressional hearings. (Photo by Kevin Hancer)

libraries and colleges. He also quoted at length from a successful defense of the book in a 1949 obscenity prosecution in Canada.

Two of the most informed and eloquent members of the paperback community, Freeman Lewis and Victor Weybright, filed statements on behalf of their firms. Lewis wrote:

> We take our responsibilities as publishers seriously. We try to publish only books which we consider to be worthy of our imprint. Because we have thus made so very many good books available at low prices, students, teachers, farmers, factory workers — American citizens throughout the land — are able to enjoy the heritage of our fine literature. We trust the judgment of the American public as a whole and its duly constituted judicial system.

Lewis sent a copy of his statement to the wholesalers, many of whom were responding to local pressures to limit the distribution of certain paperback titles. Lewis's statement had also addressed a controversy raised during the hearings that touched the wholesalers, the question of "tie-in sales." Several people had testified that national distributors of paperback books forced the dealers and wholesalers to take books they did not want. One dealer claimed, for instance, that Curtis salesmen threatened to cut off deliveries of the *Saturday Evening Post* or *Ladies' Home Journal* if the dealer did not carry Bantam Books as well. Lewis guaranteed that any dealer or wholesaler could refuse any or all of the Pocket Books sent to him.

He also offered legal assistance to any wholesalers who were facing difficulties with local authorities.

> In the course of our history we have been challenged twice; once in Dubuque, Iowa, where the case against our publication was thrown out, and once in a New England city where the matter has never been brought to trial. If you, as our enfranchised wholesalers, are challenged by local *legal authority* on any of our publications, you can be assured of our support in their defense. I strongly doubt that any of the publications of this company now or in the future will be prosecuted by your local legal authorities. It is quite possible, however, that minority pressure groups without legal standing and for interests of their own may attempt to prevent you from distributing certain titles. This form of extra-legal pressure is one which I hope you will resist with every means available to you. No greater danger to freedom of the press exists today than the efforts of well-meaning individuals or groups to deny other citizens the opportunity to choose what they may wish to read.[9]

Victor Weybright's defense of the industry was a vigorous mani-
festo that explained the workings of the reprint business and outlined its contribution to contemporary American culture. Although
it suffered from an extreme case of self-righteousness, his statement
was forceful and eloquent.

Reprints make universally available, for the first time in our history,
the entertainment, information, instruction and inspiration that formerly were available only to the well-to-do who could afford to pay
from two dollars to ten dollars for a hard-cover book and who had
access to rather limited sources of book supply. They have performed
a notable public service by turning into regular readers, and hence
better educated citizens, countless millions who had little or no previous access to books. . . .

While we are justly proud of the special accomplishments of the
reprint industry, we are proud primarily because we have succeeded in
bringing a new life and vigor to the American press as a whole by
opening up new channels for development. I believe that we have done
many genuinely creative things, but our contribution has been funda-
mentally not in creation but in distribution. . . . Our books are the
same books as those sold at higher prices in the bookstores and circulating on the library shelves. And for this reason the reprint is not a
separate problem to be singled out for attack without regard to its
relation to the publishing industry as a whole. . . .

The books brought to readers by the reprint industry represent a
cross section of the better literature being written today, with an ad-
mixture of the great works of earlier days. Let me repeat — reprints
are not new books; they are books you have seen before at four to
twenty times the price. Reprint fiction deals with sex and sin to the
same extent as the trade fiction of which it is a reproduction, and no
more. A large proportion of the better fiction being written today, and
therefore a substantial proportion of the fiction appearing in reprint
form, belongs to the realistic or naturalistic school, depicting life in
realistic detail as sordid and ugly in those aspects where life *is* sordid
and ugly. This presentation of the seamy side of human life shocked
the Victorians when it was introduced by Zola, but it has long since
won public acceptance. . . .

Of course our writers are more outspoken today than they were forty
years ago. Whether this is an evil depends on one's view of the function
of literature as a whole. The courts, the critics and the public have
swung increasingly toward the view that the truth cannot hurt. . . .

The same principles are applicable with respect to covers. Those
which are indecent, obscene or filthy are subject to prosecution. If

there are any such, the present law is thoroughly adequate to cope with them. But in the case of the great majority of covers, the only issue is one of taste. I do not believe that it is the function or the intention of Congress to legislate in matters of public taste. These are matters to be settled by the force of public opinion, operating in a free market place.[10]

Although many trade publishers were convinced that the paperback houses had exceeded the limits of taste and propriety, they were not ready to join the lynch mob. It was not difficult for them to see that a successful attack on paperback books would only be followed by an assault on books in general. And as Lewis and Weybright had pointed out, their paperbacks weren't appearing out of thin air; they were originated by legitimate trade houses. Accordingly, the rest of the publishing industry came to the defense of the paperback. In a *PW* editorial, the magazine stated:

> An industry which now produces nearly 1000 titles annually and is distributing 260,000,000 books or more this year could not possibly be given a fair appraisal by the Committee's sketchy and at times clearly hostile methods of inquiry.
>
> More disturbing than the inadequate method of investigation was the alacrity with which several members approved various proposals for censorship. Plans of control were seemingly acceptable without question or discrimination. Police pressure upon distributors without prior appeal to the courts was favored. So was the kind of industry code which has proved so controversial in the film industry. So, apparently, was the sort of local censorship by self-appointed committees which completely side-step the judicial process. . . . An appeal to cheap sensationalism eventually backfires against him who makes it — hearings certainly demonstrate at least this much. But while the industry re-examines its own procedures, as we believe it is doing, it must also fight, as an industry, against ill-considered charges and extra-judicial censorship.[11]

The other major statement in support of the paperback industry came from Douglas M. Black, president of the American Book Publishers Council. Black's statement — he was not asked to testify before the committee — acknowledged the excesses in paperbound books and favored enforcement of existing federal laws. However, he also launched a vigorous attack on the committee's prejudices and methods. His statement clearly outlined the committee's three major shortcomings.

First of all, he complained that the committee had confused legal standards with matters of taste. "There is no question of law. We know of no standards by which taste can be legislated. Where materials exist which offend the taste of some, the remedy is not to be found in passing a law."

Second, Black pointed out, the committee had misrepresented many of the books cited as objectionable by quoting excerpts taken out of context, a direct contravention of the whole-book rule used by the courts. Ignoring this standard, the committee was flouting all accepted legal understanding of obscenity at the time. "While we realize how arduous, and perhaps in some instances unpleasant, it would have been for the members of the committee to read each of the books under consideration, it remains true that there is no short cut to the objective evaluation of a book."

Finally, Black expressed his dismay at the obvious prejudices expressed by several of the committee members, illustrated best by the prehearing statement released by the committee, which said that paperback books "had deteriorated into media for the dissemination of artful appeals to sensuality, immorality, filth, perversion and degeneracy." Given this stated notion of the paperback industry, it was impossible to imagine that the paperback would get a fair hearing or that the committee would be swayed by anything it heard. The committee was much less a jury deciding guilt or innocence than a mob determining the means of execution.

Black concluded his statement by saying, "One of the most important cultural and educational forces in the past dozen years has been the paperback book industry. It has made widely available to our citizens, at very low prices, a large proportion of the best writing not only of the present day but also of the past, not only of American authors but also of the great figures in all literature. Never before has our whole population had the opportunity to examine and purchase so wide a range of books in their own localities."[12]

Despite these spirited responses in defense of the paperback and the freedom guaranteed under the First Amendment, the publishers were clearly sailing against the prevailing winds. The strength of those winds was evident when the Gathings committee released its majority report signed by six of the nine committee members. (A minority report signed by Emanuel Celler and Carroll D. Kearns was also issued; Representative George F. Miller declined to sign either report.)

The report echoed and expanded upon the sentiments expressed in the prehearing statement, which included such judgments as these:

- "The so-called pocket-size books, which originally started out as cheap reprints of standard works, have largely degenerated into media for the dissemination of artful appeals to sensuality, immorality, filth, perversion and degeneracy. The exaltation of passion above principle and the identification of lust with love are so prevalent that the casual reader of such literature might easily conclude that all married persons are adulterous [the committee was apparently not familiar with Dr. Kinsey's work] and all teenagers are completely devoid of any sex inhibitions."
- "Some books expiate upon homosexuality. . . . Other books extol by their approbatory language accounts of homosexuality, lesbianism, and other sexual aberrations. Books which deal with various phases of these subjects, introduced into the record as evidence include . . . *The Tormented, Women's Barracks, Spring Fire, Unmoral, Forbidden, Artists' Models* and *The Wayward Bus.*"
- "Other paper-bound books dwell at length on narcotics and in such a way as to present inducements for susceptible readers to become addicts out of sheer curiosity. As an example of how this subject is handled by current books, one need only read *Marijuana Girl*, by N. R. de Mexico. A more appropriate title would be: 'A Manual of Instructions for Potential Narcotic Addicts.' It even has a glossary of the jargon used by dope peddlers and their customers. . . . Even the evil effects of drug addiction are made to appear not so very unattractive by artful manipulation of the imagination. While the analysis of this book has been directed chiefly to its narcotic phase, that should not be construed as implying that it is not replete with lewdness and vulgarity."
- "Literary fashions in speech change from time to time. In Shakespeare's day great plainness and coarseness of speech was prevalent. The ascendancy of Puritanism in England promoted a pious reserve in language as in conduct. The Restoration tended to reinstate a licentious diction. The Victorian Era was a time of literary restraint. Two world wars have certainly impaired social morality, and this condition was quick to be reflected in literature. It may be that the time has come for the pendulum to swing back again toward decency, a consummation devoutly to be wished, particularly in view of the industrial potentiality of the modern press and its consequent prolific output of pornographic literature, especially in pocket-size books."

- In commenting on the *Ulysses* case, the committee majority said that it could not abide by the court's rule, calling the whole-book rule "elastic as rubber." "It is quite impossible," said the majority, "to reach a decision on obscenity without considering the questioned parts as such as related to the text as an entirety; and in so doing, the questioned parts must be taken out of context to evaluate, and that the committee has done." (The minority report said, "Such reasoning is rather bizzare.")
- In another rich vein of twisted reasoning, the committee said it was opposed to censorship, even though by all its actions it was working to suppress books it had found objectionable.

The minority report was far less condemnatory, even congratulating paperback publishers for improving the availability of literature. In a rebuke to the majority, the minority report said:

> While the Committee concludes that "censorship definitely is not a practicable answer to the problems in the field of obscenity," in its proceedings and reports it has nevertheless sat as a high congressional tribunal which has arbitrarily labeled as "obscene" a vast array of books, magazines and other publications. The Committee, in so doing, has blundered not only into the area of literary criticism but also into an area which the Supreme Court of the United States has declared to have a preferred position in our entire scheme of constitutional government. . . .
>
> The Committee has seen fit not only to criticize the content by which obscenity may be judged, but has also directed unfavorable comment toward ideas themselves contained in cited publications. This comes dangerously close to book burning.
>
> For example, *The Haters* by Theodore Strauss . . . was entered into the record with the objection . . . "Author obviously trying to cash in on the Scottsboro pro-Negro agitation which was Communist-inspired." *Cage of Darkness* by René Masson, was criticized by counsel because . . . the "Author does not seem to like the upper classes or law enforcement officers." Another book, *The Harem* by Louis Royer, is condemned by the Committee because the author personally advocated polygamy.

Whether the committee's recommendations had no real base of support in Congress, or whether Washington was preoccupied with Ike's inauguration and chasing Communists, none of the committee's proposals became law. But they didn't need to. The spotlight of a congressional hearing thrown on the paperback business triggered a definite chilling effect. In the years that followed, the paperback came under intensive pressure as local groups and police censors, seemingly acting with the full blessings of the Gathings committee, began a purge of the paperback racks, launching broad assaults on the newsstands where paperbacks were sold. In Brooklyn, the Decent Literature Committee of Our Lady Help of Christians Roman Catholic Church began to visit stores in the Flatbush section with a list of books it deemed "objectionable," asking storeowners to remove these books from the shelves. The merchants who complied were given a certificate to be displayed in the window; those who did not were faced with the loss of business. Bantam Books — which had published only a few of the titles on the list — took out advertisements in local papers answering the ban. Headlined WE CAN'T PLEASE EVERYBODY, the ad pointed out that among the books under attack was one by a recent Nobel Prize winner and another judged the best novel of 1950. "We know that no publisher can please everybody with every book. The issue, therefore, is our right to publish and your right to select books you want to read . . . in fact, everybody's right to freedom itself."

In Chicago, the powerful Archdiocese Council of Catholic Women produced a list of books that was publicized throughout the country and became the basis for many of the police bans and organized boycotts. In many other states, there were proposals put forth to suppress paperbacks. Georgia created a commission to investigate sales of literature which it considered "detrimental to the morals of the citizens of the state." Texas passed a law mandating fines or imprisonment for anyone who simply wrote advertising or designed covers for books considered obscene, as well as for the authors of such books. An Ohio proposal required prior approval by a review board before publication of any magazine, which the sponsor also wanted to apply to paperback books. There were police actions in Detroit and vigilante-type actions in Minneapolis, Augusta (Maine), Chattanooga, Scranton, Akron, and Manchester (New Hampshire).[13]

While most of these efforts were aimed at limiting books considered obscene, there were also cases of ideological and political suppression. In Texas, the legislature passed an "anti-red oath" that required an author to sign a declaration that he "is not or never has been" a member of the Communist party, and is not or never has been during the preceding five years a member of any organization on the attorney general's list of subversive organizations, before the state would adopt or purchase a textbook he had written. The bill went on to propose other stringent measures, adding the warning that state-supported institutions may, "contain communist propaganda and books which may poison the minds of many of our young people." In another incident, Bucklin Moon, a novelist and fiction editor at *Collier's*, was dismissed by the magazine after someone circulated a letter among the magazine's advertisers labeling Moon a subversive. It was the classic McCarthyist attack. Anonymous witnesses produced shadowy "evidence" showing a connection, however loose, to some "subversive organization." The burden of proof was then on the accused, who rarely met his accuser. The evidence against Moon included the fact that one of his novels had been favorably reviewed by the *Daily Worker* and that another of his novels had been advertised by the Worker's Bookshop. Moon told the *New York Times*, "I am not a martyr. I probably shall find another job. But this is a terrifying business that can happen to anybody."[14]

Happily, the publishers were winning some victories as well. The first came in March 1953 in New Jersey. The case actually began almost three years earlier when Matthew F. Melko, the prosecutor in Middlesex County, issued a list of objectionable publications based upon the recommendations of a local Committee on Objectionable Literature. In May 1950, Melko wrote to the New Brunswick News Dealers Supply Company of Elizabeth, New Jersey, sending a copy of the list of books "of such a nature that they should be withdrawn from circulation." The company manager, Ben Gelfand, later testified that he regarded the letter as a mandate to remove the books and he immediately did so. Among the books was Vivien Connell's *The Chinese Room*, reprinted by Bantam Books in 1948.

Bantam asked the prosecutor to review the titles he had asked to be removed. He did so and cleared four of them but kept the ban on *The Chinese Room*. Bantam sued. In a decision favoring Bantam that was handed down in 1953, Judge Sidney Goldman outlined the issues: Did the prosecutor have the authority to ban the sale of books? Did he in fact issue an order banning the sale of *The Chinese Room*? Should the prosecutor be restrained from further notifying distributors of the book that it should not be sold in Middlesex County? Was his action illegal and beyond the scope of his authority?

On these questions and several related points of law, the answers were completely in Bantam's favor. In an enlightened opinion that included highlights from the history of censorship to that point, Judge Goldman authorized an injunction against the prosecutor's interference with the sale of the book, his official use of the list of objectionable books, his delegation of claimed authority to censor books, and his threat to prosecute dealers of objectionable materials. And in a blow against the self-appointed citizens' committees, Judge Goldman wrote, "I hold that neither the prosecutor nor the committee constituted by him had the authority to proscribe the distribution or sale in Middlesex County of books deemed by them, or either of them, to be objectionable." Finally, Goldman found *The Chinese Room* not obscene by all the standards established in earlier cases, including the Woolsey, Hand, and Bok decisions. Wrote Goldman, "It [*The Chinese Room*] cuts a rather poor and pale figure in the colorful company of recent 'historical' novels of the *Forever Amber* type, which may be found in almost any public or circulating library, fresh from the best-seller lists."

While Judge Goldman's ruling seemed a clear-cut repudiation of local censors and autocratic prosecutors, a decision made on appeal muddied the waters. After the prosecutor appealed, the New Jersey Supreme Court upheld Judge Goldman's decision that *The Chinese Room* was not obscene. In doing so, however, they ruled that all other issues in the case were moot. The prosecutor interpreted this decision — mistakenly, it later turned out — to mean that he was still free to ban books under his own authority.

But the decision in the *Chinese Room* case would have an impact on a second victory in 1953. The scene was Youngstown, Ohio, where Police Chief Edward J. Allen had banned from newsstands more than four hundred paperback books, alleging that "all such books were obscene." Many of the books cited had been published by New American Library and NAL promptly filed suit against the police chief, seeking a court injunction to restrain him from further actions. In August 1953, Federal Judge Charles J. McNamee of the U.S. District Court in Cleveland enjoined Chief Allen from acting on his own authority in banning the books from Youngstown newsstands. In reaching his decision, Judge McNamee cited the *Bantam Books v. Melko* decision, saying the two cases were similar in many respects. Judge McNamee noted, "Freedom of the press is not limited to freedom to publish but includes the liberty to circulate publications. . . . Freedom of the press is also guaranteed by the Constitution of the State of Ohio. Censorship in any form is an assault upon the freedom of the press. A censorship that suppresses books in circulation is an infringement of that freedom."[15]

While establishing significant precedents, the victories in New Jersey and Ohio did little to stem the tide of suppression that was sweeping the paperback racks. One result of the spotlight thrown on paperbacks by the Gathings committee and the subsequent bannings was a definite toning down in the area of cover illustrations. Although the gradual desensualizing of covers probably had as much to do with changing trends in illustration as with censors, the mid and late fifties saw a noticeable shift toward lighter, less stark covers, particularly by the major houses. The cover artists who had come out of the pulp school of illustration were giving way, and a relative sophistication was replacing the harsh realism and blatantly deceptive covers of a few years before. In some cases, the changes involved doctoring old covers by zipping up models and adding some clothing. But there was also a change in philosophy. Leonard Leone, who joined Bantam Books in 1955 as art director, was one of the leaders in the move away from what he called "climbing clinches." "Years ago," recalled Leone, "most of the artwork was heavy on the idea of a man and a woman in dark rooms with a bare light bulb. But we discovered that people don't believe in 'climbing clinches.' They don't believe that people make love in the dark. So we put a lot more believability into the package."

The improvement in cover design was not enough for some communities where content was still regarded as far more dangerous than covers. Late in 1953, *From Here to Eternity*, winner of the National Book Award two years earlier, was the object of the Jersey City police chief's "suggestion" that dealers remove the book. Detroit became the second capital of censorship — after Boston — when the police there brought intensive pressure to bear on dealers under an old obscenity statute. Among the novels that were pulled from the racks in Detroit was *Auntie Mame* by Patrick Dennis (Popular Library). Another book forbidden in Detroit was *The Devil Rides Outside* by John Howard Griffin (Pocket Books), a novel described by the author as dealing primarily with modern and medieval Christianity.

One of the most persistently censored authors in Detroit and elsewhere was John O'Hara. In 1953, his novel *The Farmers Hotel* was banned in Detroit because one of the characters used the word *fuck*, to the great displeasure of police censors who were no doubt shocked by that word's appearance in black and white. *A Rage to Live* was removed from the Illinois State Library in 1953, and the powerful National Organization for Decent Literature, which provided a list that was used by local groups across the country to ban books in their cities, placed *Butterfield 8* on the hit list. As late as 1957 in Detroit, O'Hara's *Ten North Frederick* was banned in paperback. That was followed shortly by a banning in Albany, New York, where a grand jury indicted Bantam Books, along with eleven magazine publishers and local newsdealers, for conspiracy to distribute and sell obscene literature. On December 13, 1957, O'Hara himself was added to the indictment. Bantam's attorneys used the whole-book rule to get the indictment dismissed when court papers showed that the grand jury had read only selected passages from the novel. In 1958, the Albany indictment against O'Hara and Bantam was dropped.

A little later that year, the Detroit police censors were curbed by Wayne County Circuit Judge Carl M. Weideman, who issued a permanent injunction against the Detroit police commissioner and the director of police censorship. The injunction directed the Detroit Police Department to withdraw its ban on the sale of *Ten North Frederick* in Detroit and restrained the police from ordering any person to stop selling the book and from threatening to prosecute any person who sold the book. In his ruling, the judge held that the acts of the police chief and the police censor in calling the book obscene constituted a ban of the book and that they possessed no legal power to ban its sale until its obscenity was determined by a trial. In other words, it was becoming increasingly apparent that paperbacks were finally receiving the full protection under the law they were entitled to; a book could not be found obscene and banned simply because it was distributed more widely than a more expensive hardcover edition. The only remaining obstacle was some valid test of obscenity that would expand upon the whole-book rule and extend the protection of the First Amendment to a book that was plainly arousing. Such a test came as the fifties waned, with the trial of *Lady Chatterley's Lover.*

The bête noire of censors since Lawrence self-published the book in Italy in 1928, *Lady Chatterley's Lover* was under a Post Office ban in America. However, on May 4, 1959, Grove Press published a hardcover edition of the unexpurgated *Lady Chatterley's Lover.* (An expurgated version had been published by Knopf with the approval of Lawrence's literary executors, and New American Library had reprinted the Knopf edition in 1948.) Barney Rosset, Grove's publisher, knew exactly what he was doing and the risks he was taking but nonetheless went ahead, enlisting the aid of attorney Charles Rembar. Rembar knew that the *Ulysses* formula would not work, nor did he want to use the whole-book rule as the basis for his defense of *Lady Chatterley's Lover.* As he later wrote:

> To be sure, Lawrence put a lot in his novel besides the sex. But sex is its theme, and the presentation of the theme involved the specific description of sexual experience. The "erotic passages" took up much more of the book than those in *Ulysses.* Indeed, if impact as well as extent was considered, it was the nonsexual passages that might be deemed isolated. Nor could Lawrence's descriptions be said to make sex unattractive. What Mellors and Connie were up to sounded pretty good. Certainly not emetic and, to most people, probably aphrodisiac.[16]

On May 6, inspectors at the New York Post Office, acting on instructions from Washington, impounded twenty-four cartons of the book and denied Grove the use of the mails for sending it. The Post Office complaint against the book read that it was nonmailable in that it was "obscene, lewd, lascivious, indecent and filthy in character" and its "dominant effect appeals to prurient interest."[17]

The use of the phrase *prurient interest* was crucial to the case. The concept of prurience as a test of obscenity had emerged from an important 1957 Supreme Court ruling known as the *Roth* decision for publisher (some would say pornographer) Samuel Roth, who went to jail for producing and selling erotica and other books including *Lady Chatterley's Lover.* In deciding the *Roth* case, the majority ruled that obscenity did not enjoy the protection of the First Amendment and that the test of obscenity — called the "triple test" — was appeal to *prurient* (lustful) *interest,* judging the book in the light of *community standards* by its effect on the *average person.* While libertarians saw the decision as a setback, others felt it raised more questions than it answered. What did *prurient* mean? Which community? Who is average? Although Samuel Roth had gone to jail on account of the Court's decision, Rembar would base his defense of *Lady Chatterley's Lover* on the *Roth* decision and what he saw as the cracks in its foundations.

That defense came in a one-day hearing before a Post Office judicial officer, Charles D. Ablard. Witnesses for the defense included Rosset and literary critics Malcolm Cowley and Alfred Kazin. The prosecution offered only the book as evidence. Ablard abdicated the decision on the book and passed it along to Postmaster General Arthur Summerfield, a former auto dealer from Michigan, who affirmed the Post Office's ban on the novel. Rembar and Grove — at great expense to Barney Rosset — appealed the postmaster general's decision and were upheld in a historic ruling by Judge Frederick Van Pelt Bryan. In his thirty-page opinion, Judge Bryan ruled that the postmaster had no "special competence or technical knowledge" of the subject of obscenity. Far more significant was his ruling that the book was not obscene by the prurient interest rule ("a shameful or morbid interest in sex" was Bryan's definition) and confirmed the whole-book rule.

Another factor in the book's nonobscenity was the manner in which Grove had published the book. Bryan wrote, "The format and composition of the volume, the advertising and promotional material and the whole approach to publication treat the book as a serious work of literature. The book is distributed through leading bookstores throughout the country. There has been no attempt by the publisher to appeal to prurience or the prurient minded." Finally, Judge Bryan ruled, "I hold that, at this stage in the development of our society, this major English novel does not exceed the outer limits of the tolerance which the community as a whole gives to writing about sex and sex relations."

Grove's success was greeted by cheers from the literary world and howls from the proponents of censorship. The case was a major breakthrough for free expression. However, there was an unfortunate postscript to *Lady Chatterley*'s deliverance that became a sordid chapter in the history of the paperback. Within a few weeks of Judge Bryan's ruling, a flock of publishers were at each other's throats over paperback editions of the novel. New American Library, which had been continually publishing its expurgated edition since 1948, announced its plans to publish an unexpurgated edition in the near future. Grove, in the meantime, filed suit against NAL, charging that NAL's promotion of the expurgated edition was deceiving the public. Rosset also announced that Grove would release its own fifty-cent mass market edition, complete with the preface by Archibald MacLeish and introduction by Mark Schorer, which would be distributed by Dell. Grove and NAL were not alone. Since the book was out of copyright and technically in the public domain, it was fair game. Pocket Books produced one million copies of an edition on a record-setting schedule and had the first books on sale in New York only eight days after Judge Bryan's ruling. Pyramid also announced it would publish an edition that would include the complete text of Judge Bryan's decision.

In what became known as the Lady Chatterley Sweepstakes, all the books were rushed to the bookstores, leaving booksellers and readers somewhat bewildered as to who the real *Lady Chatterley* was. On strictly legal grounds, NAL said it had contracted with Knopf and Lawrence's executor for exclusive reprint rights to the novel in either expurgated or unexpurgated form; Knopf, however, announced that the contract covered only the expurgated version.

Morally, Rosset felt that Grove had won the right to publish the book. He had taken all the risks, including jail if Rembar's unorthodox defense failed, and had the blessing of Lawrence's widow, Frieda. Booksellers across the country agreed with Rosset, some calling the rush by other paperback houses to get their editions out "a stab in the back to booksellers." Frances Steloff, the legendary owner of the Gotham Book Mart in New York and a front-line soldier in the war for free expression, said at the time, "We are concerned about the case of *Lady Chatterley's Lover* and feel that booksellers owe a debt of gratitude to Grove Press for making an important writer available. We applaud the courage and the efficient, dignified manner in which the publication was handled and believe it is a bookseller's moral obligation to support the Grove edition."[18]

The situation grew ugly — Rosset called it a "publishing cat fight" — as NAL countersued Grove, charging the company with misrepresenting the Grove paperback edition. Then, in October, the Grove-NAL suits were settled out of court. The companies agreed that both versions were equally complete, unexpurgated, and valid presentations of the author's work, based upon the Orioli edition arranged by Lawrence himself. They agreed to pay royalties to the Lawrence estate and even papered over their differences by saying some nice things about how the other had worked so hard to rid the book of suppression.

In the war against censorship, the *Lady Chatterley's Lover* case was certainly D-day. A major beachhead had been taken, but the fighting wasn't over. Two more landmark victories, in the cases of *Tropic of Cancer* and *Fanny Hill*, made clear to at least a majority of the Supreme Court that a book could not be suppressed unless it failed on three counts: prurient appeal, patent offensiveness, and lack of social value. (The last of these three tests, social value, was set in 1966 in the case of *Fanny Hill*.)

Prior to these decisions, the Supreme Court had made another ruling that directly involved paperback censorship. The case was brought by four publishers — Bantam, Dell, Pocket Books, and New American Library — who were challenging the constitutionality of the Rhode Island Commission to Encourage Morality in Youth. The commission had been created to educate the public about any book containing allegedly obscene language and to recommend to the state attorney general books that he might prosecute. The publishers contended that such "education" had quickly become de facto censorship in violation of the First Amendment. In March 1963, the Supreme Court ruled eight-to-one in favor of the publishers. The decision, known as *Bantam v. Sullivan* (Joseph Sullivan was chairman of the commission), found the Rhode Island Commission's extrajudicial censorship activities unconstitutional.[19]

It is easy to look at the newsstands and theater marquees in any city, the bookstores in a suburban shopping mall, or the nightly offerings of network television and be convinced that censorship has breathed its last. Then along comes word that a school board in Maine has banned a book because it contains "obscenities." Or that a public library is being pressured by the Moral Majority to turn over records about which patrons have been borrowing a particular film. Throughout the 1960s and 1970s — and now into the 1980s — censorship remains as certain as death and taxes. The courts have provided limited support. It has been said that the Supreme Court follows the results of the last election. In 1973, the Burger Court rewrote the censorship rules; community standards were interpreted as local standards rather than national ones and a work that appealed to prurient interests had to possess some serious value.

Meanwhile, the list of books that one community or another considers offensive changes and lengthens. *God's Little Acre* and *Butterfield 8* are consigned to nostalgia. New books take their place. For a long time, number one on the hit list has been *The Catcher in the Rye*. Parents who don't know who Holden Caulfield is, let alone what he stands for, are certain that J. D. Salinger's 1951 novel will be the ruination of their children. Cited in *Library Journal* in 1978 as the most censored book in educational institutions, *The Catcher in the Rye* led a list of paperbacks that included in the Top Ten Eldridge Cleaver's *Soul on Ice,* Claude Brown's *Manchild in the Promised Land, Go Ask Alice* (by Anonymous), Heller's *Catch-22,* Steinbeck's *Of Mice and Men,* Vonnegut's *Slaughterhouse-Five,* Harper Lee's *To Kill a Mockingbird,* and Piri Thomas's *Down These Mean Streets.* These books appear in news reports with monotonous regularity as being censored by one local group or another. It is like the line from *Casablanca*: "Round up the usual suspects." Usually, the parents doing the yanking haven't read the books. It is censorship by reputation, a self-perpetuating image of a "dirty book."

That was essentially the situation in the most notable recent case of school board censorship. It took place not in some Deep South or Midwest backwater but in New York City's back yard. In 1976, on Long Island, the school board in Island Trees pulled eleven books from the school library after several of its members attended a meeting sponsored by a group called Parents of New York United. The group distributed a list of books it considered offensive. The Island Trees school board took their word for it. The board, many of whose members had not read the books in question, called these books objectionable, vulgar, anti-American, anti-Christian and anti-Semitic. The books removed were: *Go Ask Alice, A Reader for Writers* by Jerome W. Archer and A. Schwartz, *A Hero Ain't Nothin' but a Sandwich* by Alice Childress, *Soul on Ice, Best Short Stories by Negro Writers,* edited by Langston Hughes, *The Fixer* by Bernard Malamud, *The Naked Ape* by Desmond Morris, *Laughing Boy* by Oliver La Farge, *Black Boy* by Richard Wright, *Down These Mean Streets,* and *Slaughterhouse-Five.* (*Laughing Boy,* which had won the Pulitzer Prize in 1930, was returned to the library shelves; *The Fixer* was also a Pulitzer Prize winner but was not returned.)

The American Civil Liberties Union filed suit on behalf of the students in the community, and after a series of lower court rulings, the case reached the Supreme Court in 1982. The case seemed a clear-cut one of First Amendment principles. However, the Court did not see it that way. A five-to-four decision ordered a lower court to hold a trial to decide whether the school board was in violation of the First Amendment. Although the school board relented after this decision and returned the books to the library with the proviso that students receive parental permission to read them, the Court had not made a broad decision limiting the board's right to censor. In fact, Chief Justice Warren Burger, a member of the minority, wrote, "Never before today has the court indicated that the government has an obligation to aid a speaker or author in reaching an audience. . . . In short, even assuming the desirability of the policy expressed by the plurality, there is not a hint in the First Amendment or in any holding of this court, of a 'right' to have the government provide continuing access to certain books."[20]

There it stands. Some twenty years after *Lady Chatterley's Lover*, *Tropic of Cancer*, *Fanny Hill*, and *Bantam v. Sullivan*, the laws seem to shift with the tide of public opinion. The majority in the Island Trees case held the line in saying that school boards had discretion in their libraries, but "that discretion may not be exercised in a narrowly partisan or political manner. Our Constitution does not permit the suppression of ideas." However, it gives pause to consider what the result might have been if the present Court had been in place on those earlier cases. Following the election of 1980 and the supposed swing to the right in America — a shaky supposition at best — the Court has shown itself to be more conservative, and that conservatism was bolstered by Ronald Reagan's appointment of Sandra Day O'Connor to the high court. In a Court where one vote would turn the tide, the likelihood of another replacement to be made by Reagan sends icy fingers down the spines of First Amendment libertarians.

NINE

The New Age Dawns

Indian Summer is like a woman. Ripe, hotly passionate, but fickle.
— Grace Metalious, *Peyton Place* (1956)

James Bond: "They told me you only liked women."
Pussy Galore: "I never met a man before."
— Ian Fleming, *Goldfinger* (1959)

T HE CHANGES wrought upon the editorial face of paperback publishing during the late 1950s had been accompanied by significant shifts in who was doing the publishing. As the business grew increasingly complex and more sophisticated, with distribution evolving and competition intensifying, there was a gradual shakedown among the competitors. The paperback was now discussed in terms of the Big Four. In rough though shifting order they were Pocket Books, New American Library, Dell, and Bantam. (It became the Big Five after Fawcett expanded into reprinting in 1955.) Among the lower ranks were Popular Library, Avon, Ballantine, Permabooks, Pyramid, and Berkley.

If there was a visible symbol of the change among the ranks of publishers and the transition from the pioneering days to a more modern — if not thoroughly businesslike — business, it was the retirement of Robert de Graff in 1952. Known for his streak of stubbornness, de Graff and his partners had been bucking heads in a productive way for ten years. But it was time for new blood. Hailed as the father of the mass market paperback, de Graff was already less visible in the operation of Pocket Books by 1949. By 1953, he was no longer on the scene. Made a director of the company, he was, in short, kicked upstairs, where his function was increasingly ceremonial.

The business had outgrown the era of seat-of-the-pants flying that characterized earlier days when a publisher could play fast and loose, experiment a little, and eat a mistake because the risks were lower. No more. An increasingly sophisticated organization demanded more controls and efficiencies. At Pocket Books, a four-man team grew to provide that control. At the top was Leon Shimkin, the diminutive fireplug of a man who had proven himself a master of financial dealings and company marriages. While he was president of Pocket Books, Shimkin was an absentee leader, concentrating his attention on Pocket Books' sister company, Simon & Schuster — both still owned by Marshall Field. Beneath Shimkin was Freeman "Doc" Lewis, the executive vice president in charge of the overall publishing program. James "J.J." Jacobson headed the sales and merchandising side of Pocket Books. Herbert Alexander, also a vice president, handled most of the negotiations for reprints. (Vance Bourjaily, who edited *discovery* under Alexander's sponsorship, once said of him, "He had all the qualities of a great man except the wish to be one.")

One observer on the scene was Larry Hughes, who started at Pocket Books in 1949 in the mailroom ("It's a great place to learn the flow of business and get to know everyone, especially if you read other people's mail."), later moving into sales (as a "stoop, squint, and squat" man who checked Pocket Books' inventories at the local wholesale and retail level) and finally into the editorial department. (He remained there for ten years until he moved to William Morrow, where he eventually rose to become the head of the company.) Hughes later recalled the setup. "In effect, Doc and Herb had control of what was bought and Jimmy Jacobson of how it was sold. Doc and Jimmy had input into how it was packaged. Doc, of course, was knowledgeable about how books were sold because he came out of the hardcover reprint business. Jimmy was not a well-read man, but he had a nose for what would sell."

The territory inherited by this second generation at Pocket Books was not the easy-pickings gold mine it had been just a few years earlier. Larry Hughes recalled that Doc Lewis said at the time, "We're like Coca-Cola. We keep growing but our share of the market is falling." The reason was added competition leading to another downturn, just as there had been in 1946 when Pocket Books alone recalled 8 million books from the wholesalers. In 1953, the situation was just as grim. Lewis estimated paperback inventories in the field at 175 million copies. Costs were rising. Books were being produced faster than they could be sold. Nearly ninety new titles were being released each month, which meant they either never made it to the racks or they often supplanted a book that might still have a life if it were allowed a little more time. And sales were not increasing in pace with title production as the number of racks available to the paperback publishers began to level off.

Although these problems were afflicting all of the paperback publishers, they were nowhere more apparent than at Bantam Books. In addition to the general problems facing all the other publishers, Bantam had been racked by internal differences culminating in the dismissal of Ian Ballantine in 1952. A leadership vacuum lasting eighteen months had been created by his departure. Despite its powerful publishing-house ownership and the Curtis field force, Bantam was in the red in 1953. Walter Pitkin, the editor in chief, was made acting president, but it was a temporary appointment. John O'Connor, the head of Grosset & Dunlap and director of Bantam's executive board, headed the search for a successor to Ballantine. He was rewarded by the coincidental appearance of Oscar Dystel.

Oscar Dystel knew nothing about paperback books when he took the job as president of Bantam in 1954. A bulldog of a man who commanded instant attention, he had a wide reputation as a magazine marketing innovator. Born on the Lower East Side of New York, he graduated from New York University and then went to Harvard Business School, where he wrote a paper on controlled magazine circulation. After graduating, he worked for a series of magazines starting with a trade journal, *Fuel Oil and Air Conditioning Journal*, and including *American Golfer*, *Esquire*, and *Coronet*. As circulation manager and later editor in chief at *Coronet*, he boosted the digest's circulation from 80,000 to 2,750,000 readers. During the war, Dystel applied his magazine expertise to the war effort, starting the Office of War Information magazine *U.S.A.* and heading the psychological warfare leafleting program for the Mediterranean from Cairo. After the war, Dystel returned to *Coronet* and then held positions at *Collier's* and *Flair*; he later became assistant publisher at *Parent's* magazine.

But he was a man with an entrepreneurial itch. Casting around for backing for a new magazine concept, Dystel approached O'Connor to see if Grosset would be interested in his proposal. O'Connor, troubled by his Bantam headaches, declined. (The proposal that Dystel made in 1954 was for a digest-sized magazine that would spotlight celebrities and other interesting personalities, to be called *People*.) Following O'Connor's rejection of the idea, Dystel was surprised several months later when the Grosset chief called and offered him the Bantam position. After weeks of secretive negotiations, Dystel took the job with a promise of a percentage of the earnings. That arrangement must have suited O'Connor because Bantam was then losing money. As Larry Hughes, then of Pocket Books, said, "Bantam was a sleeping giant until Oscar Dystel began to make it move. They had the backing of the hardcover houses, whose books they could have locked up, and Curtis. We could never understand why they didn't wipe the floor with us."

Bantam's problems were illustrative of the industry's as a whole: overproduction, underpromotion, an overwhelming reliance on categories (especially Westerns and mysteries), and inefficient distribution. And the greatest of these was distribution. Between 75 percent and 80 percent of the paperback business — for some companies it was closer to 90 percent — was flowing through the independent magazine wholesalers, or, in the case of Dell, Avon, and Popular Library, the American News Company. In general, the wholesaler's order was predetermined by the publishers, perhaps after occasional consultation with the wholesaler, a method that came to be known as force-feeding. The wholesaler in turn parceled out the books to the local retailers based on his assumption of what the drugstore or corner newsstand could sell. The process was obviously less than scientific. There were no computers tracking orders, no experienced bookmen trained to ascertain what was selling where. Dealers merely collected money for the books and kept their 20 percent. No precise controls over how many books were printed and who would get them existed other than experience and guesswork. At best, the publishers would send out men like Larry Hughes to "stoop, squint, and squat," visually checking inventories at the local level. By 1953, it was obvious that this inexact science was seriously flawed. The wholesaler's warehouses were overflowing with books, many of which never even got out of the cartons. In one celebrated incident, a distributor near Buffalo, New York, took piles of unsold books and carted them away to be used as landfill.

Oscar Dystel quickly discovered this problem in his first weeks with Bantam when he went out into the field to meet with the wholesalers. His first stop was the District News Company in Washington, D.C., home base of Joe Ottenstein, one of the "godfathers" of the independent wholesalers. Dystel later told how Ottenstein took him out to the warehouses and showed him a pile of paperbacks as big as a city dump. "And you want me to order new merchandise? You must be crazy. I ought to throw you out of here," he told Dystel.

Instead, Dystel told Ottenstein and the other wholesalers to return the books. Bantam's returns had been running in the ten-million-per-year area. Suddenly, the field inventories were reduced by another two million copies. But bringing the books back was only part of the solution. Dystel's long-term prescription was controlled distribution. In the famous equation he called the Chinese Soldier theory, Dystel said, "We were sending out a thousand soldiers to take an objective and getting nine hundred killed." To put a brake on overshipments, Dystel instituted a conservative initial-order program under which books were actually undershipped. It became the bedrock of Bantam's distribution program for years to come. Instead of force-feeding the magazine wholesalers large quantities of books simply to allow larger initial printings (which meant cheaper unit costs), many of which then came back as returned books, the emphasis was switched to smaller initial orders and efficient service to fill reorders as books were sold. Dystel explained, "The idea was to get books out in a controlled, methodical manner. There is a psychology of scarcity. As a consumer, if you see a pile of books that never goes down, although the initial big display is impressive, you think the book is not selling. Seeing those books go down works for you. It says success. I thought it was better in most cases to initially ship fewer copies, fill reorders, and have fewer returns. The bottom line was getting returns down." By the end of 1955, using this undershipping strategy, Bantam had increased reorders from wholesalers by 348 percent over 1954. Returns were down 38.7 percent and sales went from 15,364,000 in 1954 to 18,124,000 (an 18 percent increase) in 1955.

Turning his attention to the content of the books, Dystel promoted Saul David, whom he had known in Cairo where David worked for *Stars and Stripes*, to the editor in chief slot, vacated when Walter Pitkin left after Dystel's arrival. (This left Sidney Kramer as the only remaining member of the triumvirate that had started Bantam in 1945.) One of their first decisions was to cut back on Westerns, which were Bantam's strongest suit but which threatened to overload the list. At David's suggestion, Dystel hired Leonard Leone as art director and made him an officer of the company. Leone, who came from the advertising field, had earlier been art director at *Argosy* and *True*. Under his direction, Bantam's covers moved toward a fresher, lighter approach than was common in paperbacks. In 1957, the Society of Illustrators mounted a display of Bantam covers with their light, clean look, a considerable improvement over the condemnation of only a few years earlier.

Dystel's next key move was to allow David to bring in some big books. Dystel believed the bell-ringing quality of excitement created by a best seller was necessary to any sound publishing program. So together they negotiated rights for Leon Uris's novel *Battle Cry*, for which they bid $25,000. Although Pocket Books, the paperback leader, had submitted the same bid, Dystel was able to win the book by having prepared well in advance of the meeting a promotional outline for the Bantam paperback. He had first contacted the people at Warner Brothers who would be handling the film version to discover their promotional plans; then he got the Curtis organization to push the book as well. When Dystel fished this four-page plan out of his pocket during lunch with the woman selling rights to *Battle Cry*, she was astonished at his preparation. Dystel later recounted, "We didn't think we would get the book. But that afternoon, a messenger arrived with the news that we were awarded the rights. The place went wild. That was the beginning of the turnaround at Bantam." By combining the movie promotion with the Bantam and Curtis efforts, Dystel had begun what became the hallmark of Bantam's success during the coming years — big books, coordination with Hollywood, and promotional savvy. *Battle Cry* quickly went over the million-copy mark and was followed by two more million-sellers, Pierre Boulle's *Bridge Over the River Kwai* and *East of Eden*, by John Steinbeck, a Bantam author since the company's inception. Dystel soon had the company in the black.

By 1957, paperback books had become more diversified editorially. The categories that had so dominated earlier output were giving way to more nonfiction and "permanent" or backlist fiction, such as classics and major contemporary novels. Movie tie-ins were growing in importance as Hollywood and the paperback took stock of each other. (Of the top five paperback sellers in 1955, three were movie tie-ins: *Battle Cry* from Bantam and Warner; *The Blackboard Jungle* from Pocket and MGM; and *To Hell and Back* from Pocket and Universal.) And the big, heavily promotable super seller had arrived, although Bantam wasn't the first to push this idea. Signet had done heavy promotions for its Double Volumes such as *Forever Amber* and *The Naked and the Dead* and its Triple Volumes including *From Here to Eternity*. Bantam, however, soon became the best in the business at pushing the big titles, a fundamental change from the days when books were shipped out to the wholesalers and onto the racks, where exposure alone was expected to sell them. At twenty-five cents there was simply no margin available for expensive promotions, publicity, and advertising. That began to change as paperback publishers learned that they could safely raise prices, beginning a cat-and-mouse game to see what the market would bear. In 1953, two-thirds of paperback books were still priced at twenty-five cents. But in 1957, more than half of the new titles were priced at thirty-five cents or higher. That reflected two things: the growing disposable income of Americans and the impact of higher-priced quality, or trade, paperbacks that made the mass market paperback seem more of a bargain.

In addition, the independent distribution chain was coming of age. With increasing frequency, the best and brightest of the wholesalers were separating their book business from their magazine business as paperbacks became a growing source of revenue for them. It now made economic sense to send a specially trained driver out in a truck that carried only books rather than simply dumping off a week's supply of books with the latest bundle of newspapers and magazines. In addition, these drivers were being trained how to "dress" the racks more efficiently, pulling slow-moving stock from the racks and replenishing hot titles rather than simply taking old books out and replacing them with new ones. This move to control distribution and improve service to the retail accounts helped a sputtering revolution get back on the fast track.

More potent changes were taking place in the paperback distribution business involving the long-running battle between the independent distributors and the American News Company. The once all-powerful American News Company and its retail subsidiary, the Union News Company, were being pressured on all sides by the independents and by changes in the magazine and paperback business. A few magazine publishers had already left American News, casting their lot with the independent distributors, when the paperback publishers, starting with Pocket Books, decided that the future was with independent distribution. A major blow to the American News Company was struck in 1952, when a civil antitrust suit was brought against the American News Company and the Union News Company, charging restraint of trade because the Union News stands refused to handle any magazines that were not funneled through the American News Company. A consent decree in 1955 broke the back of these monopolistic practices, and Union News was forced to consider all magazines impartially.

American News was also being racked by internal wars. In 1955, a group of dissident shareholders took over the company. They were led by Henry Garfinkle, a one-time newsstand operator who started with the newspaper concession on the Staten Island Ferry and parlayed that small business into a chain of newsstands that formed the Garfinkle News Company. A high school dropout, Garfinkle was hustling papers on the ferry when he encountered S. I. Newhouse, then the publisher of the *Staten Island Advance.* Garfinkle did some favors for Newhouse and got a loan from the publisher. With the money he began to build a string of newspaper stands, eventually possessing such key locations as the Newark airport and other major terminals. It was often suggested that Garfinkle had built his little empire with more than a loan and business smarts. He was often accused of employing strong-arm thugs as intimidators in the circulation wars that raged around independent distribution.

At the same time, the magazine business was changing. A sales technique never used before, cut-rate subscriptions, was hurting ANC's newsstand sales as magazine publishers came to rely on advertising revenues built on circulation numbers rather than single-copy sales. The independent wholesalers, with more paperbacks, grew stronger, and more magazines began to desert American News in favor of local independents. The stampede away from the ANC culminated in 1955 when Time, Inc., switched from American News to Select Magazines as its national distributor to the independent magazine wholesalers. Select Magazines, started in 1919, also distributed *McCall's, Popular Science,* and *Reader's Digest.*

A similar series of switches began to take place on the paperback side of the business. In a minor body blow, Avon Books left the American News Company in 1954, turning instead to the Hearst company's International Circulation Distributors. This left American News with only Dell and Popular Library and some smaller lines as its paperback suppliers. None of these was a major factor in paperback publishing. Popular Library had not had a million-seller since it published *Duel in the Sun* in the late 1940s. Dell had never had a million-seller. But in 1955, Dell rocked the industry by announcing its plans to use *both* the American News and independent distribution, shattering what had been an unbreakable either-or policy until then. It threw the paperback business into a period of chaotic scrambling to win accounts. Bud Egbert, then a regional sales manager for Pocket Books, recalled the situation. "Dell was a real vicious sort of thing in the minds of everybody after they went through the independents and ANC. Dell looked and saw which was best in a town and waved a stick between the two. It was considered a very evil thing to do at the time because everybody should have their franchised territories. For a multitude of reasons, the ANC was in trouble and declared what came to be called the 'Open Door' policy, which meant that they would take any line. Other publishers started to do what Dell had done and go into a town and say to the wholesalers, 'Look, if you don't do X, Y, and Z for me, I may go to American News.' " What followed was a period of circulation wars, localized switching back and forth between American News and the independents by the publishers. Then, in 1957, American News told Dell to either stay with them or pull out. Dell chose to leave.

They were able to do so for two simple reasons: *Bonjour Tristesse* and *Peyton Place*. Before 1956, Dell had had no best sellers to speak of. Their regular releases of Westerns, mysteries, and romances sold in predictable quantities each month. Occasionally, a successful title would go back for a second or third printing. However, sales and editorial policies had been dictated by the needs and wishes of the American News Company. All that changed with the arrival of the new editorial teams led by Frank Taylor for Dell reprints and Knox Burger for Dell First Editions. Dell was now diversifying its output. That program paid off when Allan Barnard purchased rights to these two books.

Françoise Sagan was only eighteen years old in 1954, when *Bonjour Tristesse* was published in the United States by Dutton. The young Frenchwoman became an overnight literary sensation that year. Her novel of young lovers was more than a little scandalous, helping to place it fourth among the year's fiction best sellers, with sales of 120,000 copies (behind Herman Wouk's *Marjorie Morningstar*, *Auntie Mame* by Patrick Dennis, and MacKinlay Kantor's *Andersonville*, the Pulitzer-winning Civil War novel). After Barnard bought the rights to the book in advance of publication for a $4000 guarantee, Dell reprinted it in 1956. The cover was amazingly chaste, featuring a photograph of the waiflike Sagan gazing forlornly into the distance. It was a long road traveled from Dell's earlier days when a book with half as much sexual content would have received red-hot art and a titillating cover blurb. In paperback *Bonjour Tristesse* sold over one million copies in 1956. But bigger things lay ahead.

Frank Taylor recalls the day that Allan Barnard came into his office and said, "I have something I want to buy, but I don't want you to read it." Without pursuing the matter, Taylor gave Barnard the green light, and he bought Grace Metalious's first novel, *Peyton Place*, also in advance of publication, for a guarantee of $11,000. Afterward, Taylor asked why Barnard had not wanted him to read the book first and was told, "Because you wouldn't have let me buy it." *Peyton Place* was published in hardcover in 1956 by Julian Messner (where, coincidentally, it had first been read by a young woman named Leona Nevler, who by the time *Peyton Place* was published was an editor at Fawcett), and it became the third-best-selling hardcover novel of the year. It had the "legs" to carry over into 1957 when it finished in second place behind James Gould Cozzens's *By Love Possessed*. Yet even its sizable hardcover sales and a six-figure movie deal provided no real indication of how spectacularly the paperback would sell.

Dell reprinted the book in 1957, the year the company left American News. Had it not been for *Bonjour Tristesse* and the excitement surrounding *Peyton Place*, Dell would have had a much more difficult time fighting for space in the independent distributors' racks. There were plenty of other companies producing category books that were already crowding the paperback racks in the mass market outlets. Instead, these two enormous best sellers greased Dell's way into independent distribution and out of the clutches of the American News Company. In 1957, American News dropped out of magazine and paperback distribution entirely. The independents had won the war — but that war was not without casualties. In making the switch from ANC distribution to independent distribution, Popular Library lost a million dollars in 1957 and almost went under. Lion Books did go under; in 1957, NAL picked up some of its titles, but the company, dependent upon American News, was finished.

In 1957, Dell sold three million copies of *Peyton Place*. By the middle of 1958, they had printed more than seven million copies, and by 1966, more than ten million copies had been sold. Yet *Peyton Place* is one of those pop culture phenomena that must be measured in terms other than simple sales figures and its impact on paperback profit and loss columns. Was *Peyton Place* simply a much-talked-about "good read"? Or does a book that reaches out to an audience of such breadth say something about the people who buy it and the place and time in which it appears. Twenty-five years after the novel was published, the words "Peyton Place" have become fixed in the language. The book that "lifts the lid off a small New England town" still conveys an aura of illicit sexuality. The town of Peyton Place, blessed with traditionally endearing local landmarks and characters, seemed an American idyll, a Norman Rockwell painting come to life. But Grace Metalious's melodramatic soap opera of the greed, vengefulness, and destructive pettiness of a respectable small town said that Peyton Place was not a single New England make-believe hamlet, but Anytown, America.

Today, the book seems quite harmless in terms of its sexual content. In fact, blatantly explicit sexual passages barely exist in *Peyton Place.* Far more interesting in retrospect are the three main characters: Allison MacKenzie; her mother, Constance (née Standish); and Selena Cross, the gypsylike girl from the poor neighborhood who is Allison's best friend. In marked contrast to most best-selling novels that preceded it — certainly any written by men — *Peyton Place* presented the rather audacious view that women had sexual feelings. They were not simply adjuncts to the whims, needs, and desires of men. If people wanted a sociological context for what the three *Peyton Place* women represented, they had only to look to Dr. Alfred Kinsey's second report, also a best seller. Published in 1953, *Sexual Behavior in the Human Female* shocked America with the effrontery of revealing that most American women had experienced orgasms before adolescence, half were not virgins if single or had not been virgins before marriage, one in four married women had committed adultery, many unmarried mothers expressed no regrets, and the chaste conceded only that they had lacked opportunity.

This news came as a major challenge to the polite notion that "good girls don't." What was important about *Peyton Place*'s women (although Allison and Selena are only teenagers, they are both more womanly than girlish) is that they represented this unspoken reality. To go a step further, they were on the cutting edge of a movement that had not yet arrived and still had no voice. They wanted more than to simply find the right man, settle down, and begin breeding and keeping house. Constance Standish had escaped the constraints of Peyton Place for New York, where she had been the lover of a married man; she had borne his child, the daughter she named Allison MacKenzie, using the father's last name. In Peyton Place, she runs her own shop and manages quite nicely without a man. ("Men were not necessary, for they were unreliable at best, and nothing but creators of trouble. . . . If at times she felt a vague restlessness within herself, she told herself sharply that this was *not* sex, but perhaps a touch of indigestion.")

Allison MacKenzie, in awe of her beautiful but distant mother and yearning for the dead father she never knew, dreams of escaping Peyton Place one day, as her mother did, and becoming a writer. In her emerging sense of womanhood, boys have a place, but they are clearly runners-up to her visions of a profession. And Selena, victimized by her brutal stepfather, is destined to be a strong, independent, fearless woman who will break all the laws of Peyton Place and get away with it.

For perhaps the first time in popular fiction, a writer was saying that women wanted sex and enjoyed it but they wanted it on their own terms. They were not passive receptacles for dominant men. To a generation fed on Mickey Spillane, for whom women counted as little more than animals, or Erskine Caldwell, whose Southern women were for the most part sluttish trash, the women of *Peyton Place* presented a new image. Independent, self-fulfilling, strong yet capable of love and desire, they were far from the perfect exemplars of the shining new woman that eventually followed with the onset of the feminist movement, but they were a breakthrough, a first faint glimmering that women were preparing to break out of the mold carefully prepared for them by centuries of male domination. Without overstating the case for *Peyton Place*, which as literature ranks considerably beneath *Jane Eyre*, the book addressed the nascent awakening of the modern American woman. The astonishing reception of *Peyton Place* made apparent the fact that Grace Metalious had touched some deeper nerve than the simple vicarious thrill of a good read.

Following the success of *Peyton Place* in 1957 and 1958, Dell caught the golden ring a third and fourth time. In 1959, the company reprinted *Anatomy of a Murder* to tie in with the film version of this novel based on a true story. The book caused some legal problems for Dell. "Robert Traver," the book's author, was actually the pen name of John Voelker, the defense attorney who successfully defended a policeman accused of murdering a tavern owner in Big Bay, Michigan. The dead man's widow filed a $9 million libel suit against Dell and the movie company, charging that the book had held her and her daughter up to public contempt and shame. The U.S. Court of Appeals ruled that neither the wife nor her daughter had a basis for a legal claim because they did not possess the "disreputable characteristics" of the characters in the novel.[1] For Dell, *Anatomy of a Murder* sold over three million copies in 1959. The following year, *Return to Peyton Place,* a sequel (paperback rights had been purchased for a new record $265,000), was issued, and it also became a multimillion-seller.

For five years running, Dell had held a valid claim to having published the leading paperback best seller of the year. The sales of these titles went alongside a growing list of accomplishments. Although the company was not especially innovative, Dell was proving resourceful. Dell First Editions (where *Collier's* contributor Kurt Vonnegut's *The Sirens of Titan* appeared as a paperback original in 1959) continued to perform well; the growing diversity of the Dell reprint list was improving the company's image and visibility; the emergence of the Dell Laurel list for the educational market added new strength in an area of rapidly expanding significance; and the publication of long-term backlist books with perennial sales potential expanded with such titles as *The Dell Crossword Dictionary* and *The James Beard Cookbook,* a 1959 Dell original that resulted from Frank Taylor's encounter with Beard at a party and a suggestion that the celebrity chef write a basic cookbook that would start with how to boil water. As the 1950s faded, Dell had broken out of the pack and moved up with the leaders in a very short time.

Such success, however, often breeds discontent. So it was at Dell. In 1959, Knox Burger left Dell First Editions for Fawcett's Gold

Medal Books. He made the switch because the Fawcetts promised him the freedom that was being curtailed at Dell. While still at Dell, Burger had to constantly contend with the demands made upon Dell by the American News Company, which really controlled Dell's output until the company broke away to independent distribution. As the paperback business grew more profitable for Dell and the comic book business began to shrink, the Dell management began to take a firmer hand in the editorial operations. Specifically, Helen Meyer, who had been functioning as Dell's chief executive but was more involved in its comic and magazine business, began to exert her influence in paperback matters. Meyer, who has been described as imperious and demanding, tightened her control over editors more accustomed to freedom. Their freedom had been symbolized by the fact that although they were editing Dell books, they worked for Western Printing and worked out of separate offices, only coming in contact with Dell for occasional editorial meetings.

But in November 1960 that changed. Dell took over the responsibility for its own editorial functions, transferring the editorial staff to its headquarters at 750 Third Avenue. The laissez faire control over editorial policy once exercised by Dell's management was gone, replaced by direct control. The departure of Burger in anticipation of this change was the first tremor. The second upheaval came when Frank Taylor, Allan Barnard, and Marc Jaffe (whom Taylor had hired away from New American Library after Jaffe had served there for ten years) stayed with Western Printing and set up the short-lived imprint called Racine Press. After working for Popular Library for two years, Donald Fine, once Burger's associate editor, returned to Dell as editor in chief in January 1961. Arlene Donovan, the one-time receptionist, was made the editor in chief of Dell First Editions, and Ross Claiborne was named editor in chief of Laurel Editions, the educational, or quality, line Dell launched in 1957.

The takeover of editorial functions at Dell in 1960 mirrored a similar situation that had occurred a few years earlier at Fawcett. A magazine publisher like Dell, Fawcett had seen its magazine business shrink while the paperback profitability mushroomed. After tasting the sweetness of paperback success, first as New American Library's distributor and then as publisher of the all-original Gold Medal Books, Fawcett was eager to become a full-fledged competitor to the other reprinters. In 1955, when their ten-year distribution contract with New American Library lapsed, the Fawcett family decided that they could do better by themselves. With Ralph Daigh at the helm of an expanding book department, Fawcett set up two new imprints. Following the New American Library lead, they created the Crest line for fiction and the Premier line for nonfiction. In addition to Daigh, the Fawcett editorial staff included William Lengle. A lawyer who had been admitted to the Missouri bar, Lengle came to New York to be an actor but answered an ad for an editor's assistant. The editor turned out to be Theodore Dreiser, and Lengle worked for the curmudgeonly writer for several years. Later he moved to *Cosmopolitan,* where he was an associate editor. Lengle liked to recall his 1925 trip to Paris, where a bartender in the Ritz pointed him to a sour-faced American. Lengle went over, struck up a conversation that lasted the night, and came back with Ernest Hemingway's story "Twenty Grand."[2] The third member of the new Fawcett editorial staff was Leona Nevler, who had worked previously at Little, Brown and had done freelance scouting for a number of publishers, including Julian Messner, where she picked *Peyton Place* out of the "slush pile." Nevler started as an associate editor with Fawcett in 1955. Two years later she was appointed managing editor of the two imprints. ·

At first, Crest books were little different from Gold Medal Books. In fact, many of the Gold Medal authors were switched over to the Crest list. In a business that was being sharply divided into the haves and have-nots, Fawcett's Crest had no visibility when it arrived on the scene and was therefore treated lightly by the trade hardcover houses. When it came to major titles, the hardcover publishers preferred dealing with the emerging elite of the business: Pocket Books, Bantam, Dell, and New American Library. So the early Crest lists included such titles as *Best Cartoons from True, The Best from Captain Billy's Whiz Bang,* and *The Education of a French Model.* Crest finally had a success when William Lengle picked up on a book that had been violently disliked by an earlier Fawcett reader. Figuring that any book that could provoke such a reaction might be worth a look, Lengle read the story set on a Southern plantation, a little-noticed hardcover that had sold about five thousand copies. The novel was Kyle Onstott's *Mandingo,* a steamy melodrama of plantation life in the ante-bellum South with an emphasis on the sexual relationships between slaves and masters. This "sleeper," as an unknown hardcover that becomes a major paperback success is called, was reprinted by Crest in 1958 and eventually sold over four million copies, launching a genre unto itself, the plantation novel.

Yet success alone did not guarantee Fawcett's acceptance into the inner circle. Instead, like so many of the nouveau riche, Fawcett did the practical thing and bought its way into the club. Loosening the Fawcett family purse strings, Daigh, Lengle, and Nevler went on a small shopping spree, buying a succession of major hardcover best sellers at head-spinning prices. First came the $101,000 advance guarantee that went for *By Love Possessed* by James Gould Cozzens, topping the old record of $100,000 shelled out by NAL for *From Here to Eternity*. Winner of the 1948 Pulitzer Prize for *Guard of Honor*, Cozzens had never cracked the best-seller list before. *By Love Possessed*, a novel about the professional and emotional dislocation of a New England lawyer, had sold just over two hundred thousand copies in hardcover and was the leading fiction seller in 1957. As a Fawcett Crest paperback, it quickly went over the million-copy mark. The flow of money out of Fawcett in exchange for best sellers continued with Vladimir Nabokov's *Lolita*, every paperback editor's dream come true. Here was a novel that carried impeccable literary credentials and was also a "sexy" book. The book could be marketed for its sex appeal and at the same time be held up as an example of how the paperback had expanded the audience for a major contemporary novelist. The story has it that Ralph Daigh asked Nabokov's publisher, Walter Minton of Putnam's, if he would take $100,000 for the book, which had been on the hardcover best-seller list during 1958 and 1959. When he received an affirmative reply, Daigh said, "Then you've sold it." *Lolita* sold more than three million copies in its Crest edition.[3] Also in 1959, Leona Nevler bought Jean Kerr's humorous look at suburban family life, *Please Don't Eat the Daisies*, which topped two million copies in paperback, and *The Ugly American* by William J. Lederer and Eugene L. Burdick, a prescient novel about an American diplomat in a small Southeast Asian country where anti-American sentiment was about to erupt into revolution. In 1960, the big Fawcett acquisition was D. C. Jarvis's *Folk Medicine*, another multimillion-seller (and still an active Fawcett title).

This gush of money being paid out for best sellers reached a temporary climax in 1961 when Fawcett broke Dell's *Return to Peyton*

Place record by advancing $400,000 for William L. Shirer's massive history of Nazi Germany, *The Rise and Fall of the Third Reich.* This long and heavy book, priced in hardcover at an equally hefty $10, sold more than a hundred thousand copies in hardcover during the last months of 1960 (plus an additional two hundred thousand book club copies) and another two hundred thousand copies in 1961. The book was hotly sought-after by every major paperback publisher at the time. But there was one great sticking point — how to publish such an enormous book in paperback. The largest paperback that had been bound until this time was one inch thick. Given the available presses and binding machinery, there was simply no way to produce the Shirer book in paperback in a single volume. But two-volume paperbacks had seen a short and inglorious history. They had simply never worked. From the time Pocket Books issued *The Hunchback of Notre Dame* in two volumes in 1939 to Ian Ballantine's unfortunate experiment with *Roosevelt and Hopkins* in 1950, the two-volume paperback was clearly the Edsel of the industry.

Just as the bidding for the book was about to begin, Fawcett learned that its printer, W. F. Hall in Chicago, had acquired a new binding machine capable of handling a two-inch-thick paperback. Whether it took friendly persuasion or some more direct means of convincing, Hall honored Fawcett's request not to share this information with Bantam, New American Library, or any of the other paperback houses whose books Hall produced. Secure in the knowledge of its ability to publish the book in a single volume, Fawcett went ahead with its record bid. It won the rights and immediately set another record by pricing the Premier edition of *The Rise and Fall of the Third Reich* at $1.65, the first mass market paperback to break the dollar barrier. The book became a major success, with long-term sales for Fawcett, and firmly established the company as one of the Big Five paperback houses at the beginning of the 1960s.[4]

In its free-spending rush to join the crème de la crème of the paperback business, Fawcett had simply exploited the strategy used earlier by NAL's Victor Weybright (who spent lavishly to acquire *Forever Amber, The Naked and the Dead,* and *From Here to Eternity*) and Oscar Dystel, whose largesse went for Leon Uris's *Battle Cry* and *Exodus* and many of John O'Hara's novels during the 1950s. The outpouring of hard cash by paperback publishers represented a vast and fundamental realignment in the dynamics of the publishing business. The shift in publishing power from the trade houses to the paperback reprinters had gained full momentum now. The paperback publishers were proving themselves far more aggressive and innovative in marketing and promoting their books, a "commercialization" of the publishing business that served only to heighten the condescension expressed by many trade publishers toward paperback people. The availability of cash for these large outlays also clearly demonstrated that the paperback was, as bank robber Willie Sutton put it, "Where the money was."

Although the era of excessive competitive bidding and two-day marathon auctions had not yet dawned, the nature of the paperback industry was evolving from one in which distribution of a large array of titles was now secondary to emphasis on the big best seller. The occasional six-figure guarantee was still the exception, but it pointed toward the future of blockbuster mania, the strategy among paperback publishers that dictated a need for titles capable of enormous sales that not only would be profitable by themselves but would have a coattail effect, bringing along a reprinter's other titles as well. This thinking was partly based upon a spoils system that was developing in independent distribution. In this case, the spoils were rack space. If a paperback publisher could put out a book that became a seller of the first magnitude, that book improved the paperback house's standing when it came to the independent distributor's allocation of racks, an allotment based upon sales volume. If Fawcett was responsible for 10 percent of a wholesaler's volume, then Fawcett got 10 percent of the wholesaler's racks. Books were not treated as individual titles, each with a sales potential based upon its merits, but as interchangeable numbers in a massive equation.

Yet sales volume was only one factor in that equation. Another widespread practice of suspect legality was also in place to assure access to the racks. These were the prevalent "promotional allowances," which were in fact kickbacks to "favored customers." In November 1959, the Federal Trade Commission issued complaints against New American Library, Dell, Bantam, and Pocket Books for giving certain chain retailers allowances that were not paid to all retailers handling those companys' publications. The publishers countered that these retailers were not their own customers but customers of the locally franchised independent magazine wholesalers. Each publisher also made the dubious claim that it was only making the payment in good faith to meet equal allowances offered by its competitors. The reality behind these payments was that the wholesalers had to offer certain customers special discounts. To compensate the wholesaler, the publishers, rather than increasing across the board the discount it allowed the wholesaler, paid the difference directly to the wholesaler. Finally, in 1962, the Federal Trade Commission said that every account must be offered the same sales terms or else it would be unfair competition and a violation of the Robinson-Patman Act (1936), which legislated against price discrimination. The major paperback publishers were all required to sign a consent decree ending the practice, but a new period of discounting wars among the publishers was opened up at great cost.[5]

Rarely do events divide decades so neatly as those of 1960 delineated the shift from the fifties to the sixties. It was the year that America got the "Pill," elected John Kennedy president, and saw sit-ins in Greensboro, North Carolina. The world seemed to be conspiring to announce a new age of vast changes: the loosening of sexual repression; the opening of the political process; the great upheaval in race relations. It was not coincidental that America elected its youngest president ever and that he promised to get the country moving again.

In paperback publishing a similar string of events set off one era from the next, a declaration that the paperback business was no longer a second-class citizen in the world of publishing. The forces that had been gathering during the fifteen years of postwar American publishing were finally unleashed with the onset of the new decade. The momentum was confirmed by a little-heralded milestone that was reached between 1959 and 1960. For the first time, dollar sales from paperbacks surpassed those of adult trade hardcover books. Although well behind textbooks, encyclopedias, and book clubs in dollar volume, the paperback was far and away the leader in numbers of books sold and was the fastest-growing segment of the publishing industry.

There were two basic reasons for this surge in paperback sales. First was the growing acceptance of the paperback by the bookstores. When Anchor, Vintage, Meridian, Evergreen, Beacon, Grosset's Universal, Viking/Compass, and a host of other imprints burst upon the scene in the mid-1950s, they opened the doors of the American bookselling scene to the paperback. Bookstore owners who once found the paperback objectionable now saw it as a practical necessity and an economic boost. Book buyers wanted paperbacks. Paperbacks increased traffic for bookstores, drawing new customers. Even though cover prices were still relatively low, buyers tended to purchase several books at once. And as cover prices rose, there seemed to be little resistance to the change, particularly when major best sellers on the order of *The Rise and Fall of the Third Reich* and *Doctor Zhivago* were being made available in inexpensive paper editions.

This was creating changes within the marketing strategy of the paperback business as well. Until this time, publishers had fought — often unsuccessfully — to retain what they called segregation. In other words, all Bantam titles were displayed together, all Pocket Books were displayed together, and so on. While this was a convenient method for publishers' representatives who wanted to keep track of inventories, it went against every rule of bookselling. Instead, bookstores were creating paperback category sections that were the equivalent of their hardcover sections. With the increasing output from a variety of publishers, it was not difficult to fill almost any subject category with a broad selection of paperback editions. There was no longer a subject area in which paperbacks were missing.

The next major step came in 1961 when Fawcett announced that it would extend a full trade discount of 40 percent to its retail customers. Other publishers followed suit and the movement toward increased direct sales to bookstores — accounts that were serviced directly from the publisher or from exclusively paperback wholesalers, or "jobbers," rather than through the independent wholesaler — marked a major evolutionary change for the paperback. Even though there were still shamefully few full-service bookstores in America at the end of the 1950s, these stores catered to an audience that bought books out of proportion to its numbers. In addition, the phenomenon of the paperback bookstore had been born. In New York City, several of these had sprung up around subway entrances and railroad terminals. As the number of titles proliferated from a growing number of publishers, other existing bookstores began to cultivate a paperback audience. Two shops represented this spirit. In New York's Greenwich Village, the Eighth

THE POCKET POETS SERIES

HOWL

AND OTHER POEMS

ALLEN GINSBERG

Introduction by

William Carlos Williams

NUMBER FOUR

The City Lights edition of Ginsberg's *Howl*, one of the best-selling and most influential volumes of poetry published in paperback. (Photo by Jerome Frank; by permission of City Lights Books)

Street Bookshop became a mecca for the emerging underground of beats. On the West Coast, a landmark was established in 1952 when Lawrence Ferlinghetti opened the City Lights Bookshop in San Francisco. It became the most famous all-paperback bookstore in America and also emerged as a lightning rod for the avant-garde literary set known as the San Francisco group. That notoriety was heightened when Ferlinghetti, himself a poet of some following, began to publish paperback books under the City Lights imprint. Among the first in the series was Allen Ginsberg's *Howl and Other Poems* (1956), the beat anthem and surely the most influential collection of poetry published in the 1950s. Subsequent to its publication, the book was seized by U.S. Customs and the San Francisco police for alleged obscenity. It was the first in a series of run-ins between City Lights and the law. The subject of an extended court trial that became a platform for a vigorous defense of *Howl* by academics and critics, the book was cleared and went through twenty-four printings and more than 250,000 copies by the end of the sixties.

The second major factor in expanding paperback sales was the growing use of paperbacks in education. Teachers had discovered the paperback, with the flexibility and options it offered as a teaching tool. Students realized that they could own the books they were required to read rather than borrowing (or stealing) them. The growth was greatest at the college and high school level, where trade paperbacks, with their academic emphasis, were making major inroads. Other than NAL's Mentor series — the only mass market trademark that had any visibility within the college market — few paperback reprinters had anything to offer educators in the way of college-level adoptions on a broad scale. They might have a few titles suitable for the classroom, but no paperback house had an entire line that could be profitably marketed. (Pocket Books and Bantam had attempted to penetrate the primary education field and were successful in using the Teen-Age Book Club, which operated through *Scholastic* magazine, but this was not a broad-based educational program.)

Throughout the 1950s, New American Library was the only paperback house with an educational sales department specifically aimed at penetrating the college bookstore and classroom adoption market. However, with the burgeoning of the trade paperback lines with their obviously academic titles, the paperback gained a whole

new constituency. Following the lead of Mentor and the other quality paperback publishers, several of the mass market houses took
aim at the growing college market. Somewhat surprisingly, Avon
became the first to set up a separate educational imprint by introducing its Bard line in 1955. Taking books from its own backlist,
Avon put such titles as *The Rubaiyat of Omar Khayyam* and several of Somerset Maugham's novels into the new line. But Avon's
efforts lacked a strong editorial focus and the backing of a concen-
trated educational sales department, and Bard lay dormant for many
years after its inception.

   In 1957, Dell made a far more substantial effort. At Frank Taylor's
instigation, the company set up a "quality" imprint called Laurel
Editions (after Allan Barnard's daughter). Ross Claiborne, a Yale
graduate with ambitions to become an editor but whose publishing
experience was limited to sales, was hired as the first educational
sales manager. After the departure of Taylor and Barnard, Claiborne
advanced to the Laurel editorial slot in 1961. The early Laurel releases were for the most part anthologies and titles in the public
domain that could be obtained for little advance cost and therefore
printed and sold in smaller quantities because there was no large
up-front investment to recoup. Among the first Laurel titles were
Four Plays by George Bernard Shaw; *Great English Short Stories*
(edited by Wallace and Mary Stegner); *Six Centuries of Great Poetry*
(edited by Robert Penn Warren and Albert Erskine, the famous Random House editor who had worked with Frank Taylor at Reynal &
Hitchcock); and a complete series of Shakespeare's plays.

   During the same period, Pocket Books accelerated its development of the school market. At the time, Leon Shimkin, an alumnus
(and later a major benefactor) of New York University, was also on
the board of NYU Press, which was attempting to publish commercially as New York University Press, Inc. When that commercial
program began to encounter difficulties, Shimkin decided to buy it
for Pocket Books and relieve the university of its commitment. As
he later commented:

>   I was thanked very much for it by the university but I had my own
> little reason for doing so. I could deduct it as capital loss of operation.
> So I acquired the NYU Press but didn't call it that. Instead, I was
> walking through the Square [Washington Square, home of the NYU
> campus] one day, and I looked up at the arch and said Washington
> Square Press was a good name. It was desirable that we publish books

that would represent us to the university, so we published studious books at first. Later we went in and published more for the high school audience.

The first Washington Square Press books, issued in 1959, were titles that came from elsewhere in the Pocket Books and Cardinal lists. They included dictionaries and language reference books, plays by Sophocles and Marlowe, some classic novels, and the verse of Edna St. Vincent Millay. However, the crowning achievement of the Washington Square Press line was the Folger Shakespeare Library. Working in association with the Folger Library in Washington, D.C., one of the world's largest and most respected centers for Shakespearean scholarship and memorabilia, Pocket Books began to issue the complete works of Shakespeare in uniform editions with full annotations, introductions by scholars, and historical information.

Although Pocket's Washington Square Press was a major entrant into the educational market sweepstakes, the company found itself in the unfamiliar position of playing catch-up. While Mentor held its acknowledged monopoly on academic nonfiction in the mass market, Pocket Books had been content to stay out of that market, concentrating instead on what it had always done best, general nonfiction for a broader audience: self-help, cookbooks, reference works, gardening and other how-tos. But now interlopers like Dell and even Ace Books, which in 1959 started a quality line it called Ace Star Books, had stolen a march on Pocket Books by getting a start in the quality mass market area. Like so many who reach the pinnacle of success, whether they are big businesses, football teams, or tennis players, Pocket Books was losing some of the edge from its competitive drive. When success abounds, it is easy to get complacent and forget about taking the risks that got you to the top in the first place. Pocket Books, built on initiative and innovation, had gotten fat and a little lazy.

There had also been a conscious decision within Pocket Books' management to stay out of the growing competition for expensive reprint properties. With its rich backlist, Pocket Books was content to continue racking up strong sales on such titles as *Baby and Child Care*, the Erle Stanley Gardner mysteries, and Dale Carnegie's books, along with the list of standard fiction that had been developed since 1939. It was a policy dictated by Leon Shimkin, who

spoke with more authority than ever at Pocket Books because he
was now the majority owner of the company. When Marshall Field
died suddenly in 1956, the trustees of Field Enterprises decided to
sell off Pocket Books. Well connected to the Field Enterprises management, Shimkin went to Chicago to arrange to purchase Pocket
Books for himself. With James Jacobson, Pocket Books' vice president in charge of sales, as a minority partner, and the backing of
Prudential Insurance, Shimkin was able to raise the $5 million he
needed to buy Pocket Books, and in 1957 he did so.

The Field estate's decision to sell Pocket Books was not a case of
a company dumping an unprofitable load. On the contrary, exactly
how successful and dominant Pocket Books was in the industry at
the onset of the sixties became a matter of public record when the
company took a major step — one of the significant paperback publishing events of 1960. Pocket Books stock went public at the end
of the year. Ronald Busch, then the assistant sales director at Bantam Books, recalled the reaction in the industry when Pocket Books
made the financial disclosure required for a public stock sale:

> The big shock came when Pocket Books went public. They were the
> first to go public and they indicated in their prospectus that they had
> sold sixty million books in the prior year. And here we were at Bantam
> thinking we were doing pretty well and we hadn't even sold twenty
> million. We didn't even believe the figures. We thought that they were
> gross and not net figures. But we found out that they were net figures
> and we began to realize what the scope and opportunities were. We
> didn't realize at the time that Pocket Books represented such a lion's
> share of the business. There were no figures around to show what
> anybody was doing, so everybody assumed we were doing about the
> same. But they weren't. There was no question that Pocket Books was
> way ahead of everyone else not only in terms of being there, but they
> had a lot of exclusive accounts where you didn't see any other paper-
> back lines. For instance, Walgreen's was an exclusive Pocket Books
> account for many, many years.

While that level of sales at Pocket Books was revealed, it was
difficult to separate out exactly how profitable the paperback sector
of Pocket Books' business was, because under Shimkin and Jacobson the company had expanded into several allied businesses. In
addition to publishing paperbacks under the various Pocket Books
imprints, Jacobson set up a subsidiary called Affiliated Publishers,
which distributed Pocket Books, Simon & Schuster books, Guild

Press, Golden Key comics, and the incredibly successful Golden Books, formerly published by Simon & Schuster but jointly acquired by Pocket Books and Western Printing. They became a major contributor to Pocket's corporate profits, with unit sales far exceeding even those of Pocket Books' paperbacks. From this diversification, it was apparent that the leadership of Pocket Books saw themselves as more than simply paperback publishers. It was a major step in taking the paperback in the direction of comprehensive publishing.

That movement gained further confirmation when Pocket Books set up a hardcover imprint of its own in association with Simon & Schuster. In 1961, the Trident Press was formed as a general trade publishing line, but its salient feature was the author Harold Robbins. In 1962, the first Trident–Simon & Schuster effort, *The Carpetbaggers*, became the fifth-best-selling novel of the year. It was the first time Robbins had cracked the hardcover best-seller list. All of his earlier books, published during the 1950s, had been successful in paperback, mostly for Pocket Books, although one title, *Never Leave Me*, was an Avon paperback original in 1954. By 1967, Pocket Books had sold in paperback 5.5 million copies of *The Carpetbaggers;* more than 3 million of *79 Park Avenue;* 2.7 million of *Never Love a Stranger;* and 1.9 million of *A Stone for Danny Fisher.* In 1966, Pocket Books' Trident Press published *The Adventurers*, which became the second-best-selling hardcover novel of the year (behind Jacqueline Susann's *Valley of the Dolls*) and Pocket Books issued the paperback edition in an initial printing of 1,625,000 copies, a new Pocket Books record.

Despite its success with Robbins and the rest of its three thousand–odd titles, Pocket Books was apparently encountering some difficulties, as its publicly published profit statements began to show. In August 1961, the company reported an increase in sales from $14.4 million to $15 million, but net income had declined from $1,208,000 to $881,000, and earnings per share were down from 39.1 cents to 28.8 cents. (At the same time, Pocket Books reported that sales from its 50 percent–owned subsidiary, Golden Books, were $43.5 million, a gain of 59 percent over the previous year, and profits had risen 57 percent to $2,381,869 from $1,521,580.) For the fiscal year 1961, Pocket Books posted all-time-record sales of more than $22 million and additional distribution fees of $5.9 million, but net income was down.

To counter this slide, Pocket Books first made a shift in its distribution. Select Magazines, which had taken over Pocket Books' sales to the independent distributor market in 1957 when Shimkin and Jacobson bought the company from Field Enterprises, was dropped in 1963 in favor of the establishment of a new Pocket Books sales force that would contact the independent wholesalers directly. But in mid-1964, Pocket Books made another switch, moving this time to Curtis Circulation Company, previously the national distributor (and half-owner) of Bantam Books. The Curtis arrangement with Bantam had come to an abrupt end for a variety of reasons. First of all, the great suckling teat of the Curtis Publishing Company, the *Saturday Evening Post*, had fallen on hard times. The magazine was slipping badly, out of touch with America as it entered the sixties. Consequently, to raise cash for its magazine operations, Curtis sold a substantial portion of its stock back to Grosset & Dunlap, its partner in Bantam. Once Curtis had less proprietary interest in Bantam's profits, it became more concerned with making money as Bantam's distributor by demanding larger brokerage fees. Bantam resisted. Then the Curtis management, no longer the same group of men who had helped give Bantam its start, decided that they also wanted to publish paperbacks. However, their contract with Bantam prohibited them from doing so. That proved to be the last straw and Bantam looked for an alternative, first considering Triangle Publications, distributor of *TV Guide* (owned by Walter Annenberg), but ultimately turning to Select Magazines, which was looking for a paperback line to distribute after its association with Pocket Books came to an end in 1963.

New distribution for Pocket Books, however, was not the answer. Another part of the problem was the shift in emphasis to the blockbuster best seller, an area in which Bantam, Dell, and Fawcett were becoming far more aggressive than Pocket Books, which apart from Harold Robbins was still relying more on its old standbys. As a result, an eight-year sales summary released in 1966 showed that Pocket Books' sales, after reaching a peak of $23,259,000 in 1962, had slipped down to $19,639,000 by 1965, with net income dipping to $637,000 in that year. But these setbacks were no hindrance to Leon Shimkin's empire building. This diminutive man with horn-rimmed, owlish glasses had his fingers in a great many pies. Besides acquiring Washington Square Press in 1959, Shimkin bought All Saints Press, a Catholic publishing house, in 1962. In 1965 he added

Julian Messner to Pocket Books' holdings. A small firm known best for its publication of Grace Metalious's novels, including *Peyton Place,* but also a publisher of children's books, Messner gave Pocket Books an additional hardcover line.

Pocket Books assumed the distribution of the Ballantine Books list in 1963. After the initial success of the simultaneous hardcover-paperback concept, Ian Ballantine's luck had changed. He was plagued by distribution problems through the late 1950s, switching from one small national distributor to another. In addition, there had been some questionable publishing decisions. So Ballantine came to Pocket Books looking for financial backing as well as distribution. He got both, but at a price: a measure of independence. Pocket Books was willing to distribute Ballantine Books, but only those titles it wanted Ballantine to publish. Accordingly, the Ballantine list began to be screened by Pocket Books' management.

But the major coup for Shimkin came in 1966. In addition to his holdings consolidated under Pocket Books, Shimkin was also a 50 percent owner of Simon & Schuster, which had also been repurchased (for $1 million!) from Field Enterprises after Marshall Field's death. In a dazzling sequence, Shimkin first sold off Pocket Books' half-share in Golden Books to Western Printing for almost $6 million in 1964. Then, in 1966, he used $2 million from Simon & Schuster's operating funds to buy Max Schuster's half of Simon & Schuster, thus leaving himself in total control of S&S. Pocket Books and Simon & Schuster, closely linked since the birth of Pocket Books in 1939, were now merged into a single company in which Leon Shimkin, once the bookkeeper, now owned a majority of shares. (The corporate name became Simon & Schuster, Inc.) Finishing off his conquests with a small pièce de résistance, Shimkin bought Regents Publishing Company, an educational publisher, and Pocket Books created a new division, PB Specials, that published paperbacks in non-rack-sized formats at a higher price. (One of the first and most successful of the PB Specials was the *Royal Canadian Air Force Exercise Plans for Physical Fitness.*)

By the time he had finished his master plan in 1967, Leon Shimkin had built a one-man empire, a complex of companies with annual sales of more than $40 million. There were many in publishing who resented the man for his dollar-oriented publishing, and there was also criticism of the manner in which the two founders of the company had been supplanted. Within his own company, the resentment was strong enough to lead to the resignation of three of Simon & Schuster's top people, Robert Gottlieb, Anthony Schulte, and Nina Bourne, who left together and reappeared at Alfred Knopf. But few people inside publishing begrudged Shimkin his financial savvy, and it was soon acknowledged that the way of the shrewd businessman was the track that the publishing business was heading down as it moved through the sixties and seventies. The genteel business of publishing — if it had ever existed — was being supplanted by the business school dynamics of go-go growth and the boom times of America's new age.[6]

The transformation of publishing, represented by the institution of more bureaucratic corporate-management practices and corporate or public ownership as opposed to individual ownership, was becoming widespread as time went by. But in the highly visible, tightly circumscribed world of paperback books, the trend seemed more pronounced. The shift from "cottage industry" to Big Business, as symbolized by the public offering of Pocket Books stock in 1960, was highlighted by the other turning point of the year: the first corporate takeover of a paperback publishing house by an outside business interest since Marshall Field had acquired Pocket Books in 1947. (With one small exception. After the death of Joseph Meyers in 1957, Avon Books was bought by the Hearst Corporation in 1959. At the time, Avon was little more than a statistical blip when compared with Pocket Books.) This time the prize was New American Library, second to Pocket Books in size and power, and the eager suitor was the Times Mirror Company of Los Angeles, owned by the Chandler family, publisher of the *Los Angeles Times*. In this case, unlike the Field acquisition of Pocket Books, the sale would have unpleasant repercussions.

The company that was placed on the block in 1959 had come a long way since its 1948 inception, which developed out of the breach between Penguin Books Limited and Penguin Books, Inc. Kurt Enoch, the guiding hand behind the direction of NAL's business, sales, production, and distribution, and Victor Weybright, who molded its unique editorial profile, had built New American Library to a point not only of great profits but also of unparalleled prestige. The Signet and Mentor lines had won the admiration of critics, writers, educators, and readers. It was often the case that when a book was available for reprint, its hardcover publisher favored New American Library simply for the cachet of inclusion in the line.

That was the case with *Doctor Zhivago*, Boris Pasternak's great novel of the Russian Revolution, which was spirited out of Russia and published in the United States in 1958, the year Pasternak was forced by Soviet authorities to refuse the Nobel Prize for literature. A best seller for two years in the United States, the book had been published here by Pantheon, the house founded by émigrés Kurt Wolff, Jacques Schiffrin, and Kyrill Schabert, who had provided Enoch the capital he needed to get a start in America many years before. However, the reprint rights were controlled by Collins-Harvill, the British publisher, which wanted NAL as the American reprinter. After a long stretch of negotiations, the book was acquired for a guarantee of $100,000, practically a bargain in light of some of the money that was being paid out by Fawcett and Dell.

NAL's list of accomplishments during the 1950s was exemplary. Enoch and Weybright had managed to maintain the delicate balance between commercial success and literary innovation and adventurism, the mark of any great publisher. They had pioneered publishing serious literature in paperback, typified by the works of Wolfe, Faulkner, Farrell, and a host of others (some critics said Weybright bought dirty books that happened to be good, but that assessment was unfair); they promoted the overwhelming notoriety and sales of Erskine Caldwell; they demonstrated a marvelous commitment to the modern in the *New World Writing* series guided by Arabel Porter, who had become something of a high priestess among the young writers of America; and they pressed the ongoing development of Mentor Books, the finest collection of nonfiction in paperback. This was all done with an amazingly small editorial staff. During the 1950s, besides Weybright and Porter, it included Weybright's stepson, Truman "Mac" Talley, who was Weybright's chief aide-de-camp and was being groomed as his successor; Marc Jaffe, who edited Mentor Books as well as Westerns and mysteries; Brad Cummings, a good editor with social connections, a trait Weybright found appealing; and Walter Freeman, the resident Southern editor. Apart from their specific duties and specialties, each editor handled the output from a number of hardcover houses.

But at the center was Weybright, always appreciative of the spotlight he focused on himself. The man was an enormous bundle of contradictions. Universally derided as vain, pompous, affected, and a bit of a social climber, he was also acclaimed as a brilliant editor with a flair for both the literary and the commercial. He was at home corresponding with Sir Isaiah Berlin, playing the part of the Old School don, or talking tough with Mickey Spillane. More than one Jew who knew him professionally said he had a touch of the anti-Semite in him, surely a complicating factor in his relationship with Enoch. Yet he was charming, zestful, and, by every account, a prodigious reader. Marc Jaffe, a Weybright protégé for ten years, recalled the Monday morning editorial meetings. "We all approached with a sense of dread because we were supposed to report on what we had read over the weekend. Each of us would have a couple of books in front of us on the table. Then in would walk Victor with an enormous stack of books that he had read." In addition, Weybright also had near-total recall and could cite page and paragraph where a certain passage from a book he had read earlier could be found.

When Marc Jaffe left NAL in 1959 after being hired away by Dell's Frank Taylor, his place on the editorial board was taken by a young man with aspirations of becoming a writer. Edgar L. Doctorow had been a reader for the Columbia Pictures story department when he first met Victor Weybright, who later offered what Doctorow said was known as "the Jewish seat on the NAL editorial board," vacated by Marc Jaffe. When he arrived, Doctorow found NAL full of energy and excitement. "For a young editor it meant a chance to work on books of all kinds, from garbage to rather erudite works of scholarship. [The first book he recalls handling was a translation of Xenophon from the University of Michigan Press.] My colleagues were terrific. First of all, my office was next to Arabel Porter's. To a young writer, she was legendary because of *New World Writing*. She was a lovely, generous person and a wonderful old-line book editor."

Weybright, in Doctorow's view, had grave failings and great virtues. "He saw the idea of the paperback book as something technologically wonderful. And he saw the way for the paperback to thrive was to become the primary contractor of books, reversing the process. He had a good restless mind and loved to wheel and deal. He wanted to raise the status of the paperback to something as honorable and culturally significant as any hardcover house." On the other hand, said Doctorow, Weybright could be "suckered" by people who knew he wanted to be one of the "big boys."

One way in which NAL pursued elevated status for the paperback was by contracting for books that were then placed with a regular trade hardcover house. Between 1950 and 1963, this was done with more than ninety books. In fiction, it was accomplished most successfully with Irving Wallace, whose novels *The Chapman Report*, *The Prize*, and *The Three Sirens* were contracted for by NAL and then placed with Simon & Schuster, each becoming a best seller in hardcover and paperback. In the nonfiction area, many of the serious books commissioned to fill gaps in the Mentor and general nonfiction lines were also placed with trade houses. Among these were Anne Freemantle's *The Age of Belief;* Max Dimont's *Jews, God and History;* Isaiah Berlin's *The Age of Enlightenment;* Richard D. Heffner's *A Documentary History of the United States;* Isaac Asimov's *The Genetic Code, The Human Brain,* and *The Human Body;* and Victor Van Hagen's *The Realm of the Incas* and *The Realm of the Mayas.*

While the editorial policy pursued under Weybright was vigorous, eclectic, and certainly the most sophisticated of any paperback house, it had its equal in the efficiency and dynamism of the sales and distribution program developed under Enoch. A cultivated, experienced European publisher, Enoch realized better than most American-born publishers the importance of developing the export market. In the late 1940s he set the company on a course that would bring it alongside Penguin Books as a paperback publisher of international repute. If Penguin was synonymous with paperbacks in the world outside America, Mentor and Signet were not far behind. With the exception of Pocket Books, which had aimed its exports primarily at South America, New American Library was the most aggressive American paperback house in developing international distribution of its books. The first step in that program came when the United States government established the Economic Cooperation Administration in 1949, a program designed to subsidize the sale of American books first in Germany and then in the rest of postwar Europe. Under the plan, an American publisher shipped books that would be paid for in deflated marks (or other local currency), which the ECA then converted into dollars to pay the publisher. The titles eligible under the ECA program had to be considered useful in representing "the American scene and the American way of life"; in other words, they were serving a propaganda purpose. To ensure that its books met with approval, New American Library enlisted a screening committee to select 150 titles. It was composed of Eduard C. Lindeman (editorial consultant to NAL since its beginnings), Norman Cousins of the *Saturday Review of Literature,* Charles B. Shaw, the librarian at Swarthmore College, Bryn J. Hovde, president of the New School for Social Research, and Atwood H. Townsend, chairman of the Committee on College Reading of the National Council of Teachers of English. Enoch got the first ECA contract, worth $100,000; Pocket Books got the second.[7]

In 1950, Enoch set off for Europe for the first time since he had left as an exile nearly ten years earlier. In a bittersweet return, marked by reunions with former colleagues and employees who had survived the devastation of Europe, he began renewing his contacts in the European publishing community, or what was left of it. Continental publishing was in ruins, leaving Europe ready for imported books. In addition, English was becoming the lingua franca, and basic books in English were much sought after. There was also a large contingent of Americans as occupation forces who constituted an additional market in Europe.

In the course of that exploratory overseas trip, Enoch visited Denmark, Sweden, Switzerland, France, Holland, Austria, and Germany. In each country, he appointed a local distributor who would handle NAL books, sometimes on an exclusive basis. In Germany, the ECA's first target country, NAL sold 250,000 books between June 1949 and the end of 1950. In succeeding years, Enoch traveled the world over, expanding NAL's reach to the South Pacific, Southeast Asia, the Middle East, India, and Japan. In the latter two countries, Enoch provided financial backing to the best local book wholesalers, enabling them to emerge as the largest distributors in their respective countries.

Weybright also began to travel widely, both men in essence becoming ambassadors not only for NAL but for the American paperback industry as a whole. This was reflected in NAL's ambitious attempts to publish foreign writers, fulfilling its corporate name as the New American Library of *World* Literature. In addition to fiction by many of the leading Continental writers, NAL met this goal by publishing the poets of several Asian and African nations in *New World Writing.* Enoch and Weybright had also gained near-celebrity status and were usually accorded VIP treatment in their travels, often being interviewed by local newspapers and radio stations.

By the end of the fifties, New American Library had built a considerable empire with international reach. Its 1959 gross sales hit

$12,117,000, with more than thirty-three million books sold, approximately double its 1955 volume. However, as is the case with many privately held companies, the two partners began to have fears about the fate of the company after them, particularly regarding estate taxes. Enoch was nearing his seventies and Weybright was only slightly younger, although both men were still in their prime in terms of health and motivation. Enoch commented about the circumstances, "We both felt it was an unhealthy situation. If something happened, then we were at the mercy of the tax people. They could say, 'Your share is worth $50 million,' and tax our estate. To prove the contrary, we thought of going public." On the advice of a consultant who said that Securities and Exchange Commission requirements would leave them little time for publishing, overtures were instead made to the Times Mirror Company, which was seeking to diversify into the book publishing arena. Besides the *Los Angeles Times*, which accounted for about 60 percent of the company's 1959 gross income of more than $50 million, the Times Mirror Company owned another, smaller Los Angeles newspaper (the *Mirror-News*); a controlling interest in a paper company with large timberland holdings; a newsprint mill; the company that produced telephone directories in southern California; KTTV in Los Angeles; a share in an oil and cattle company; and extensive real estate holdings in California. Besides its vast economic powers, the Chandler family — conservative Republican back to its earlier union-busting days — held enormous sway in California politics.[8] And Norman Chandler's wife, Dorothy, was a central figure in California social, art, and charitable circles. (Enoch later recalled how Dorothy Chandler, after the merger, put the finger on both Weybright and him for $25,000 each for her pet project, the music center that was later built as the Dorothy Chandler Pavilion.)

As the business-oriented half of the NAL partnership, Enoch handled the negotiations with the Times Mirror Company, which was represented by Charles Bates "Tex" Thornton, the head of Litton Industries and later one of the Defense Department "whiz kids" of the McNamara circle. They finally reached an agreement that went into effect on March 24, 1960. Under the plan, officially a merger but in fact a total absorption of NAL by Times Mirror, the Times Mirror Company received all of NAL's stock. Weybright and Enoch in return got 138,888 shares of Times Mirror stock and an additional $1 million in Times Mirror stock between 1963 and 1965 at the market price then prevailing. There were also provisions for further stock payments if NAL met certain specified conditions related to sales and profits.

Almost immediately, the merger was productive for Times Mirror, which saw its stock rise overnight — a benefit to Enoch and Weybright as well — and the NAL profits added considerably to the corporation's profits. But the seemingly well arranged merger soon opened a wound between Weybright and Enoch that never healed. One of the terms of the agreement was that an NAL representative would sit on the Times Mirror board of directors. Initially, Weybright and Enoch planned to alternate this duty on a yearly basis. It soon became apparent that Enoch was preferable to the Times Mirror management as the NAL representative. This became one of a series of sore points that eventually left Weybright embittered and angry, forcing his eventual resignation from NAL and prompting a scathing attack on Enoch in his memoir, *The Making of a Publisher.* According to Weybright, the first sign of trouble was the institution of corporate-style controls on NAL's editorial program. To a man who prided himself on his independence and individualism, bottom-line management constraints stuck in his throat. He said he found himself in an Orwellian bureaucracy. Then Enoch was told to search for a successor as chief executive officer of the company, and it was made clear that Weybright was not the choice of the Times Mirror management. Additionally, Enoch was charged with creating an entire book division for Times Mirror through acquisition of existing publishing companies.

Relations between the two partners deteriorated quickly. Although Weybright later wrote that he faced repeated attempts by Enoch to stifle his editorial approach and that the two were practically antagonists during their highly successful partnership, evidence suggests otherwise. Letters in Weybright's own files (donated to New York University) and correspondence from Weybright to Enoch indicate that they had once enjoyed a more congenial spirit. While the two were so starkly different as to limit the chances for a warm social friendship, their relationship seemed to have always been cordial and obviously of mutual benefit. For instance, in a 1952 letter from Rome while vacationing and scouting, Weybright wrote to Enoch, "It's wonderful to behold how our NAL has grown as a result of our combined vision and hard work."

E. L. Doctorow, who joined NAL just as the merger was being

negotiated, remembers that Enoch was rarely present at editorial meetings, unless a great deal of money was at stake. "There were rumors that they did not get along, but it was always kept very correct." By the time the merger was concluded, the correctness was a ghost of the past. There were no cordial sentiments in Victor Weybright's memoirs.

When Kurt Enoch, now president of the Times Mirror book division and a vice president of the Times Mirror Company, moved to the book division's new offices on Park Avenue and began to search for a successor, the die was cast. NAL was also moved to new offices, which Weybright found distastefully decorated, and he saw his company slipping from his grasp. Seeing the changes being forced upon the company, Weybright rightfully balked. Yet in the early 1960s NAL did some highly successful and creative publishing. At this time, the company instituted its Signet Classics series. Both Pocket Books and Bantam had classics lines, but when NAL introduced its series, with distinctive covers and a uniform border surrounding each, they quickly overwhelmed the competition. NAL made vigorous searches to find the most reliable existing edition of each of the classics in the series and commissioned introductory essays by major contemporary critics. When *Native Son* was later included, E. L. Doctorow went to *Commentary* critic Ted Solotaroff for an introduction to the book. Solotaroff himself would later become the key figure in the *New American Review* series, the spiritual descendant of *New World Writing* that was begun by NAL in 1967. The Signet Shakespeare series was also initiated, and it quickly equaled the Pocket Books Folger series in critical stature. In addition, the Signet Shakespeares were given strikingly original illustrations by Milton Glaser, a series of line drawings on a white background with a splash of color highlighting some element within the drawing.

It was also at this time that Truman Talley brought in the writer who would replace Mickey Spillane as the company's best-selling writer and carry the company through the sixties. That writer was Ian Fleming, and his creation, James Bond, Agent 007, became part of the pop iconography of the sixties.

Casino Royale introduced James Bond to the world back in 1953. After being rejected by three publishers here, it was published by Macmillan to unspectacular sales and reprinted by Popular Library to little notice. The succeeding three titles, *Live and Let Die, Moon-*

CD171 50c
The Signet Classic
Shakespeare

A Midsummer Night's Dream

Graphic designer Milton Glaser created the singular look of the Signet Shakespeare series. (Photo by Jerome Frank)

raker, and *Diamonds Are Forever,* were reprinted by Pocket Books, again to humdrum reception. The time was not yet ripe. In 1957, Talley offered to buy the next Bond novel, *From Russia with Love,* if Pocket Books' offer was unsatisfactory to the hardcover publisher. NAL succeeded in getting that title as well as the four earlier books. When Viking picked up Fleming's next three-book hardcover contract, NAL paid for those as well, its paperback guarantee covering the cost of Viking's advance to Fleming. It was exquisite timing on NAL's part. Bond was just about to break out. Between 1957 and 1963, NAL sold five million Bond books in Signet editions. Then, in 1963, the company announced its plans to undertake a hardcover program and that Fleming's next thriller, *On Her Majesty's Secret Service,* would be the first book issued under a three-book deal between NAL and the author.

According to Truman Talley, the thirteen Fleming thrillers featuring Bond that NAL eventually published in paperback accounted for one-third of the firm's revenues during a four-year stretch through the mid-1960s. Concurrent with Fleming's success, John Le Carré, the pseudonymous master of the thinking man's spy novel, hit the best-seller lists with *The Spy Who Came in from the Cold* (the number-one hardcover novel in 1964, the same year that *You Only Live Twice,* NAL's second Fleming hardcover, was number eight), which sold two million paperback copies in 1965, and *The Looking Glass War* (number four in 1965 to Fleming's *Man with the Golden Gun,* number seven). The two joined fellow countryman Len Deighton, whose *The Ipcress File* (1962) and *Funeral in Berlin* (1964) had not achieved best-seller status in hardcover but had built Deighton a paperback audience.

Suddenly, a pent-up American interest in the world of spies was unleashed. The spy novel had never been a particularly American genre, although Gold Medal and Dell First Editions both used espionage thrillers in their originals program. The British, better practiced at spying than Americans, were also superior at espionage fiction, with a tradition that included Kipling's *Kim,* Maugham's *Ashenden,* Conrad's *The Secret Agent,* Eric Ambler's thrillers, and Graham Greene's entertainments, a line-up that indicated that the British took the world of spies more seriously than America took its detectives. (On the other hand, the British never produced a hard-boiled detective writer of Hammett's rank, though they excelled in the classic mystery. Class distinctions? British policemen don't carry guns?)

It may have been a sequence of events that eventually made the difference. First of all, the hard-boiled detective had been around since the 1930s without any fresh blood (no pun intended) as the Gardners and Spillanes churned out one repetitious exercise in detection and mayhem after another. By the end of the fifties, their work was starting to show its age, wrinkling around the edges with signs of wear and tear. It was a new era and people wanted something a little fresher and more modern. Then in 1960 came the U-2 incident, when American pilot Francis Gary Powers was shot down over Russia in his sophisticated spy plane and sentenced to ten years for espionage (he was later exchanged for a Russian). For the first time, Americans realized that we were in the spy game too. Until this point, the American image of spying was that it was the purview of the godless Russians, intent on stealing Russian bomb secrets by using "untrustworthy" Jews (Julius and Ethel Rosenberg) and intellectuals (Alger Hiss) who were really Commie dupes and not true Americans. The cold war, once thought of as a battle of brute forces facing across Eastern Europe or on the windy highlands of Korea, was shown to be a war of nerves and duplicity. Then the Russians built a wall dividing Berlin. Kennedy faced down Khrushchev in Vienna. The Bay of Pigs fiasco stunned America in 1961. In 1962, the Cuban missile crisis, in which we "stood eyeball to eyeball and the other guy blinked," had the world on the brink. This succession of events put espionage on the front pages. Then came the crowning moment. President Kennedy announced that he too was a James Bond fan. The floodgates opened.

In the dawning era of the jet plane and space travel, James Bond was simply a high-tech Mike Hammer. And Fleming was only a few notches or so above Mickey Spillane on the evolutionary ladder. Secret agent James Bond, with his notorious double-zero license to kill, was at best clever, amusing, and a sexual champion. At worst, he was (shades of Spillane) a racist, anti-Semitic, sexist xenophobe, a relic of Britain's colonial Old School past as the shrinking British Empire passed from the glorious days of Queen Victoria to a new era of trade unionism, the dole, and Labour government.

Like Spillane and Gardner, Fleming adhered to a calculated and specific plot formula, beginning with a violent prelude in which Bond kills or otherwise wreaks destruction upon an enemy and then calmly dresses for dinner. Bored by inactivity, he is summoned by

M, the chief of intelligence. The villain and Bond then confront each other in a social situation (a card game, a golf match). An alluring woman, usually in league with the villain, is introduced and seduced. Bond is captured and tortured. Bond escapes and kills the villain. Bond and the woman end up in bed. In addition, Fleming provided an "insider's look" at the technology and gadgetry of modern killing. (A member of British intelligence during the war, Fleming had come up with some absurd notions, including freezing clouds so they could be used as anti-aircraft gun mounts and sinking a block of concrete in the Channel so men with periscopes could observe France.) He had a compulsive use of brand-name goods and took the reader to exotic places, making the books a palatable geography lesson.

Although Bond had a champion in President Kennedy — and was enlarged as a pop icon by the spectacularly successful series of James Bond films beginning with *Dr. No* — he also had his detractors. It was more than a little ironic that E. L. Doctorow, whose political views were diametrically opposed to those of Fleming's, ended up as Fleming's editor after the writer was signed by New American Library. "I was sometimes very critical, but he dismissed what I had to say. I was prepared to dislike him because of the noxious things in his books. The racism and sexism was the helpless symbolism of a sexually disturbed person. When I met the guy he was terrific. On brief acquaintance, we got to be pals. He read my first novel [*Welcome to Hard Times*, a parody of the hundreds of Westerns Doctorow was compelled to read for Columbia Pictures], and he was generous in his praise." Doctorow also found a certain fascination in Fleming's meticulous attention to detail. "He spent more time on the caliber of some firearm than with a sentence." The obsession with precise dimensions and the specific brand names mentioned in the books were meant to give the works a sense of realism. Doctorow commented, "He was very shrewd to ground these ridiculous fantasies in factual precision."

The fortune that Ian Fleming bestowed upon NAL did little to prevent the company's eventual fracturing. Weybright and Talley, increasingly disgusted at what they saw as corporate interference with their editorial freedom, prepared to abandon ship. By 1966, they were both gone, later establishing a hardcover imprint, Weybright & Talley. Talley later commented, "Conglomeratization

meant that a great talent like Victor Weybright was lost or smoth-
ered. It was now the corporate manager rather than the independent, cantankerous, immensely irritable entrepreneur, who saw
some things differently. The individuality got lost."

In addition, the once-proud NAL editorial staff had been pretty
well dismantled by other departures. Marc Jaffe was long gone, having emerged at Bantam, where he was teaming with Oscar Dystel
to make that company the new power in paperback publishing.
E. L. Doctorow had moved on to the Dial Press, a small, prestigious
hardcover publisher acquired by Dell in 1963. Arabel Porter had
moved on to Houghton Mifflin, but not before discovering a first
novel called *The Graduate,* which was published under the NAL
hardcover line. The other editors of the earlier generation were also
gone. Enoch's replacement as chief executive, John Budlong, came
from McGraw-Hill but had little experience with trade publishing,
let alone mass market publishing, and he was gone by 1967. As a
replacement for himself, Weybright had first turned to David
Brown, formerly of *Cosmopolitan* and Twentieth Century–Fox,
husband of Helen Gurley Brown, author of *Sex and the Single Girl.*
But he did not stay. Timothy Seldes of Doubleday (son of critic
Gilbert Seldes and brother of actress Marian Seldes) came in to head
the hardcover program, but he soon departed as well. A succession
of editors in chief followed, including Edward T. Chase, a friend of
Talley's and a magazine writer of some repute (who is also the
father of comedian Chevy Chase).

By 1968, however, Weybright was gone and Enoch had given up
his positions with the Times Mirror Company book division, taking
up a consultancy in his semiretirement. The old guard at New
American Library had passed. It was true of most other paperback
houses as well. Few of the founding fathers were still active in the
business by the middle of the sixties. Ironically, Sidney B. Kramer
was one who was. One of the founders of Bantam Books, he left
there in 1966 and moved to NAL in 1967 to become its president in
an attempt to pull the company together again.

While the once mighty New American Library seemed to be slipping, as had the industry-leading Pocket Books, there were certainly
others to take their place in the latter half of the decade. At the
same time that America was beginning to undergo the massive
social changes of this era the paperback business was already moving along with it.

Paperback Best Sellers:
The First 25 Years

18½ MILLION

Baby and Child Care by Benjamin M. Spock, M.D. (1946)

15½ MILLION

The Merriam-Webster Pocket Dictionary (1947)

10 MILLION

Peyton Place by Grace Metalious (1957)

8 MILLION

God's Little Acre by Erskine Caldwell (1946)

6½ MILLION

Webster's New World Dictionary of the American Language (1958)

6 MILLION

University of Chicago English-Spanish, Spanish-English Dictionary (1950)
In His Steps by Charles Sheldon (1960)

5½ MILLION

Exodus by Leon Uris (1959)
To Kill a Mockingbird by Harper Lee (1962)
Roget's Pocket Thesaurus (1946)
The Carpetbaggers by Harold Robbins (1962)

5 MILLION

How to Win Friends and Influence People by Dale Carnegie (1940)
Return to Peyton Place by Grace Metalious (1960)

4½ MILLION

The Pocket Cook Book by Elizabeth Woody (1942)
Profiles in Courage by John F. Kennedy (1947)
The Big Kill (1951), *I, the Jury* (1948), *My Gun Is Quick* (1950) by
    Mickey Spillane
1984 by George Orwell (1950)
Thunderball by Ian Fleming (1962)

4 MILLION

The Dell Crossword Dictionary by Kathleen Rafferty (1951)

3½ MILLION

Duel in the Sun by Niven Busch (1946)
Anatomy of a Murder by Robert Traver (1959)
The Pocket Book of Short Stories edited by M. E. Speare (1941)
Four Tragedies of Shakespeare (1955)
Larousse French-English, English-French Dictionary (1955)
The Diary of a Young Girl by Anne Frank (1955)
The Ugly American by William J. Lederer and Eugene L. Burdick
    (1960)
Lolita by Vladimir Nabokov (1959)
Tropic of Cancer by Henry Miller (1961)
Lady Chatterley's Lover by D. H. Lawrence (1962)

(Source: *New York Times*, February 27, 1966. Copyright © 1966 The New York Times
Company)

TEN

The New Age:
From Roth to Robbins

I'd like to meet Philip Roth. But I wouldn't want to
shake his hand.
— Jacqueline Susann, to talk-show host Merv Griffin

Frodo Lives!
— Ballantine Books button circa 1965

W HEN THE CLOCK struck midnight, ushering in 1960, the
world did not rise to its collective feet in awe of the
dawning of the Age of Aquarius. It was soon apparent,
however, that something was in the air. One set of signals heralding
the changes taking place in American society came from the emerging trends and fresh voices in fiction and letters. The literary styles
and social criticism that appeared in the middle and later fifties
pointed in new directions. This was evident in the widespread acceptance of such books as Kerouac's *On the Road;* Mailer's 1959
Advertisements for Myself, an essay collection that showed the
esteemed novelist moving into the realm of his unique, highly personal brand of sociopolitical reportage (including the epochal "The
White Negro"); the poetry of Ginsberg in *Howl;* Vonnegut's *The
Sirens of Titan* (a 1959 paperback original passed off as science fic-
tion by Dell); the later stories of Salinger in *Franny and Zooey* and
Nine Stories, with their increasing mysticism and exploration of
Zen; maverick social critic C. Wright Mills's *White Collar, The
Power Elite* (both Galaxy Books from Oxford University Press), *Lis-
ten, Yankee: Revolution in Cuba* (a Ballantine original), and *The
Causes of World War Three* (Simon & Schuster trade paperback;
Ballantine mass market); and the social writings of Paul Goodman

collected in the crucial *Growing Up Absurd* (Random House and Vintage, 1960). All were straws in the wind. As Morris Dickstein wrote in *Gates of Eden,* his comprehensive study of American culture in the sixties, "The fifties were the seedbed of our present cultural situation and the ground against which the upheavals of the sixties sought to define themselves."[1]

Along with these new voices of rising discontent, there was a new audience eager to listen to what they were saying. The first phalanx of the heralded youth movement so often associated with the contentious sixties was coming of age. Unlike their mothers and fathers, they had lived through no depression and had fought no wars. They had enjoyed the fruits of America's growing affluence but were beginning to chafe at the demands it placed upon them — demands that were echoed in titles like *The Lonely Crowd, The Organization Man, The Status Seekers, The People Shapers, The Man in the Gray Flannel Suit,* and in the increasing pressure to fit in and conform. They were also the beneficiaries of the great push for more education dollars that came after the Russians put Sputnik in space while America's efforts, actually the work of "rehabilitated" Germans, fizzled on the launching pad.

The surging tidal wave of youth was ready to crash the perfect sand castles prepared for them. Again Dickstein: "The 'young intelligentsia' whom [C. Wright] Mills had identified as the agents of change were to become an amorphous mass spread out across thousands of colleges and communes, in the country and in the city, whose culture enshrined music and films and drugs more than books, but who adopted certain books that helped them articulate a new set of values."[2]

And the books they adopted were, for the most part, paperback books. By this time, both trade and mass market paperbacks had achieved ubiquity in the campus bookstores and on classroom reading lists (at least those that did not require specific textbooks) and were filtering down to high schools. College reading and the college audience soon became linked to the paperback. The notion of "cult books" and "cult writers" entered the realm of publishing. In January 1962, the *New York Times Book Review* devoted an entire supplement to the paperback. It was a culturally valid — if somewhat tardy — recognition of the impact that paperbacks were having, not on the publishing industry but on the reading habits of America. (It also generated new advertising revenues for the *Times Book Review* from all those paperback publishers who didn't regularly advertise because there was no margin in paperback cover prices for promotional budgets.) In this supplement, Princeton professor and critic Carlos Baker wrote an article called "On Campus, It's the Generation of the Mixed Book Bag." In it he had made an admittedly unscientific sampling of student reading at several major colleges. The leading author was, of course, J. D. Salinger, and it seemed that most college students had read *The Catcher in the Rye* by this point and were now at work on the later stories. (One side effect of Salinger's interest in Zen was the increase in sales for Alan Watts's books *Nature, Man and Woman, Psychotherapy East and West,* and *The Way of Zen,* all Mentor books.) The other names prominent among college paperback readers included Mailer, Capote, Baldwin, Malamud, Styron, McCullers, Ellison, and Roth.

The last of these, Philip Roth, had not yet supplanted Salinger — and perhaps never would — as *the* novelist to read, but with his first book, *Goodbye, Columbus,* he marked out a piece of the college turf as his own. With an agreeable nod of acceptance, the literary world had also said yes to the young puncturer of the new Jewish middle class. Critic Irving Howe, certainly a representative in good standing of the literary establishment, said of Roth, "What many writers spend a lifetime searching for — a unique voice, a secure rhythm, a distinctive subject — seem to have come to Philip Roth totally and immediately. At 26 he is a writer of narrow range but intense effects. He composes stories about the life of middle-class American Jews with such a ferocity it would be idle to complain about, so thoroughly do they pour out of his own sense of things."[3]

A collection of short stories that had appeared variously in *The New Yorker, Commentary,* and the *Paris Review,* Roth's *Goodbye, Columbus* had won its first literary stripes by earning Roth (University of Chicago by way of Newark, New Jersey) the prestigious Houghton Mifflin Literary Fellowship, which meant a grant of $5000 in addition to the usual advance against royalties. Published in the spring of 1959, the book won solidly admiring reviews, and Houghton Mifflin went back to press five times by September. The title story, actually a novella, is about Neil Klugman ("clever fellow") and his summer love affair with Brenda Patimkin, daughter of nouveau riche Jews — fortune made in bathroom sinks — who have graduated from Newark to the posher suburbs where they attempt to emulate the WASP American dream. Neil's ultimate

1961 Paperback Best Sellers

FICTION

1. *Hawaii* by James Michener (Bantam)
2. *Advise and Consent* by Allen Drury (Pocket)
3. *The Catcher in the Rye* by J. D. Salinger (NAL)
4. *Exodus* by Leon Uris (Bantam)
5. *Tropic of Cancer* by Henry Miller (Grove)
6. *The Ugly American* by William J. Lederer and Eugene L. Burdick (Fawcett)
7. *The Devil's Advocate* by Morris West (Dell)
8. *The Alexandria Quartet* by Lawrence Durrell (available from Pocket Books in mass market and Dutton in the first paperback boxed set)
9. *The Last of the Just* by André Schwarz-Bart (Bantam)
10. *For Whom the Bell Tolls* by Ernest Hemingway (Scribner's)

GENERAL

1. *Folk Medicine* by D. C. Jarvis (Fawcett)
2. *The Status Seekers* by Vance Packard (Pocket)
3. *The Conscience of a Conservative* by Barry Goldwater (MacFadden)
4. *Masters of Deceit* by J. Edgar Hoover (Pocket)
5. *The Organization Man* by William H. Whyte (Anchor)
6. *May Man Prevail?* by Erich Fromm (Anchor)
7. *Profiles in Courage* by John F. Kennedy (Pocket)
8. *The Peace Race* by Seymour Melman (Ballantine Books)
9. *The Lonely Crowd* by David Riesman (available in an abridged edition by Anchor and complete from Yale University Press)
10. Three books *(Deliver Us from Evil, The Edge of Tomorrow,* and *The Night They Burned the Mountain)* by Tom Dooley (NAL)

(Source: *The New York Times Book Review,* January 14, 1962. Copyright © 1962 The New York Times Company)

Although this list is an interesting one, it should be noted that it was gathered from bookstores and does not reflect newsstand or drugstore sales. Thus it is skewed toward trade paperback publishers and away from mass market titles that certainly sold in greater numbers. However, the fiction list is fairly representative. A final point of interest is the number of backlist books published several years earlier that were still selling well. Paperback books, even from the mass market houses, were obviously staying in print much longer than they had been. The *Times Book Review* did not begin regular coverage of paperbacks until 1974. A weekly paperback best seller list did not commence until 1976.

falling out with Brenda, in which a diaphragm is the deus ex machina, is an inevitability. For Neil, who works in the library, life as a Patimkin is as unthinkable as life with his aunt Gladys. He shares far more with the young black boy who comes into the library to look at "Go-Again's" paintings of Tahiti (in the library's "heart" section). In another of the stories, "The Conversion of the Jews," the theme of *non serviam* is repeated in the story of a young boy who unflinchingly questions rabbinical wisdom. For Ozzie Freedman (freed-man), nonconformity comes in an act of rooftop defiance in which he gets the whole world to bend its knee before him. New American Library expressed some interest in reprinting the book, but partly out of friendship, partly because of the cachet of the quality paperback, Roth instead chose Meridian Books as his paperback publisher.

Meridian was started as the paperback arm of Noonday Press, founded by Cecil Hemley and Arthur Cohen. In 1956, their partnership broke up and Cohen kept Meridian while Hemley took Noonday Press (which was later sold to Farrar, Straus). During its first few years of existence, Meridian was the quintessential "egghead" paperback publisher. Concentrating on works in history, philosophy, and religion, the company had reprinted such writers as Arnold Toynbee, Edmund Wilson, Lionel Trilling, William James, and theologians Jacques Maritain and Paul Tillich. In addition, they had originated works by Reinhold Niebuhr (*Essays in Applied Christianity*); Walter Kaufmann (*Existentialism from Dostoevsky to Sartre*); Johan Huizinga (*Men and Ideas*); Daniel Boorstin (*America and the Image of Europe*); and, somewhat incongruously by comparison, Kate Simon (*New York Places and Pleasures*). In 1959, Meridian published the first and only authorized American edition of Edmund Wilson's *The Scrolls from the Dead Sea*.

In 1958, Cohen had been joined by Aaron Asher, whom he had hired away from Knopf (where Asher had been working on Vintage Books, which simply meant managing the smooth movement of Knopf titles into paperback), with the offer of more money and more editorial opportunity. At the time, Meridian was publishing a series called Living Age Books dealing with Catholic theology, which did not interest Asher. But soon they also had an agreement with the Jewish Publications Society for a series on Jewish history and theology. There was no place for fiction on the Meridian list until Cohen found an "angel" who was interested in backing a line of Meridian fiction. Louis Strick had been successful on Wall Street and then bought a failing typewriter ribbon company in Brooklyn that he turned around to profitability. In 1959, with only his love of literature and a checkbook, Strick joined Cohen and Asher in creating the Meridian fiction list. As Asher later recalled, "Louis Strick was a guy who loved books and publishing and fiction. Arthur sort of conned him into supporting the Meridian fiction list." (Strick later bought the Taplinger Publishing Company, which he still owns and runs.)

The Meridian fiction list made its debut in February 1960 with Simone de Beauvoir's *The Mandarins*, Randall Jarrell's *Pictures from an Institution*, Sybille Bedford's *A Legacy*, and *The Collected Stories of Isaac Babel*. The raison d'être of the list was purely and simply literary resuscitation. As Asher described the series, they were personal favorites of the three men and not the kind of novels that would ever be reprinted for the mass market. The second group of titles, appearing in March, was *The Middle Age of Mrs. Eliot* by Angus Wilson, *A Long Day's Dying* by Frederick Buechner, *The Towers of Trebizond* by Rose Macaulay, and *Goodbye, Columbus*.

Asher later recalled, "I met Roth when he was in New York, but I was not in a position to do anything. After *Goodbye, Columbus* was published, he had an offer from NAL — three or four thousand — and we offered less. But he gave it to us because of friendship partly and because, apart from the Mentors, mass market books wouldn't be around long. At the same time, there was the prestige of the 'quality paperback.' Our books were in bookstores, not in drugstores. He didn't think that young people in drugstores would buy his books. Those were his assumptions."

Just as Meridian was going to press with the plates for the book borrowed from Houghton Mifflin, Roth was announced as the winner of the 1960 National Book Award. Asher said, "Houghton Mifflin started screaming because they needed the plates to go back to press. We refused until we had printed. And we were the ones in the stores. Our edition benefited from the award." (At about the same time that he bought the rights to *Goodbye, Columbus*, Asher also bought *The Little Disturbances of Man* by Grace Paley. But Roth's book was clearly the biggest success in Meridian's fiction series.)

While Meridian was embarking on its idealistic fiction series (which proved to be short-lived, finally comprising only some twenty titles), the company also launched a second experiment cast in the image of the now-defunct *New World Writing.* The idea came from writer Herbert Gold, whose spoke on behalf of Saul Bellow and some other Chicago-based writers. They wanted to edit a magazine that would include fiction, essays, and reportage and came to Meridian for backing. *New World Writing* had folded its tent in 1959 (at NAL; Lippincott published a few more issues in trade paperback) but had been replaced by several other periodically published paperback reviews including the *Anchor Review* and Grove's *Evergreen Review.* It was, according to Asher, a "crazy idea from Meridian's point of view," but they went ahead, calling the new publication *Noble Savage.* Although its list of contributing editors included Ralph Ellison, Arthur Miller, Wright Morris, and Harvey Swados, the crush of submissions that naturally followed the announcement of the magazine fell mainly upon Saul Bellow and Keith Botsford, the editors. The contributing editors basically contributed their own works, and the first issue of *Noble Savage* included work by Ellison, Miller, and Morris, along with that of Mark Harris, Edward Hoagland, and Jack Ludwig, another of the original proponents of the idea.

Noble Savage went the way of most noble savages, meeting extinction after five appearances. Its demise came at about the same time that Arthur Cohen left Meridian, which was then selling about one million books a year, and sold it to the World Publishing Company. Owned by Ben Zevin, World was best known as a publisher of Bibles, reference books, and children's books, although it also produced some general trade books. Subsequently, World was bought by the Times Mirror Company's book division, in a move that was meant to strengthen New American Library's hardcover production by blending the NAL hardcovers into the World list. It was a plan that ended dismally and was undertaken just as Weybright was on his way out at NAL. Asher, who had stayed on to run the Meridian imprint after Cohen's departure, soon decided that his future was not with New American Library. He moved on to Viking, where, he later pointed out in comparing the current publishing scene with that of the early 1960s, he served as senior editor, managed the company's trade paperback line of Compass Books, and acted as subsidiary rights director. Today each of those jobs requires a separate department.

Philip Roth was but one of the new novelists embraced by the younger generation. As Joseph Heller, another member of the emerging group, later said:

Without being aware of it, I was part of a near movement in fiction. While I was writing *Catch-22*, J. P. Donleavy was writing *The Ginger Man*, Kerouac was writing *On the Road*, Ken Kesey was writing *One Flew over the Cuckoo's Nest*, Pynchon was writing *V.*, and Vonnegut was writing *Cat's Cradle*. I don't think any one of us even knew any of the others. Certainly I didn't know them. Whatever forces were at work shaping a trend in art were affecting not just me, but all of us. The feelings of helplessness and persecution in *Catch-22* are very strong in Pynchon and in *Cat's Cradle*.[4]

What Heller was singling out was a new literature of rebellion and protest. But it was a different sense of alienation than had been expressed by the earlier generation whose disaffection was revealed in angrier, more darkly brooding, and often violent terms. Instead, the group that was breaking out in the early sixties was turning its vision of the absurd into a literature of mordant humor.

A World War II bombardier, Joseph Heller was a graduate of Columbia and a Fulbright scholar who taught English for two years at Penn State and then returned to New York, where he wrote copy for an advertising agency. His short stories had appeared in *Esquire*, the *Atlantic Monthly*, and *Story*. Heller's first novel, *Catch-22* (originally planned as *Catch-18* until Leon Uris's *Mila Eighteen* was published and Robert Gottlieb, Heller's editor at Simon & Schuster, suggested the change) was seven years in the making. In the first published excerpt, in *New World Writing* No. 7 (1955), *Catch-18* was simply a rule that required every officer who censored letters to sign his name to those letters he had approved. Heller's hero, Yossarian, who was assigned to censoring duties while in the hospital, assaults the rule through creative censorship. One day he blacks out all the articles, the next day all the modifiers, and finally he expunges all words except *a*, *an*, and *the*. In addition, he signs his work "Washington Irving" or sometimes "Irving Washington." Eventually the concept that became Catch-22 was broadened to include the wider range of absurdities and self-contradictions that were peculiar to the army — but not exclusively so.

Catch-22 was published in hardcover by Simon & Schuster in 1961. Don Fine, then Dell's editor in chief, negotiated for the paperback rights to the book with its editor, Robert Gottlieb. Fine later recalled:

This was a book lovingly and carefully prepared by Bob Gottlieb. But the book did not take off in hardcover. We paid $32,000 or $34,000 for

In its Dell paperback edition, *Catch-22* caught on as opposition to the Vietnam War was beginning to coalesce. (Photo by Jerome Frank)

it, around there. The publication of *Catch-22* in paperback gave the book its impact. The success of that book in the first few months was astonishing. I remember when I sent the contract information to Bill Callahan [Dell's vice president in charge of sales], he wrote to me saying, "What the hell is a *Catch-22*?" I wrote back and said, "It's a World War II novel." We so-called "packaged" it so it could pass as a big important World War II novel. We had a quote from Nelson Algren that it was the best World War II novel since *The Naked and the Dead.* We had an aviator's head — not very good art — for the cover instead of the dangling man, which was the trademark of the hardcover. It would have destroyed the paperback with that on the cover. And this was the magic of paperback publishing in those days. We didn't have any television spots. We probably didn't have much point-of-sale stuff. But people read it. Young people read it and war veterans read it and goddammit, it worked! The paperback public took over this book and made it a very big success because of its availability through the much-maligned wholesalers. This was the way books got talked about and became household words.

Between its first paperback appearance in September 1962 and the late sixties, *Catch-22* was reprinted by Dell more than thirty times. The phrase "Catch-22" had entered the language and soon came to mean a no-win situation of highly absurd dimensions.* Some people eventually came to believe that Heller had named the book after the phrase. The book was taken to heart particularly by the young, who undoubtedly found parallels in their dealings with college registrars and draft boards. Like so many other paperback successes, *Catch-22* appeared at the right moment in American history and indeed became part of that history. Its antiwar, anti-authority theme hit readers across the country just as America's involvement in Vietnam was deepening. The book's success accelerated with the rising tide of opposition to the war. Heller later commented:

> Virtually none of the attitudes in the book — the suspicion and distrust of officials in the government, the feelings of helplessness and victimization, the realization that most government agencies would lie — coincided with my experience as a bombardier in World War II. The antiwar and antigovernment feelings in the book belong to the period following World War II. The Korean War, the cold war of the

The American Heritage Dictionary (Second College Edition) defines "Catch-22" as "a difficult situation or problem whose seemingly alternative solutions are logically invalid."

fifties. A general disintegration of belief took place then, and it affected *Catch-22* in that the form of the novel became almost disintegrated.[5]

At the time of *Catch-22*'s paperback publication, Dell was on the upswing. Despite the repeated successes it had published a few years earlier, the company had gone through a period of upheaval after Dell took over its own distribution and editorial functions, leaving the company at least temporarily in chaos. But the situation was eventually resolved, and in editorial matters, Dell was making some of its most impressive moves forward. The Laurel list of quality books was by now well established, and Dell was also branching out into the area of paperbacks for teenagers with a line it called Laurel Leaf, launched at the end of 1962. Later in 1963, Dell started two children's paperback lines, one for simplified language books and another called Clover Books (later changed to Seal Books). In 1962, Dell instituted a trade paperback line called Delta Books under the direction of Don Fine and Ross Claiborne. Developed for both reprints and originals in fiction and nonfiction, the Delta list's first titles included Katherine Anne Porter's *The Leaning Tower and Other Stories*, James Baldwin's *Nobody Knows My Name*, Robert Benchley's *The Benchley Roundup*, and a revision of William Miller's *A New History of the United States*. Dell also set up under the Delta banner a $5000 prize for an original work of fiction and named novelists Mary McCarthy and Walter Van Tilburg Clark and critic Leslie Fiedler as judges. However, there was no winner in the 1962 contest and the money was held over until the next year, when the $10,000 prize went to Jeremy Larner for his first novel, *Drive, He Said*.

By this time, Dell could also publish books in hardcover. In 1963, the company bought 60 percent of the Dial Press, a thirty-nine-year-old trade publisher best known for its association with *The Dial*, the famous literary magazine. Then, in 1964, Dell went a step further and set up its own hardcover imprint, Delacorte Press, which premièred with Burton Wohl's novel *The Jet Set*. Other early Delacorte titles included Gael Greene's *Sex and the College Girl*, *For Women Only* by Dr. Bernard L. Cinberg, four other novels (unmemorable), and an anthology, *A Century of Science Fiction*, edited by Damon Knight. Like Ian Ballantine's plan for simultaneous hardcovers and paperbacks more than ten years earlier, the Delacorte plan made waves. Under Delacorte's contract terms, Dell acquired the paperback rights to the book automatically and the author kept 100 percent of the paperback royalties. The arrangement was the key inducement in Don Fine's two major coups, the signing of Irwin Shaw, a long-time Random House author, and his buddy James Jones, out of the Scribner's fold.

The final piece in building the Dell book empire was the establishment of a separate hardcover imprint for editor Seymour Lawrence in 1965. Formerly with the *Atlantic Monthly*, then the Atlantic Monthly Press, and later Alfred Knopf, Lawrence came to Dell in one of the first independent personal imprint arrangements in publishing. (The only other one existing at the time was that of Helen and Kurt Wolff with Harcourt Brace Jovanovich, begun in 1962). Under this arrangement, Lawrence acquired and edited books that were then produced, distributed, and advertised by Dell with Lawrence's supervision. In other words, Lawrence existed like a small publishing house within the context of a larger one. Under the Seymour Lawrence/Delacorte Press imprint, the list of writers grew to include J. P. Donleavy, Thomas Berger, T. Berry Brazelton — author of the classic *Infants and Mothers* — and, later on, Kurt Vonnegut.

Player Piano, Vonnegut's first book, was published in hardcover by Holt in 1952 to little success. Knox Burger, who had edited Vonnegut's stories while at *Collier's*, brought Vonnegut to the Dell First Editions list in 1959 with *The Sirens of Titan*. Mistakenly classed as a science fiction writer in his early career, Vonnegut was simply using the devices and trappings of science fiction to weave his unique, playful brand of visionary satire and express his dissatisfaction with militarism and greed. His succeeding novels, *Mother Night* (a devastating exploration into the psyche of an American Nazi), *Cat's Cradle, God Bless You, Mr. Rosewater*, and *Welcome to the Monkey House*, had begun to attract a small clique of devoted fans. But it was not until *Slaughterhouse-Five* appeared in 1969 that Vonnegut gained his widest recognition.

This was the first of the books published under the Seymour Lawrence/Delacorte Press imprint. Prior to *Slaughterhouse-Five*, Vonnegut's publishing history had been desultory as he moved around to a variety of publishers. Then it became known that he and his agent were seeking a better financial deal. Both Don Fine and Sam Lawrence wanted to provide it, Fine for Delacorte and Lawrence for his own imprint. According to Fine, "Sam Lawrence was interested. I was interested. I remember meeting with the Dell management and I said I thought Sam should have this. They were all stunned. I was not known for my selflessness. But it would have been very wrong in the state Delacorte was in. Vonnegut needed special attention. Sam Lawrence did a good job."[6]

Dell was of course still a beneficiary of the deal. All Seymour Lawrence books, like Delacorte Press books, were automatically published by Dell in paperback. So all of Vonnegut's books were eventually published by Dell, some first as Delta trade paperbacks and later as Dell mass market books. As Vonnegut's reputation grew, particularly among the young during the late sixties, his body of work became a major success for Dell. Vonnegut also became a pre-eminent example of how paperback success can pave the way for hardcover success. Most of Vonnegut's recent books have become instant best sellers, owing to the enormous built-in audience for his books, an audience created out of paperback readers who probably buy few hardcover books besides Vonnegut's.

With all of these imprints and subsidiary lines in place, Dell Books emerged from the mid-sixties with a full-fledged publishing operation. The company's metamorphosis from ugly-duckling re-printer to a comprehensive publishing operation confirmed the growing trend among paperback houses toward becoming full-line book publishers and not simple reproducers of the output of trade houses. Pocket Books had its hardcover line, trade paperbacks, and mass market capabilities (as well as the luxury of kinship with Simon & Schuster), and NAL did as well. But Dell's alignment of the various rack-sized imprints plus the Delta trade books, the Dial Press, Delacorte Press, and Seymour Lawrence gave the company more depth and eventual staying power. Long after Trident Books, the Pocket Books imprint created almost exclusively for Harold Robbins, was gone and NAL's hardcover program was folded into that of World (after its acquisition by Times Mirror), the Dell combine still published vigorously.

Besides publishing new fiction styles as represented by Heller and Vonnegut — as well as continuing to publish strictly commercial fiction such as *Return to Peyton Place* and *The Tight White Collar* by Grace Metalious and Morris West's best sellers, *The Devil's Advocate*, *The Shoes of the Fisherman*, and *Daughter of Silence* — all paperback successes — Dell was in step with other changes in the American social landscape. Shortly after Dell published *Catch-22*,

the company reprinted a book that was to have powerful consequences for American women and the way they were viewed by
themselves and by men.

A summa cum laude graduate of Smith College, Betty Friedan
was a mother of three and a magazine journalist when she wrote
The Feminine Mystique, a devastating look at American women in
the postwar generation. Describing the malaise and disillusionment
felt by the American woman trapped in her housewife/mother role
with all its modern conveniences, Friedan wrote:

> The new mystique makes the housewife-mothers, who never had a
> chance to be anything else, the model for all women; it presupposes
> that history has reached a final and glorious end in the here and now,
> as far as women are concerned. Beneath the sophisticated trappings, it
> simply makes certain concrete, finite, domestic aspects of feminine
> existence — as it was lived by women whose lives were confined, by
> necessity, to cooking, cleaning, washing, bearing children — into a
> religion, a pattern by which all women must now live or deny their
> femininity.[7]

At Dell Books, it was again Don Fine who was responsible for the
acquisition of rights, although at the urging of several female colleagues. Fine recounted:

> Long before publication in hardcover, the subsidiary rights director at
> Norton sent us the book. I was away, and when I came back, there
> were memos on my desk from every woman in the office. "This is the
> book we've been waiting for. You've got to buy it." I had a built-in
> resistance. I told Betty Friedan later that I didn't agree with everything
> in it. I thought Freud was misread — I still think Freud is misrepre-
> sented by the women's movement. But I was bulldozed into it by
> Arlene Donovan [then editor in chief of Dell First Editions] and Marcia
> Nasatir [assistant editor at Dell Books]. We didn't pay much, but it
> was considered a lot for a book of its kind. Within months after it was
> published, there was an interesting sign. I think it was Vassar that
> bought copies of the Dell edition for its freshman kits for the incoming
> class. That's a hell of a tip-off. It had already become something for
> young, intelligent women. And then it just spread. Garden clubs
> started calling to talk to Betty. She was all over the country. Again it
> was the exposure of the books. It sold millions of copies.

It is a sign of the times when Dell published *The Feminine Mystique* that the 1961–62 *Paperbound Books in Print* had no such
category as women's studies. There were, however, more than forty

child-care and development books; close to two hundred cook-books; about fifty gardening titles; more than forty books about marriage and sex; and about fifty house and home paperback titles. One paperback publisher, Pyramid Books, had instituted a line of books for women in 1960. They included *Beauty Today, The New Italian Cookbook, Tell Me, Doctor* — dealing with gynecological problems — and *The Miracle of Growth*, about conception. In other words, women's concerns were considered beauty, cooking, sex, and babies. On the plus side, fiction by major women novelists was plentiful, and *The Second Sex* by Simone de Beauvoir had been reprinted by Bantam.

The multimillion-copy sale of *The Feminine Mystique* in its Dell edition was concrete proof that Friedan had touched a very sensitive nerve. A great many women, despite their increasing level of edu-cation, had married young in the years after the war and were being forced by every element of society to accept the role of wife, mother, and housekeeper. *The Feminine Mystique* documented how this was being accomplished through the media, education, and the medical community, and the immense psychic costs borne by dis-consolate professional women for whom a career meant they had failed as women and by frustrated mothers cheated out of the op-portunity to achieve anything besides motherhood. Until Kate Mil-lett's *Sexual Politics* (1970) and Germaine Greer's *The Female Eunuch* (1970) joined *The Feminine Mystique* in the canon of the women's movement, Friedan was a voice in the wilderness. But her voice was soon heard throughout America, and it was her book that became the catalyst and first gospel of the modern American femi-nist movement. Twenty years after *The Feminine Mystique* ap-peared, Friedan wrote, "I am still awed by the revolution that book helped spark. . . . Even now, women — and men — stop me on the street to reminisce about where they were when they read it — 'I was in the maternity ward with my third kid, and then I decided to go to law school.' I keep being surprised, as the changes the wom-en's movement set into motion continue to play themselves out in our lives."[8]

Key Paperbacks: 1960–1965

1960

The Adventures of Augie March	Saul Bellow (Viking/Compass)
The Dangling Man	Saul Bellow (Viking/Compass)
The Ugly American	Eugene Burdick and William Lederer (Fawcett)
The Manchurian Candidate	Richard Condon (Signet)
Spartacus	Howard Fast (Bantam)
Growing Up Absurd	Paul Goodman (Vintage)
A Separate Peace	John Knowles (Dell)
A Canticle for Leibowitz	Walter Miller (Bantam original)
Listen, Yankee: The Revolution in Cuba	C. Wright Mills (Ballantine original)
From the Terrace	John O'Hara (Bantam)
Doctor Zhivago	Boris Pasternak (Signet)
We the Living	Ayn Rand (Signet)
In the Labyrinth	Alain Robbe-Grillet (Grove)
Drugs and the Mind	Robert S. De Ropp (Grove)
Goodbye, Columbus	Philip Roth (Meridian)
Walden Two	B. F. Skinner (Macmillan)
Elements of Style	William Strunk, Jr., and E. B. White (Macmillan)
Rabbit, Run	John Updike (Fawcett)
The Once and Future King	T. H. White (Dell)
The Case Against Adolf Eichmann	Henry Zeiger, ed. (Signet instant book)
Noble Savage No. 1	Saul Bellow et al., eds. (Meridian)

1961

Nightwood	Djuna Barnes (New Directions)
Advise and Consent	Allen Drury (Pocket)
Kaddish	Allen Ginsberg (City Lights)
Black Like Me	John Howard Griffin (Signet)
Folk Medicine	D. C. Jarvis (Fawcett)
The Tropic of Cancer	Henry Miller
The Status Seekers	Vance Packard (Pocket)
The Rise and Fall of the Third Reich	William L. Shirer (Fawcett)
West Side Story	Irving Shulman (Pocket)
Mother Night	Kurt Vonnegut (Dell)

1962

Another Country	James Baldwin (Dell)
Reinhart in Love	Thomas Berger (Dell)
From the Back of the Bus	Dick Gregory (Avon)
Catch-22	Joseph Heller (Dell)
One Flew over the Cuckoo's Nest	Ken Kesey (Signet)
To Kill a Mockingbird	Harper Lee (Popular Library)
Lolita	Vladimir Nabokov (Fawcett)
Function of the Orgasm	Wilhelm Reich (Noonday)

1963

Silent Spring	Rachel Carson (Fawcett)
The Feminine Mystique	Betty Friedan (Dell)
Why We Can't Wait	Martin Luther King, Jr. (NAL originated)
Power, Politics and People	C. Wright Mills (Galaxy)
One Day in the Life of Ivan Denisovich	Aleksandr Solzhenitsyn (Bantam, NAL)
Cat's Cradle	Kurt Vonnegut (Delta)

1964

A Confederate General in Big Sur	Richard Brautigan (Grove)
I Never Promised You a Rose Garden	Hannah Green (Signet)
Understanding Media	Marshall McLuhan (Mentor)
V.	Thomas Pynchon (Bantam)
City of Night	John Rechy (Grove)
Call It Sleep	Henry Roth (Avon)
Franny and Zooey	J. D. Salinger (Bantam)
Last Exit to Brooklyn	Hubert Selby, Jr. (Grove)
Crisis in Black and White	Charles Silberman (Vintage)
Candy	Terry Southern and Mason Hoffenberg (Lancer, Dell)
The Report of the Warren Commission	(Bantam instant book)

1965

In Cold Blood	Truman Capote (Signet)
The Wretched of the Earth	Frantz Fanon (Grove)
The Autobiography of Malcolm X	Malcolm X and Alex Haley (Grove)

Everything That Rises Must Converge	Flannery O'Connor (Signet)
The Fellowship of the Ring	J.R.R. Tolkien (Ballantine)
The Kandy-Kolored Tangerine-Flake Streamline Baby	Tom Wolfe (Bantam)

The American feminist movement of the sixties and seventies was one of two powerful forces of social change in postwar America. The other was the struggle for the rights of blacks. Not coincidental to the feminist movement, but another expression of the hunger for justice and freedom that characterized the times, the emerging conflict over the rights of blacks in the United States was reaching its boiling point as the sixties dawned. The stepping-off point for the civil rights movement must be dated 1954 with the landmark *Brown* v. *Board of Education* Supreme Court decision that ended legal segregation of public schools. But it was in the sixties that the racial question gained its greatest urgency, a pressing call for racial justice that was being sounded loudly and clearly by an increasing number of black writers. As the books of Harriet Beecher Stowe had led the abolitionist movement of the previous century, writing about the cause of black freedom was leading the way in the sixties.

Until this time, the number of books by black writers appearing in mass market paperback editions had been limited to those published by New American Library. In this field, however, NAL's record had been superior. James Baldwin's *Giovanni's Room* and *Go Tell It on the Mountain* and the novels of Ellison, Wright, Lillian Smith, and Chester Himes had all been widely and successfully distributed as Signet paperbacks. In 1964, Victor Weybright and Martin Luther King's literary agent initiated King's *Why We Can't Wait*, published simultaneously with a Harper & Row hardcover edition. The book was conceived on a crash basis to capitalize on the 1963 March on Washington, and the Mentor edition was issued in a half-million-copy first printing, in the year that King was awarded the Nobel Peace Prize. The book stands as one of the significant documents of the civil rights struggle.

Two years earlier, NAL had published a book by a white writer about the status of blacks in America that also had a profound impact on the racial question. John Howard Griffin was a novelist from Texas who had been blinded during World War II. (His best-known novel, *The Devil Rides Outside,* was reprinted by Pocket Books and had been the object of censorship in Detroit in the fifties.) After regaining his sight, Griffin continued to write, and in 1959, with the blessing of the publisher of *Sepia* magazine, a black magazine similar to *Life,* Griffin crossed the color line — literally. In order to pass himself off as a black man, Griffin shaved his head and underwent medical treatment to darken his skin. He then traveled through the Deep South, recording his experiences and observations.

It would be easy to mock Griffin's mission as the misguided Amos 'n' Andy attempt of a white liberal to clear his conscience by trying to experience the meaning of living under Jim Crow. After all, Griffin knew that he would eventually return to his home, family, and race. There also must have been considerable black resentment that it had taken the witness of a white man to tell the world of the fear and hatred American blacks lived with daily. But to Griffin's credit, it must be remembered that he took his life into his hands to accomplish this assignment. Had Griffin's true identity been uncovered and his purpose revealed in some small Southern backwater, his life would not have been worth a nickel. A rope over a tree or a roadside ditch might easily have been the end of his daring act. If nothing else, then, his was a mission of considerable courage. But the book succeeded as more than simply a tale of one man's brave adventure skirting death. Unlike any book before it, perhaps with the exception of Richard Wright's *Black Boy,* Griffin's *Black Like Me* woke America to the truth of its ugly underside. The book became a five-million-plus best seller, vividly demonstrating that its message was being received. As social historians Douglas Miller and Marion Nowak wrote:

> Griffin feelingly illuminated the monstrous cruelty of the whole racial scene, the sexual exploitation, emotional destruction, arbitrary white violence. He also told of the way blacks welcomed and helped each ' other. . . . It was the shock value of the act — the witness, transformed back and forth — that gave the book its vast importance. And this shock value would not have existed if it were not for one terrible truth. Even sympathetic liberals were bigoted enough to never have listened to black anguish.[9]

If Griffin had illustrated for white America the anguish of black America, black writers soon gave the country a taste of black anger.

Three men in particular emerged in the sixties to catalogue the tyranny, injustice, and separateness of the lives of American Negroes (the noun of preference before "black" gained vogue later in the sixties): James Baldwin, Malcolm X, and Eldridge Cleaver. Each was a vastly different, complex man with a different style, whose ideas occasionally clashed with those of the others, creating a kind of internecine warfare among them. However, their works were read widely in paperback and radically influenced the perception and outcome of the race question as black awareness and militancy rose in the middle sixties.

Of the three, Baldwin was the one most accepted by white America — if true acceptance can be given to a black, a homosexual, an intellectual, a writer, and an expatriate. Baldwin was a writer of great power, erudition, style, and insight. His early novels *Giovanni's Room, Go Tell It on the Mountain* (both reprinted by NAL) and *Another Country* (Dell) had helped to cast him as the successor to Ellison and Wright as the artistic spokesman for the American black. But it was in his nonfiction that he gained his strongest voice. Beginning with *Notes of a Native Son* (1955) and through *Nobody Knows My Name* (1961) and *The Fire Next Time* (1963), Baldwin emerged as the most gifted polemicist on black America, a stirring voice of rising anger.

In these books, Baldwin wrote with the moral urgency and fearful tone of warning of an Old Testament prophet. His wrenching picture of the terrors that were part of daily life *in simply getting by* was complemented by his fearsome vision of the potential for vengeance that these terrors might soon provoke.

In strictly commercial terms, Baldwin's emergence as a widely read and much-admired essayist and messenger from the other America also provided a striking example of how Dell could operate with its full capacities. Baldwin was published in hardcover by the Dial Press. His books (including those that had earlier been reprinted by NAL, Grosset's Universal Library, and Meridian and were recovered by Dell) then moved into Delta trade paperback editions, starting with *Nobody Knows My Name.* Finally, they appeared as Dell mass market paperbacks and got full distribution. Dell's strategy and success with Baldwin's books were among the foremost examples of the paperback publisher's growing potential to publish across a broad spectrum, reaching the widest possible audience with books that were no longer the second-rate trash that paperback publishers, Dell being one of the principal culprits, were once accused of creating.

Dell later became the paperback publisher of a writer completely different in style — in both his life and his writing — from Baldwin. An admirer of Baldwin who nonetheless attacked him, Eldridge Cleaver was breathing the "fire" that Baldwin had predicted. Born in 1935, he was arrested while in junior high school for stealing a bicycle and sent to a boys' school, where he learned about hustling pot (so much for *reform* school); not surprisingly, it was for possession and sale of marijuana that he was sent to prison for the first time in 1954. While there, Cleaver, a man of obvious intellect, began to read eclectically, and soon formulated his notion of the rape of white women as an "insurrectionary act." Upon his release, he rehearsed this theory on black women before putting it into practice. He was sentenced to Folsom Prison after being convicted of assault with intent to kill. Recognizing the folly of his theory, Cleaver later became a follower of the rabidly antiwhite Black Muslim sect and started writing the prison letters that made him notorious.

Though it was eventually Dell that made a two-million-plus paperback seller out of *Soul on Ice* in both Delta trade and Dell mass market editions, the book was first published in hardcover by (incongruous as it might seem) McGraw-Hill, where it had been acquired by Frank Taylor, Dell's former editorial director. Far better known as a publisher of text, business, and professional books than as a trade publisher, McGraw-Hill was as much a bastion of the capitalist ethic as any publishing house and would seem an unlikely place for Eldridge Cleaver's diatribe against white capitalist America to be published. Nonetheless, critic Maxwell Geismar sent Cleaver's attorney, Beverly Axelrod, to Taylor with the collection of letters he had written in prison to her and fellow lawyer Charles R. Garry. As Taylor later recalled:

> One day this rather radical looking woman appeared in my office. She said she represented an astonishing writer and wanted a contract. I asked what the book was and she said it was not really written yet, but the author needed $7500 to get out of prison. I asked how I could know if he can write and she said she would share something very private with me. She opened her purse and brought out Eldridge Cleaver's letters to her. And I read. I didn't want to read them because they were so personal and so beautiful. I thought it was an invasion of

The paperback edition of *Soul on Ice* became one of the basic documents of the Black Power movement during the late 1960s. (Photo by Jerome Frank)

privacy. I was astonished by them and said, "here's $7500." That's the way it began.

Portions of the book first appeared in *Ramparts*, a radical muck-raking magazine. When the book was ready, Taylor was prepared for McGraw-Hill to be "blown up the wall." (He had already shaken the foundation there a bit when he acquired and published Desmond Morris's *The Naked Ape*). Yet the book turned into an unexpected success for McGraw-Hill and was a best seller during 1968, though it was not one of the year's top ten books. Delta editor Richard Huett bought the paperback rights for $2000, and the book became Delta's first commercial success. It appeared when America's racial situation was at its hottest. Three successive "long, hot summers" had torn the country's ghettos apart. There were black militants talking with deadly earnest of war with "whitey." Martin Luther King and Bobby Kennedy had been gunned down. At the same time, the protest against the war in Vietnam was reaching its peak, and the frenzied Democratic convention in Chicago had turned into a nightmare. The threads all seemed to be coming loose. Yet, in Frank Taylor's opinion, the book may have had the opposite of its expected effect:

> The value of that book — this is an idiosyncratic conclusion — looking at that time in the sixties when it was published, was that the rhetoric was such a safety valve for black people. I think there were fewer riots because of that book, despite the fact that many people thought it was inciteful — a call to arms. The rhetoric in which it was constructed was so strong. But the deepest feelings had been expressed in the vernacular.

Although he had written admiringly of James Baldwin — though criticizing Baldwin's dismissal of Mailer's essay "The White Negro" — Cleaver's true mentor and predecessor was Malcolm X. Born Malcolm Little, Malcolm X had seen the institutionalized racism in America from his earliest memories, became involved in street lowlife, and eventually rose to a position of power within the Black Muslim organization. It is reasonable to say that, at one point, alongside Martin Luther King, Malcolm X was the most powerful and admired black man in America (though the two did not admire each other, it seems). If he had not been assassinated in 1965 after a feud within the Black Muslim leadership, at a point in which his views seemed to be moderating, the history of the racial issue in

America might have been very different. Malcolm X had acquired notoriety as a speaker and was a brilliant public relations man if nothing else. But it was through *The Autobiography of Malcolm X* that his fame and legend grew even greater after his death.

The Autobiography of Malcolm X (as told to Alex Haley, then a well-known journalist who had interviewed Malcolm X, American Nazi George Lincoln Rockwell, Martin Luther King, and Cassius Clay for *Playboy,* and later famous as the author of *Roots*) was a document of seminal importance to the period. Published in 1965, just after Malcolm X's death — which he had predicted in the early pages of the book — it was an evocative account of his rise from country boy to city slicker, criminal, convict, and, finally, leading spokesman for militant blacks in America. As a narrative, it hinged on a string of frequently haunting, often bitter remembrances and observations that brought him to his separate conversions: the first to the Black Muslim sect, the second to the moderation of his views that was partly responsible for the fracturing of his relationship with the Black Muslims, which eventually led to his murder.

Like Malcolm X himself, the book's publishing history was complex. Alex Haley had spent a long time simply convincing Malcolm X to agree to tell his story — as Malcolm X later told Haley, he only trusted the writer 20 percent when they began. They spent much of the next two years together, Haley taping and taking notes, Malcolm X revising and approving the drafts as he moved through the turbulent period that preceded his death. Initially, the book was under contract to Doubleday, Haley's publisher. However, Doubleday never published the book. Grove Press did. According to Barney Rosset, Grove's owner, "Mr. Doubleday had bought the book, but wouldn't publish it. I don't know what happened, but there were two stories. One was that he had said he didn't want the store windows smashed; the other, that he didn't want the receptionists' faces smashed. Anyway, we called the agent and said we'd do it. I think we paid $20,000."

Grove first published the book in a hardcover format that was only modestly successful. Nat Sobel, who was Grove's sales manager at the time, recalled the difficulties of selling a book about a man who had professed hatred for the entire white race:

> It was a sales manager's nightmare. Too many people remembered his comments at the time of JFK's assassination about the chickens com-

ing home to roost. But in the years I have been in publishing, that was one of the only books that really electrified me. It was a book not only about Malcolm X but about the whole black experience, what it meant to be black. Then there was the famous incident. On publication date for *The Autobiography*, the *New York Times Book Review* reviewed Sammy Davis, Jr.'s autobiography on the front page and they totally ignored Malcolm X. They had obviously chosen the more acceptable black.

Although the book was published at a moment in Grove's history when the company was on a roll with successive best sellers, and Sobel could say that Grove was thoroughly committed to what they felt was an important book, *The Autobiography* did not sell well in hardcover. Grove received no offers from mass market houses to do a paperback edition. Instead, Grove itself issued the paperback, with Dell providing the initial distribution to the wholesalers. However, by the time Grove's paperback edition was issued, the book was beginning to be discussed. As Sobel recalled:

> People were beginning to say that this is one of the more important books they had read. When the paperback was published there was a new editorial group at the *Times Book Review* and *The Autobiography of Malcolm X* was given a page-three review, I think. A major review for a paperback reprint. I think that the *Times* was recognizing its omission. A seminal work was being covered. The other real breakthrough for the book came when the Scholastic Book Club took it. Considering the language and the theme, some very brave people at Scholastic took a stand. It didn't mean a lot of money, but it did mean a lot of young people were being exposed to the book. Then it was word of mouth. It was phenomenally successful in paperback.

It was not surprising that Grove Press had stepped in to resuscitate the book after Doubleday turned it down. Rosset had already made a name for himself as an iconoclast and rebel with little regard for conventions or laws he didn't accept. In many respects, the Grove Press he created, with an editorial staff that included two esteemed editors, Richard Seaver and Fred Jordan, was the quintessential publisher of the sixties. Grove was often outrageous, daring, avant-garde, and disrespectful of authority. Rosset had made his name and Grove's reputation by taking chances on writers that others were not willing to risk. For the first ten years of the company's existence, such bravado had meant that Grove was surviving only from Rosset's considerable personal assets. But with the coming of the sixties, that changed. The publication of *Lady Chatter-ley's Lover* was the first step in putting Grove on the map as a publisher. (Rosset, who got into publishing almost by fluke, later recalled that as a child he had, perhaps presciently, always crossed out the "G" in Grosset & Dunlap on his schoolbooks.) After the battle to allow the publication of the Lawrence novel and the sub-sequent legal haggling over the numerous competing editions, Grove had done quite well with *Lady Chatterley's Lover*, the com-pany's first major financial success.

Rosset followed the *Lady Chatterley* court test by audaciously publishing another underground classic banned in the United States for its sexual content. Henry Miller's *Tropic of Cancer* was written in Paris in 1934 but never released here by Miller's American pub-lisher, New Directions. According to one biography of Miller, Vic-tor Weybright, while still at Penguin, had offered Miller a $1000 advance for an expurgated edition of *Tropic of Cancer* in an attempt to "capitalize on the *sub rosa* notoriety of the novel."[10] NAL did eventually publish three of Miller's books, *A Devil in Paradise, The Intimate Henry Miller*, and *Nights of Love and Laughter*. Miller once told Truman Talley when the editor visited him in Big Sur that writers should "pay for the privilege of being published in paperback." Given Miller's generally desperate financial straits, he was probably just being nice.

Rosset had admired Miller since he was a college freshman and had written a class paper on Miller's work. He convinced Miller's publisher, and a reluctant Henry Miller, to allow Grove to publish the book and assume financial liability for all actions brought against the book, Miller, or booksellers who sold the book. The publication of *Tropic of Cancer* led to dozens of cases all across the country in which Grove did spend more than $250,000 to defend the book until it was cleared by the United States Supreme Court in 1964. (Another legal footnote: Miller and Rosset were charged with conspiracy to write, publish, and distribute *Tropic of Cancer* in Miller's hometown of Brooklyn, New York. Rosset appeared and explained to the court that Henry Miller wrote the book in Paris in 1934. At the time, Rosset was twelve and living in Chicago. When the prosecutor asked if Rosset knew the book was being sold near a school, the publisher read aloud one of the more infamous sections and told the court, "I congratulate you if your children are literate enough to read the book and understand it." The jury laughed, as did the district attorney, and the indictment was dropped.) *Tropic of Cancer* became Grove's second-best seller, after *Lady Chatterley,* eventually selling more than three million copies in hardcover and paperback.

In 1961, Grove had started a mass market paperback line called Black Cat books to complement its Evergreen trade paperbacks, and *Tropic of Cancer* was the tenth book in the line; Miller's *Sexus, Nexus,* and *Plexus* were Black Cat books 99, 100, and 101. Other early Black Cat editions were generally books that Rosset believed might have the potential to reach a wider audience — although that was not always the case; distinctions were often arbitrary. The line eventually grew to include works diverse and provocative, among them the plays of Bertolt Brecht; the novels of William S. Burroughs; *Drugs and the Mind* by Robert S. De Ropp; Albert Ellis's *Sex Without Guilt;* the experimental novels of Alain Robbe-Grillet (then an editor at Editions de Minuit, Beckett's French publisher, a company created by the French Resistance and so named because its books "came out at midnight"); Hubert Selby, Jr.'s *Last Exit to Brooklyn;* and a book version of *I Am Curious (Yellow),* the film that brought full frontal nudity to the American screen. (That project came about as a result of Rosset's decision to get involved in film distribution, a scheme that resulted in the loosening of film censorship, just as the *Lady Chatterley* and *Tropic* cases had done for books, but almost broke Grove in the end.)

Most of the books that made it into the Black Cat editions were, like *The Autobiography of Malcolm X,* ones that no other mass market house was interested in or brave enough to publish. One of the most astonishing instances of this came when Grove published in hardcover a work by a little-known California psychiatrist named Eric Berne. In 1964, Grove published Berne's second book, *Games People Play,* in a 3500-copy first printing. The book caught on and remained on the annual best-seller lists through 1965, 1966, and 1967. Yet Grove received no offers from mass market houses and published it as a Black Cat edition with distribution by Dell. As a paperback it sold several million more copies.

Another of the major Black Cat works was a book that stood alongside *The Autobiography of Malcolm X* as one of the crucial documents of the black revolutionary movement in America. Frantz Fanon was a black psychiatrist born on Martinique. His first book, *Black Skin, White Masks,* was based upon his psychiatric experience in the Antilles. Fanon was in Algeria during the war against the French and his experiences soon brought him to sympathize with the rebel cause, spawning two more books, *L'An V de La Revolucion Algerienne* (published by Grove as *A Dying Colonialism*) and *The Wretched of the Earth,* the critical work that not only gave voice to the demands of black Americans but was a blueprint for revolutionary movements throughout the Third World. First published by Grove in 1968, with a preface by Jean-Paul Sartre, *The Wretched of the Earth* went through more than twenty printings by 1982 and, along with *The Autobiography of Malcolm X* and *Soul on Ice,* stood as one of the key works behind the Black Power movement of the late sixties.

Despite Rosset and Grove's success in publishing the major new dramatic and fiction writers and expanding social and psychological consciousness in this period, the label that Rosset was branded with was "smut peddler" and "dirty book man." Certainly the die was cast when he pioneered the publication of *Lady Chatterley's Lover* and *Tropic of Cancer.* The controversy surrounding those books was the foundation of the reputation he (unfairly) acquired. But the literary value of both of those books was apparent. Artistic merit was less clear to some people when Rosset began publishing the works of the Marquis de Sade, Pauline Reage's *The Story of O* (another Grove best seller), and the classics of anonymous Victorian erotica *The Pearl, A Man with a Maid,* and *My Secret Life.* But the publishing of pornography or erotica — the distinctions are open to debate — was simply another expression of Rosset's disdain for convention. Said Nat Sobel:

> The sixties were a period of experimentation, revolt, throwing-off of earlier concepts. *The Autobiography of Malcolm X* and *The Wretched of the Earth* did that to social awareness and *Games People Play* did that to our understanding of personal relationships the way *Tropic of Cancer* and *The Story of O* did to our sexual awareness. Barney Rosset attracted a bunch of guys totally dedicated to working at Grove. His concept was to experiment. Be audacious. Craziness. We all picked up on that. We didn't have a lot of meetings; they bored Barney. I'm not sure I could characterize him as a great businessman, but he had great instincts and a great ear for what was happening. He also had a curiosity for a wide range of interests — the hallmark of a great publisher. When I once asked him why we were publishing a simultaneous Spanish-English bilingual edition of Neruda's poetry when I can't sell

poetry, let alone bilingual poetry, Barney said, "Because it's important. We made a lot of money with this and that and we've got to give a little of it back to the business that made us the money." It was one of the few times he ever waxed philosophical. He hardly ever talked about it as a crusade. He didn't take a holy attitude. He just went his own way.

Rosset and Grove had distilled the essence of the defiance and free-spiritedness of the period into an unstated publishing philosophy. Perhaps equally representative of the sense and sensibilities of the late sixties and early seventies was a single publishing project of great ambition and sometimes great achievement, *New American Review* (later *American Review*). Through ten stormy years, three publishers, and twenty-six occasionally sublime but always interesting issues, this series of fiction, essays, and poetry stood at what Lionel Trilling had called "the bloody crossroads where art and politics meet." Its vibrancy, daring, willingness to strip away pretense and often shock, were a tribute to *NAR*'s editorial Svengali, Theodore Solotaroff.

Solotaroff was among the first ranks of young men and women whose literary education had come in part through paperbacks, the first children of the Paperback Revolution who had bought their copies of *The Naked and the Dead* in drugstores, read Anchor Books in college, or unearthed the riches offered in *discovery, Noble Savage,* and, particularly for Solotaroff, *New World Writing.* "I remember seeing a copy of the first *New World Writing* in a local drugstore in Ann Arbor, and it blew me away — the idea that there could be a paperback with all these terrific pieces of writing in it. I was a loyal reader, an envious reader." A self-described "Depression kid," Solotaroff came out of college with plans to become a writer himself, an ambition he achingly described in his sole written contribution to the magazine (other than sporadic introductory notes) called "Silence, Exile and Cunning" (*NAR* No. 8). Following an aborted and frustrated career as a writer living the bohemian dream in New York while waiting tables, Solotaroff returned to graduate school and eventually found his voice as a book critic. That was how he came to the attention of E. L. Doctorow, then the editor in charge of Signet Classics at NAL, who commissioned Solotaroff's introduction to *Native Son.*

It was NAL's *New World Writing,* once the object of Solotaroff's envy, that was largely responsible for the impulse to begin *New*

American Review, an impulse that Solotaroff was not disposed toward. The year was 1964 and the new editorial group at NAL was interested in moving the company in the direction of comprehensive trade publishing with a full hardcover line. The suggestion to revive *New World Writing* as a sort of "farm team" for the company's hardcover program came from Robert Gutwillig, one of two editors (the other was Ed Kuhn) who had come to NAL from McGraw-Hill along with the new publisher, John Budlong. Solotaroff initially rejected the suggestion that he edit a resuscitated *New World Writing* and went to Berkeley instead, but he later accepted their offer. However, it was under his own terms. He said, "I wasn't interested in reviving *New World Writing* because it did not pay to revive a corpse — it was already dead." Solotaroff was also well aware of the life span of the various other attempts to publish paperback small magazines — usually five or six issues.

If it was to be done, Solotaroff wanted a new and different editorial concept that would be less concerned with recruiting the next generation of writing talent for NAL's hardcover program:

I wanted to start a magazine that would not only publish fiction, poetry, and literary criticism but would be a genuine journal of literature and ideas. They were reluctant when I started talking about people like David Riesman and Conor Cruise O'Brien. The really important issue was not a matter of taste in fiction. It was 1966. The civil rights revolution was at its height. The Vietnam situation was brewing. A whole sense of alternative points was taking place. I was saying that any magazine that was not political or sensitive to the political and social changes the country was going through was beside the point. They decided that I might do something interesting and probably might drop the idea of being ideological, and they let me go ahead. Then a funny thing happened on the way to publication. As fast as New American Library went into hardcover publishing, they went out. I think they lost seven million dollars. They made tremendous mistakes.

In an attempt to shore up its investment in NAL, the Times Mirror Company brought in paperback veteran Sidney Kramer as a consultant, and he later became publisher. One of his first pronouncements, according to Solotaroff, was "Let's get rid of that cockamamie magazine." At this point, the first issue was ready to go to press. Since Solotaroff had an interesting line-up, the first *NAR* was given an eleventh-hour reprieve. Then success took over.

The first issue of *New American Review* was published in September 1967 and became the literary event of the year. It was widely reviewed and well received and soon went back to press for two additional printings, for a total of about 120,000 copies.

In his opening remarks in the issue, Solotaroff paid homage to his predecessor, *New World Writing,* but emphasized that the new magazine would be different in that it was "broadening the concept of a writer's magazine for the common reader to include imaginative writing in various fields and in providing somewhat more explicit and topical connections between contemporary literature and culture-at-large." *New American Review* came along just as the "new journalism" was bringing the techniques of fiction to reporting and writers like Barthelme and Doctorow were bending facts into new forms of fiction. The connections between literature and current events became apparent from the opening story in the first *New American Review,* Victor Kolpacoff's "The Room," a vividly realistic story of the interrogation of a suspected Vietcong in which it became apparent that the interrogators were the ones being imprisoned. The group of Americans trapped inside a sheet metal hut surrounded by fencing was a metaphor for America's involvement in Vietnam, while the possibility that Americans were capable of brutality provided an awful dose of reality in 1967.

The essays in the first issue also demonstrated the connections that Solotaroff was trying to make. Richard Gilman wrote a stinging rebuke of *MacBird!,* the off-Broadway sensation that intimated that LBJ was responsible for Kennedy's death; Benjamin DeMott and George Dennison wrote on the question of homosexuality and art; Stanley Kauffmann (the former Bantam and Ballantine editor and later film critic for the *New Republic*) discussed his brief and controversial stint as drama critic of the *New York Times,* an essay that raised questions of power, influence, and their place in art and criticism; Theodore Roszak criticized the academic world's failure of conscience; Keith Botsford wrote from the wrong side of the much-discussed "generation gap"; and Conor Cruise O'Brien discussed the impact of Marx and Burke on the modern world.

The fiction and poetry were equally impressive. In addition to Kolpacoff's chilling Vietnam tale, there were stories by Grace Paley, Mordechai Richler, Ronald Sukenick, and William Mathes (his "Swan Feast" was a powerful story in which the performance of a staged sex act leads to an apocalyptic orgy of violence). But the fictional highlights were William H. Gass's "In the Heart of the Heart of the Country" and Philip Roth's "The Jewish Blues," an early section of the unpublished *Portnoy's Complaint.* Edited by Stanley Moss, the poetry included selections by Anna Akhmatova, John Ashbery, Richard Eberhart, Robert Graves, and Anne Sexton.

With no discernible decline in quality, the second issue — with stories by E. L. Doctorow, John Barth, and Robert Coover, an essay by Nat Hentoff, two discussions of Marshall McLuhan, and antiwar poetry of Günter Grass — sold only half as well as the first. Part of the reason was that the uniqueness of the first issue had contributed to the wide attention it had received in the press; once it was no longer "new," it was no longer news. With the third issue, however, there was a major rebound. The key to success this time was the inclusion of twenty-eight thousand words by Philip Roth that were essentially the central portion of *Portnoy's Complaint.* Roth had submitted the section under the same title that later appeared in the book, "Cunt Crazy." When Ed Kuhn saw that, he said it couldn't be used even though Solotaroff argued that they would spell it "Kunt Krazy." Kuhn said no and Roth proposed "A Nice Jewish Boy" instead, which Kuhn said wasn't sexy enough. Solotaroff then proposed "Civilization and Its Dis*cunt*ents," also not acceptable, and it was finally published as "Civilization and Its Discontents." In his introduction, Solotaroff felt compelled to address the question of Roth's second appearance in three issues, a contradiction of his own editorial ideal for *New American Review.* Writing that *NAR* was not becoming a "coterie magazine," Solotaroff commented:

> This objection is likely to be aggravated by the feeling that the contents of this story, "Jewish" consciousness *in extremis,* is hardly new these days, that indeed, it is part of a vogue which already takes up an undue amount of print and attention. But against our own reservations on these scores, there stood the specific quality of "Civilization and Its Discontents"; its extraordinary wit, candor and power; its ready ability to touch bottom, the point at which ethnic singularities take on the universal implications of human life itself. In the end, the desire to publish the best writing we receive won out, a decision which should please all but the most "trendentious" of our readers.

The success of *NAR* No. 3 (which also included Donald Barthelme's "Robert Kennedy Saved from Drowning," R. V. Cassill's

"The Rationing of Love," and Leonard Michaels's "Crossbones") gave the magazine a new infusion of life. But going into its third year, *NAR* developed a problem. Copies of the first two issues, which had been floating around the wholesalers' warehouses, began to come back as returns. In an effort to stanch the flow, print runs were reduced and distribution was fine-tuned. Solotaroff also tried mightily to make the series succeed on a subscription basis, but this idea didn't catch on with readers and there were never more than five thousand subscribers. No matter how much they reduced the print runs, NAL always seemed to get stuck with about 50 percent returns of the magazine. Yet, to its credit, NAL remained committed. After No. 3, the next big success was *NAR* No. 7, primarily because it included a section of Kate Millett's *Sexual Politics*, in which she savaged Henry Miller, Norman Mailer, and Jean Genet for their debasement of women (or in Genet's case, the feminine male homosexual).

By the time the tenth issue was being prepared, however, *NAR*'s grasp on life had become somewhat more tenuous. The final falling-out between Kramer and Solotaroff came over another Philip Roth contribution. *On the Air* is a bitingly funny story of a Jewish shoe salesman who manages a "colored" tap dance team and has the idea of convincing Albert Einstein to become a Jewish version of radio's popular "Answer Man," whom the shoe salesman considers a goy-ish schmuck. After all, who's smarter than Einstein? The story descends into a surrealistic, zany nightmare as the salesman takes his wife and son to Princeton to try to meet Einstein. When he saw the story scheduled, Kramer wanted Solotaroff to promote it on the front cover as a new story by the author of *Portnoy's Complaint*, which was by that time a major best seller. Solotaroff objected on the grounds that to do so would debase the magazine's integrity, identity, and tone and turn it into another "mass market product." Solotaroff later recounted, "He was making it a magazine that had to tell its readers that this story was by the man who wrote *Portnoy's Complaint*. When you say that, you embarrass the reader. The magazine loses what it is — a magazine of standards."

NAR No. 10 was published, but it was the last to be produced by NAL. Returns were mounting and Solotaroff was asked to find another publisher. Fortunately, Simon & Schuster agreed to take over, but the company tried a new strategy by changing from a mass market to a trade paperback format for the five issues it published (numbers 11 through 15). In 1973, *NAR* was transplanted once again, this time to Bantam Books, where it was returned to rack size and the name was shortened to *American Review*. (The words "New American" obviously sounded too much like Bantam's competitor.) After four years at Bantam, through *AR* No. 26, Solotaroff decided it was time to pack it in. He later said it was his own decision to do so, but nobody begged him to reconsider.

Looking back at *NAR/AR* provides a kaleidoscopic retrospective of the cultural currents abroad in the land, particularly from the series' beginnings as the Vietnam and civil rights protests came to a head, right through the Watergate period. Later issues, said Solotaroff, became collections of interesting fiction. Reading the early issues today is a little like finding one of those time capsules buried at a World's Fair, with a copy of *Time* magazine, some Beatles records, and a miniskirt inside. The essays were certainly all of their time and carried the sense of immediacy and urgency that was prevalent in the period in which they appeared. At its best, much of the work in *NAR* remains fresh, lively, and provocative and has more to say about understanding where we were as a culture than simply dusting off a memento found in the attic. The pieces that had the greatest shock value — and sexual explicitness was no small part of *NAR*'s daring and controversial profile — seem far less shocking today. But Harold Brodkey's "Innocence" remains a pretty high voltage account of a Harvard woman's first orgasm. Among some of the other highlights that retain their electricity and timeliness are Nat Hentoff's "Reflections on Black Power"; Albert Goldman's "The Emergence of Rock"; "Illumination Rounds" by Michael Herr, *Esquire*'s Vietnam correspondent, which later became part of his acclaimed *Dispatches;* and Jane Jacobs's critique of the misspent millions of the urban renewal program, "Why Cities Stagnate."

The best pieces of fiction were also tuned into the times yet have remarkable staying power: among them Alan Friedman's "Willy-Nilly," the story of a young hermaphrodite confused over his/her sexual identity; Max Apple's imaginative tale of Howard Johnson's empire building in "The Oranging of America"; and the debut of a section from E. L. Doctorow's *Ragtime.* The magazine was ultimately filled with the names of some of the most prominent and some of the least known writers of the decade between 1967 and 1977. Solotaroff bridged the old and new generations. One of the best examples of the magazine's cross-generational flavor came in one of the last issues, *AR* No. 24, which featured Norman Mailer's homage to Henry Miller, "Genius, Lust and Narcissism." Here was Mailer, the outlaw writer of the fifties and sixties, now an éminence grise, writing about the grand old man, the outlaw of an earlier day. In the same issue appeared "The Chink and the Clock People," a story by Tom Robbins, the wunderkind of the mid-seventies who had attained cult status with his novel *Another Roadside Attraction.* A major disappointment to Doubleday in hardcover, the book had become a slow, steady seller in its Ballantine paperback edition. But unhappy with both Doubleday and Ballantine, Robbins's agent went to Solotaroff with his next book, which was signed by Bantam and licensed back to Houghton Mifflin. *Even Cowgirls Get the Blues,* from which the story in *AR* No. 24 had been excerpted, was published in a simultaneous hardcover–trade paperback edition in an extremely successful use of that publishing strategy (170,000 trade paperback copies are in print). Bantam later issued the mass market edition, which extended the book's reach and Robbins's growing popularity even further. Nonetheless, Robbins's third novel, *Still Life with Woodpecker,* which Solotaroff also acquired for Bantam with the notion of licensing the hardcover edition, was rejected by several New York houses, and Bantam eventually issued the novel in one of the company's first hardcover undertakings.

Robbins was the latest in a line that had its beginnings with Salinger, Heller, and Roth and ran more directly through such counterculture favorites as Vonnegut, Thomas Pynchon, and poet-novelist Richard Brautigan, all writers who held almost mystical sway over the young. With Robbins, plot is loosely described at best. *Another Roadside Attraction,* for instance, centers on a hot dog stand in Washington State and the mummified remains of Jesus Christ. *Even Cowgirls Get the Blues* describes the odyssey of Sissy Hankshaw, the world's most proficient hitchhiker because of her generously endowed thumb. Robbins was the counterculture poet laureate, the satirist of the spaced-out age, a writer perfectly tuned in to a generation weaned on rock and roll, "recreational" drugs, and television. The comparisons to Vonnegut and Pynchon (whose *Gravity's Rainbow* had been successfully published in simultaneous hardcover and trade paperback by Viking) were inevitable. More unlikely was a comparison to Mark Twain. But to pigeonhole Robbins into the counterculture bin is something of a disservice.

He is read by a fairly wide audience and has certainly left cult status behind, entering the mainstream of the mass market, even if there were plenty of critics who found his writing sophomoric if not incomprehensible. While his literary credentials and perhaps his ultimate longevity are open to question, there is little doubt that Robbins is a prime example of the way paperbacks can bring a new writer to his audience.

Robbins's appearance in the same issue with Mailer's paean to Miller and Robert Penn Warren's poetry was an example of the range and diversity that Solotaroff had been aiming to capture in the series. It was not dedicated to high, low, or any specific brand of pop culture but to American culture in the widest sense — the exchange of ideas and the presentation of alternative points of view. Perhaps the best last words on *NAR/AR* were those that Solotaroff provided in a sort of elegy written for *AR* No. 26, in which the editor assessed his goals:

> More than anything else, diversity is what *NAR/AR* has been about — no relatively fixed corps of contributors, no literary cults or ideological coteries, no sense of the chosen few talking to each other, but rather a free and open house, a democratic mingling of interests and ideas, classes and religions, generations and reputations, styles and tastes — reacting, reverberating, contrasting. . . . An abundance of talent going this way and that. . . . I hoped that the magazine would develop a kind of community spirit in which the literary and the literate could meet on the grounds of mutual concern. I wished to appeal to rather than exclude the common reader who has been relegated by the elitism of modernism to the position of being a distrusted or ignored bystander of literature. . . . I believe *NAR/AR* was useful because it trusted that the culture would provide each issue with what one reviewer characterized as a "vital dialogue between public concern and private imagination."

One of the magazine's appeals — and certainly no small part of its diversity — was the refusal to accept blindly the new idols of the counterculture. Though liberal to leftist in its politics, *NAR* could still publish Gilman's dismantling of *MacBird!* or Marshall Berman's "Sympathy for the Devil," a critique of the sixties. Another example of the magazine's willingness to puncture the trendy and the faddish was evident in Mary Ellman's essay "Growing Up Hobbitic" (*NAR* No. 2), a wry appraisal of the Middle-earth mania that was sweeping America from the campuses outward, a devotion to

J.R.R. Tolkien, *The Hobbit,* and *The Lord of the Rings* that superseded simple faddishness or cult status among the few knowledgeable members of the claque. The extraordinary response to Tolkien's work cut across the usual demarcation of predictable literary and social lines, firing the imagination of an entire generation.

All the hobbitic hoopla must have amused the stately, white-haired Oxford don who was responsible for starting the whole thing. J.R.R. (for John Ronald Reuel) Tolkien was born in South Africa on January 3, 1892. He came to England at age four and moved through the proper educational ranks to Oxford, served three years with the Lancashire Fusiliers during the First World War, worked as an assistant on the *Oxford English Dictionary,* and became a lecturer and professor of English literature at Oxford. His specialties included Middle English, Anglo-Saxon myths, and philology — all hinting at what was to come — and his first books were befitting a proper academic: *A Middle English Vocabulary, Sir Gawain and the Green Knight, Chaucer as a Philologist, Beowulf: The Monsters and the Critics.* Then, in 1937, he produced a whimsical little volume called *The Hobbit,* a story of the Halflings who inhabited the Shire, a land remarkably like the English countryside, placed, however, in a world called Middle-earth. Although *The Hobbit* was published as a children's book (and won the New York *Herald Tribune's* 1938 children's book award), Tolkien would later say that it was not written for children. Said the author, "If you're a youngish man and you don't want to be made fun of, you say you're writing for children. *The Hobbit* was written in what I should now regard as bad style as if one were talking to children. There's nothing my children loathed more. They taught me a lesson."[11]

Of course, *The Hobbit* was but a prelude — a loosening-up exercise, of sorts — to Tolkien's masterwork, his fourteen-year-long effort (with two-fingered typing, no less) at creating a universe, several languages, a mythology, an epic quest pitting the elemental forces of evil against innocence: the trilogy called *The Lord of the Rings,* comprising *The Fellowship of the Ring, The Two Towers,* and *The Return of the King.* The first two volumes were published in 1954 and the third followed in 1955. Houghton Mifflin, the American publisher, imported books from England rather than printing them here, a distinction that was to cause considerable problems when it came to paperback publication. It is more than a little ironic that the benign Tolkien became a prize as sought after

as the Ring of Power itself in a hard-fought battle between Ballantine Books and Ace Books, both of which sought to be Tolkien's
paperback publisher. Since Houghton Mifflin had exceeded the al-
lowable limit of books that could be imported, *The Lord of the
Rings* was technically out of copyright in this country. In such
situations, it was usual for a paperback house to honor the conventions of copyright law and pay royalties in good faith. Ace announced its plans to publish the trilogy in three volumes without
honoring such accepted rules. At almost the same time, Ballantine
announced its arrangement with Houghton Mifflin to publish the
authorized edition, with full royalties going to Houghton Mifflin,
the British publisher, and Tolkien. Tolkien himself issued an appeal
to readers printed in the Ballantine edition to buy only the Ballantine edition, and Ace eventually was forced to withdraw its books.
There was a repeat of this duel between the two companies over
the rights to publish the works of Edgar Rice Burroughs, both the
Tarzan novels and the science fiction featuring John Carter. In that
case also, the books were technically out of copyright and Ace
planned to issue them. The Burroughs estate turned to Ballantine,
and after considerable haggling, Ballantine won the Tarzan and
Martian novels while Ace was granted some of the lesser science
fiction titles. Burroughs proved to be a small gold mine for Ballantine.

The publishing controversy over *The Lord of the Rings* prompted
an initial flurry of press interest in the books, which gave the trilogy
national attention. (The hardcover editions had not sold well.) Ian
Ballantine picked up the ball and ran with it, as he was prone to do
when something caught his fancy. In a grassroots publicity campaign, Ballantine produced maps of Middle-earth like travel posters,
which said, "Come to Middle-earth." Buttons reading "Frodo Lives"
became the campus rage. The books took off suddenly and became
an overnight campus sensation, quickly spreading to larger segments of the mass market. Soon a Tolkien Society came into being
(numbering W. H. Auden among its members). Critics also took to
the books, admiring Tolkien's creation of a universe, a language,
and an epic fantasy in which the ordinary, reluctant hobbit, Frodo
Baggins — Everyman, if you will — and his fellows embark on an
odyssey to destroy the Ring of Power — the absolute corruptor —
in a quest that ultimately became a cosmic confrontation between
the forces of good and evil.

The books obviously operate on more than one level. But foremost they were tales of high adventure and the heroism of the ordinary man, the sort of riveting exploits that have captivated listeners since the days of Gilgamesh. A devout Christian, Tolkien was also using fantasy for allegorical purposes, just as his friend and colleague C. S. Lewis had done in *The Chronicles of Narnia*. In this sense, the evil lord of Mordor, Sauron, can be seen as the fallen angel; with his defeat and the destruction of the Ring of Power, the King is returned, ushering in a new millenium in Middle-earth history. On still another level, the trilogy could be interpreted as a reflection of contemporary history, with both the Second World War and the potential catastrophe of nuclear weapons as the real context. One of Tolkien's admirers was the late novelist John Gardner (no stranger to mythologizing as he showed in *Grendel*, also a Ballantine book), who wrote of the trilogy in his controversial work *On Moral Fiction*, "J.R.R. Tolkien in his Ring Trilogy sums up more powerfully than any realist could do the darkness of total war and the essential opposition of evil and good in the shadow of some monstrously destructive power. The Ring Trilogy presents, among other things, Tolkien's understanding of the threat of English annihilation and his intuition of still more terrible things to come."[12] Tolkien himself denied that the story had any allegorical intentions — "general, particular, or topical, moral, religious, or political" — and that his only intention had been to invent several languages. The stories, he claimed, were made to provide a world for the languages rather than the reverse. Tolkien once commented, "I should have preferred to write in 'Elvish.' "[13]

His millions of readers undoubtedly did not agree. Ian Ballantine — whom Tolkien once called "Frodo-like," in reference, no doubt, to his hobbitish nature — later said of the trilogy and the extraordinary reaction to it among America's youth:

> Many people took to thinking that this was some kind of *escape* — the reader was avoiding reality. But I believe Tolkien had that property that is so important in communicating any book that is pivotal or influential in changing people's thinking; he drew the audience into the work. They became participants. They added to the story. We soon saw paintings, maps, stained glass, songs, and poetry that had been inspired by Tolkien. People learned the language of *The Lord of the Rings*. In this time, young people could be observed stretching their skills much more so than my generation of young people had. The

individuals who were attracted to Tolkien were in one way or another finding dissatisfaction in their own time. Tolkien was a catalyst. He inspired people to think for themselves. The fact that Tolkien was a moralist and believed in right over wrong, that he posed problems about power at a time when the world was experiencing concerns about the concentration of power, contributed to his impact on people and on the times.

It was not surprising that a work of the trilogy's grand imaginative scale and with its system of values had come from Ballantine Books. Perhaps more than any other paperback publisher, the career of Ian Ballantine — and that of his wife and partner, Betty, who became an indispensable and widely admired editor — could be seen as part of a continuum that stretched back to World War II. That was when he began publishing the Penguin Specials dealing with the war. It continued through his years at Bantam, where he attempted new publishing strategies and began his commitment to the prevention of nuclear war, and into the Ballantine Books era, when the science fiction Ballantine published was an expression of his concern for staying ahead of the social currents in America. As Ballantine commented:

> Beginning at Bantam and more strongly at Ballantine, we took an interest in writers who were writing about what was going to happen next. Obviously, that meant science fiction and fantasy. I don't know if any of these books all by themselves changed the world or in connection with some important issue became a factor in starting opposition to atomic energy and weaponry. One gets the feeling with these kinds of books that if you get visibility and circulation, their points of view will not go unnoticed by people. If the point of view is important, it will have its proper weight in what happens.

Though Ballantine may have been the only paperback publisher who approached the subject so philosophically, there were other paperback houses publishing important science fiction — which may be abbreviated as *sf* but never *sci-fi*, a heinous affront to its practitioners and readers — throughout the fifties and sixties, a period that sf maven Lester del Rey describes as the "Age of Acceptance" and the "Age of Rebellion" in his history, *The World of Science Fiction.* Besides Ace, the sf leader alongside Ballantine Books, Dell had issued science fiction as paperback originals in its First Editions line. Among them was Jack Finney's *The Body*

Snatchers, which had first appeared in *Collier's* and was the basis for that classic film of fifties paranoia, *Invasion of the Body Snatchers*. New American Library was Isaac Asimov's paperback publisher — as well as the originator of some of his straight science books in the Mentor series — and also reprinted some books by Robert Heinlein, generally considered to be one of the four or five best writers in the field. Ironically, Heinlein's most successful and influential novel was the one purists liked least, *Stranger in a Strange Land*, in which a messianic hero brings a message of free love and universal peace to mankind, which rejects both message and messenger. Like Tolkien's trilogy, *Stranger in a Strange Land* attained a degree of success that went far beyond the bounds of science fiction and fantasy cultdom. *Stranger* was first issued in paperback by Avon and later by Berkley, one of the paperback houses more committed to science fiction, whose position as a major publisher of sf was strengthened when the firm was bought in 1965 by G. P. Putnam, an established trade hardcover house and itself a leading publisher of science fiction. As with Dell, the Putnam-Berkley pairing could offer authors the hardcover-paperback contract with 100 percent of the paperback royalties to the author, rather than the fifty-fifty split with the hardcover publisher.

It was at Ballantine, however, that the concerns voiced by science fiction writers about such issues as peace, the environment, and power were complemented by a commitment to serious nonfiction about these same issues. As early as 1948 at Bantam, Ian Ballantine had been publishing books like *Hiroshima* and *No Place to Hide*, expressing his concern over the nuclear weapons dilemma. The concern over pressing social and political issues became even stronger when Ballantine was free to publish at his own Ballantine Books, where he published such works as Seymour Melman's *The Peace Race*; C. Wright Mills's pro-Castro book, *Listen, Yankee*; *The Un-Americans* by Frank J. Donner, an account of the abuses of power committed by the House Un-American Activities Committee (a 1961 Ballantine original); J. W. Schulte Nordholts's *The People That Walk in Darkness*, a history of the Negro in America; and Alan Guttmacher's *The Complete Book of Birth Control*, which in 1962 successfully challenged the Post Office ban on articles "designed for preventing conception."

One of the most successful, and in a way revolutionary, examples of Ballantine's commitment to publishing in a socially conscious way came through the relationship that developed with the Sierra Club environmental group and its head, David Brower (the "Archdruid" in John McPhee's *Encounters with the Archdruid*). Sierra Club Books had been publishing beautiful photographic books accompanied by the writings of the great naturalists. They were priced at $25 and, even at that, subsidized by the Sierra Club. Ballantine approached Brower with a plan to reprint the books in oversized quality paperback editions that would be mass distributed. As Ballantine later said of Brower and the project, "David Brower's vitality had an immense role in the project. He had a wonderful interest in reaching the mass audience. I was thinking like a mass market publisher so I projected five-hundred-thousand-copy printings. He did the smart thing by giving me the rights to his best book first, *In Wildness Is the Preservation of the World.*" At the time of the project's inception, 1967, Simon & Schuster still held control over what Ballantine could publish and how. Initially, the Simon & Schuster people were reluctant to go along with Ballantine's rather grandiose plans and wanted to do the book in a fifteen-thousand-copy printing that would be sold at $9.95. Ballantine felt that would have defeated his purpose — reaching a wider audience with books that he believed would have a significant impact on the conservation movement. "I wanted to go through mass market channels. We had already stimulated the college bookstore constituency. Leon Shimkin decided in my favor, and we sold out right away on the first book. The order of success was amazing." After two years, there were one million of the so-called Ballantine Gift Books in print with *In Wildness* leading the list. From a social point of view, the books were important because they served to raise consciousness about the environment just as the ecology movement was gaining momentum, culminating in Earth Day in 1970 and the subsequent passage of the major environmental acts. In publishing terms, the books represented another step in the evolution of the paperback, bringing the concept of the gift book to paperback. Ballantine expanded the illustrated paperback idea into a series of art books, and one of the company's outstanding successes was a paperback edition of M. C. Escher's work, making the artist something of an idol for the psychedelic generation, who found fascination in his illusionary paintings.

However, the most important book to emerge from the Ballantine/Sierra Club collaboration was not a picture book. Stanford University biologist Paul Ehrlich's *The Population Bomb*, published in

1968 as a paperback original, was a frightening look at the consequences of unlimited population growth, including its impact on
the world's food supply and ultimately on the fate of the world. A
call for population control, it was published just months before
Pope Paul VI issued a major decree condemning birth control and
abortion. A prophet of the apocalypse if the world did not take heed,
Ehrlich became a sought-after figure on the talk show circuit as the
book became a widely discussed best seller. His advocacy of birth
control and abortion was fairly daring at a time when the subject
still bordered on the taboo. In assessing the book's impact, Ian Ballantine believed that it had been a major force in the liberalization
of American attitudes toward contraception and abortion and certainly a factor in the move toward zero population growth that took
hold in the late sixties and early seventies.

In the year that Ballantine published *The Population Bomb*, the
rest of the industry had helped to sell more than 350 million books
worth an estimated $65 million, representing approximately 15 per-
cent of the publishing industry's income. *Paperbound Books in
Print* now showed more than twelve thousand new titles contributing to a total of more than sixty-three thousand paperbacks available from hundreds of different publishers. The Paperback
Revolution, which had brought more books to more people for less
money, seemed to be going at full tilt. Or was it?

If the industry was so healthy why did the *New York Times Book
Review* in 1969 ask, "Is the Paperback Revolution Dead?" Taking a
closer look at the statistics pumped out by the "Revolution's ministry of propaganda," the *Times Book Review* said there were signs
that the revolution was "standing still — and may have even
slipped into reverse gear." Such a possibility seemed ludicrous to a
casual observer. As the sixties faded, more and more big dollars
were being paid out for rights to reprint best sellers. Names like
Jacqueline Susann, Arthur Hailey, and Harold Robbins had become
household words. And paperback houses like Bantam and Fawcett
seemed to be making record profits each year. Why, then, had the
Times Book Review asked such a seemingly implausible question?
Because while dollar volume continued to rise, it was an illusory
performance based on increasing cover prices. The number of copies
sold in 1968 was not much higher than it had been in 1959, even
though the population was 15 percent higher. Had Marshall Mc-
Luhan's electronic birds finally come home to roost?

Another indication that the patient was in trouble was that the number of paperback outlets had not substantially increased in the ten years since they topped one hundred thousand. For many years, the growth of the paperback had been due to the expansion of outlets. Now that the limit had been reached, the industry had to look for more sales out of a limited and possibly declining universe.

Finally, the *Times* article asked, "Have the paperback revolutionaries gotten tired? The industry today wears a middle-aged look. The men in power entered the field a dozen or more years ago, during its great period of expansion. More editors and salesmen in close touch with members of the younger generation might result in titles with greater attraction for the under-36 readers." And if that did not happen, warned the *Times*, "Not only paperbacks but the whole publishing industry is in trouble, not to mention the intellectual life of the nation."[14]

It was a discouraging note on which to end the Age of Aquarius.

Key Paperbacks: 1966–1969

1966

Naked Lunch	William S. Burroughs (Grove)
The Fixer	Bernard Malamud (Dell)
The Crying of Lot 49	Thomas Pynchon (Bantam)
Hell's Angels	Hunter Thompson (Ballantine)

1967

Rivers of Blood, Years of Darkness	Robert Conot (Bantam original)
Games People Play	Eric Berne (Grove)
The Essential Lenny Bruce	Lenny Bruce (Ballantine original)
Trout Fishing in America	Richard Brautigan (Delta)
Black Skin, White Masks	Frantz Fanon (Grove)
The Medium Is the Massage	Marshall McLuhan with Quentin Fiore (Bantam original)
The Story of O	Pauline Reage (Grove)
The Harrad Experiment	Robert Rimmer (Bantam)
New American Review No. 1	Theodore Solotaroff, ed. (Signet)
Strike Zion	William Stevenson (Bantam instant book)
Quotations from Chairman Mao Tse-Tung	(Bantam instant book)

1968

A Man with a Maid	Anonymous (Grove)
The Teachings of Don Juan	Carlos Castaneda (Ballantine)
Soul on Ice	Eldridge Cleaver (Delta)
The Population Bomb	Paul Ehrlich (Ballantine original)
The Algiers Motel Incident	John Hersey (Bantam instant book)
Revolution for the Hell of It	Abbie Hoffman (Simon & Schuster)
Democracy and the Student Left	George F. Kennan (Bantam)
Where Do We Go From Here?	Martin Luther King, Jr. (Bantam instant)
The Armies of the Night	Norman Mailer (Signet original)
Miami and the Siege of Chicago	Norman Mailer (Signet original)
Couples	John Updike (Fawcett)
Report of the National Advisory Commission on Civil Disorders	(Bantam instant)
Rights in Conflict	(Bantam instant; Signet Broadside)

1969

The Sot-Weed Factor	John Barth (Bantam)
The Strawberry Statement	James Simon Kunen (Avon)
Portnoy's Complaint	Philip Roth (Bantam)
The Making of a Counter Culture	Theodore Roszak (Anchor original)
Joy: Expanding Human Awareness	William Schutz (Grove)
Slaughterhouse-Five	Kurt Vonnegut (Delta)
Violence in America	(Bantam instant)
We Reach the Moon	(Bantam instant)

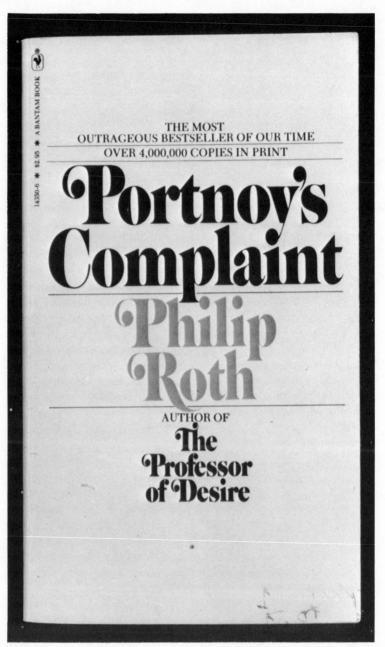

Roth's best seller about the masturbatory fantasies of his hero made the writer's name a household word. (Photo by Jerome Frank)

ELEVEN

A Million Dollars
for a Jewish Bird?

There is real hope for a culture that makes it as easy to
buy a book as it does a pack of cigarettes.
— Professor Eduard C. Lindeman
Editorial consultant to Penguin Books and New American
Library

IN THE YEAR that the *Times Book Review* wondered about the
liveliness of the Paperback Revolution, Avon got out 1.9 million copies of Haim Ginott's *Between Parent and Child;* Bantam printed 4 million copies of Arthur Hailey's *Airport;* Delta sold
more than 1 million copies of *Soul on Ice;* Anchor Books sold
107,000 copies of Peter Berger's *Invitation to Sociology;* Noonday
Press (now owned by Farrar, Straus & Giroux) sold 125,000 copies
of Hermann Hesse's *Narcissus and Goldmund,* and New Directions
sold more than 270,000 copies of Hesse's *Siddhartha;* Grove sold
610,000 copies of *The Autobiography of Malcolm X* and 300,000
copies of *I Am Curious (Yellow);* the Jerry Kramer–Dick Schapp
collaboration about the Green Bay Packers, *Instant Replay,* went to
2.75 million copies and the late Robert F. Kennedy's *Thirteen Days*
topped 1 million copies, both for New American Library.

In the following year, the successes reached even greater magnitude as New American Library set a record initial printing of
4,350,000 copies for Erich Segal's tear-jerking *Love Story.* Fawcett
printed Mario Puzo's *The Godfather* and it became the fastest-sell-
ing paperback in history, with more than 5 million copies sold
within one year of publication. Bantam continued to maintain
household-name status for Jacqueline Susann and Philip Roth with,

respectively, *The Love Machine* (4.2 million copies in print) and *Portnoy's Complaint* (3.2 million copies in print). Even that old (anti)warhorse Dr. Spock was keeping up with the million-copy Joneses as *Baby and Child Care* sold another 1,043,801 copies in 1970. Not bad for a dying swan. Or to paraphrase Mark Twain, the reports of death were greatly exaggerated.

Clearly, the paperback was going through boom times as the sixties gave way to the seventies — with no discernible change in the nation's atmosphere. The political turmoil of the late sixties — the Black Power movement and the antiwar demonstrations — was still raging in violent confrontations, climaxing with the killings at Kent State and Jackson State in 1970. Economically, there were also problems; *inflation* and *recession* were added to the average American's vocabulary. However, the book industry — and specifically the paperback business — seemed to be adhering to the old saw that books are recession- and depression-proof, and the business continued to grow.

1969 Paperback Best Sellers

ACE

Dune by Frank Herbert

APOLLO

Dutchman and The Slave by LeRoi Jones
Speeches of Malcolm X at Harvard by Malcolm X

AVON

Between Parent and Child by Dr. Haim Ginott (1.6 million in print)
Vanished by Fletcher Knebel
Christy by Catherine Marshall (a 1968 holdover with 2.2 million in print)
The Arrangement by Elia Kazan (also a 1968 holdover with more than 3 million in print)

BALLANTINE

The Lord of the Rings by J.R.R. Tolkien
Appointment on the Moon: The Inside Story of America's Space Venture by Richard S. Lewis

BANTAM

Airport by Arthur Hailey (4 million in print)
Coffee, Tea or Me? by Trudy Baker and Rachel Jones (1.5 million in print)

BERKLEY

Stranger in a Strange Land by Robert Heinlein

DELL/DELTA

Soul on Ice by Eldridge Cleaver (1 million sold in Delta edition)
The President's Plane Is Missing by Robert J. Serling
Pretty Maids All in a Row by Francis Pollini
Nicholas and Alexandra by Robert K. Massie
The Naked Ape by Desmond Morris

DOUBLEDAY

The New Testament of the Jerusalem Bible (Anchor/Image; 272,653 sold)
Invitation to Sociology by Peter L. Berger (107,000 sold in 1969; total sale 412,824)
The Making of a Counter Culture by Theodore Roszak

DUTTON

I Ching (a holdover from 1968; 100,000 in print)

NOONDAY

Narcissus and Goldmund by Hermann Hesse (125,000 sold)
Journey to the East by Hermann Hesse (102,000 sold)
Beneath the Wheel by Hermann Hesse (50,000 sold)

FAWCETT

Couples by John Updike
The Salzburg Connection by Helen MacInnes
Snoopy and the Red Baron by Charles M. Schulz
Testimony of Two Men by Taylor Caldwell

TEMPO (GROSSET & DUNLAP)

The Super Joe Story (525,000 sold)

GROVE

The Autobiography of Malcolm X by Malcolm X and Alex Haley (610,000 sold)
Joy: Expanding Human Awareness by William C. Schutz (365,000 sold)

I Am Curious (Yellow) by Vilgot Sjoman (300,000 sold)
Games People Play by Eric Berne (200,000 sold)

HARCOURT, BRACE & WORLD

The Little Prince by Antoine de Saint-Exupéry
The Waste Land and Other Poems by T. S. Eliot
A Passage to India by E. M. Forster

LANCER

The Exquisite Thing by Joyce MacIver
The Fortunate Pilgrim by Mario Puzo

NEW AMERICAN LIBRARY

Instant Replay by Jerry Kramer and Dick Schaap
The Beautiful Couple by William Woolfolk
Thirteen Days by Robert F. Kennedy
(The Graduate, I Never Promised You a Rose Garden, and *2001: A*
   Space Odyssey all sold over a million copies)

NEW DIRECTIONS

Siddhartha by Hermann Hesse (1 million in print)
A Coney Island of the Mind by Lawrence Ferlinghetti (490,000 in
   print)
Nausea by Jean-Paul Sartre (320,000 in print)

PENGUIN

The Other America by Michael Harrington (320,000 in print)
Before the Mayflower by Lerone Bennett (110,000 sold)

POPULAR LIBRARY

To Kill a Mockingbird by Harper Lee (backlist best seller, total copies in print: 9,950,000)

PYRAMID

To Sir, With Love by E. R. Braithwaite

VINTAGE

Post-Prison Writings by Eldridge Cleaver
The Trial by Franz Kafka

SCRIBNER'S

The Forsyte Saga by John Galsworthy
The Great Gatsby by F. Scott Fitzgerald

SIMON & SCHUSTER

The Worldly Philosophers by Robert Heilbroner (103,000 sold;
1.1 million in print)

VIKING/COMPASS

Death of a Salesman by Arthur Miller (150,000 sold)
A Portrait of the Artist as a Young Man by James Joyce (160,000
sold)

YALE UNIVERSITY PRESS

Long Day's Journey into Night by Eugene O'Neill (250,000 sold)
The Lonely Crowd by David Riesman (400,000 in print)

(Source: *The Publishers' Weekly*, February 9, 1970)

Nowhere was the glow of success more evident than at Bantam
Books, which had emerged as the clear industry leader by 1970.
Bantam had undergone enormous changes since 1945 when it was
founded as the offspring of Grosset & Dunlap (itself owned by several publishing houses and the Book-of-the-Month Club) and Curtis
Publishing Company, the magazine publisher and distributor.
While there had been some bad times in the early fifties as two of
the three founders departed (Ballantine and Pitkin left; Kramer
stayed until 1967), Bantam had nearly always been a consistent
moneymaker from the day the company opened its doors. Born with
the silver-spoon luxury of its corporate parents Random House,
Scribner's, Harper & Brothers, and Little, Brown, Bantam had been
able to acquire a strong backlist of contemporary writers whose
books would be perennial sellers. With the ability to withhold copies of the *Saturday Evening Post* unless Bantam Books were also
ordered, the potent Curtis Circulating Company had almost dictatorial powers. When Oscar Dystel arrived in 1954 to fill the leadership void left in the wake of Ballantine's departure and Marc Jaffe
replaced Saul David — who went to Hollywood in 1961 — as the
architect of Bantam's editorial future, the company's reputation and
stature quickly flourished. Bantam grew into a profitable powerhouse, overtaking a declining Pocket Books with a dynamism in
acquiring, packaging, promoting, marketing, and distributing paperback books.
One of the keystones in Bantam's rise to pre-eminence was its

early and continuing reliance on big, juicy, promotable novels by big-name authors. It was a tradition that was part of Bantam's character before Dystel arrived, but he nurtured and institutionalized it. Through Bantam's earlier years, the strategy could be seen in such titles as *The Grapes of Wrath; Green Mansions; A Farewell to Arms* and *For Whom the Bell Tolls; This Side of Innocence;* J. P. Marquand's *H. M. Pulham, Esq.; The Keys of the Kingdom* and *The Citadel* by A. J. Cronin; *The Moon and Sixpence* by Maugham; *The Fires of Spring* and other early Michener work; and *The Confidential Agent* and other novels by Graham Greene.

But more than any other author, the best example of this type of novelist at Bantam during the fifties and into the sixties was John O'Hara. As the author of *Appointment in Samarra* and *Butterfield 8,* O'Hara had enjoyed critical and popular success during the thirties for these hard-boiled novels of manners, tinged with his reporter's sense of realism and devastating dialogue. The sexual candor of his books contributed to their scandalous reputation and was no small part of O'Hara's appeal. But he had never attained true bestselling status. After 1938, he took a long hiatus from novel writing while continuing to contribute short stories to *The New Yorker,* where he had been a fixture since 1930.

Unhappy with his publisher, O'Hara moved to Random House in 1947 and was published there for the rest of his life: twenty-three years in which he produced twenty-three books (many of them collections of short stories). His first book with Random House was *Hellbox,* a collection of stories that was reprinted by Avon. Then, in 1949, Random House published his first novel in eleven years, *A Rage to Live.* It was the first of O'Hara's books to achieve bestsellerdom, although the critical acclaim he once enjoyed deserted him. After *The New Yorker*'s reviewer savaged the novel, O'Hara didn't write for the magazine again for many years. (O'Hara was also bitterly disappointed that he never won the Nobel Prize, which he felt he deserved.) The Random House edition of *A Rage to Live* went through eight printings in 1949, plus two book-club printings and a Grosset & Dunlap hardcover reprint. Ian Ballantine paid a then-heady advance guarantee of $25,000 for the novel, and in 1951 it was reprinted by Bantam and went through thirty-three large printings. O'Hara followed with *The Farmers Hotel,* which was less successful in hardcover and paperback initially, although it sold far better when reissued in 1957 in conjunction with the paperback edition of *Ten North Frederick*, and it eventually went through eighteen paperback printings at Bantam.

In 1960, O'Hara's *From the Terrace*, which had sold a hundred thousand copies in hardcover, was reprinted by Bantam, and it eventually became his best-selling paperback title. Although O'Hara never quite attained the star magnitude in total numbers of books sold reached by Caldwell, Gardner, or Spillane, his performance in paperback was nonetheless impressive. Critic-biographer Matthew J. Bruccoli calculated O'Hara's record:

> Like *Ten North Frederick* and *A Rage to Live*, *From the Terrace* enjoyed remarkable distribution in paperback, for the Bantam edition went through at least thirty-four printings. It is patently absurd to attribute these paperback reprint sales to John O'Hara's reputation for lubricity. People do not read 500- or 900-page novels to find a few erotic passages. The prurient can find what they want in more concentrated form. *From the Terrace* became O'Hara's most widely-read paperback with 2½ million copies of the Bantam edition sold by 1966. His other big sellers were *A Rage to Live* (2 million copies by 1966), *Butterfield 8* (1,800,000) and surprisingly *The Farmers Hotel* (902,000). The guarantees paid by Bantam rose from $50,000 for *Ten North Frederick* to $185,000 for *Elizabeth Appleton*. . . . Through 1966, Bantam paid $1,186,750 in guarantees for O'Hara paperback rights and during this period more than 15½ million copies of O'Hara titles were sold by Bantam.[1]

O'Hara's value as a paperback "property," as well as the changing order of the paperback business, became apparent in 1967 when NAL paid either $500,000 — according to Bruccoli — or $700,000 — according to Bennett Cerf — for *The Lockwood Concern* in an attempt to wrest all of O'Hara's books away from Bantam.

O'Hara was obviously aware of his value. As early as 1958, he was pressing Random House for a larger share of his paperback royalties than the customary even split. In 1961, the often testy, hard-drinking O'Hara wrote to Cerf, "I now serve notice on you that the 50-50 reprint deal is a thing of the past, and if you are going to repeat all the answers you had three years ago, don't bother to answer this letter. I know all those answers. You and Donald [Klopfer, Cerf's partner] and whoever else is involved are going to have to come up with a new deal, more favorable to me. . . ."[2] Even after O'Hara's death in 1970, his stock had considerable value. Popular Library paid $500,000 to O'Hara's estate for all of his works. By the seventies, however, O'Hara was out of vogue; his reputation had slipped considerably. (Recently Vintage has begun to reissue some of his books, and *Appointment in Samarra* and *Butterfield 8*, perhaps his two best novels, are once again available in paperback.)

Led by the likes of O'Hara, Michener, and Leon Uris — whose *Battle Cry* was the first major acquisition under the Dystel regime — Bantam had continuing success with name writers. In 1960, Arthur Hailey was added to the list with his book *Runway Zero-Eight* (co-authored by John Castle), the predecessor to *Hotel* and *Airport*, both major successes for Bantam. But none of these writers, despite their exceptional sales in paperback, ever quite attained the cult of personality that became attached to the writer most associated with Bantam's success in the late sixties and early seventies: Jacqueline Susann. Before Susann's arrival on the scene in 1966, the idea of major promotional tours with author appearances on television talk shows was almost nonexistent. Jacqueline Susann changed all that almost single-handedly. Whatever her skills as a writer, she was — with the assistance of her husband, television producer, and agent, Irving Mansfield — unquestionably a genius at self-promotion.

Susann's arrival at Bantam came in a roundabout way — ironically, because of the loss of another major best seller. Oscar Dystel recalled having dinner with Hollywood producer David Brown and his new bride, who regaled the dinner guests with stories of her unmarried life. Dystel was a little taken aback at her candor but still had the presence of mind to suggest that she put her experiences into a book. He even gave her the title, *Sex and the Single Girl*. Thus was the world given Helen Gurley Brown, who later transformed *Cosmopolitan* from a sinking Hearst disaster into one of the major magazine success stories in recent history, with its blend of sex, sleaze, man-catching hints, and diet tips. When the manuscript came in to Bantam, it was read and rejected by several editors, and Dystel passed it along to Bernard Geis, a former Grosset & Dunlap editor who had gone into business on his own, signing up celebrities — including Harry Truman, Groucho Marx, and Art Linkletter — and promoting their books through unorthodox relationships with television and magazines. *Sex and the Single Girl*, a Bernard Geis hardcover with Random House distribution, became a best seller in 1962, and the rights were then auctioned off, with Bantam losing out to Dell. Geis sent Dystel a case of Scotch, a note of regret, and a promise that he would make it up to him.

The pledge was fulfilled when Dystel received from Geis the manuscript of Jacqueline Susann's first novel, *Valley of the Dolls.* Dystel bought the book immediately and the Geis hardcover went on to become one of the major sellers of 1966. Susann's face and name were everywhere. She was a press agent's dream come true. She had a sharp tongue, a saucy wit, and loved to gossip. Talk show hosts and gossip columnists ate her up. Her roman à clef about drugs, dreams, and ambitious Hollywood starlets had the sex and scandal, all told in Susann's breathless style, that spelled instant success in the mass market. She quickly became one of the best-selling writers in the world, and her string of Bantam successes included *The Love Machine, Once Is Not Enough,* and *Dolores,* the thinly veiled (and posthumously published) novel about Jackie Kennedy. (Bantam acquired the prime contract on both *Once Is Not Enough* and *Dolores,* as they did with Uris's *Topaz,* all of which became hardcover best sellers and then went on to additional paperback success.)

Despite its estimable million-sellers and growing profits, Bantam could not rightfully be called an innovator in the paperback field. Instead, like Sony, Bantam excelled at taking existing concepts and perfecting them. NAL, for instance, had been the leader in cover price changes, using the Giant, Double, and Triple volumes to go to thirty-five, fifty, and seventy-five cents. NAL had also initiated the concept of acquiring prime contracts to books and licensing hardcover rights back to trade houses, a strategy later developed by Bantam with such major successes as the two Susann books, *The Exorcist, Serpico,* and *The Complete Scarsdale Medical Diet.* Fawcett and Dell had been much more vigorous in original publishing programs. Movie tie-ins were as old as the business itself, but Bantam seemed to have the knack and the titles to be tied in to the right movie at the right time. The strategy of promotions and marketing was not unheard of, but Bantam perfected them, becoming the consistent leader for more than twenty years by producing the right publicity angle to get its books into the news.

The prime example of Bantam's ability to fine-tune an existing publishing concept and make it seem like a Bantam innovation was the "instant book," which at Bantam was christened the Extra. In a very short time, the Extra became an integral part of the Bantam mystique. The instant book was a marriage of the worlds of journalism and mass marketing; truly topical material and information was published more quickly and distributed more widely than could be done by any hardcover house, and it was treated in greater depth and detail than by any newspaper or newsmagazine. The instant book concept can be traced to Allen Lane's Penguin Specials, the books related to the crisis in Europe before and during the Second World War that were produced on a faster-than-normal publishing schedule. In New York, Ian Ballantine had adapted the format to a degree with the Fighting Forces–Penguin Specials, but they lacked the elements of quick turnaround and universal distribution.

The first true American-produced instant books came from Pocket Books: *Franklin Delano Roosevelt: A Memorial*, which was off the presses six days after Roosevelt's death, and *The Atomic Age Opens*, on sale three weeks after the first atomic bomb was dropped on Hiroshima. NAL had published an instant book more typical of the genre in 1960 when it produced *The Case Against Adolf Eichmann* in the wake of his capture in Argentina by the Israelis.

But Bantam made the instant book its exclusive territory when it produced its first Extra in September 1964, *The Report of the Warren Commission on the Assassination of President Kennedy*. It was produced and on sale eighty hours after the commission's 385,000-word report, complete with photographs, notes, and index, was released to the press. The suggestion to do the book had come from Bantam editor Marcia Nasatir (formerly with Dell, later with United Artists) who pushed the idea when the speculation about the assassination was at a peak and leaks about the report's findings were flooding the papers. Prior to the report's release, President Johnson often said that he thought the finished report should get the widest possible audience in order to quell the rumors about the assassination (a self-serving statement, since many of those rumors revolved around Johnson). After making the decision to publish as soon as the report was released, Bantam sold hardcover rights to its edition to McGraw-Hill and the Book-of-the-Month Club, both to appear after the Bantam edition.

Though considerable preparation was made in order to complete the book quickly, the amount of editing, indexing, proofreading, and design work, as well as the typesetting, printing, and binding, was a mountainous task. Anticipating a document that might range from 150,000 to 300,000 words, plus notes and illustrations, all the guesswork went out the window when the report came out at 385,000 words. Bantam editors picked up the report upon its Friday afternoon release and were editing in the car that took them to the airport. An indexer had to work through the night rekeying the index to Bantam's paging. The *New York Times* was also involved in the project, and there were supplementary articles by assistant managing editor Harrison Salisbury, Washington bureau chief Tom Wicker, Supreme Court correspondent Anthony Lewis, and associate editor James Reston, all of which were teletyped to Chicago. The initial print run was set at 300,000 copies, raised to 500,000 and then again to 700,000. W. F. Hall produced 12,000 copies per hour of the eight-hundred-page paperback, the first of which were sent to the airport for distribution to Europe. Then planes took copies to Washington, Boston, and New York. There was a rush of sales as soon as the book hit the newsstands, and it ultimately went to three printings totaling 1.6 million copies. Bantam followed up on that first Extra in December 1964 with *The Witnesses: The Highlights of Hearings Before the Warren Commission on the Assassination of President Kennedy,* again prepared in association with the *New York Times.*

In years to come, Bantam produced as many as three Extras a year, a process that extended to its limits the entire Bantam editorial, production, and sales organization, as well as its suppliers. The Extras came as events warranted. Some of them were successful; others were not. One of the failures was *The President's Trip to China,* produced after Nixon's historic trip to the People's Republic of China and his meeting with Mao. But many of the Extras were extremely significant documents for their times, examples of paperback publishing at its most conscientious. This was so, for instance, with *The Algiers Motel Incident,* John Hersey's reconstruction of the events surrounding the shooting deaths of three blacks during the 1967 Detroit race riots. Published simultaneously with a Knopf hardcover edition, the book was a major journalistic account of one of the most heated episodes in the tense racial atmosphere of the late sixties. Hersey's book is said to have influenced the trial of the three policemen later convicted in the murders of the three black men.

Some of the most important Extras in terms of their timeliness or influence were *The Report of the National Advisory Commission on Civil Disorders; The Diary of Che Guevara; Rights in Conflict: The Walker Report* (following the violence at the 1968 Democratic Convention in Chicago), which NAL also published as an instant book, called a Broadside; *We Reach the Moon*, published seventy-six hours after the splashdown of Apollo 11; *The Tales of Hoffman*, excerpts from the comic-opera conspiracy trial of the Chicago Seven, in which Yippie Abbie Hoffman locked horns with eighty-year-old judge Julius Hoffman, published eleven days after the verdict was announced; *The Report of the Commission on Obscenity and Pornography*, which debunked most of the myths about pornography and was summarily ignored by President Nixon, who commissioned it; and *Soledad Brothers: The Prison Letters of George Jackson*.

Perhaps the most significant Extras of all were three that came in the turbulent final days of Nixon's second presidency, when there was open warfare between president and press. *The Pentagon Papers*, the complete and unabridged version of the *New York Times* series on the top-secret Vietnam study, was published eight days after the Supreme Court decision lifting the ban on publication of the documents. (The Bantam edition eventually sold 1.5 million copies.) *The Watergate Hearings* was published right after the Senate hearings were completed, and *The White House Transcripts* was in paperback six days after President Nixon relinquished the transcripts of the tapes that led to his eventual downfall.

Bantam could also trivialize the concept of the Extra by publishing such superfluities as *Golf Step by Step; Hoax: The Inside Story of the Howard Hughes–Clifford Irving Affair; The Watergate Follies* (photos with humorous captions); *The Streaking Book;* and *William Peter Blatty on The Exorcist: From Novel to Film*, a blatant attempt to hype Bantam's already successful paperback edition of *The Exorcist*.

Despite the lapses in choice of material for Extras, the concept was an important factor in bestowing legitimacy upon the paperback and specifically on Bantam Books, which became most closely associated with instant books even though Dell, New American Library, Berkley, Avon, and Ace all produced some. But they were important for a less visible reason. Marc Jaffe compared the Extras to New American Library's *New World Writing*, on which he had worked for seven years, in the sense that they were projects that gave the staff a sense of identity and esprit de corps. With projects like these, people could feel that they were working for the best, an attitude that often produces the best. The idea of an entire organization pulling together in a vast team effort was a significant ele-

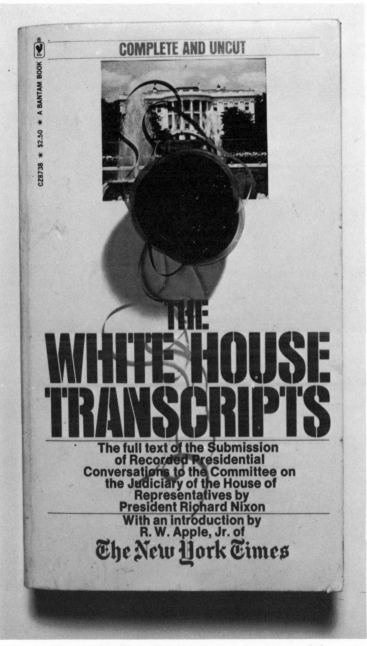

COMPLETE AND UNCUT

THE WHITE HOUSE TRANSCRIPTS

The full text of the Submission
of Recorded Presidential
Conversations to the Committee on
the Judiciary of the House of
Representatives by
President Richard Nixon

With an introduction by
R. W. Apple, Jr. of
The New York Times

A Bantam Extra, *The White House Transcripts* was one of the more successful and significant "instant books." (Photo by Jerome Frank)

ment in the cohesion that was outwardly characteristic of Bantam's prominence in the industry, perhaps even more important in the long run than its ability to acquire, package, and promote major commercial successes.

It is this same cohesion, pride, or sense of identity that character- ized many of the most successful publishing operations — which is probably true of business in general. Those companies that flour- ished in an unusually prominent way were places with a sense of direction and purpose that flowed naturally from the top down, usually from dominant personalities who were able to place their distinctive stamp upon the publishing program and surround them- selves with equally creative individuals. In the hardcover world, Alfred Knopf was the prime example. At Pocket Books it could be seen with the original de Graff–Howe-Simon-Schuster-Shimkin grouping, later replaced by the Freeman Lewis–Herb Alexander– James Jacobson–Larry Hughes combination. At New American Li- brary, it emanated from the dominant personalities of Kurt Enoch and Victor Weybright, who could attract first-rate people like Marc Jaffe, Arabel Porter, and E. L. Doctorow. With Grove Press, it was the unique individualism of Barney Rosset, with his editorial staff of Richard Seaver and Fred Jordan. And at Bantam, Oscar Dystel was the focal point, yet he surrounded himself with astute editors such as Marc Jaffe and Allan Barnard, marketing men like Ron Busch, the dean of paperback art directors Leonard Leone, and pub- licity maven Esther Margolis. This is not to say that an atmosphere of cooperation reigned supreme in these places. The opposite is true. Enoch and Weybright were not exactly kindred spirits, and meet- ings at Bantam often took place in the high-decibel range with the air colored blue. But the clash of wills allowed for expression of opinion and exercise of talent. Individual strengths emerged, and the strong inevitably survived.

At Bantam, the results of this process could be seen in the succes- sive stages of ownership the company underwent. The first step in these changes had come in 1961, when the trade publishers who owned Grosset & Dunlap (which in turn owned half of Bantam) announced their plan to offer Grosset stock publicly by reducing their holdings from 85 percent to 51 percent. At the time of the offering, Bantam's net sales for 1960 were more than $8.5 million, a $1.5 million improvement over 1959. The reason for the public sale was to enable Grosset to raise the capital it needed to buy 20 percent of the Bantam stock that was held by the Curtis Publishing Company. Curtis was eager to sell its shares because it desperately needed cash. The *Saturday Evening Post,* long the mainstay of the Curtis fortunes, was beginning to fail in the sixties. The magazine was of an earlier era and was out of touch with the changing American lifestyles of the sixties. Curtis sold its valuable stock in Bantam for cash with which to prop up its magazines. It also wanted to be able to publish its own books, something it could not do under its distribution contract with Bantam.

In 1963, when Curtis and Bantam finally severed their distribution contract, Curtis did set up a short-lived paperback line. Bantam, in the meantime, turned to Select Magazines for distribution to the independent wholesalers, with the understanding that Select would establish a separate sales force just for books, something that Curtis had resisted. In addition, Bantam was able to create its own in-house sales force that would sell Bantam Books on a direct basis to the growing number of bookstores that carried paperbacks and to the variety and chain stores. Under the Curtis agreement, Bantam had been shut out of direct sales. In 1964, looking for more cash, Curtis sold its remaining 30 percent interest in Bantam, and the company became a wholly owned subsidiary of Grosset & Dunlap.

By 1968, the original hardcover partners in Grosset & Dunlap decided to leave the reprint business and cash in on their share of Bantam. Grosset & Dunlap was put on the block. Oscar Dystel tried to raise the capital to buy it himself, but was knocked out by a major bid from a Los Angeles company, the National General Corporation, an insurance-related firm that had holdings in motion picture production and movie theaters. National General paid a little less than $50 million for Grosset & Dunlap, $35 million of which was earmarked as the cost of Bantam. The presence of National General, a conglomerate, along with the Times Mirror Company, which held New American Library, marked the first takeovers of paperback operations by non–book publishing conglomerates that became prevalent later in the sixties and seventies. Optimists said that these companies would bring an infusion of new cash and sound management principles to the business; pessimists said that such corporate owners would be the ruin of publishing as the emphasis was placed more heavily on "bottom-line" efficiencies rather than good publishing policy.

At the time of the sale to National General, Oscar Dystel antici-

pated that the relationship with the parent would mean new opportunities to tie up with Hollywood in book promotions. Bantam did
become more aggressive in seeking out screenwriters who might be
novelists. There was also heightened interest in turning screenplays
into books, the so-called novelization that failed more often than it
worked. But this "synergy," which was the popular corporate jargon
of the day, never materialized. Perhaps the most important thing to
come out of the Los Angeles connection was Marc Jaffe's introduction to screenwriter William Peter Blatty, which resulted in Bantam's acquisition of the prime contract on *The Exorcist,* later sold
back to Harper & Row for hardcover publication. It became one of
the top-selling paperback books in history.

Three years after National General acquired Bantam, it went public with 10 percent of the Bantam stock. Included in the prospectus
was a revealing summary of Bantam's earnings. The paperback
house that had net sales of $8.5 million in 1960 had reached sales
of $19 million by 1966 and $38,198,000 in 1970, with net income
rising from $1.5 million in 1966 to nearly $4.3 million in 1970. And
the growth appeared to be continuing into 1971. By this point, the
company's catalogue included more than 1400 titles, 700 of which
were listed in Bantam's various educational catalogues, an indication of the breadth of its rich backlist. Almost 150 Bantam books
had gone over one million copies in sales and 45 of these had surpassed two million copies. In addition, the list of sellers over the
three million mark included *Hotel* and *Airport, The Catcher in the
Rye, Exodus, Everything You Always Wanted to Know About Sex*
(over six million sold), *Portnoy's Complaint,* the classic Western
Shane, The Grapes of Wrath and *The Pearl* by Steinbeck, and Susann's *Valley of the Dolls* (more than nine million sold). It seemed
that just about everything that Bantam touched was turning to gold.
The Exorcist was followed by *Jaws,* both books moving to the top
of the list of all-time paperback sellers.

But Bantam also balanced best sellers with a broad range of titles.
In 1968, they had begun a series called Modern Classics, which
included *Goodbye, Columbus, Man's Fate* by Malraux, and other
contemporary novels. Erich Fromm's *The Art of Loving* went over
one million copies before reverting back to Harper & Row, which
reissued it in a trade paperback edition. Then, in the early seventies,
Bantam had stunning successes with *Future Shock,* Alvin Toffler's
exciting book about the postindustrial age; *The Greening of Amer-*

ica by Charles Reich, which began as a *New Yorker* article and
became a major best seller; and perhaps the most unlikely paperback best seller of all, *Zen and the Art of Motorcycle Maintenance,*
Robert Pirsig's philosophical speculation undertaken while the
writer took a motorcycle tour with his disturbed son. If nothing
else, the success of these three complex, controversial, and challenging books in paperback provided evidence that the Paperback
Revolution was still capable of bringing difficult and serious work
to the mass market.

Key Paperbacks: The Early Seventies

1970

The Making of 2001	Jerome Agel (Signet original)
Understanding Human Sexual	Fred Belliveau (Bantam instant)
Inadequacy	
Soledad Brothers	George Jackson (Bantam instant)
Sexual Politics	Kate Millett (Avon)
The Godfather	Mario Puzo (Fawcett)
Do It!	Jerry Rubin (Ballantine)
The Electric Kool-Aid Acid Test	Tom Wolfe (Bantam)
Earth Day: The Beginning	(Bantam instant)
The Report of the Commission	(Bantam instant)
on Obscenity and Pornography	
The Tales of Hoffman	(Bantam instant)

1971

The Last Whole Earth Catalog	Stewart Brand, ed. (Portola Institute)
Deliverance	James Dickey (Dell)
Steal This Book	Abbie Hoffman (Grove)
The Sensuous Woman	"J" (Dell)
One Hundred Years of Solitude	Gabriel Garcia Marquez (Avon)
The Greening of America	Charles Reich (Bantam)
Everything You Always Wanted	David Reuben (Bantam)
to Know About Sex	
Future Shock	Alvin Toffler (Bantam)
The Pentagon Papers	(Bantam instant)

1972

Bury My Heart at Wounded   Dee Brown (Bantam)
  Knee
Fire in the Lake   Frances FitzGerald (Vintage)
The Best and the Brightest   David Halberstam (Fawcett)
The Happy Hooker   Xaviera Hollander (Dell original)
Who Runs Congress?   Mark Green and James Fallows
                                     (Bantam instant)
Diet for a Small Planet   Francis Moore Lappe (Ballantine
                                     original)
The Bell Jar   Sylvia Plath (Bantam)
Fear and Loathing in Las Vegas   Hunter Thompson (Popular
                                     Library)

1973

Watership Down   Richard Adams (Avon)
Jonathan Livingston Seagull   Richard Bach (Avon)
The Exorcist   William Peter Blatty (Bantam)
I'm OK—You're OK   Thomas Harris (Avon)
Open Marriage   George and Barbara O'Neill
                                     (Avon)
Gravity's Rainbow   Thomas Pynchon (Viking
                                     simultaneous hardcover/trade
                                     paperback)
Bob Dylan   Anthony Scaduto (Signet original)
The Making of the President: Theodore H. White (Bantam
  1972   instant)
The Watergate Hearings   (Bantam instant)

1974

The Joy of Sex   Alex Comfort
Ladies and Gentlemen, Lenny   Albert Goldman and Lawrence
  Bruce!!!   Schiller (Ballantine)
Fear of Flying   Erica Jong (New American
                                     Library)
Serpico   Peter Maas (Bantam)
I. F. Stone Weekly Reader   Neil Middleton, ed. (Vintage)
S.D.S.   Kirkpatrick Sale (Vintage)
The White House Transcripts   (Bantam, Dell instants)

1975

Jaws   Peter Benchley (Bantam)

Helter Skelter	Vincent Bugliosi (Bantam)
Something Happened	Joseph Heller (Ballantine)
The War Between the Tates	Alison Lurie (Warner)
The Total Woman	Marabel Morgan (Pocket)
The Palace Guard	Dan Rather and Gary Paul Gates (Warner)
Alive	Piers Paul Read (Avon)
Working	Studs Terkel (Avon)
All the President's Men	Bob Woodward and Carl Bernstein (Warner)

In 1973, National General was itself acquired by the American Financial Corporation, which immediately announced its intention to sell Bantam Books. On Thanksgiving Day 1974, Bantam was bought by a foreign company owned by Italian auto magnate Giovanni Agnelli, of FIAT fame. Agnelli's holding company, IFI (Istituto Finanzario Industriale), paid $70 million for Bantam, a 100 percent increase in Bantam's stated value at the time of National General's purchase of Grosset & Dunlap in 1968. The international dealing did not end there. In 1977, IFI sold a controlling 51 percent interest in Bantam to the West German Bertelsmann Group, the largest publishing combine in the world. Although Bertelsmann reported that it had paid more than $36 million for its share of Bantam, one insider said that the figure was more than $50 million. By this time, Bantam had reached $85 million in annual sales and controlled an estimated 22 percent of the American paperback market. In May 1981, Bertelsmann went the rest of the way and became sole owner of Bantam Books.

But a short time after Bertelsmann bought into Bantam in 1977, some of the gilt seemed to be wearing thin. The successive years of record sales and profits had begun to flatten out. In addition, the predictable statements about noninterference with Bantam and no changes in personnel had all been made by Bantam and Bertelsmann management, but within a short span of time the faces at Bantam were very different. The chief difference was Oscar Dystel's shift to a role as "consultant." Louis Wolfe, who had been a vice president at Avon Books in the sales and marketing area, replaced him as chief executive officer. Soon after that, Marc Jaffe, the chief of Bantam's editorial department who had been elevated to president and publisher, moved over to Random House as its executive vice pres-

ident and editor in chief at Ballantine Books (a role he relinquished
in 1983 to establish Villard Books, his own hardcover imprint at
Random House). Jaffe's leaving and the exiling of Dystel to a
"golden cage" came after the departures of a number of top executives. Ron Busch, Stanley Reisner, Victor Temkin, Rena Wolner,
and Esther Margolis, all key players in Bantam's success, left to
head up or launch different companies. The strings seemed to be
coming loose. Years of continuity in management unraveled all at
once. These changes came just as Bantam was losing an edge on its
competitive sharpness. By 1980, the company's sales had exceeded
$100 million annually, but its share of the market had slipped
sharply. The old formula of big best sellers was no longer the key to
success in the changing market of the mid to late seventies, and
Bantam lagged behind some of its competitors in the areas of original publishing, trade paperbacks, science fiction, and, perhaps above
all, the new styles in women's romances. Younger companies and
new forces in mass marketing were chipping away at the once gran-
itelike monolith of Bantam's position atop the mass market field.

The best example of the young lions in the paperback business
was a mercurial, aggressive, dynamic — some would say frenetic —
editor and publisher named Peter Mayer, who was responsible for
the transformation of Avon Books from near obscurity to a position
as the most innovative and influential mass market house of the
seventies. His techniques were simple and set the form and fashion
for paperback publishing in the seventies. Publish more and better
original paperbacks. Spend lots of money for the *right books.* And
use mass marketing techniques to sell trade paperbacks as they had
never been sold before.

Mayer joined Avon in 1963 when he was in his early twenties,
hired by Frank Taylor as "education editor" at a company that had
published precious little of educational value in more than twenty
years of paperbacking. At the time of Mayer's hiring, Avon was still
turning out a dreary monthly list of a dozen or so mysteries, Westerns, and sensational exploitation novels. The Bard line, halfheart-
edly begun in 1957 as Avon's answer to Mentor and other quality
paperbacks, was defunct. In fact, Avon itself was practically defunct
since the time of its purchase by the Hearst Corporation in 1959,
when it was turned over to be run by ICD, Hearst's magazine distributing subsidiary. In an attempt to bring some life and respectability back to the house, Hearst hired Frank Taylor in 1963, and he

brought with him Allan Barnard. As a team, the two men had been behind the editorial success of Dell Books in the fifties until they left Dell and set up the short-lived Racine Press. Soon after their arrival, Mayer was hired. The son of a successful glove maker — an émigré from prewar Europe — Peter Mayer was raised in Queens, New York, graduated summa cum laude from Columbia University, and later attended Oxford, Indiana University, and the Free University of Berlin. He had also been a cabdriver before working for a small hardcover house called Orion Press.

When he first came to Avon, Peter Mayer was taken under the wing of Allan Barnard, who became his paperback mentor and taught him the ropes of acquisition. When Mayer made his first reprint acquisition, Barnard sat beside him and nursed him word-for-word through the entire telephone conversation with the subsidiary rights director of the hardcover house. His first acquisition was Van Wyck Brooks's *The Writer in America.* It lost money.

Not long after that inauspicious beginning, Mayer made a discovery that not only compensated for his first mistake but also provided an indication of the direction in which his career as a paperback publisher would move. As a cabdriver, he had worked with another cabbie who was a writer and lived near Mayer on the Lower East Side. (His name was Eddie Adler and he later wrote *Notes from a Dark Street.*) Adler told Mayer that a great novel had been written about their neighborhood. Published in 1934, the book was Henry Roth's *Call It Sleep* and was widely praised upon its appearance. But the Depression had ruined its publisher and the novel had long been out of print. Mayer found a copy at the library but it was not available for circulation, so he had to read it in installments each day. When he went to Avon, he remembered the book and set out to learn who held the rights. It turned out that the copyright had come into the hands of two used-book dealers, whom Allan Barnard knew. So Mayer and Barnard went to see them, and in the midst of thousands of dusty used books, they acquired paperback rights to *Call It Sleep* for $2500, Mayer's budgetary ceiling. So much for the excitement and glamour of the paperback world.

Instead of simply reissuing the novel in the midst of a dozen or so typical Avon books, Mayer pushed to have the book prepared as if it were an original publication, with bound galleys sent to book reviewers in advance of publication; this was a highly unusual undertaking for a paperback house in 1964. Roth's novel was set in turn-of-the-century New York, in the Jewish tenements of the Lower East Side. It vividly portrayed that world through the eyes of a young Jewish boy and invoked comparison to Joyce's *A Portrait of the Artist as a Young Man* or Farrell's *Young Lonigan*. Although out of print, the book was discussed in literary circles as one of the "most neglected books in American literature" and had considerable standing in the critical world. That was no indication, however, of the reception it would receive in paperback. The *New York Times Book Review* gave the novel a front-page review when it was issued in October 1964, an unprecedented event in paperback history. (Avon was almost caught off guard by postponing publication. Alerted to the review, Mayer had Avon rush off twenty-five thousand books.) *Call It Sleep* quickly passed the million-copy mark and became one of Avon's first commercial successes, putting both the company and Peter Mayer on the map. (The other distinctive feature of the book when first published was its "circumcised" corners. In an attempt to distinguish Avon from its competitors, Frank Taylor had two machines built that rounded the corners of the books. However, the machines were expensive and slow. They also prevented Avon from staining the books' edges — a process used to camouflage the cheap paper on which paperbacks were printed — and more expensive paper had to be used. The machines were scrapped soon after Taylor's departure.)

Besides the boost that the book gave Avon at the time, Peter Mayer learned some important lessons from the *Call It Sleep* experience. To Mayer, the success of the novel as a paperback without the stamp of hardcover-best-seller recognizability opened up new possibilities for the use of paperback originals. The much-maligned and abused original had been a significant element of the paperback business in earlier years at such companies as Gold Medal, Dell, and Ballantine — and in a different context at Mentor Books, where serious nonfiction was often commissioned to fill a specific need. But in the years that the inexpensive reprint flourished in importance, the original had been shunted to the side of the paperback business.

Too ambitious to remain an education editor, Mayer became editor in chief after Barnard left for Bantam in 1964 and then supplanted Taylor as publisher in 1965. At the age of twenty-six, he was in charge of Avon, pushed ahead by Richard Deems and John R. Miller, Hearst executives who recognized his potential. Still wet behind the ears in the ways of the paperback business, Mayer found an important ally in an unheralded man from the distribution end of the business, Gene Kaiser. Kaiser had begun his career with the old American News Company and had survived the breakup of the ANC after the distribution wars of the fifties by coming to work for Hearst's ICD. He became Mayer's major-domo, handling every aspect of the business except selecting the books and designing the covers. For choosing the books, Mayer began to surround himself with a small group of talented editors that included Paula Diamond, Robert Wyatt, and Nancy Coffey. Timidly at first, Mayer began to acquire books. His first major acquisitions, purchased in advance of hardcover publication, were Robin Moore's *The Green Berets* and Bel Kaufman's *Up the Down Staircase.* Both became major paperback successes for Avon, each selling more than three million copies, figures then unheard of at Avon.

Soon after, he set Avon on its original publishing course, a path that would practically revolutionize the trade publishing industry in the seventies. Instead of simply publishing books to fill out the bottom of a list, Mayer promoted the original to the lead position usually occupied by a major hardcover best seller for which a large advance had been paid. It worked successfully from the very start with such commercial writers as Jack Hoffenberg and Burt Hirschfeld, and Mayer and his staff gradually expanded the concept to more literary work and serious nonfiction including the *Rights of . . .* series, a group of books with a question-and-answer format (inspired by David Reuben's book *Everything You Always Wanted to Know About Sex*) containing legal advice for various minority and special interest groups, published in association with the American Civil Liberties Union. By 1972, Avon could fill an entire month's list of twenty-six titles with paperback originals. At the same time, Mayer was expanding Avon's publishing sphere by launching new imprints to fill out the undernourished backlist. To the basic Avon line was added a revitalized Bard series for distinguished fiction, under which the novels of Saul Bellow, Heinrich Böll, Elie Wiesel, Thornton Wilder, and others were published in uniform editions. Also under Bard, editor Robert Wyatt continued to develop the critically and commercially successful program of publishing the wave of contemporary South American fiction begun with *One Hundred Years of Solitude* by Gabriel Garcia Marquez, which Mayer had acquired from Harper & Row. Then, in neat al-

The first in a series of Latin American novels published by Avon, *One Hundred Years of Solitude* achieved cult status that was partly responsible for Marquez's Nobel Prize in 1982. (Photo by Jerome Frank)

phabetical order, Mayer created Camelot for young adult books; Discus for serious nonfiction in a rack-sized format, which included Freud's *Interpretation of Dreams,* Fromm's *Escape from Freedom,* and Lillian Ross's controversial *New Yorker* profile of Hemingway extended to book form; Equinox, a trade paperback format for quality books such as *Sexual Politics;* and finally Flare for oversized "gift books" in trade paperback, inspired by Ian Ballantine's success with the Sierra Club books. Mayer also began to experiment with issuing trade paperbacks to go through the independent wholesalers and had major success with *Sylvia Porter's Money Book* and *The Best of Life,* which sold hundreds of thousands of copies each, many of them through the mass market outlets that had not carried trade paperbacks before.

Avon's big burst, however, came in 1971 when Nancy Coffey, who was responsible for the Camelot line as well as adult books, picked out of the "slush pile" of unsolicited manuscripts that litter every publisher's office a book called *The Flame and the Flower* by an unknown writer, Kathleen Woodiwiss. Taking a chance on a newcomer, Avon scheduled the book as its Spectacular, or lead title, in April 1972 without the benefit of the hardcover success, author celebrity, prestigious reviews (or any reviews at all), and massive publicity that are usually attendant to a major paperback release. Nevertheless, the book touched a hidden nerve — or slumbering erogenous zone — in the American heartland. It eventually sold millions of copies. *The Flame and the Flower* (or *TFTF* in the trade) was soon followed by another unsolicited manuscript simply addressed to "The Editor of *The Flame and the Flower.*" This time, it was Rosemary Rogers and her first novel, *Sweet Savage Love.* The two books became the forerunners of the publishing sensation of the seventies, the historical romance specifically aimed at the women's paperback market.

There was nothing new about the existence of a women's market for paperbacks. The paperback had begun as an essentially male-oriented business — who, after all, passed the newsstands, airport terminals, and cigar stores more often during the forties and fifties? — with the heavy emphasis on hard-boiled mysteries, Westerns, and thrillers. But the pendulum had gradually swung toward women, and they gradually equaled and then surpassed men as paperback buyers. There were a number of reasons for this shift. Obviously, as time went by, the woman's role in America changed and many more women were in the workplace rather than at home. The paperback had also begun to penetrate the supermarkets, where women were the principal shoppers, so appropriate titles had to be made available to them. In addition, the number of women's magazines featuring light fiction had declined. Perhaps most significant was the emergence of women as editors in the paperback field. At Fawcett Books, for instance, the most prominent of women editors was Leona Nevler. She had spun the romantic suspense novels of Mary Stewart, Victoria Holt, and Phyllis Whitney into paperback gold. Another veteran, actually the doyenne of women paperback editors, was Grace Bechtold, who had been with Bantam since 1949 and brought to Bantam such early romance writers as Emilie Loring and Inglis Fletcher. Bantam had also had numerous successes in the sixties with a category called nurse books, soap opera stories with a hospital setting.

Prior to the rush for historical romances, the paperback rage had been the so-called Gothic romance, which traced its roots to *Jane Eyre,* but the apple had fallen far from Miss Brontë's tree. Without the stylistic sensibility or thematic seriousness of that classic, the Gothic was essentially a packaging phenomenon. Every Gothic romance came in exactly the same format, give or take a few alterations. A terrified young woman in a white nightgown was seen under a gloomy sky, running away from a darkened castle or manor house. And always, repeat *always,* there was a light on in one of the castle's windows. Without that light it was almost scientifically proven that a Gothic was as good as dead. The Gothic was a proven moneymaker through the late sixties and was joined by a number of other successful romance categories, including the Regency, Victorian, and contemporary, all girl-meets-loses-gets-man stories with only the settings to differentiate them. All of these books, whatever time or background, were formulas as predictable as pudding. But in none of them did a four-letter word cross a heroine's lips or a heaving breast come out of hiding.

All that changed with the coming of the historical romance (a.k.a. the "erotic historical," "bodice ripper," "take-and-rape" or "sweet-savage") à la Woodiwiss and Rogers. In the new age of romances, the emphasis was on the tempestuous and voluptuous, wickedness, torment, desire, tumult, passion, and the wild fires of lust. The heroine, kept from her true love by wars or indentured servitude, was abducted, betrayed, ravished, brutalized, and raped in a smorgasbord of ingeniously conceived and deliciously meted-out punishments by enough hard, cruel men to fill out a Mongol horde. Although Avon initially had its finger on this curious pulse, the success of the Avon Ladies soon opened the floodgates for a deluge of imitations and variations in the paperback marketplace.

By the end of the seventies, the romance — not just the erotic historical — was the most significant single category within paperback publishing. In 1981, romance sales were estimated at upwards of $200 million, representing as much as 40 percent of the domestic paperback business. While Avon had led the charge of the erotic romance, an even more successful liaison was brewing at the opposite end of the sexual spectrum where Harlequin Books held court. A Canadian company, Harlequin published demure contemporary romances with exotic scenarios. The Harlequin romance invariably involves a vulnerable young woman, usually in some subservient position, who meets the man of her dreams, usually older and somewhat callous. Their stormy affair is never consummated but always brought to the dangerous borders of passion until the climax (no pun intended) in which the couple marry and the woman gives up her job. The idea of the schoolteacher wife of Harlequin's publisher who considered most paperbacks too sexy, the concept was good for sales of about 14,000 books in 1966. Then Harlequin took a new strategy and began to work its magic. Using the same techniques employed by Procter & Gamble to promote a new line of soap or toothpaste, Harlequin spent a bundle of money building brand-name identity for its line of books.

It was a method previously untried in an industry where most of the "products" were unique and had to be promoted for their individual merits. It was also impossible to mount a meaningful television advertising campaign for a book priced under two dollars and whose shelf life might be only ten to thirty days long. But with the Harlequins, it was not individual books that were being sold but a dependable, consistent formula, quickly identifiable to a loyal group of readers. The names, locales, and subplots might change, but the Harlequin reader could expect the same experience with every Harlequin, each month. Perhaps in a world of tremendous upheaval and change, such a consistently familiar pattern provided some sense of stability. Whatever the reason, Harlequin soon developed a stranglehold on its particular and extremely lucrative market. All original books by unknown authors and written to very strict specifications,

Harlequins went from nowhere to second place in sales (behind Bantam) in 1979 with U.S. sales estimated at $63 million to $70 million, representing approximately 10 percent of the domestic market and with a profit margin of 25 percent to 30 percent, far exceeding even the highest of its general mass market competitors. The reasons were simple: low costs because of small advances, inexpensive production values, and minimal returns. The extent of Harlequin's success soon promoted its American distributor, Simon & Schuster / Pocket Books, to end the distribution agreement and establish its own version of the Harlequin called Silhouette Books, promoting the series with a lavish television advertising budget. Within two years, Silhouette was challenging Harlequin, and between them the market seemed to be expanding without limits. Their success inevitably led other mass market houses to enter the romance sweepstakes with their own versions of the Harlequin theme, many of which, like Bantam's Circle of Love and Fawcett's Coventry, went belly-up at the cost of several million dollars.

There was no denying, however, that the paperback romance in all its guises was where the action was to be found. Ironically, its emergence dovetailed very neatly with the acceleration of the women's movement in America. And at the same time that the fictional heroines were either defending their virginity or losing it against their will, novels like Erica Jong's *Fear of Flying* and Marilyn French's *The Women's Room* were selling extremely well, along with increasing numbers of books about women and business, money, and power. In the midst of the most cataclysmic changes in the way men and women behaved toward and viewed each other, why was a genre that pigeonholed women into the centuries-old image of subservient chattel so enormously successful? Obviously, the markets were not the same; the readers of Erica Jong were not the readers of *Love's Tender Fury* and *Wicked, Loving Lies*. Perhaps like the men who turned to the routinely formulated world of Mickey Spillane and Ian Fleming, with their sadomasochistic women hating, the readers of romances were looking for a predictable, undemanding escape — a fantasy that was both romantic and erotic. *Village Voice* critic Walter Kendrick, in assessing the romance, maintained this idea. "Escapist, masturbatory, exploitative — romance is all these things. It's a typical mass-produced American product, catering to a public so dull and timid that even when it dreams, it can only conceive what it's dreamt before. All the lines of thought romance seemed to initiate lead straight to the expected conclusion, without a twist or turn or spark of interest."[3] Taking Kendrick's thesis a step further, Columbia professor Ann Douglas had harsher words for the genre, calling it typical of the degradation of women found in "soft-porn culture." In an article for the *New Republic*, Douglas wrote, "The timing of Harlequin's prodigious success has coincided with the appearance of the women's movement, and much of its increasingly anti-feminist content reflects this symbiotic relationship. A Harlequin heroine gives up a job more easily than her maidenhead; better yet, she abandons them simultaneously. As in male weepies and hard porn, female identities are obligingly so much tinder in the crucible in which the male ego is to be re-forged."[4]

The antifeminist theme, whether intentional or not, became even more disconcerting when the standard romance began to be targeted toward the teenage reader. The themes of submission, male dominance, and man (or boy) chasing as the woman's ultimate goal became predominant in these books, whose covers were squeaky clean yet carried an oh-so-subtle hint of kiddie-porn sleaze about them. One of these lines, First Love, an offshoot of Silhouette Books, also provided an interesting indication of the operative mentality in book publishing at the outset of the eighties. In 1981, Jack Gfeller was named president of Silhouette Books. Previously he had worked for General Foods, the Squibb Corporation, Liggett & Myers Tobacco, and Consolidated Cigars (a subsidiary of Gulf & Western, Pocket Books' corporate parent). Upon his arrival at Silhouette, Gfeller talked about the idea of marketing lingerie under the First Love name. The possibilities are endless: from First Love training bras, one could move to First Love diaphragms and after that to First Love maternity wear. Given Gfeller's background, there was even the potential of a new brand of cigarettes called — what else? — First Love. Often called the garment district of publishing, paperback publishers were seemingly out to prove that they deserved the name.

Though it is implausible that the promotion of the romance was a concerted antifeminist act on the part of the publishers (especially unlikely given the preponderance of women editors in the paperback business), a much larger excuse for their success was the backlash against feminism among the "total woman" segment in America's heartland, the same women who helped defeat the Equal

Rights Amendment. Harmless diversion or subtle forms of woman-hatred, the romances, with their spectacular profit performance, were indicative of major changes in the paperback business, especially the shift toward original paperbacks and away from reprints. Along with romances, the entire spectrum of books being issued as original paperbacks was a direct response to the overheated competition for major hardcover best sellers and the related skyrocketing costs of acquisition. By the mid-seventies, it was less risky and far more profitable to buy an inexpensive original manuscript and promote it to mass market paperback best-sellerdom. The paperback publisher not only improved the book's chances for success but also retained the rights to the book for the length of copyright rather than a limited license term under the typical reprint arrangement. The success of originals had proven that smart packaging and powerful promotions were a more than adequate substitute for hardcover notoriety. And publishing originals removed the terrible risk taken on a book bought before hardcover publication, with its chances for success unassured. The author also benefited by keeping 100 percent of the paperback royalties rather than splitting them with the hardcover publisher.

The move to stepped-up original publishing was forced by the predicament that the paperback industry had brought upon itself in the mid-seventies. As with free agency in major-league baseball and basketball, often mediocre properties were attracting bigger and bigger dollars. Pushed by the intensifying competition among paperback houses, more aggressive authors' agents, and subsidiary rights directors who played upon the psychology and egos of the reprinters, advances shot through the six-figure range into the million-dollar arena. Ironically, it was Peter Mayer, the man responsible for revitalizing original paperback publishing as the wave of the seventies, who helped stimulate what became known as the Big Book Syndrome or the Blockbuster Complex.

In 1972, Mayer caught the paperback industry by surprise when he shelled out $1 million of the Hearst Corporation's money on two separate occasions for two very different books. The first was Thomas Harris's *I'm OK — You're OK*, a simplified guide to transactional analysis, the subject of the earlier Eric Berne best seller, *Games People Play*. A few days later, Mayer came back and put the squeeze on Hearst once again for a slim volume of text and photos called *Jonathan Livingston Seagull*. The inspirational story of a seagull who dares to be different, the book had already become a runaway best seller in hardcover, and there was some doubt whether Macmillan would even offer it for paperback reprint when the company's rights director contacted all the paperback houses and told them that the book would be sold for $1 million. The Avon staff was apparently the only group willing to go to such heights, and Mayer and Gene Kaiser then had to cajole and bully the Hearst management to reach down deep once again. After Hearst president John Miller approved the advance, an older Hearst executive, Richard Berlin, said in amazement, "John, you spent a million dollars for a Jewish bird?" Said Mayer, "I think his hearing was not so good, and when he heard 'Seagull' he thought it was 'Siegal.' "

Both books became multimillion best sellers in paperback, completely justifying Avon's gamble, which at the time was considered foolhardy by most other reprinters. In fact, the two books were not only successful for themselves but also helped tiny Avon Books receive enhanced representation in the competitive world of the independent wholesalers, when the majority of the rack space was still completely dominated by the Big Five — even though some of these five were decidedly down at the heels. In 1973, Avon's business increased by more than 140 percent over the previous year, which had not been a bad year, and the company's creaking distribution system threatened to collapse from the weight of orders. *Jonathan Livingston Seagull* alone commanded a million-plus first printing and three days later went back to press for an additional million copies. Practically overnight, Mayer and company had turned an insignificant Avon Books into a major force in mass market paperback publishing. He added to the company's million-dollar string by acquiring Piers Paul Read's *Alive,* the story of an Andes plane crash in which the survivors had to resort to cannibalism, and Richard Adams's *Watership Down* — another seemingly unlikely candidate for mass market popularity — the story of a group of rabbits that sets out to find a new warren and undergoes a terror-filled journey cross-country. Mayer wrote into the reprint contract the following stipulations: the book must be published by Macmillan as an adult book, not a children's book; Macmillan had to print one hundred thousand copies; they had to spend $100,000 on advertising for the book; and Avon reserved the right of approval of the hardcover jacket. All these were unprecedented demands, a further signal in the shift of publishing power.

A book of "pop" psychology — before the term was in vogue. An allegory about a messianic seagull. An epic about rabbits initially planned as a children's book by its American hardcover publisher. And the story of a plane crash. Perhaps with the exception of *Alive,* none of these books had the makings of typical mass market durability. Yet each was unique in its own way and touched nerves in the American public, a quality that the Avon staff was proving to be tuned in to. As Mayer later reflected, *Jonathan Livingston Seagull, Watership Down,* and *Alive* were all books concerned with survival — specifically, group survival — at a time when that issue was being widely expressed, which also accounted for the sales of *The Population Bomb* and *Diet for a Small Planet* for Ballantine Books at roughly the same time. All of them were concerned with dwindling resources and seeking alternative lifestyles. As for *I'm OK — You're OK,* Mayer said the book had appeared when interest in transactional analysis was "incandescent" and had the additional appeal of strong underpinnings in Christianity just as there was the beginning of the reawakening of spiritual interest in America. That same spiritual concern spilled over to *Jonathan Livingston Seagull,* regardless of the book's shallow thinking. Avon had also discovered that *Alive* sold especially well among parochial schools and other Catholic groups because the survivors of the crash had perceived their acts of cannibalism in sacramental terms.[5]

Hurtling headlong down the track toward expensive acquisitions was not Peter Mayer's innovation. The $35,000 and $100,000 guarantees Victor Weybright had made in the late forties and early fifties for Norman Mailer and James Jones were as startling as Mayer's millions in the early seventies. Fawcett had become the big bidder during the early sixties, paying out six-figure sums for Cozzens, Nabokov, and Shirer. Under the new management team that replaced Weybright, NAL picked up the pace in the mid-sixties by bidding between one-half and three-quarters of a million dollars for Capote's *In Cold Blood,* O'Hara's *The Lockwood Concern,* and Kathleen Winsor's *Wanderers East, Wanderers West;* they were, respectively, a smash success, a break-even deal at best, and a dismal failure. In 1965, Fawcett again tipped the scales by winning *The Source* by James Michener, who until then had been successfully published in paperback by Bantam, with an advance guarantee of $700,000. Yet these were isolated freaks, and even the $400,000 Fawcett advanced in 1968 for Mario Puzo's *The Godfather,* which quickly became one of the best-selling paperbacks of all time, was considered an unseemly amount of money at the time.

Within a few short years, however, advance guarantees of $500,000 or more were becoming commonplace within the paperback industry. This acceleration represented two basic changes in the structure of the business. The first involved marketing philosophy. With the major paperback successes of the late sixties, such as *Airport, Hawaii, Valley of the Dolls, The Godfather,* the novels of Harold Robbins, and other multimillion sellers, there was greater pressure applied by the independent distributors for these fast-turning books. The industry was pushed — without much resistance from the publishers, it should be said — toward concentration on a few major titles rather than a broad range of books getting widespread distribution and representation in the wholesalers' racks. The push was on inside the paperback houses to meet this demand by acquiring the major best sellers, which not only took the lion's share of the rack space for themselves but had a coattail effect, bringing the publishers' other books into the racks as well. Soon the big hundred-copy racks were filled with more copies of fewer titles in multiple displays.

The second factor, more controversial and more widespread throughout the publishing business, was the increasing influence of non–book publishing corporations that were buying into the publishing business and pressing their publishing operations to maintain targeted profit goals. To do so, it was assumed, meant buying more of the big best sellers. That, in turn, meant feeding the paperback houses infusions of corporate dollars with which to make their mark. Undoubtedly they were lured by the record-setting performance of Bantam Books, the cachet of publishing, and the promise of exploiting the gush of federal dollars that was flowing into the educational systems in the Johnson and Nixon administrations — a mistaken notion, as it turned out, because many school administrators decided to spend their new-found wealth on "teaching machines" and audio-visual equipment instead of books. In other cases, the cash-rich conglomerates were simply looking for investments, and the glamour held out by publishing, with its famous authors who were seen on the myriad television talk shows, seemed attractive. Many of these large corporations also had extensive holdings in the media and entertainment world, and they were looking for the notorious "synergy" between their television and movie companies and publishing, which was expected to supply the raw materials for movie and television productions. Whatever the specific reasons for the individual takeovers, they occurred in a blitz during the seventies. Although it was a pattern that had quietly begun in 1959 when the Hearst Corporation bought Avon Books, in 1960 when Times Mirror acquired NAL, and in the changes at Bantam previously discussed, the trend accelerated in the seventies. By the end of the decade, all the major paperback houses had been taken over by large corporations.

The impact of these corporate takeovers was immediate and obvious. Just as Hearst had bankrolled Peter Mayer's freewheeling, albeit wise, purchases, the other corporations began to demand visible actions and put up the cash to pay for them. Where there once had been the Big Five paperback houses bidding for the significant reprints, there were now a dozen houses all armed with overstuffed purses and corporate management that demanded results. Small companies that were once completely out of the running for a major hardcover reprint were suddenly in the thick of the action, and they hoped to buy recognition and respectability overnight.

One example of what lay in store for the paperback business was the overhaul of Warner Books (née Paperback Library). When the company was acquired by Warner Communications in 1972, it was for all practical purposes nonexistent in the paperback galaxy. Its output was a predictable blend of mysteries, Westerns, and Gothics. When Warner took over, the new head of the company, Howard Kaminsky, who had worked at Random House, was given a mandate to make the company visible. Along with that mandate, he was also initially staked to a $3 million editorial budget in 1972. Without Warner Communications' backing, Paperback Library would never have been able to secure that kind of working cash. Trying to go from the paperback basement to the top floor in one easy step, Warner Books paid out a flurry of six-figure advances. In rapid succession, they bought rights to *What Every Child Would Like His Parents to Know* by Dr. Lee Salk, *The Coming of Age* and *A Very Easy Death* by Simone de Beauvoir, and Robert C. O'Brien's *Report from Group 17*. A $101,000 advance was also made to playwright Imamu Baraka (formerly LeRoi Jones) for an autobiographical novel that would be licensed back to a hardcover publisher. Warner also made a series of smaller, but still substantial, five-figure acquisitions. At the time of this spree, Howard Kaminsky

Chronology of Takeovers
of Paperback Publishers

1968: Intext (with textbook and other educational interests) acquires
Ballantine Books.

1971: CBS acquires Popular Library.

1972: Warner Communications (including Warner Brothers film stu-
dios) acquires Paperback Library, renamed Warner Books.

1973: Random House (itself owned by RCA since 1965) acquires
Ballantine Books, badly mismanaged by Intext; the company's founders, Ian and Betty Ballantine, are forced out,
and veteran sales and marketing man Ron Busch is brought in
from Bantam.

1974: Harcourt Brace Jovanovich acquires Pyramid Books; renamed
Jove Books.

1975: Gulf & Western acquires Simon & Schuster/Pocket Books.
(Both companies are placed with the company's leisure-time
division, which includes Paramount Pictures and Madison
Square Garden.) Peter Mayer is hired in 1976 to bring a stag-
nating Pocket Books back to life; he departs in 1978 and is
replaced by Ron Busch.

1976: Filmways (owner of Grosset & Dunlap) acquires Ace Books.
Doubleday acquires Dell Books.
CBS acquires Fawcett Books (Justice Department files suit to
undo the purchase as anticompetitive.)

1979: Putnam's, owner of Berkley Books (both owned by MCA Inc.),
acquires a limping Jove from Harcourt Brace Jovanovich.

1982: Putnam's, owner of Berkley-Jove, acquires Playboy Press (part
of Hugh Hefner's troubled empire) and the failing Grosset &
Dunlap, owner of Ace and Tempo Books.
Random House, owner of Ballantine, acquires assets of Fawcett.
Warner acquires assets of Popular Library.

told *Publishers Weekly,* "Before the year is out you can look for us
to buy two or three books for over two hundred or three hundred
thousand dollars."[6]

He kept his promise when Warner paid a $700,000 advance in
1973 for Robert Crichton's novel *The Camerons,* published by
Knopf. Set in a Scottish mining town, it is the story of one proud
mining family and their struggle upward. Full of old-fashioned fictional virtues and light on trendy overt sexual content, the book

was compared to *Sons and Lovers* and *How Green Was My Valley*. Although it was not among the top ten best sellers of the year, it had been on the *New York Times* list for twenty-one weeks. Besides its hardcover success, the book also had going for it the stamp of Crichton's earlier successes, *The Great Imposter* and *The Secret of Santa Vittoria*. Nonetheless, the size of the advance and its having come from the former Paperback Library were a surprise. More surprising still was Warner's attempt to promote the novel with television advertising, a first for a paperback. Unfortunately, it was not enough. Warner printed 1.6 million copies of the novel, but it never gained the sales needed to cover the sizable advance and promotion costs. Neither did Warner do well with the Beauvoir books in the mass market. A magazine wholesaler–oriented company, Warner simply did not yet have the marketing know-how to move books that were not their usual fare.

These failures were part of a process Kaminsky later described as "falling down on our ass." But the expensive lessons paid off when Warner tried another unorthodox maneuver. After buying prepublication paperback rights to *Sybil*, a nonfictional account of a seriously disturbed young woman with sixteen personalities, Warner paid the hardcover publisher, Henry Regnery, $60,000 above the advance to promote and advertise the book in hardcover. It eventually paid off when *Sybil* became Warner's first major best-selling book. The paperback edition had even greater sales when a television version, starring Sally Field, was successfully produced. Warner Books also turned to one of its sister companies within the Warner family, *Mad* magazine, and sewed up a deal to continue the series of successful books adapted from the magazine. (After Ballantine had published the first five *Mad* books in the fifties to great success, NAL took them away with a sizable advance and published forty-seven more. Then, in 1974, Warner Books began releasing sixteen *Mad* books a year.)

The company's initial failure to make its expensive books perform the kind of tricks that were being done by other major paperback sellers did not make Howard Kaminsky shy. He got Warner to join the Millionaires' Club (see the accompanying chart) in 1974 when he bought the rights to Woodward and Bernstein's *All the President's Men* for $1 million in advance of publication, a prepublication record. Initially this gamble did not pay off, as the paperback did not have the sales impact of the hardcover edition. How-

The Millionaires' Club

1972:	*I'm OK—You're OK*	$1 million	(Avon)
	Jonathan Livingston Seagull	$1.11 million	(Avon)
1973:	*The Joy of Cooking*	$1.5 million	(NAL)
1974:	*Centennial*	$1 million	(Fawcett)
	All the President's Men	$1 million	(Warner)
1975:	*Ragtime*	$1.85 million	(Bantam)
1976:	*The Final Days*	$1.55 million	(Avon)
1977:	*The Thorn Birds*	$1.9 million	(Avon)
1978:	*Love Signs*	$2.25 million	(Fawcett)
	Fools Die (and *The Godfather*)	$2.55 million	(NAL)
1979:	*Princess Daisy**	$3.2 million	(Bantam)

The books cited above were all record-setters at the time of their acquisition for paperback. Some of the other notable members of the Millionaires' Club include: *Serpentine* ($1 million, Dell); *Sophie's Choice* ($1.5 million, Bantam); *The Investigation* ($1.595 million, Pocket Books); *The Old Neighborhood* ($1.45 million, Bantam); *Donahue* ($1.633 million, Fawcett); *Oliver's Story* ($1.41 million, Avon); *Full Disclosure* ($1.375 million, Ballantine); *A Stranger Is Watching* ($1 million, Dell); *Your Erroneous Zones* ($1.1 million, Avon).

ever, when the Robert Redford–Dustin Hoffman movie version (a Warner Brothers film; there's "synergy" for you) was released, the book took off as a movie tie-in. Warner then proved it was above partisan politics by buying the paperback rights to Richard Nixon's memoirs and licensing the hardcover rights to Grosset & Dunlap. Warner later began its own hardcover imprint, a resurgent trend in the late seventies, and signed two more Nixon books to be published in Warner hardcover editions.

The presence of a financially strong Warner Books in paperback publishing was indicative of the entire paperback industry. The key factor in the raising of the stakes in the acquisition frenzy of the mid-seventies was the ability of almost any paperback publisher to secure the cash to make a big bid. Like farmers at the county fair with the family egg money, paperback publishers were caught up in the roulette-wheel gamble to acquire books, often throwing caution

---

*Princess Daisy, the all-time record holder, will probably not be surpassed unless the industry takes a drastic turn for the better.

and the rule book to the winds. Like most crapshoots, it sometimes paid off; more often, it did not. With one million-dollar auction following another, the paperback soon found itself the unaccustomed center of attention, making front-page headlines. But the burst of major auctions was a deceiving sign of the industry's health. Instead, it was a symbol of the necessity to maintain stature in an increasingly competitive business, in which visibility mattered more than what was actually being published. No more could the large powers of paperback publishing overlook the small fry. All that mattered was the macho shoot-out that resulted in these record-setting advances.

Eventually, it was the consumer who had to pay for the publishers' profligacy. Accordingly, paperback cover prices shot sky-high during the mid-seventies. The motivating principle behind the creation of the paperback — the most books for the most people at the lowest possible price — was a forgotten dream. In purely business terms, *margin* had replaced *volume* as the basis for paperback profitability. Of course, rising cover prices gave the paperback the semblance of increasing sales. But in the midst of the seeming plenty of the seventies, when new records for printings, advances, and revenues were being set, definite problems lay ahead.

In addition to the rising costs of acquiring books, the royalty rates being sought by agents and authors — and agreed to by publishers willing to offer a huge sum for the right book or even the wrong book — and other costs were going up. The stagflation of the seventies also hit the publishing business with a vengeance — perhaps in retribution for the myth about books being recession-proof. Paper shortages also became a severe problem when the paper industry ran into trouble around 1973 and 1974. (Remember when it was difficult to get toilet paper?) Then the paper manufacturers determined that disposable diapers were more profitable to produce than book paper, further tightening the screws. The oil crunch of 1973 also hurt the paperback business, as shipping costs rose dramatically. The independent magazine wholesalers, whose lifeblood was fuel for their trucks, were forced to cut back on deliveries, hurting sales efficiency. The cost of ink, an oil-based product, also rose. During the good times, paperback companies had also grown physically, moving into exclusive buildings in midtown Manhattan, meaning that overhead, payrolls, and general expenses were pushed upward.

On top of the other problems, the number of outlets selling paperbacks — one of the key elements in the growth of the business when it was increasing — was beginning to level off, and it later declined. That meant a smaller number of outlets had to sell more books, which were becoming more expensive. The increases became frightening. While the price of a paperback had remained stable for more than a decade, new price barriers were being broken with depressing regularity. *Ragtime* broke the $2 barrier in 1976 and between 1976 and 1982, the $3 and $4 high-water marks were topped. The obvious result was that fewer copies of books were being sold. The fewer books that were sold, the higher prices had to be raised to compensate for the unit sales drop-off. The higher the price, the fewer the books. On and on it went, like a snake trying to swallow its own tail.

The increase in dollar volume camouflaged these problems. But toward the end of the seventies, reality was setting in. The business was approaching a crisis. In 1969, the *New York Times*'s uncertainty regarding the Paperback Revolution's vigor was not far from the mark. Few people were harsher realists than Oscar Dystel, who had managed Bantam's push to the summit. In 1977, Dystel was asking what had become of that revolution. To a group of periodical distributors, who had seen their sales of paperbacks diminish in importance as men's "sophisticates" (a fancy word for dirty magazines) led a resurgence in their magazine business and their book business was being taken away by national bookstore chains, large national book distributors, and local book distributors, Dystel said:

> Since 1973, net unit sales have remained static. Last year unit sales were down 3% and unit sales have shown little change so far this year. . . . What has masked this sales plateau is the rising dollar volume of the paperback business. Net dollar billing has been up an average 13% annually in the last five years and much more sharply since 1975. . . . But higher dollar sales cannot cover up the steadily eroding profit margins for most publishers and distributors. . . . One significant cause of the tight cash condition has been the rise in mass market paperback cover prices. Bantam has been no exception in this sharp increase which has amounted to almost double the rate of increase in the Consumer Price Index. The CPI rose 44% in the last five years while the price of rack-size paperback books jumped 77% from an average cover price of 93 cents to $1.65. And mass market cover prices continue to climb.[7]

The uncomfortable truth of Dystel's speech soon hit home. In a few short years, the paperback business went from boom to bursting bubble. By the beginning of 1980, the situation had deteriorated further still. Some of those conglomerates that had come in on the crest of the wave wondered how they got beached. There was no better example of the troubles than Fawcett Books. In the 1981 Annual Report of CBS, Fawcett's corporate parent, appeared these words: "The discontinuation of mass market paperback publishing operations was an important _strategic action_ by the [Publishing] Group. This business has been _operating at a loss_, showed _little potential for growth_ and _did not fit_ into the Group's _long-term business strategy_." (Emphasis added.)

The depth of Fawcett's plight became apparent after a rash of top-level executive and management firings and corporate changes that took place in 1981. The magnitude of the losses at Fawcett was made apparent in the CBS Annual Report. CBS noted that Fawcett Books had lost $759,000 in 1980 and $6,486,000 in 1981. In addition, there was a stated loss of more than $20 million on the "disposal" of the company.

Disposal was an appropriate word, because CBS literally tossed Fawcett aside like trash, selling the company's assets to Random House on January 29, 1982.[8] The news of the deal shook the industry at its foundations. Although rumors of changes at Fawcett and perhaps the sale of the company had been in the wind for some time, the terms and execution of the sale came as a shock. Under the agreement, Random House purchased Fawcett's assets — books under contract, backlist, and inventory — but not its people. In a sense it was like Chrysler locking its plants, throwing out its workers, and selling its stock of cars to General Motors at distress prices. A one-time powerhouse of the paperback business had ceased to exist as an independent entity.

With the sale of Fawcett Books and the subsequent sale of Popular Library to Warner Books, CBS was out of the mass market paperback business. Although CBS retained a publishing group consisting of a magazine division (including _Woman's Day, Field & Stream, Cuisine_, and other specialty magazines) and a book operation (comprising Holt, Rinehart & Winston, W. B. Saunders, Cassell's, and Praeger), their amputation of the paperback operations raised serious questions about an ailing paperback industry. In addition, the abrupt and callous handling of the Fawcett sale by the CBS management confirmed the worst fears about the role of conglomerates in book publishing.

Fawcett's poor performance in the period under CBS ownership cast a long shadow over the industry. With the continuing recession, high interest rates, and many retail accounts paying their bills by returning books for credit, the overwhelming question was who would be next and when. There was no doubt that there would be others. The answer came when Playboy Press and Grosset & Dunlap, with its Ace paperback line, were folded and sold to Putnam's, owner of Berkley-Jove. The sale of Fawcett made the industry wonder out loud if other conglomerates, burdened by marginally profitable or hemorrhaging book operations, would follow the CBS lead, cut their losses, and abandon ship.

But lingering above the other speculation was one troublesome question: what had happened to a company that only a few years earlier was one of the Big Five, with a sales force acknowledged to be among the best and an editorial staff that was respected and admired throughout the industry? What went wrong at Fawcett Books?

Immediately after the sale, there was a wave of finger pointing about Fawcett's demise and who was to blame. Most commonly cited as the key to Fawcett's downfall were the excessive guarantees the company had paid for books that ultimately failed in the marketplace. However, former Fawcett employees and executives asserted that the company's troubles were far more complex and deep-seated than a few bad buys. Every company in the business was sporting black eyes from over-guarantees that had backfired. Another more convincing view of Fawcett's demise was the opinion held by one successful paperback veteran who maintained that Fawcett's problems were essentially long-term editorial failures. "They had no original leaders when the industry was moving in that direction. No children's books. No trade paperbacks. The failure goes back five years before CBS even bought the company. Then when CBS took over, they appointed as publisher someone with no editorial vision." In addition, corporate politics, general economic conditions, and the woes of the paperback business all played a part in Fawcett's long tumble. Above all, the refrain heard most often was that of corporate mismanagement. As one former Fawcett editor put it, "Many things caused Fawcett to disappear. Mismanagement is one. It is the single most important thing. If a company is not properly managed, forget about it. There were people who worked there who insinuated themselves into the business, who were smart enough to see where the problems were, where the holes were. But there were also people who didn't bother, who may have been careless in the way they made changes in the company."

There had been many changes in the Fawcett organization since January 1977, when CBS had purchased the company for $50 million in cash. But change came hard to a place that had for many years been a stable, family-owned, private company with sizable profits. Just how sizable was a well-kept family secret, and the Fawcetts had a reputation for spending much of their time finding ways to hide their profits from the government. Like other paperback houses, Fawcett's roots were in the magazine business, and at the time of the sale to CBS, the more than thirty Fawcett magazines played a large part in the company's $135 million annual sales. In fact, the magazines were assumed to be the real prize in the acquisition of Fawcett by CBS. The book side of Fawcett emerged in the sixties when the company showed its willingness to pay big money and had done so on a number of occasions, eventually building a list that included James Michener, the thrillers of Alistair MacLean and Helen MacInnes, the mysteries of John D. MacDonald (originated under the Gold Medal line), the enormously popular "Charlie Brown" cartoon books, the dominant women's writers Mary Stewart and Victoria Holt, and more literary novelists such as John Updike and Joyce Carol Oates.

All of this had made the Fawcett family very wealthy, but by the seventies, the surviving brothers were ready for retirement. CBS, which already had a publishing group that included the magazines and Popular Library, was especially interested in Fawcett because of *Woman's Day*, the centerpiece of the Fawcett magazine group and a powerful force in the supermarkets, and the Fawcett distribution operation. Ironically, it was Fawcett's strength, its sales force, that was most adversely affected by the sale. Either by choice or by purge, a large number of the veteran Fawcett sales reps left the company after the CBS purchase. Always known as a "wholesaler-oriented" company — in other words, strongest in the magazine distribution market — Fawcett soon began to suffer serious reverses in this area. Instead of depending upon the veterans, CBS went outside the business to bring in salespeople guided by the Gospel According to the Harvard Business School. The belief that books could be marketed like toothpaste soon informed the company's sales policies. Any understanding of the extremely willful independent wholesalers was completely lacking, and Fawcett soon began to slip badly in this market. This change was accompanied by the upheaval in the upper echelons of CBS corporate management: John Backe, the man responsible for the acquisition of Fawcett, left CBS after being groomed as William Paley's successor but failed to succeed in the role of heir apparent. When Backe left, a number of other CBS executives committed to the Fawcett operation went as well, and a new group replaced them without the same interest in Fawcett that their predecessors had felt.

In the midst of these internal changes, the industry was being buffeted by problems. Declining unit sales, rising cover prices, a fragmented market where competition for rack space was blast-furnace hot — all resulting in larger discounts to wholesalers, a further chipping-away at the margin of profit — and more and more big dollars going to questionable acquisitions all took their toll. Things were bad enough at paperback houses that had strong central leadership, so they had to be worse where there was no one to take charge. Ultimately, CBS had no responsibility to book publishing, only to its stockholders. Recognizing that mass market paperback publishing was not an area of maximum profits, CBS decided to get out before it lost any more than it already had. As one former Fawcett employee put it, "What it says to somebody who cares about the book business is that CBS saw the sale as an entry on its balance sheet. Originally CBS saw mass market publishing as a potential growth area. They didn't realize or know enough to see that it was not a growth opportunity."

Could more enlightened management have saved Fawcett Books (and Popular Library) without the loss of hundreds of jobs and the cannibalization of two paperback houses? It's a debatable question at best. But it seems likely that responsible ownership, committed to the idea of book publishing rather than bottom-line performance, could have salvaged Fawcett Books. Certainly the company had strengths: its reputation within the industry, the expertise and energy of its employees, and the reservoir of respect that the company had acquired. Once lost, though, these things are irretrievable. They cannot be transferred with the company's "assets." What is also certain is that the dismembering of one of the most powerful paperback companies haunts the business like the ghost of Hamlet's father. The paperback industry is walking a tightrope. Ron Busch, the acerbic and somewhat dyspeptic head of Pocket Books, who is generally considered one of the more savvy people in the business today, told a meeting of paperback publishers in late 1982, "There is a huge fire burning within the paperback business. And I don't think that anybody gives a damn. I'm not saying that we are innocents or poor city church mice. But we have got a big problem on our hands and I don't think anybody is listening." At the same meeting, Warner's Howard Kaminsky stated the problem more prosaically. "Last year the paperback business was in a toilet; now it's in the hospice."[9]

One essential reason for this situation is the myth — or perhaps the misnomer — of the mass market. There are still books that reach millions of readers, although the last of the big best-selling paperback novels, *The Thorn Birds* in 1977, fell several notches below the level of the paperback superstars. And books like these are fewer and farther between. The mass market paperback isn't really mass anymore. At Pocket Books, for instance, there was jubilation when the tie-in edition of Herman Wouk's *The Winds of War* sold a few million copies after the television series was aired. Compare that to the hundred or so million people who watched the series. Or the number of people who watched the last episode of *M*A*S*H* or the Super Bowl. Or the number of people who buy *TV Guide* or *Reader's Digest.* That is the mass market. The paperback industry is far more like the cable television business or the specialty magazines that fill the newsstand racks, catering to smaller, elite groups. This is entirely in keeping with the fracturing of America. The neatly homogenized American marketplace and society of the forties and fifties went out with the Eisenhower administration.

But far worse than the problems of economics, a changing marketplace, falling sales, rising returns, and increasing cover prices is the problem of the "product" itself. And *product* is the only fair term to describe the current output of the paperback industry. The paperback business in the 1980s is characterized by a failure of nerve and creativity. The result is a monthly outpouring of "lists" highlighted by artless imitation, a frightful lack of imagination, crass pandering to lowest-common-denominator tastes, and a slavish adherence to supposedly sound management practices that limit creativity and risk taking. To be fair, the same can be said of most major trade hardcover houses. In fact, the point of meaningful dis-

tinction between trade hardcover house and mass market publisher
was passed long ago. Bantam, New American Library, Pocket Books,
and Warner Books all publish regularly in hardcover now, producing
books that often make the best-seller charts and become fodder for
their mass market lists as well. Other paperback houses have either
Byzantine or indirect relationships with hardcover houses, usually
through mutual corporate ownership. Berkley Books, which now
includes the paperback lines of Jove, Playboy, and Ace Books, is
owned by Putnam's, which also owns the hardcover imprints Grosset & Dunlap and Coward, McCann & Geoghegan, as well as the
Perigee trade paperback imprint (all in turn owned by MCA, Inc.).
There is hardly a major trade house that does not publish trade
paperbacks under a special imprint.

All of this has led to a fearfully homogenized output from American publishers. Always an imitative field, publishing — paperback
publishing in particular — has become dominated by me-too-ism
and an alarming dependence on ephemera. There are successes
today, but where are the books that will still be read five, ten, or
twenty years from today? If someone publishes a successful cut-
out-doll book or a collection of cartoons about dead cats, there are
five more beside it in the stores the next day. These quickie rip-off
books are then imitated ad nauseam. Ian Ballantine, the crafty old
pioneer of the paperback who is still actively pursuing paperback
projects, graphically described the problem as "publishers devour-
ing each other's genitals."

One measure of this sad state of affairs can be seen in the list of
best-selling paperbacks of 1982 compiled by *Publishers Weekly.* As
the mass market listing shows, serious fiction and nonfiction simply do not sell in the numbers they once did. With the exceptions
of John Irving and James Michener, to be charitable, novels of any
dimension or challenge are completely absent, and in any case Irving's *The Hotel New Hampshire* was an admitted million-dollar
write-off for Pocket Books despite its two-million-in-print figure.
Not until *The White Hotel* by D. M. Thomas, with an in-print figure
of 1.4 million copies, does a novel of literary merit and distinction
appear. This is not merely a problem endemic to the paperback. The
hardcover best-seller lists are little improvement in either fiction or
nonfiction. The top fifteen sellers of the year in fiction are dominated by the "brand-name" best-selling commercial authors, none
of whom lays any claim to literary seriousness. The other remark-

able point about the fiction list is the preponderance of science fiction writers, including Arthur C. Clarke, Isaac Asimov, and Stephen R. Donaldson. Along with these three, it is fair to say that Stephen King, Sidney Sheldon, John Jakes, and Danielle Steel are all creations of the paperback; that is, these novelists achieved hardcover success by building paperback success and an audience that has crossed over to hardcover buying. These writers' shift from paperback to hardcover success is more evidence of the paperback's pervasive influence on readers and the impact it has had on publishing.

The trade paperback best-seller list offers little consolation. Created as a viable means of publishing quality works of fiction and nonfiction in a paperback format, the trade paperback has largely evolved into an extension of the mass market. The field of trade paperback publishing has become totally dominated by original romances; health, beauty, and fitness books; humor and cartoon books; and other ephemeral categories. Among the top fifty best-selling trade paperbacks, there are only two books of real seriousness: *At Dawn We Slept*, a history of the attack on Pearl Harbor, with 140,000 copies in print; and *In the Belly of the Beast*, the prison writings of Jack Henry Abbott, the literary protégé of Norman Mailer who was released from prison with the support of several notable writers and publishers and committed a murder while on parole (133,075 copies in print). In fiction, the sole noncategory novel of literary merit was Toni Morrison's *Tar Baby*, with 90,000 copies in print. There was a day when all three books would have been eagerly reprinted as mass market paperbacks with hundred-thousand-copy printings.

1982 Best Sellers

MASS MARKET PAPERBACK

If There Be Thorns (occult fiction) by V. C. Andrews
Rage of Angels (fiction) by Sidney Sheldon
Firestarter (occult fiction) by Stephen King
Goodbye Janette (fiction) by Harold Robbins
The Key to Rebecca (suspense fiction) by Ken Follett
Cujo (occult fiction) by Stephen King
Noble House (fiction) by James Clavell
Surrender to Love (romance) by Rosemary Rogers

Gorky Park (suspense fiction) by Martin Cruz Smith
The Covenant (fiction) by James Michener
An Indecent Obsession (fiction) by Colleen McCullough
A Perfect Stranger (romance) by Danielle Steel
Random Winds (fiction) by Belva Plain
The Ring (romance) by Danielle Steel
The Hotel New Hampshire (fiction) by John Irving

TRADE PAPERBACK

A Rose in Winter (romance) by Rosemary Rogers
Thin Thighs in Thirty Days (fitness) by Wendy Stehling
Real Men Don't Eat Quiche (humor) by Bruce Feirstein
Richard Simmons' Never-Say-Diet Cook Book (fitness) by Richard
    Simmons
Garfield Weighs In (humor) by Jim Davis
Garfield Takes the Cake (humor) by Jim Davis
Color Me Beautiful (beauty) by Carole Jackson
Items From Our Catalog (humor) by Alfred Gingold
Once in a Lifetime (romance) by Danielle Steel
Here Comes Garfield (humor) by Jim Davis
Thirty Days to a Beautiful Bottom (fitness) by Deborah Cox and
    Julie Davis
This Calder Range (romance) by Janet Dailey
Garfield Bigger Than Life (humor) by Jim Davis
Garfield Gains Weight (humor) by Jim Davis
The Dark Crystal (movie tie-in) by A.C.H. Smith

HARDCOVER FICTION

E.T. The Extra-Terrestrial Storybook by William Kotzwinkle
Space by James Michener
The Parsifal Mosaic by Robert Ludlum
Master of the Game by Sidney Sheldon
Mistral's Daughter by Judith Krantz
The Valley of the Horses by Jean M. Auel
Different Seasons by Stephen King
North and South by John Jakes
2010: Odyssey Two by Arthur C. Clarke
The Man From St. Petersburg by Ken Follett
The Prodigal Daughter by Jeffrey Archer
Foundation's Edge by Isaac Asimov
Crossings by Danielle Steel
The One Tree by Stephen R. Donaldson
Spellbinder by Harold Robbins

HARDCOVER NONFICTION

Jane Fonda's Workout Book by Jane Fonda
Living, Loving and Learning by Leo Buscaglia
And More by Andy Rooney by Andrew A. Rooney
Better Homes and Gardens New Cookbook
Life Extension by Durk Pearson and Sandy Shaw
When Bad Things Happen to Good People by Rabbi Harold S.
    Kushner
A Few Minutes with Andy Rooney by Andrew A. Rooney
The Weight Watchers Food Plan Diet Cookbook
Richard Simmons' Never-Say-Diet Cook Book by Richard Simmons
No Bad Dogs by Barbara Woodhouse
Weight Watchers 365-Day Menu Cookbook
The Fall of Freddie the Leaf by Leo Buscaglia
The G-Spot and Other Recent Discoveries about Human Sexuality
    by Alice Kahn Ladas, Beverly Whopple and John D. Perry
An Uncommon Freedom by Charles Paul Conn
Megatrends: Ten New Directions Transforming Our Lives by John
    Naisbitt

(Source: *Publishers Weekly*, March 11, 1983)

There are two ways of viewing this alarming decline in quality as represented by these best sellers. Either the broad American public is completely disinterested in books of merit or American publishers have forsaken these books. Are these lists truly reflective of American tastes in the eighties? Has the broad audience for serious literature in paperback shrunk to a hundred thousand readers? What became of the audience that made million-sellers of *Hiroshima, The Naked and the Dead,* the novels of James T. Farrell, *The Catcher in the Rye, The Feminine Mystique, Soul on Ice,* the novels of Hermann Hesse, *Future Shock, Zen and the Art of Motorcycle Maintenance,* and *The Last Whole Earth Catalog*?

The answer may lie in another question. Why is there always such surprise and amazement when the public responds to something of quality, whether it is a book, a film, or a television series (such as *Masterpiece Theater, Civilization,* or *Cosmos*)? The problem may be the existence in the inner halls of America's culture centers a dangerous elitism that presumes that the people "out there" demand less than the best. This is partly due to an island mentality on the part of cultural decision makers who see Manhattan as different from (and better or smarter than) the rest of America. There is also the bottom-line factor; there is no denying that these ephemeral books do sell. The problem comes from the fact that their success means they are cultivated to the exclusion of other books. Most of the publisher's energy goes into creating and selling more of these quickies — which would probably sell by themselves without the effort. There is a strange logic operative that calls for the expenditure of money and creativity on the marketing of books that have either attained success or seem destined for it. The less-certain books are orphaned or tossed into the pool, there to sink or swim. Thus they are not promoted. Therefore they don't sell. The original premise is neatly confirmed, convincing the publisher exactly how smart he was in the first place.

Ironically, this method of operation is contrary to the spirit of the most successful paperback publishers, particularly if success is defined not in terms of dollars and cents but in the ability to communicate ideas and new truths and make some meaningful contribution to the culture and society — which publishing, ideally, is meant to do. Historically at least, the most "successful" publishers in paperback have been those who mingled quality with commerce, the essence of the Paperback Revolution. In most cases, that mix came from powerful individuals with the scope and vision that went beyond reading the bottom line of a profit-and-loss column. It did not come from management by committee. Nor does it come from a philosophy of marketing that looks at the market, decides that women buy 70 percent of the books and decrees that 70 percent of the books published will therefore be aimed at women. That is the way to self-fulfilling prophecies.

Some publishers have suggested that the failure lies elsewhere, that in an age of commonplace functional illiteracy and video games in every candy store (where paperback racks once stood), America is not producing writers capable of firing the imagination. To that, most writers would say that unless they write in the image of Judith Krantz, Harold Robbins, or Rosemary Rogers, they don't get published. The truth lies somewhere between. Obviously, good books still get published. Many find their way into paperback, although in fractions of the numbers that once meant mass market paperback publishing. Why don't they get the full-scale distribution they once might have enjoyed? Publishers don't push, taking an elitist notion of what the market wants. Wholesalers don't want to carry them in expensive inventories unless they are "like" something else already successful that promises quick turnover. Booksellers, if they carry them, consign these books to the back of the store, leaving the front for the humor, cartoons, best sellers, and other ephemera that are expanding at a geometric rate. The spirit of risk taking and innovation that characterized the Paperback Revolution seems almost extinct, except in some of the smaller independent publishers, whose books are rarely carried by the large chain bookstores. The concept of "Good Reading for the Millions," once an article of faith at New American Library, has been replaced by "Fast-Food Reading for the Millions."

What does that say about the future of the paperback and, by extension, all of publishing. From the current vantage point, the outlook is not bright. In simple business terms, the likelihood of more failures of paperback houses is real, although many companies are now realizing substantial profits. Part of this stems from the disillusionment of large corporations with their publishing subsidiaries, as CBS was unhappy with its Fawcett and Popular Library investment. Yet such a realistic observer as Oscar Dystel remains optimistic. "This business has gone up and down for almost fifty years. The excitement, innovation, and discovery have dimmed. But it is a good business. The revolution created a new form of publishing." The grim truth, however, seems to be that there is little reason for optimism that a return to quality and seriousness in paperback *on a mass scale* is possible. Of course, books of seriousness continue to be published. But it seems far less likely that they will ever reach a "mass market." Increasingly, these books are being published under quality imprints selling to a shrinking elite of interested readers. The concept of the most books for the most people at the lowest possible price, the driving principle of the Paperback Revolution, is a lost ideal — a publishing dinosaur.

Can that revolution be rekindled? It seems unlikely. The elements that made it work — inexpensive advance guarantees, widespread distribution, low costs — are all things of the past. But these elements were only the raw materials. The inspiration came from individuals who saw these raw materials and realized what could be done with them. In doing so, they reshaped literature and culture in America during the past forty years. They were people who knew that success depended upon taking chances on untried methods and ideas and then plowing back some of the wealth that they had uncovered.

Can such a revolution come again? Certainly. But it is likely that the paperback will not be the vehicle driving it. Perhaps books will play only a small role in the next wave. One vision of the future rests with the twelve-year-old who is not merely playing with a computer but programming it. The time has come when the computer has begun to take the raw materials of the Paperback Revolution — low production costs, accessibility, and inexpensive materials or software — to make a new and probably more radical revolution. One can only hope that there are people wise enough to take these elements and see what can be made of them. Will they be adulterated to create another narcotizing diversion? Or will they, like the best books, open up new worlds? You pays your money and you takes your choice.

APPENDIX:

Fifty Paperbacks
that Changed America

Notes

Bibliography

Index

APPENDIX

Fifty Paperbacks that Changed America

I SET OUT to list the ten most consequential paperbacks ever published — that is, books that in their paperback format reached a broad audience and had some basic impact on American culture and consciousness. Ten was impossible, so I tried for twenty-five. Twenty-five books was still too difficult a selection to make. I have settled for these fifty. They are books that I believe made some fundamental alteration in the way Americans thought and deeply reflect the major changes in American society during the past forty years. There are, of course, many other books that could and should be on this list. Most of them appear elsewhere in this history as having had some consequence. (Dates following the titles are the year of the book's first paperback appearance. The listing is in order of chronological appearance, not relative importance.)

1. *How to Win Friends and Influence People* by Dale Carnegie (1940).
2. *Baby and Child Care* by Dr. Benjamin M. Spock (1946).
3. *Patterns of Culture* by Ruth Benedict (1946).
4. *God's Little Acre* by Erskine Caldwell (1946).
5. *Hiroshima* by John Hersey (1948).
6. *1984* by George Orwell (1951).
7. *The Naked and the Dead* by Norman Mailer (1951).
8. *Brave New World* by Aldous Huxley (1952).
9. *The Fountainhead* by Ayn Rand (1952).
10. *The Catcher in the Rye* by J. D. Salinger (1953).

11. *New World Writing* and *discovery* (1953).
12. *Fahrenheit 451* by Ray Bradbury (1953).
13. *The Diary of a Young Girl* by Anne Frank (1953).
14. *The Lonely Crowd* by David Riesman (1953).
15. *Waiting for Godot* by Samuel Beckett (1953).
16. *Death Be Not Proud* by John Gunther (1957).
17. *Siddhartha* by Hermann Hesse (1957).
18. *Profiles in Courage* by John F. Kennedy (1957).
19. *Peyton Place* by Grace Metalious (1957).
20. *The Organization Man* by William H. Whyte (1957).
21. *On the Road* by Jack Kerouac (1958).
22. *Lord of the Flies* by William Golding (1959).
23. *Lady Chatterley's Lover* by D. H. Lawrence (1959).
24. *The Rise and Fall of the Third Reich* by William L. Shirer (1961).
25. *Black Like Me* by John Howard Griffin (1961).
26. *Tropic of Cancer* by Henry Miller (1961).
27. *Catch-22* by Joseph Heller (1962).
28. *One Flew over the Cuckoo's Nest* by Ken Kesey (1962).
29. *To Kill a Mockingbird* by Harper Lee (1962).
30. *The Feminine Mystique* by Betty Friedan (1963).
31. *Silent Spring* by Rachel Carson (1963).
32. *One Day in the Life of Ivan Denisovich* by Aleksandr Solzhenitsyn (1963).
33. *The Report of the Warren Commission* (1964).
34. *In Cold Blood* by Truman Capote (1965).
35. *The Fellowship of the Ring* by J.R.R. Tolkien (1965).
36. *The Harrad Experiment* by Robert Rimmer (1967).
37. *New American Review/American Review* (1967).
38. *Soul on Ice* by Eldridge Cleaver (1968).
39. *The Armies of the Night* by Norman Mailer (1968).
40. *The Population Bomb* by Paul Ehrlich (1968).
41. *Slaughterhouse-Five* by Kurt Vonnegut (1969).
42. *The Electric Kool-Aid Acid Test* by Tom Wolfe (1970).
43. *The Last Whole Earth Catalog* (1971).
44. *Future Shock* by Alvin Toffler (1971).
45. *The Pentagon Papers* (1971).
46. *Sexual Politics* by Kate Millett (1971).
47. *Fire in the Lake* by Frances FitzGerald (1972).
48. *I'm OK — You're OK* by Thomas Harris (1973).
49. *The Watergate Hearings* (1973).
50. *The White House Tapes* (1974).

H<small>ONORABLE</small> M<small>ENTION</small>
The following books were all candidates for top fifty:

A Streetcar Named Desire (1951); Invisible Man (1953); Go Tell It
on the Mountain (1954); The Sea Around Us (1955); Why Johnny
Can't Read (1956); Bonjour Tristesse (1956); Notes of a Native Son
(1957); From Russia with Love (1968); On the Beach (1958); The
Myth of Sisyphus (1959); Childhood's End (1959); Exodus (1960);
The Sirens of Titan (1959); Spartacus (1960); Elements of Style
(1960); Doctor Zhivago (1960); Goodbye, Columbus (1960); A
Separate Peace (1960); The Status Seekers (1961); Lolita (1962);
Cat's Cradle (1963); Candy (1964); I Never Promised You a Rose
Garden (1964); The Wretched of the Earth (1965); The
Autobiography of Malcolm X (1965); The Story of O (1967); The
Teachings of Don Juan (1968); The Godfather (1971); The Sensuous
Woman (1971); The Greening of America (1971); The Best and the
Brightest (1972); The Bell Jar (1972); Diet for a Small Planet (1972);
Jonathan Livingston Seagull (1973); Our Bodies, Ourselves (1971).

Notes

ONE IN THE BEGINNING, THERE WAS SPOCK

1. Landon Y. Jones, *Great Expectations: America and the Baby Boom Generation* (New York: Coward, McCann & Geoghegan, 1980). Ballantine Books paperback edition, p. 54.
2. Quotes from Dr. Spock are taken from a telephone interview with him conducted on April 15, 1982.
3. Jessica Mitford, *The Trial of Dr. Spock* (New York: Alfred Knopf, 1969), p. 11.
4. Benjamin Spock and Mitchell Zimmerman, *Dr. Spock on Vietnam* (New York: Dell, 1968), p. 9.
5. William Manchester, *The Glory and the Dream* (Boston: Little, Brown, 1974). Bantam Books paperback edition, pp. 1187–89.
6. Douglas T. Miller and Marion Nowak, *The Fifties: The Way We Really Were* (Garden City, N.Y.: Doubleday, 1975), pp. 270–71.
7. Harvey Wasserman and Norman Solomon, *Killing Our Own: The Disaster of America's Experiment with Atomic Radiation* (New York: Delacorte/Delta, 1982). The excerpt is from Dr. Spock's introduction to the book.

TWO COMPLETE AND UNABRIDGED

1. "Experiment in New York," *The Publishers' Weekly*, June 24, 1939.
2. "Pocket Books Make Good Start," *PW*, July 1, 1939.
3. "Pocket Books on Sale Nationally After Success in New York," *PW*, July 29, 1939.
4. "Pocket Books Sell Outside New York," *PW*, August 19, 1939.
5. O. H. Cheney, *Economic Survey of the Book Industry* (New York: National Association of Book Publishers, 1931). Fifty years later, the Cheney Report makes instructive reading for those critics of today's book industry who long for the "good old days" when publishing was in the hands of

"enlightened" individuals instead of profit-motivated conglomerates. With the exception of the radicals and reformers — Knopf, Liveright, Reynal, Hitchcock, Cerf and Klopfer, Simon and Schuster, to name a few — the business was in the hands of crusty conservative gentlemen who ruled their fiefdoms with a sense of divine right. While this is hardly meant to be taken as a defense of the large corporations that control publishing in the 1980s, the point remains that there are enlightened corporations under which some publishing houses have flourished and other conglomerates that have ruined their book operations. Similarly, there are good and bad individual owners.

6. Wallis Howe, "The First Half-Billion," *Bestsellers*, September 1962.

7. Kurt Enoch, "The Paperbound Book: Twentieth Century Publishing Phenomenon," *The Library Quarterly*, July 1954.

8. J. E. Morpurgo, *Allen Lane: King Penguin* (London: Hutchinson, 1979), p. 79. Although this book focuses on the growth and importance of the American paperback industry, the role and impact of Penguin Books in England was seminal. *Allen Lane: King Penguin* is an objective and fascinating account of this extraordinary personality and the effect he has had on twentieth-century publishing. Morpurgo's definitive biography is a wonderful portrayal of an empire builder. I am indebted to Morpurgo for his account of the rise of Penguin Books.

9. Morpurgo, *King Penguin*, pp. 92–94.

THREE WINNING FRIENDS AND INFLUENCING PEOPLE

1. "Cheap Books," *Time*, July 7, 1939.

2. Letter from Robert de Graff, *The Publishers' Weekly*, April 22, 1939.

3. Louis P. Birk, "The Market For Paper Bound Books," *PW*, September 29, 1939.

4. "Robert de Graff Starts Publication of 25-cent Reprint Series," *PW*, May 27, 1939.

5. Wallis Howe, "The First Half-Billion," *Bestsellers*, September 1962.

6. Robert de Graff letter to Frederic Melcher, dated August 14, 1939, in *PW* files.

7. Cass Canfield, *Up and Down and Around: A Publisher Recollects the Time of His Life* (New York: Harper & Row, 1971), p. 140.

8. John Cooney, *The Annenbergs: The Salvaging of a Tainted Empire* (New York: Simon & Schuster, 1982), pp. 31–32.

9. Lindsay Chaney and Michael Cieply, *The Hearsts: Family and Empire — The Later Years* (New York: Simon & Schuster, 1981), p. 192.

FOUR THEY WERE EXPENDABLE

1. "Pocket Sized Books, Turned Out Like Cars, Are Turning Over Pocketsful of Money," *New York World Telegram*, April 28, 1941.

2. Copy of memo by Robert de Graff to M. Lincoln Schuster, in the Schuster Collection at Butler Library, Columbia University.

3. Wolff's publishing firm, Pantheon Books, was established in February 1942 by Wolff, Schabert, and Jacques Schiffrin, another refugee. The company became home to many of the most prominent European writers. Thus the same capital was responsible for launching two of the most significant ventures in contemporary American publishing. The impact of the German and other European refugees on the American publishing scene, as well as on every other facet of business, intellectual, scientific, and cultural life in America, has been discussed in Laura Fermi's book *Illustrious Immigrants* (Chicago: University of Chicago Press, 1972).

4. "Pocket Books that Sell Best in Army Camps," *The Publishers' Weekly*, July 11, 1942.

5. John Jamieson, *Books for the Army* (New York: Columbia University Press, 1950), pp. 143–44.

6. Jamieson, *Books for the Army*, pp. 144–45.

7. *PW*, June 27, 1942.

8. W. L. White, *They Were Expendable* (New York: Harcourt, Brace and Co., 1942), p. vi.

9. White, *They Were Expendable*, pp. 3–4.

10. John Tebbel, *A History of Book Publishing in the United States*, Vol. 4 (New York: R. R. Bowker, 1981), p. 29.

11. Jamieson, *Books for the Army*, pp. 147–48.

12. Jamieson, *Books for the Army*, p. 142.

13. "ASE Well Received by Troops," *PW*, February 12, 1944.

14. Letter from Elmer Leighton, *PW*, May 20, 1944.

15. Major General Joseph W. Byron, "A Better Read Man than His Father, GI Joe Consumes Millions of Books," *New York Post*, November 30, 1944.

16. John Jamieson, "Armed Services Editions and GI Fan Mail," *PW*, July 12, 1947.

FIVE   THE CASE OF THE MYSTERIOUS MILLIONS

1. Stephen Becker, *Marshall Field III* (New York: Simon & Schuster, 1964), p. 317.

2. "Mr. Field and the Word Business," *Time*, October 9, 1944.

3. Bennett Cerf, *At Random* (New York: Random House, 1977), pp. 195–96.

4. Lovell Thompson, "Books, Business and Finance," *The Publishers' Weekly*, November 11, 1944.

5. Donald Porter Geddes, "Books Can Be Business Too," *PW*, December 2, 1944.

6. Becker, *Marshall Field III*, p. 319.

7. Wallis E. Howe, "Breaking Into New Markets," *PW*, January 27, 1945.

8. Charles W. Morton, "The World of Erle Stanley Gardner," *Atlantic Monthly*, January 1967.

9. *Contemporary Authors*, Vol. 25–28 (Detroit: Gale Research Company, 1970), p. 420.

10. "Can Anyone Beat This?" *PW*, December 27, 1952.

11. Morton, "Erle Stanley Gardner."

12. "$100,000 Offer for Erle Stanley Gardner's Ghost," *PW*, January 27, 1958.

13. Memo by Max Schuster to Robert de Graff, Richard Simon, Leon Shimkin, Wallis Howe, and Donald Porter Geddes. Schuster Collection, Columbia University.

SIX PENGUIN HATCHES TWINS

1. Bennett Cerf, *At Random* (New York: Random House, 1977), pp. 195–96.

2. Cerf, *At Random*, p. 197.

3. *The Publishers' Weekly*, February 5, 1947.

4. J. E. Morpurgo, *Allen Lane: King Penguin* (London: Hutchinson, 1979), p. 201.

5. See Victor Weybright, *The Making of a Publisher* (New York: Reynal & Company, 1966). Weybright's memoir, written after he left New American Library following a bitter and divisive period, paints an extremely unfavorable portrait of Enoch, whom he casts as an arch-villain. Weybright suggests that their relationship was one in which he constantly had to battle Enoch's attempts to cheapen the company's output and that enmity between them was ever-present. Evidence suggests otherwise. It hardly seems likely that so successful a business partnership could be founded on such personal antagonism. Letters from Weybright as well as material in New American Library's archives point to a more amicable and even proud partnership until the sale of the company. The heat of this bitter leave-taking was certainly a factor in the vituperative nature of Weybright's attack on Enoch.

6. Morpurgo, *King Penguin*, p. 229.

7. Margaret Mead, Preface to *Patterns of Culture* (Boston: Houghton Mifflin, 1958), p. vii. In 1960, the paperback rights to *Patterns of Culture* reverted to Houghton Mifflin and the book was reissued in a higher-priced trade paperback edition under the Sentry Editions imprint. The question of rights reversions is a painful one for mass market paperback publishers who feel that they have built a market for a book only to see it reclaimed by the hardcover publisher and reissued in a more expensive edition when the reprint license expires, usually after five or seven years. Hardcover houses are simply seeking to build profitable paperback lists by turning to their own backlists. But for paperback houses, which until recently depended heavily upon reprints, the situation is seen as an injustice.

8. Carvel Collins, "Erskine Caldwell at Work," *Atlantic Monthly*, July 1958.

9. Collins, "Erskine Caldwell."

10. Alfred Kazin, *On Native Grounds* (New York: Reynal & Hitchcock, 1942), p. 380.

11. Theodore H. White, *In Search of History* (New York: Harper & Row, 1978), p. 247.

12. Donald Porter Geddes, "New Light on Sexual Knowledge" in *About the Kinsey Report* (New York: New American Library, 1948), p. 8.

13. Frederick G. Melcher, "A Cycle That Can End in Vulgarity," *PW*, June 4, 1949.

14. Piet Schreuders, *Paperbacks U.S.A.: A Graphic History* (San Diego: Blue Dolphin, 1981), p. 55.

SEVEN TWO-BIT CULTURE: THE GREAT CONTRADICTION

1. Harvey Swados, "Paper Books: What Do They Promise?" *Nation*, August 11–18, 1951.

2. *The Publishers' Weekly*, January 14, 1950.

3. *PW*, November 8, 1950.

4. Freeman Lewis, *Paperbound Books in America* (New York: New York Public Library, 1952), pp. 8–9.

5. Bennett Cerf, *At Random* (New York: Random House, 1977), p. 183.

6. "Bantam Plans Two Volume *Roosevelt and Hopkins*," *PW*, July 8, 1950.

7. Cerf, *At Random*, pp. 197–98.

8. One of Kauffmann's novels, *The Tightrope*, was the object of a celebrated obscenity case in England. Published there under the title *The Philanderer*, the book was exonerated when a judge delivered a fresh appraisal of an 1868 ruling that had influenced obscenity cases on both sides of the Atlantic.

9. Among the growing ranks of collectors of old or "vintage" paperbacks, Ace's edition of *Junkie* is a valued treasure. For these collectors, there is now a standard price guide called *The Paperback Price Guide* by Kevin Hancer (Crown/Harmony). In the first edition, the value of *Junkie/Narcotics Agent* is $30, $65 or $100, depending on the condition. This applies only to first editions; later printings are much less valuable.

10. David Dempsey, "The Revolution in Books," *Atlantic*, January 1953.

11. Kurt Enoch, "The Paper Bound Book: Twentieth Century Publishing Phenomenon," *Library Quarterly*, July 1954.

12. Bernard DeVoto, "Culture at Two Bits," *Harper's*, October 1954.

13. Douglas T. Miller and Marion Nowak, *The Fifties: The Way We Really Were* (Garden City, N.Y.: Doubleday, 1975), pp. 167–68.

14. Dwight Macdonald, "A Theory of Mass Culture" in Bernard Rosenberg and David Manning White, eds., *Mass Culture in America* (Glencoe, Illinois: Free Press, 1957), p. 68.

15. Bernard Rosenberg, "Mass Culture in America" in *Mass Culture,* p. 5.
16. Charles J. Rolo, "Simenon and Spillane," *New World Writing: First Mentor Selection* (New York: New American Library, 1952), pp. 244–45.
17. Dempsey, "Revolution in Books."
18. J. E. Morpurgo, *Allen Lane: King Penguin* (London: Hutchinson, 1979), p. 170.
19. Morpurgo, *King Penguin,* p. 171.
20. Victor Weybright, *The Making of a Publisher* (New York: Reynal & Company, 1966), p. 242.
21. Martin Mayer, "Spock, Sex and Schopenhauer," *Esquire,* April 1962.
22. "Views on Publishing," *PW,* December 16, 1974.

EIGHT THE LADY GOES TO COURT

1. Anne Lyon Haight and Chandler B. Grannis, *Banned Books: 387 B.C. to 1978 A.D.* (New York: R. R. Bowker, 1978), p. 1. My intention in this chapter is to present a survey of the censorship of paperback books rather than a comprehensive history of book censorship and the significant milestones in overcoming such censorship. Others have done so far more eloquently and competently. To the interested reader I recommend several basic texts and summaries: *The End of Obscenity* by Charles Rembar; *Banned Books: 387 B.C. to 1978 A.D.* by Anne Lyon Haight and Chandler B. Grannis; *Censorship: The Search for the Obscene* by Morris L. Ernst and Allan U. Schwartz; Harriet Pilpel's 1973 R. R. Bowker Memorial Lecture "Obscenity and the Constitution"; *The Report of the Commission on Obscenity and Pornography;* and the highly readable history of censorship woven through *Thy Neighbor's Wife* by Gay Talese. See also Frances FitzGerald's *America Revised,* which documents the ideological censorship of American textbooks, and Net Hentoff's *The First Freedom,* an introduction to the issues of free speech.
2. In *The End of Obscenity,* Charles Rembar notes that the Society for the Suppression of Vice slipped from view after the 1930s. Checking records, he discovered that the society had not disappeared but changed its name, merged, and lived on as the Police Athletic League.
3. Charles Rembar, "Censorship in America" in Haight and Grannis, *Banned Books,* p. xx.
4. Fitzgerald was referring to the Hays Office, named for Will Hays, the first president of the Motion Picture Association of America. Hays operated with dictatorial powers, using a code that kept profanity out of movies and married couples in single beds; a bedroom kiss had to be delivered with the man's feet planted firmly on the floor. There was something of an uproar when Hays allowed Clark Gable the line "Frankly my dear, I don't give a damn" in *Gone with the Wind.* Apparently, the far more provocative scene in which Rhett sweeps Scarlett up in his arms and carries her up the stairs was not a problem. Where exactly did Hays think they were going?

5. In this exchange, O'Connor would be asked about the decisions made by Judge Curtis G. Bok in Pennsylvania, a key case in which Judge Bok wrote an important ruling clearing nine paperbacks including *God's Little Acre*. It might have helped O'Connor here if he had been able to cite Bok's opinion: "It will be asked whether one would care to have one's young daughter read these books. I suppose that by the time she is old enough to read them she will have learned the biological facts of life and the words that go with them. There is something seriously wrong at home if those facts have not been met and faced and sorted by then; it is not children so much as parents that should receive our concern about this. I should prefer that my own three daughters meet the facts of life and the literature of the world in my library than behind a neighbor's barn, for I can face the adversary there directly. If the young ladies are appalled by what they read, they can close the book at the bottom of page one; if they read further, they will learn what is in the world and in its people, and no parents who have been discerning with their children need fear the outcome."

Judge Bok himself became an issue in the Gathings hearings when the general counsel mentioned that Bok was a member of the Curtis family, which retained a 42½ percent interest in Bantam Books, a fact that the committee majority noted in its report. This swipe at Judge Bok was disguised by the committee, which claimed not to doubt the judge's integrity, but stated that he was "inherently imbued with a liberal conception of the tradition" guaranteeing freedom of the press because of his relationship with the publishing industry.

6. John Tebbel, *A History of Book Publishing in America*, Vol. 4 (New York: R. R. Bowker, 1981), pp. 706–8.

7. Tebbel, *History of Book Publishing*, p. 700.

8. *The Publishers' Weekly*, December 20, 1952.

9. Freeman Lewis, statement filed in the records of the Gathings Committee, December 9, 1952.

10. Victor Weybright, *The Complete and Unabridged Statement to the Gathings Committee by The New American Library of World Literature, Inc.*, December 10, 1952.

11. Chandler B. Grannis, "The Gathings Committee and Paper-Bound Books," *PW*, December 13, 1952.

12. *PW*, December 20, 1952.

13. *PW*, June 27, 1953.

14. *PW*, May 2, 1953.

15. *PW*, August 15, 1953.

16. Charles Rembar, *The End of Obscenity* (New York: Random House, 1968), Bantam Books paperback edition, p. 23.

17. "Postal Censors to Test Lady Chatterley," *PW*, May 18, 1959.

18. *PW*, August 17, 1959.

19. *Bantam* v. *Sullivan* was significant not only from the point of view of

free expression; it also established an important precedent and was cited by the Supreme Court in 1971 in the Pentagon Papers case. In ruling against the government, the Court quoted *Bantam* v. *Sullivan:* "Any system of prior restraints of expression comes to this court bearing a heavy presumption against its Constitutional validity."

20. *PW*, July 9, 1982.

NINE THE NEW AGE DAWNS

1. The question of the legitimacy of the use of recognizable individuals in works of fiction remains unsettled to this day, and recent decisions in a number of cases involving libel brought against novelists have only produced a series of conflicting rulings, further muddying the waters. A number of large publishers have instituted the practice of providing libel insurance for all their contracted writers to protect these authors from damages. But the large legal question of libelous fiction is generally left to the discretion of a jury or the presiding judge.

2. "The Story of Fawcett World Library," *Book Production Magazine,* August 1964.

3. *Book Production Magazine,* August 1964.

4. When Fawcett's reprint license expired on *The Rise and Fall of the Third Reich,* Simon & Schuster, the original publisher, reissued it in 1981 under its Touchstone trade paperback imprint. This was yet another example of the pervasive trend among hardcover publishers to recover books previously licensed to mass market publishers that had great success in the mass market format and reissue them in more expensive editions aimed exclusively at the bookstore trade. It makes economic sense for the publisher, but it is another example of the disappearance of the inexpensive paperback, the major factor in the fueling of the Paperback Revolution.

5. *The Publishers' Weekly,* November 2, 1959; January 18, 1960.

6. John Tebbel, *A History of Book Publishing in the United States,* Vol. 4 (New York: R. R. Bowker, 1981), pp. 207–9.

7. *PW*, April 23, 1949; May 28, 1949.

8. The most fascinating exploration of the Chandlers' political clout and economic muscle, including their aid to the political ambitions of Richard M. Nixon and the fund-raising abilities of Dorothy Chandler, has been made by David Halberstam in his book *The Powers That Be* (New York: Knopf, 1979; Dell paperback). It is a penetrating study of how the media and the people who control it amass and wield power.

TEN THE NEW AGE: FROM ROTH TO ROBBINS

1. Morris Dickstein, *Gates of Eden: American Culture in the Sixties* (New York: Basic Books, 1977). Harper Colophon paperback edition, p. 27.

2. Dickstein, *Gates of Eden,* p. 69.

3. Irving Howe, "The Suburbs of Babylon" reprinted in Irving Howe, *Cele-*

brations and Attacks (New York: Harcourt Brace Jovanovich, 1979). Harvest paperback edition, p. 35.

4. Joseph Heller, "Reeling in Catch-22," reprinted in Lynda Rosen Obst, ed., *The Sixties* (New York: Rolling Stone Press/Random House, 1977), p. 50.

5. Heller, "Catch-22," p. 50.

6. For his efforts on Vonnegut's behalf, Lawrence earned a small piece of literary posterity when Vonnegut wrote his own version of events into *Slaughterhouse-Five.* "And somewhere in there a nice man named Seymour Lawrence gave me a three-book contract, and I said, 'O.K., the first of the three will be my famous book about Dresden.' The friends of Seymour Lawrence call him Sam. And I say to Sam now: 'Sam, here's the book.' " Kurt Vonnegut, *Slaughterhouse-Five* (New York: Seymour Lawrence/Delacorte Press, 1969), pp. 16–17.

7. Betty Friedan, *The Feminine Mystique* (New York: W. W. Norton, 1963). Dell paperback edition, pp. 37–38.

8. Betty Friedan, "Twenty Years After the Feminine Mystique," *New York Times Magazine,* February 27, 1983.

9. Douglas T. Miller and Marion Nowak, *The Fifties: The Way We Really Were* (Garden City, N.Y.: Doubleday, 1975), p. 211.

10. Jay Martin, *Always Merry and Bright: The Life of Henry Miller* (Santa Barbara, Calif.: Capra Press, 1978), Penguin paperback edition, p. 371.

11. Barbara Harte and Carolyn Riley, eds., *200 Contemporary Authors* (Detroit: Gale Research, 1969), pp. 276–78.

12. John Gardner, *On Moral Fiction* (New York: Basic Books, 1978), Harper Colophon paperback edition, pp. 194–95.

13. Harte and Riley, *Contemporary Authors,* pp. 276–78.

14. *New York Times Book Review,* February 16, 1969.

ELEVEN A MILLION DOLLARS FOR A JEWISH BIRD?

1. Matthew J. Bruccoli, *The O'Hara Concern* (New York: Random House, 1975), p. 247.

2. Bruccoli, *O'Hara Concern,* pp. 270–71.

3. Walter Kendrick, "Falling in Love with Love," *Village Voice,* August 3, 1982.

4. Ann Douglas, "Soft-Porn Culture," *New Republic,* August 30, 1980.

5. The Christian element cannot be overlooked in the creation of modern pop cultural icons. One of the best recent examples is the success of Steven Spielberg's *E.T.* In the film, a messenger from the heavens comes to earth, gathers a small band of followers, and is persecuted; he is killed, then raised from the dead through the power of love; and he then ascends into heaven with a promise to return. Sunday school and science fiction make a powerful combination.

6. *Publishers Weekly,* May 15, 1972.

7. Oscar Dystel, "The Paperback Revolution: Where Has It Gone?" *PW*, November 14, 1977.

8. Along with Fawcett, Random House now included Alfred Knopf, Vintage Books, Pantheon, and Ballantine Books. The company had obviously traveled a long way from the 1940s, when Bennett Cerf, motivated by the fear of Marshall Field creating an impregnable publishing combine, had organized the partnership of publishers that bought Grosset & Dunlap. What would Cerf have thought of the delicious irony that the company he had created was now precisely the type of vertical combine he feared that Field was trying to create?

9. *PW*, December 3, 1982.

Bibliography

Ballou, Robert O. *A History of the Council on Books in Wartime: 1942–1946.* New York: Country Life Press, 1946.

Becker, Stephen. *Marshall Field III: A Biography.* New York: Simon & Schuster, 1964.

Bonn, Thomas L. *Undercover: An Illustrated History of Mass Market Paperbacks.* New York: Penguin Books, 1982.

Bruccoli, Matthew J. *The O'Hara Concern.* New York: Random House, 1975.

Canfield, Cass. *Up and Down and Around: A Publisher Recollects the Time of His Life.* New York: Harper & Row, 1971.

Cerf, Bennett. *At Random.* New York: Random House, 1977.

Chaney, Lindsay, and Michael Cieply. *The Hearsts: Family and Empire — The Later Years.* New York: Simon & Schuster, 1981.

Cheney, Orin H. *Economic Survey of the Book Industry: 1930–1931.* New York: National Association of Book Publishers, 1931.

Cooney, John. *The Annenbergs: The Salvaging of a Tainted Empire.* New York: Simon & Schuster, 1982.

Cowley, Malcolm. *And I Worked at the Writer's Trade: Chapters of Literary History, 1918–1978.* New York: Viking Press, 1978. Penguin paperback.

———. *The Dream of the Golden Mountains.* New York: Viking Press, 1980. Penguin paperback.

Daigh, Ralph. *Maybe You Should Write a Book.* Englewood Cliffs, N.J.: Prentice-Hall, 1977.

del Rey, Lester. *The World of Science Fiction.* New York: Ballantine Books, 1979.

Dessauer, John P. *Book Publishing: What It Is, What It Does.* Second Edition. New York: R. R. Bowker, 1981.

Dickstein, Morris. *Gates of Eden: American Culture in the Sixties.* New York: Basic Books, 1977. Harper/Colophon paperback.

Dufus, R. L. *Books: Their Place in a Democracy.* Boston: Houghton Mifflin, 1930.

Ernst, Morris L., and William Seagle. *To the Pure . . . (A Study of Obscenity and the Censor).* New York: Viking Press, 1928.

FitzGerald, Frances. *America Revised.* Boston: Little, Brown, 1979. Vintage paperback.

Gifford, Barry, and Lawrence Lee. *Jack's Book: An Oral Biography.* New York: St. Martin's Press, 1978. Penguin paperback.

Goulden, Joseph C. *The Best Years: 1945–1950.* New York: Atheneum, 1976.

Gross, Sidney, and Phyllis B. Steckler. *How to Run a Paperback Bookshop.* New York: R. R. Bowker, 1963.

Hackett, Alice Payne, and James Henry Burke. *80 Years of Best Sellers: 1895–1975.* New York: R. R. Bowker, 1977.

Haldeman-Julius, Emanuel. *The World of Haldeman-Julius.* New York: Twayne Publishers, 1960.

Hancer, Kevin. *The Paperback Price Guide: First Edition.* New York: Harmony Books, 1980.

Hassan, Ihab. *Contemporary American Literature: 1945–1972.* New York: Frederick Ungar, 1973.

Hewison, Robert. *Under Siege: Literary Life in London 1939–45.* New York: Oxford University Press, 1977.

Howard, Gerald, ed. *The Sixties.* New York: Washington Square Press, 1982.

Howe, Irving. *Celebrations and Attacks: Thirty Years of Literary and Cultural Commentary.* New York: Horizon Press, 1978. Harvest paperback.

Hughes, Dorothy B. *Erle Stanley Gardner: The Case of the Real Perry Mason.* New York: William Morrow, 1978.

Jamieson, James. *Books for the Army.* New York: Columbia University Press, 1950.

Jones, Landon Y. *Great Expectations: America and the Baby Boom Generation.* New York: Coward, McCann & Geoghegan, 1980. Ballantine Books paperback.

Kazin, Alfred. *On Native Grounds.* New York: Reynal & Hitchcock, 1942. Harvest paperback.

Lasch, Christopher. *The Culture of Narcissism.* New York: W. W. Norton, 1979. Warner Books paperback.

McLuhan, Marshall. *Understanding Media: The Extension of Man.* New York: McGraw-Hill, 1964. McGraw-Hill paperback.

———, and Quentin Fiore. *The Medium Is the Massage.* New York: Bantam Books, 1967.

Manchester, William. *The Glory and the Dream.* Boston: Little, Brown, 1974. Bantam Books paperback.

Martin, Jay. *Always Merry and Bright: The Life of Henry Miller.* Santa Barbara, Calif.: Capra Press 1978. Penguin paperback.

Miller, Douglas T., and Marion Nowak. *The Fifties: The Way We Really Were.* Garden City, N.Y.: Doubleday, 1975.

Mitford, Jessica. *The Trial of Dr. Spock.* New York: Knopf, 1969.

Morpurgo, J. E. *Allen Lane: King Penguin.* London: Hutchinson, 1979.

Mott, Frank Luther. *Golden Multitudes: The Story of Best Sellers in the United States.* New York: R. R. Bowker, 1947.

Obst, Lynda Rosen, ed. *The Sixties.* New York: Rolling Stone Press/Random House, 1977.

Rembar, Charles. *The End of Obscenity.* New York: Random House, 1968. Bantam Books paperback.

Rosenberg, Bernard, and David Manning White, eds. *Mass Culture in America.* Glencoe, Ill.: The Free Press, 1957.

———. *Mass Culture Revisited.* New York: Van Nostrand Reinhold, 1971.

Schick, Frank L. *The Paperbound Book in America.* New York: R. R. Bowker, 1958.

Schreuders, Piet. *Paperbacks U.S.A.: A Graphic History.* San Diego: Blue Dolphin Enterprises, 1981.

Smith, Roger H. *Paperback Parnassus.* Boulder, Co.: Westview Press, 1976.

Solotaroff, Theodore. *Writers and Issues.* New York: New American Library, 1969.

Spock, Benjamin, and Mitchell Zimmerman. *Dr. Benjamin Spock on Vietnam.* New York: Dell Books, 1968.

Tebbel, John. *A History of Book Publishing in the United States. Vol. 3, The Golden Age Between Two Wars: 1920–1940.* New York: R. R. Bowker, 1978.

———. *A History of Book Publishing in the United States. Vol. 4, The Great Change: 1940–1980.* New York: R. R. Bowker, 1981.

Toffler, Alvin. *Future Shock.* New York: Random House, 1970. Bantam Books paperback.

———. *The Third Wave.* New York: William Morrow, 1980. Bantam Books paperback.

Trilling, Diana. *Reviewing the Forties.* New York: Harcourt Brace Jovanovich, 1978.

Weybright, Victor. *The Making of a Publisher.* New York: Reynal & Co., 1966.

Index